Praise for Horses For Dummies

"Where was this book when I first got MY horse? Finally, the perfect resource for the horse enthusiast and potential horse owner — written with understanding and compassion for both the human and the horse."

> —Valerie K. Angeli, Public Information Coordinator, The American Society for the Prevention for Cruelty to Animals (ASPCA)

"Audrey Pavia has done it again with *Horses For Dummies*. This talented equine writer has taken the basics of horse ownership and care, and created an easy-to-read, informative book that takes readers through all aspects of the equestrian world. Packed with tidbits of information, *Horses For Dummies* is a must-have resource for horse-lovers and novice owners."

> —Carroll Brown Arnold, Publisher/Editor *America's Cutter* and *America's Barrel Racer* magazines

"I can think of no other person I would rather see entrusted with the awesome task of presenting the ins and outs of the grand responsibility that is horse ownership than Audrey Pavia. Audrey's instinctive understanding of the equine mind and her boundless concerns for the species' well-being may lead some to wonder if perhaps she was a horse in a previous life."

> —Betsy Sikora Siino, Award-winning animal writer and co-author (with gold medalist Greg Louganis) of *For the Life of Your Dog*

"If you've always wanted a horse of your own, you could ask for no better guide than this one to make that dream a reality. Audrey Pavia and Janice Posnikoff, D.V.M., are not only experts, but also horse-lovers, and their knowledge and devotion shines through on every page."

> —Gina Spadafori, Universal Press Syndicate pet-care columnist and award-winning author of *Dogs For Dummies* and *Cats For Dummies*

"Audrey Pavia's long-standing passion for horses serves as a wellspring for providing readers with accurate, inspiring, and interesting information on equines. With 32 years of involvement with horses of all breeds and with various riding disciplines, she understands how to best reach new horse enthusiasts in a fun, easy-to-follow manner."

> —Moira Harris, Editor, *Horse Illustrated* and *Equine Athlete* magazines

 ™

References for the Rest of Us!™

BESTSELLING BOOK SERIES

Do you find that traditional reference books are overloaded with technical details and advice you'll never use? Do you postpone important life decisions because you just don't want to deal with them? Then our *...For Dummies*® business and general reference book series is for you.

...For Dummies business and general reference books are written for those frustrated and hard-working souls who know they aren't dumb, but find that the myriad of personal and business issues and the accompanying horror stories make them feel helpless. *...For Dummies* books use a lighthearted approach, a down-to-earth style, and even cartoons and humorous icons to dispel fears and build confidence. Lighthearted but not lightweight, these books are perfect survival guides to solve your everyday personal and business problems.

> **"More than a publishing phenomenon, 'Dummies' is a sign of the times."**
>
> **— The New York Times**

> **"...you won't go wrong buying them."**
>
> **— Walter Mossberg, Wall Street Journal, on IDG Books' ...For Dummies books**

> **"A world of detailed and authoritative information is packed into them..."**
>
> **— U.S. News and World Report**

Already, millions of satisfied readers agree. They have made *...For Dummies* the #1 introductory level computer book series and a best-selling business book series. They have written asking for more. So, if you're looking for the best and easiest way to learn about business and other general reference topics, look to *...For Dummies* to give you a helping hand.

IDG
BOOKS
WORLDWIDE

1/99

by Audrey Pavia
with Janice M. Posnikoff, D.V.M.

IDG Books Worldwide, Inc.
An International Data Group Company

Foster City, CA ◆ Chicago, IL ◆ Indianapolis, IN ◆ New York, NY

Horses For Dummies®

Published by

IDG Books Worldwide, Inc.
An International Data Group Company
919 E. Hillsdale Blvd.
Suite 400
Foster City, CA 94404
www.idgbooks.com (IDG Books Worldwide Web site)
www.dummies.com (Dummies Press Web site)

Library of Congress Control Number.: 99-62843

ISBN: 0-7645-5138-8

Printed in the United States of America

10 9 8 7 6 5

1O/SU/QV/ZZ/IN

Distributed in the United States by IDG Books Worldwide, Inc.

Distributed by CDG Books Canada Inc. for Canada; by Transworld Publishers Limited in the United Kingdom; by IDG Norge Books for Norway; by IDG Sweden Books for Sweden; by IDG Books Australia Publishing Corporation Pty. Ltd. for Australia and New Zealand; by TransQuest Publishers Pte Ltd. for Singapore, Malaysia, Thailand, Indonesia, and Hong Kong; by Gotop Information Inc. for Taiwan; by ICG Muse, Inc. for Japan; by Intersoft for South Africa; by Eyrolles for France; by International Thomson Publishing for Germany, Austria and Switzerland; by Distribuidora Cuspide for Argentina; by LR International for Brazil; by Galileo Libros for Chile; by Ediciones ZETA S.C.R. Ltda. for Peru; by WS Computer Publishing Corporation, Inc., for the Philippines; by Contemporanea de Ediciones for Venezuela; by Express Computer Distributors for the Caribbean and West Indies; by Micronesia Media Distributor, Inc. for Micronesia; by Chips Computadoras S.A. de C.V. for Mexico; by Editorial Norma de Panama S.A. for Panama; by American Bookshops for Finland.

For general information on IDG Books Worldwide's books in the U.S., please call our Consumer Customer Service department at 800-762-2974. For reseller information, including discounts and premium sales, please call our Reseller Customer Service department at 800-434-3422.

For information on where to purchase IDG Books Worldwide's books outside the U.S., please contact our International Sales department at 317-596-5530 or fax 317-572-4002.

For consumer information on foreign language translations, please contact our Customer Service department at 1-800-434-3422, fax 317-572-4002, or e-mail rights@idgbooks.com.

For information on licensing foreign or domestic rights, please phone +1-650-653-7098.

For sales inquiries and special prices for bulk quantities, please contact our Order Services department at 800-434-3422 or write to the address above.

For information on using IDG Books Worldwide's books in the classroom or for ordering examination copies, please contact our Educational Sales department at 800-434-2086 or fax 317-572-4005.

For press review copies, author interviews, or other publicity information, please contact our Public Relations department at 650-653-7000 or fax 650-653-7500.

For authorization to photocopy items for corporate, personal, or educational use, please contact Copyright Clearance Center, 222 Rosewood Drive, Danvers, MA 01923, or fax 978-750-4470.

About the Authors

Audrey Pavia is the former editor of *Horse Illustrated* magazine and an award-winning freelance writer specializing in equine subjects. She has authored articles on various equine topics in *Thoroughbred Times, Horses USA, The Western Horse, Veterinary Product News,* and *America's Cutter* magazines, and works as a consulting editor for *Horse Illustrated* and the producer of the Acmepet.com horse section. She has authored two horse books besides *Horses For Dummies*.

In addition to her experience as an equine writer, she is also a former managing editor of *Dog Fancy* magazine and a former Senior Editor of the *American Kennel Club Gazette*. She has authored more than 100 articles on the subject of animals and has written a several books on various kinds of pets.

Audrey has been involved with horses since the age of 9. She has owned and cared for equines throughout her life, and has trained in both Western and English disciplines. She currently resides in Yorba Linda, California.

Janice M. Posnikoff, D.V.M. is a graduate of the western College of Veterinarian Medicine, University of Saskatchewan, Canada. She is currently an associate member of Equine Medical Associates, a private equine practice in Tustin, California. Janice is coauthor of "Vet on Call," a monthly column appearing in *Horse Illustrated* magazine, and contributing author of *The Ultimate Horse Care Book*. She has been around horses all her life, has trained in dressage, and has worked as a groom for both racetracks and training barns.

ABOUT IDG BOOKS WORLDWIDE

Welcome to the world of IDG Books Worldwide.

IDG Books Worldwide, Inc., is a subsidiary of International Data Group, the world's largest publisher of computer-related information and the leading global provider of information services on information technology. IDG was founded more than 30 years ago by Patrick J. McGovern and now employs more than 9,000 people worldwide. IDG publishes more than 290 computer publications in over 75 countries. More than 90 million people read one or more IDG publications each month.

Launched in 1990, IDG Books Worldwide is today the #1 publisher of best-selling computer books in the United States. We are proud to have received eight awards from the Computer Press Association in recognition of editorial excellence and three from Computer Currents' First Annual Readers' Choice Awards. Our best-selling ...*For Dummies*® series has more than 50 million copies in print with translations in 31 languages. IDG Books Worldwide, through a joint venture with IDG's Hi-Tech Beijing, became the first U.S. publisher to publish a computer book in the People's Republic of China. In record time, IDG Books Worldwide has become the first choice for millions of readers around the world who want to learn how to better manage their businesses.

Our mission is simple: Every one of our books is designed to bring extra value and skill-building instructions to the reader. Our books are written by experts who understand and care about our readers. The knowledge base of our editorial staff comes from years of experience in publishing, education, and journalism — experience we use to produce books to carry us into the new millennium. In short, we care about books, so we attract the best people. We devote special attention to details such as audience, interior design, use of icons, and illustrations. And because we use an efficient process of authoring, editing, and desktop publishing our books electronically, we can spend more time ensuring superior content and less time on the technicalities of making books.

You can count on our commitment to deliver high-quality books at competitive prices on topics you want to read about. At IDG Books Worldwide, we continue in the IDG tradition of delivering quality for more than 30 years. You'll find no better book on a subject than one from IDG Books Worldwide.

IDG BOOKS WORLDWIDE

John Kilcullen
Chairman and CEO
IDG Books Worldwide, Inc.

Eighth Annual Computer Press Awards ≥1992

WINNER

Ninth Annual Computer Press Awards ≥1993

WINNER

Tenth Annual Computer Press Awards ≥1994

WINNER

Eleventh Annual Computer Press Awards ≥1995

IDG is the world's leading IT media, research and exposition company. Founded in 1964, IDG had 1997 revenues of $2.05 billion and has more than 9,000 employees worldwide. IDG offers the widest range of media options that reach IT buyers in 75 countries representing 95% of worldwide IT spending. IDG's diverse product and services portfolio spans six key areas including print publishing, online publishing, expositions and conferences, market research, education and training, and global marketing services. More than 90 million people read one or more of IDG's 290 magazines and newspapers, including IDG's leading global brands — Computerworld, PC World, Network World, Macworld and the Channel World family of publications. IDG Books Worldwide is one of the fastest-growing computer book publishers in the world, with more than 700 titles in 36 languages. The "...For Dummies®" series alone has more than 50 million copies in print. IDG offers online users the largest network of technology-specific Web sites around the world through IDG.net (http://www.idg.net), which comprises more than 225 targeted Web sites in 55 countries worldwide. International Data Corporation (IDC) is the world's largest provider of information technology data, analysis and consulting, with research centers in over 41 countries and more than 400 research analysts worldwide. IDG World Expo is a leading producer of more than 168 globally branded conferences and expositions in 35 countries including E3 (Electronic Entertainment Expo), Macworld Expo, ComNet, Windows World Expo, ICE (Internet Commerce Expo), Agenda, DEMO, and Spotlight. IDG's training subsidiary, ExecuTrain, is the world's largest computer training company, with more than 230 locations worldwide and 785 training courses. IDG Marketing Services helps industry-leading IT companies build international brand recognition by developing global integrated marketing programs via IDG's print, online and exposition products worldwide. Further information about the company can be found at www.idg.com.   1/26/00

Dedication

To my parents, John and Haydee, for always encouraging my love for horses.
— Audrey Pavia

Authors' Acknowledgments

Audrey: Thank you to IDG editors Kyle Looper, Stacy Collins, and Tammy Castleman; brilliant writer and friend Gina Spadafori; my husband Randy Mastronicola; my attorney Patricia Crown; technical editor Rick Oas; and my dear friend and constant support, Betsy Sikora Siino. Heartfelt gratitude goes out to Moira Harris, Lora Duckett, Jim Bennet of J. Bennet Farms; Diane Robinson, John Evangalista, Jeanne Smith, and Paddy Korb of Amber Ridge Farms; Doug Kraus, Matt Rayl, and everyone at Serrano Creek Equestrian Center; Jenny Walker, Cathy Blakesley, Susan Cox, Elizabeth McCall, Buddy Zech, and Joe Allen of the Equestrian Therapeutic Horsemanship Center; Wendy Kaufmann of Rancho Extravaganzia Paso Finos; Carroll Brown Arnold of *America's Cutter* and *America's Barrel Racer* magazines; Diana Deterding of the Dymar Agency; Leslie Thompson of Leslie Thompson Training; Stacie Moriarity, Cindy Perez, and Janet Roberts of the American Quarter Horse Association; Pam Shannon of the Arabian Horse Registry of America; Tina Ashford of the American Saddlebred Association; Susan Bavaria of the International Arabian Horse Association; and the staff at the American Morgan Horse Association.

I must also thank the horses that have taught me so much throughout my life: Rosie, Peggy, Snickers, Lucy, Spec, Molly, Monday, Tommy, Inflation, Tejano, Amorita, Miguelena, Gitano Jevon, Charlie, Autumn, Coke, Pal, and Pepper. I don't know who I'd be without them.

Janice: Thanks to Henry Dodd, Dr. Rex Leach, Dr. Bob Bettey, and most of all my mom and dad. You have all made me the vet I am today.

Publisher's Acknowledgments

We're proud of this book; please register your comments through our IDG Books Worldwide Online Registration Form located at http://my2cents.dummies.com.

Some of the people who helped bring this book to market include the following:

Acquisitions, Editorial, and Media Development

Senior Project Editor: Kyle Looper

Acquisitions Editor: Stacy Collins

Copy Editors: Tamara Castleman, Kathleen Dobie, Donna Love

Technical Editor: Rick Oas, Pollyrich Farms

Editorial Coordinator: Maureen Kelly

Editorial Manager: Leah P. Cameron

Media Development Manager: Heather Heath Dismore

Editorial Assistant: Beth Parlon

Production

Associate Project Coordinator: Maridee V. Ennis

Layout and Graphics: Linda M. Boyer, Thomas R. Emrick, Angela F. Hunckler, Dave McKelvey, Brent Savage, Jacque Schneider, Janet Seib, Brian Torwelle

Illustrator: Pam Tanzey

Photographers: Gemma Giannini, Shawn Hamilton, Sandra Hall, American Quarter Horse Association

Proofreaders: Christine Berman, Nancy Reinhardt, Jennifer Mahern, Ethel M. Winslow, Janet M. Withers

Indexer: Sherry Massey

Special Help

Janet Roberts, American Quarter Horse Association; Ann Yeiser, *Racking Review Magazine;* Lisa Roule, Acquisitions Coordinator

---

General and Administrative

IDG Books Worldwide, Inc.: John Kilcullen, CEO

IDG Books Technology Publishing Group: Richard Swadley, Senior Vice President and Publisher; Walter R. Bruce III, Vice President and Publisher; Joseph Wikert, Vice President and Publisher; Mary Bednarek, Vice President and Director, Product Development; Andy Cummings, Publishing Director, General User Group; Mary C. Corder, Editorial Director; Barry Pruett, Publishing Director

IDG Books Consumer Publishing Group: Roland Elgey, Senior Vice President and Publisher; Kathleen A. Welton, Vice President and Publisher; Kevin Thornton, Acquisitions Manager; Kristin A. Cocks, Editorial Director

IDG Books Internet Publishing Group: Brenda McLaughlin, Senior Vice President and Publisher; Sofia Marchant, Online Marketing Manager

IDG Books Production for Branded Press: Debbie Stailey, Director of Production; Cindy L. Phipps, Manager of Project Coordination, Production Proofreading, and Indexing; Tony Augsburger, Manager of Prepress, Reprints, and Systems; Laura Carpenter, Production Control Manager; Shelley Lea, Supervisor of Graphics and Design; Debbie J. Gates, Production Systems Specialist; Robert Springer, Supervisor of Proofreading; Trudy Coler, Page Layout Manager; Troy Barnes, Page Layout Supervisor, Kathie Schutte, Senior Page Layout Supervisor; Michael Sullivan, Production Supervisor

Contents at a Glance

Cartoons at a Glance

By Rich Tennant

"I read that horses are very good at picking out patterns."

page 145

A HORSE CALLED MAN

page 97

"I told you they were very social animals."

page 31

"He prefers it to trotting."

page 333

The way I see it, a visual inspection of my horse's feed just isn't enough.

page 221

"I thought you said he's been trained. He just passed after I bid 1 No Trump."

page 323

"We live in a converted barn decorated in southwestern furniture; you own a Chaps wardrobe and splash on Polo cologne each morning. How can you NOT want to own a horse?"

page 7

Fax: 978-546-7747
E-mail: richtennant@the5thwave.com
World Wide Web: www.the5thwave.com

Table of Contents

Introduction

• •

Welcome to *Horses For Dummies,* the one and only book you need to get started in the hobby of horses.

Why do you need a book on horses? If you want to ride, can't you just climb up on a horse and hit the trail? What's so complicated about letting a horse carry you around on his back, anyway?

The truth of the matter is that as simple as riding may seem, it's anything but. Here's why: With most other hobbies, your main component is something rather undynamic. For example, the racket and ball you use to play tennis, or the clubs and balls you require for golf. Without human energy to put these pieces into motion, they're nothing but unfeeling, unmoving, inanimate objects.

Horseback riding, on the other hand, relies crucially on something that is hardly passive in the process: the horse. Horses have the ability to operate on their own — they don't need a human to set them in motion. This fact is not only true of the equine body, but it's especially true of the equine mind.

So why *do* you need this book? Because we can help you understand the horse and how it functions, both physically and mentally. Because we can show you how to communicate what you want to a horse so he'll do your bidding. And so we can show you how to care for this amazing creature, which, by the way, needs much more maintenance than your average set of golf clubs!

After you're comfortable with the basics of horsemanship, you'll likely be hooked on horses for good. Then you'll be hungry to explore the world of horses in even greater depth. But to get acquainted with things equine, you've come to the right place. Whether you're contemplating riding a horse for the first time in your life, thinking about adding riding to your list of hobbies, or wondering how to care for your first horse, we're certain this book will be a great help you.

About This Book

We've designed *Horses For Dummies* to be a useful reference for beginning horsepeople. You can turn to any section of the book that interests you and begin reading at that point — and not feel lost. You don't have to remember what you read yesterday, and you don't have to read chapters or sections in order. Just find something that interests you, read it, do it, and put the book back on your shelf. We don't expect you to read from cover to cover.

If *Horses For Dummies* were a building, it would be a department store that you can enter on whatever floor you like. You don't have to walk past that smelly perfume counter to get to the housewares section on the third floor. You just walk into the housewares section.

Of course, you can feel free to read this book from cover to cover to avoid missing one pearl of horse wisdom (or horse sense) that we've painstakingly compiled for you. You won't hear us say nay to that!

We've worked long and hard to bring you what we think is the consummate beginner's reference book on horses, and we hope that you find it as fun to read as we found it to write. We also hope that you take all of our advice and thank us for the rest of eternity for all the equine wisdom we've brought you.

Seriously, though, we've found great joy, comfort, and fulfillment in our personal involvement with horses, and we hope for you the same kind of experience. We're certain that once you dive deep into the ocean of horseness, you'll never try to make it to shore.

Conventions Used in This Book

In this book, we refer to horses with the male pronoun (he, his, and him). We understand that horses aren't all male, and we don't prefer male horses to female horses particularly (Audrey's actually partial to mares). This convention is merely for readability's sake. We don't call horses "it" (not *our* horses!), and using both sexes ("his or her," "he or she," and so on) makes the text hard to read. So we flipped a coin: It came up heads — he.

What You're Not to Read

From time to time in this book, we tell you stuff that may be nice to know, but isn't essential to understanding the topic. In these cases, we place the text in a gray box, which we call a sidebar. Don't feel like you have to read these. Also, if you see a paragraph that's highlighted by a technical stuff icon, you don't need to understand that information either to function in the horsey world.

Foolish Assumptions

In this book, we assume that you know a horse when you see one. That's really about all we assume. Well, we do assume that you're interested in these magnificent creatures and that you want to treat them kindly.

We also assume that you're no dummy. You may not be an expert in the horse field, but you're not one to go around pretending that you are. You know that the best way to find out about things is to read up, ask questions of those who've been around the block, and to keep your eyes open. We think you're pretty smart; after all, you bought this book, didn't you?

How This Book Is Organized

Horses for Dummies is made up of seven parts. That's many parts, but you need a lot information to get started with horses.

The following sections look at each of these parts and what they cover.

Part I: A Horse, of Course!

To fit in with the horsey crowd, you need to know equine basics. You need to know head from tail, a trot from a canter, a star from a blaze, and withers from a fetlock. You also need to have a good idea of how the horse sees the world, and humankind.

In Part I, we give you some background on the human/horse relationship over time, and show you the parts of the horse and how to evaluate them. We also get into specific details about horse colors, markings, and gaits, and spend quite a bit of time helping you understand equine behavior — something you absolutely have to know if you are going to spend any amount of time around horses.

Part II: Choosing a Horse

Buying a horse can be a daunting experience, especially if you don't know what you're doing. The wrong decision can mean an unpleasant and costly situation — one that will sour you on horses for good.

If you're thinking about buying a horse, Part II is the place for you. In this part, we help you decide whether horse ownership is really for you at this time in your life, or whether leasing or taking lessons are better options. If you're certain you're ready to commit to horse ownership, then read here about breed, age, and gender differences before you buy. Our details on where and how to buy your horse should prove pretty helpful, too.

Part III: Stuff You're Gonna Need

A horse isn't the only thing you need in order to ride. If you plan to own your own horse, you'll have to get yourself some tack, grooming equipment, riding apparel, and, oh yeah, a place to keep the animal. Go to Part III for the low-down on all this stuff and more.

If you aren't ready to buy a horse yet but just want to ride, you still need to take a look at Chapter 6. The information on tack, grooming equipment, and riding apparel are relevant to anyone who rides a horse.

Part IV: Caring for Your Horse

If you've made the commitment to horse ownership — or are planning to — Part IV is very important to you. In these chapters, we give you all the basic information you need to take care of your horse. That includes advice on grooming, providing preventative veterinary care, recognizing common ail-ments, and figuring out exactly what to do with your horse when it's time to part.

Part IV is not only for those who own their own horse. The information here on grooming and recognizing common health problems is important to anyone interested in horse care.

Part V: Horsin' Around

Here's the payoff for the hard work: riding! In Part V, we give you details on how to handle your horse while you are on the ground and in the saddle. We show you how to put on the saddle and bridle, how to mount and dismount, and how to hold the reins. We also give you a rundown of the different riding disciplines, and alert you to the various safety issues concerning horses and riding. We also break down the different types of equine competitions, and also detail the myriad fun, non-competitive activities out there for those who ride.

Part VI: The Part of Tens

In the Part of Tens, we tackle two very different subjects: equine myths and horseback vacations. In the equine myths chapter, we strive to debunk various untruths about horses that have pervaded our culture in recent decades. In the vacations chapter, we seek to introduce you to the wonderful world of horseback holidays by presenting you with ten vacation possibilities that will help you get away from the rat race and improve your riding skills at the same time.

Part VII: Appendixes

Horses For Dummies has two useful appendixes to help you along your journey of equine discovery. Appendix A is a glossary of equine terms that you're likely to run into and Appendix B is a compendium of great horse-related resources.

Icons Used in This Book

As with all the other books in the *...For Dummies* series, this book has little icons in the margins to call your attention to specific types of information. Here's an explanation of what each of those icons means:

Procedures in the horse world may not seem to make much sense at times, yet they're written in stone and people always follow them. These types of procedures are indicated by this icon.

This icon a appears frequently throughout this book. That's because when it comes to horses, you need to do plenty of remembering. We've placed this icon next to information that we think is very important and shouldn't be missed or forgotten.

This icon alerts you to helpful hints regarding horses, pertaining to their care and handling. If you read the information so highlighted in this book, you'll find your life around horses much easier.

Occasionally, horse information gets a bit technical, hence this icon. When you see it, put the left side of your brain in high gear.

When you see this symbol, beware! It indicates something serious to watch out for.

Where to Go from Here

Go wherever you want. You can start at Chapter 1 and read all the way through to the final appendix if you want. Or, you can skip here and skip there.

If you're going to do the skipping around thing, though, can we at least ask you to do us a favor? Before you start jumping from place to place, take a few moments to read through Chapter 2, which gives you insights into the equine mind. These are issues that *every* potential horseperson should know.

Go ahead! Start hoofin' it!

Part I
A Horse, of Course!

The 5th Wave   By Rich Tennant

"We live in a converted barn decorated in southwestern furniture; you own a Chaps wardrobe and splash on Polo cologne each morning. How can you NOT want to own a horse?"

In this part . . .

In the chapters of Part I, you'll find the basic information you need to know about horses. We show you how to tell if a horse is well put-together, how to measure a horse, and how to identify the parts, colors, and markings of horses. We also explain in great detail how the equine mind works and give you pointers on how to communicate effectively with horses.

Chapter 1

The Essence of Horseness

*I*f you want to be around horses, you need to acquire some horse sense. By that, we mean that you need to understand some basic things about horses: why humans are so drawn to them, how horses affected human history, and how horses are put together physically. This chapter covers all these things.

The Equine Mystique

For some reason, horses attract human beings like magnets attract steel. This human infatuation has been going on for thousands of years. The fascination began when primitive man saw horses as food. As cavemen became more civilized, horses became valuable as beasts of burden. Basically, for most of the horse's history with humans, he has helped humans survive in a hostile world.

Nowadays, however, humans have few practical reasons for keeping horses around. Whereas humans used to use horses to provide transportation and sustenance, we now have much speedier ways to get to the grocery store.

So why do humans still keep horses? Horses are big, unwieldy creatures that eat a great deal and produce a significant amount of poop. They're also expensive to house and rather time consuming to care for. What could horses possibly offer modern humans that would make keeping *equines* — that is, members of the horse family — worth all the trouble?

You get different answers to this question depending on whom you ask. But because we're the ones writing this book, you're going to get ours:

✔ Horses are amazing, incredible creatures. They're as breathtakingly beautiful as they are powerful and fast. They're wild in their souls, yet they gladly give us their hearts. Horses offer us beauty, a connection to nature, and a quiet and dignified companionship that no other animal can provide in the same way.

✔ If you don't believe us, it's only because you haven't gotten to really know a horse yet. We guarantee that after you do, the equine mystique will reveal itself to you.

Talking the Talk: Describing Horses

If you hang around a stable for any length of time, you'll notice that horse people have a language all their own. This language — which sounds like a foreign tongue to the uninitiated — is what horse people use to describe the intricate details of the horse's body.

If you want to fit in with the horsy set, you need to know the lingo — and the basic knowledge of horses that goes with it. The horse's anatomy, and the horse's height measurements, colorations, and markings are all essential details that real horse lovers know.

Prehistoric horses

Horses did not always look like they do today. The horses you now see are the result of thousands of years of human domestication. Before humans came along, horses were considerably smaller, and in fact, didn't even have the same amount of toes as they do today.

Scientists believe that the first horse was a small fox-sized critter called Eohippus. Fossil evidence indicates that Eohippus developed around 60 million years ago. In addition to being much smaller than today's horse, Eohippus had a total of four toes on each foot — as opposed to the one toe (the hoof) on the modern horse. Carnivores of the time regularly dined upon Eohippus, a vegetarian and a prey animal.

Over the next 59 million years or so, Eohippus slowly evolved into Mesohippus, Miohippus, and a few other hippuses, losing toes along the way until only one big toe was left. The evolving horses gradually got bigger, too, until they finally ended up as an animal called Equus Przewalski. Equus Przewalski is the horse that the cave men hunted and the horse that humans eventually domesticated and turned into the modern horse.

Amazingly enough, members of the Equus Przewalski species are still alive today. You can see them in zoos, or in the wilds of Mongolia where they have recently been reintroduced.

Equines in the modern age

Before the invention of the automobile in the early 1900s, horses were everywhere. Nearly everybody had at least one — you needed a horse if you wanted to get where you were going with efficiency. But after the car showed up on the scene, horses slowly lost their practical purpose.

The reason horses are still around today is because people love them, pure and simple. Sure, horses still do plenty of work. They take dude ranch visitors on trail rides, carry mounted police officers during riots, and pull beer wagons for TV commercials. But do we really, truly *need* horses to do all this stuff? Or could these just be excuses to keep them around? We think so (see the section "The Equine Mystique" earlier for details on why).

The main function of horses today is to provide humans with recreation and companionship. Horses perform the job well — so well that they have pretty much been guaranteed a permanent place in the human heart.

Horse parts

Horses are really put together. No fooling. Nature made them to be virtual running machines who can reach speeds of nearly 40 miles per hour. The equine body is an impeccably designed combination of muscle and bone in an elegant and graceful package.

People who spend time around horses not only begin to appreciate equine anatomy, but also come to understand it. Horse people talk about their horse's bodies the way mechanics talk about cars. In the equine world, if you want to keep up with such conversations, you must know the lingo and the blueprint as well. (To get to know the parts of the horse, see Figure 1-1.)

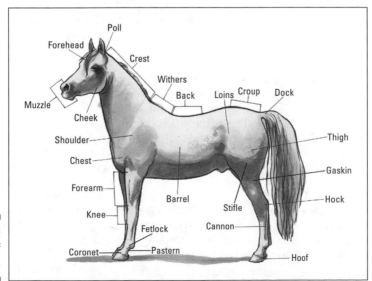

Figure 1-1:
The parts of the horse.

Hoofin' it

Heard the expression *no hoof, no horse*? Well, it's true. Without healthy hooves, horses can't function well. Becoming familiar with the parts of the horse's hoof gives you intimate knowledge of this most important part of the equine body. This knowledge helps you take better care of your horse's tootsies, too (see Figure 1-2 for the parts of the hoof).

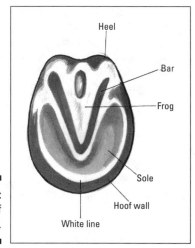

Figure 1-2: The parts of the hoof.

Heel

Bar

Frog

Sole

Hoof wall

White line

Measuring horses

The average horse weighs anywhere from 1,000 to 1,200 pounds. But horse people rarely refer to a horse's weight when describing the animal's size. Instead, the horse's height, measured in something called *hands,* is the appraisal of choice.

One hand equals 4 inches, and horses are measured from the ground to the top of the withers (see Figure 1-3). So, if a horse stands 60 inches from the ground to its withers, the horse is 15 hands high. If the horse stands 63 inches from the ground, the horse is 15.3 hands. Because a hand is an increment of 4 inches, a horse that is 64 inches from the ground to the withers would not be 15.4 hands high, but would instead be considered 16 hands. Height in hands is sometimes written as *h.h.,* which stands for *hands high.*

A horse's height is really only important if you plan to ride it — which most people do. Generally speaking, an average-sized woman can comfortably ride a horse that is anywhere from 14.2 hands to 16.1 hands in height. If you are a rather tall woman, or are a man of average male height, you'll probably want to lean toward a horse on the taller side of the range.

All this is mostly asthetics, of course. If you are a tall person, you'll look better on a taller horse. Of course, if you are above average in weight, a larger horse can carry you more comfortably. If you plan to show your horse or perform particular events with it, height may also be a consideration.

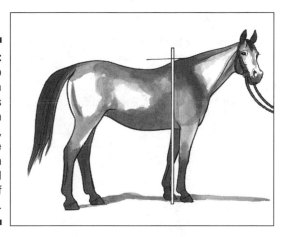

Figure 1-3:
To determine a horse's height in hands, measure the horse from the ground to the top of the withers.

You can use a regular measuring tape to determine a horse's height, as long as you're good at division, because you need to divide the number of inches you come up with by 4. If you'd rather not bring your calculator to the stable, you can buy a special horse measuring tape or a measuring stick (even more accurate) at your local tack store. These devices are labeled in hands, so you don't have to do any calculating of your own.

Horse measuring tapes are also useful for determining your horse's weight, because the tapes usually have pound increments on one side and hand measurements on the other. To determine your horse's weight, wrap the tape around the horse's girth, just behind the elbow, and up behind the withers.

A horse of a different color

Nature made horses to blend into their surroundings, so the colors you typically see in horses are meant to hide and camouflage. Based on this definition, you may think that horse colors should be dull, but the exact opposite is true. It's really amazing how many different shades and variations of coat color you find in the equine world. Knowing the different horse colors helps you describe and identify individual horses you may come across in your equine travels. Having this knowledge also permits you to converse intelligently with other horse lovers. You may even end up finding a favorite coloration that you would like to see on your own future horse!

The best way to learn horse colors is to see them. In the insert in the middle of this book, you can find color photographs of 16 of the most common horse colorations along with the names and descriptions of each.

All those markings

Leg and facial markings are great for helping to identify individual horses. Each marking has a name, and each name is universal among equine aficionados.

Figure 1-4 shows the most common horse facial markings. Keep in mind that these patterns often have subtle variations. Figure 1-5 shows typical white leg markings on horses.

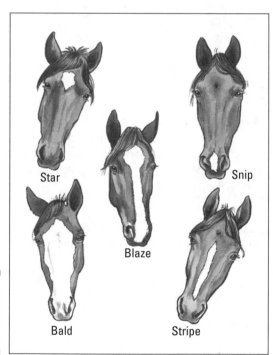

Star

Snip

Blaze

Figure 1-4:
Common
horse facial
markings.

Bald

Stripe

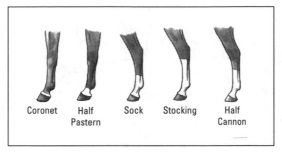

Figure 1-5:
Common
white leg
markings.

Coronet   Half   Sock   Stocking   Half
     Pastern   Cannon

Horse (Not Bill) Gaits: How Horses Move

If you've ever seen a Hollywood western, you know that horses gallop. In fact, in the movies, all horses seem to do is gallop. In real life, however, most horses have two other gaits besides the gallop: the walk and the trot.

The three gaits are considerably different from one another. One difference is speed: the walk is the slowest of the three. The trot is faster than the walk, and the gallop is faster than the trot.

A big difference in the gaits is in the way the horse positions his legs while he's moving. In the *walk,* the horse puts each foot down one at a time, creating a four-beat rhythm. In the *trot,* one front foot and its opposite hind foot come down at the same time, making a two-beat rhythm. In the *gallop,* one hind leg strikes the ground first, and then the other hind leg and one foreleg come down together, then the other foreleg. This movement creates a three-beat rhythm. When you're riding a horse, you can feel each of these different rhythms. (See Figure 1-6 for a visual sense of how this all works.)

Depending on the discipline you're riding in, you may hear other terms to describe these gaits. In English riding circles, *canter* describes a slow gallop. Western riders use the term *jog* to describe a slow trot and *lope* for a slow gallop.

Just to confuse matters, the horse world has something called *gaited horses,* which are horses who naturally possess one or more gaits in addition to the basic gaits, or instead of one or more of the basic gaits. Only horses of particular *gaited breeds* have these peculiarities. Chapter 4 contains information on various horse breeds, including gaited breeds.

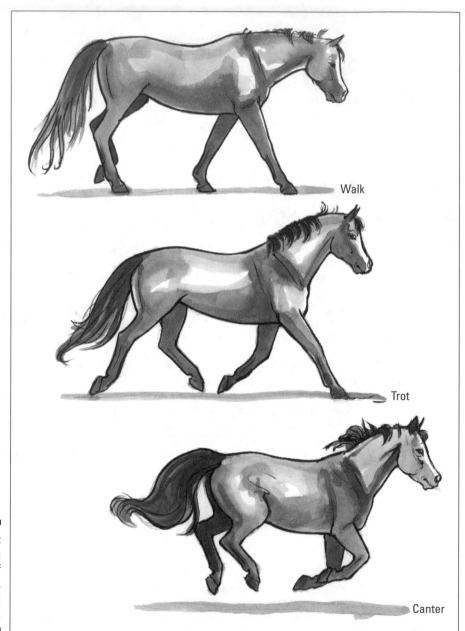

Walk

Trot

Canter

Figure 1-6:
The leg
positions of
the walk,
trot, and
canter.

Chapter 2

Understanding Your Horse

●●

●●

*Y*ou can improve your relationship with your horse a great deal if you can get into your horse's head — do a little horse psychology, if you will. Start by dragging a really large couch out to the stable and asking the horse about his relationship with his mother. Naw, not really, but this chapter gives you insight into the horse's world and the horse's mind. Using the information we give you here, you can figure out what the horse is telling you.

Although humans and horses have been interacting for literally thousands of years (we provide a short rundown of this relationship in Chapter 1), only relatively recently have humans bothered to try to really understand how horses think and feel. Instead, humans have tended to assume that horses (and other nonhuman animals, for that matter) think and feel in exactly the same ways as humans (scientists even have a ten-dollar word for this: *anthropomorphizing*).

The view that horses and humans think in similar ways, however, only causes misunderstanding and trouble between the two species. Although horses *do* share certain feelings with humans — affection, fear, pain, discomfort, playfulness, and a sense of well-being, among other emotions — quite a few of horses' thought processes are uniquely equine. What it all boils down to is this: Human understanding of life from the horse's point of view is essential to a good human/horse relationship. In this chapter, we intend to put you in the horse's shoes (but we'll pass on the nails to keep them in place).

The Horse's Psyche

To really understand the horse, you need to comprehend the world that the horse lives in. Think about it: The horse world is not composed of fast food joints, unbalanced checkbooks, and vacations to far away countries. Instead, horses live in a world made up of hay and grass, buzzing insects, and assorted horsy politics.

Looking at the world through a horse's eyes can open up all sorts of avenues for communication between you and the horse. When you finally connect with your horse, you'll find that suddenly, this huge, four-legged alien is very special.

Equine nature

Horses have a way of thinking and viewing things that is uniquely their own. The evolution of horses as prey animals has given them a very special viewpoint that helps them survive.

The components of this perspective (such as viewing the world as a series of threats, finding safety in numbers, and looking to an authority figure for guidance) make up the essence of the horse's being. The human who understands and sympathizes with these sometimes very-unhumanlike ways of looking at the world is the person who becomes most adept at conversations with the horse.

Prey, not predator

The first thing you need to know about horses to really get into their heads is that the horse is a prey animal. In the wild, horses are at the top of most large predators' dinner menus. Dogs and cats, on the other hand, evolved to be hunters. Consequently, the horse looks at the world differently than the domesticated dog and cat.

Nowadays, horses live in domestic situations where their biggest worries are horsefly bites, but try telling that to a horse. Long before humans even considered building barns, haylofts, paddocks, and arenas, bolting from a potential threat is what literally saved the horse's hide. This instinct to flee first and ask questions later is at the core of every equine personality.

You don't need to spend much time around horses to witness the equine instinct to flee: In a nutshell, horses scare easily. They often spook at what humans view as the most benign of things: a plastic bag blowing in the wind, a low-flying plane passing overhead, or a car backfiring nearby. To humans, these are minor distractions. To the ever-watchful horse, these are potentially life-threatening hazards.

The ease with which horses spook may seem ridiculous, but the instinct to flee from trouble is at the very center of a horse's psyche. Although most domestic horses don't have predators chasing them, they still have a powerful instinct to be on guard. Their brains are telling them that horse-eating monsters are out there, so they need to be on the lookout. If a real predator can't be found, then, by golly, the horse will conjure up a hunter to run from.

Togetherness

Closely associated with the get-the-heck-out-of-here-now instinct is the herd instinct, represented by the horse's burning desire to always be with other horses. This need stems from the fact that, in the wild, large numbers mean safety. It works like this: Pretend for a minute that you're a horse, and a huge, terrifying saber-toothed tiger has decided on horsemeat for his next meal. When the big cat starts chasing your herd looking for prey to take down, the chances of *you* being the horse that gets nailed are less if a whole herd of other horses surround you.

In addition to decreasing your odds of being the unlucky body in a kill, being in a herd also means that you can find out about impending danger much sooner than you would if you were alone. After all, a herdful of eyes are better than one measly pair.

The horse's love for other horses is not completely mercenary, however. You only need to watch a group of horses out in a field to discover that they genuinely enjoy each other's company. Although each horse is an individual with his own distinct personality, horses nonetheless thrive on companionship and bond strongly with their herdmates. They groom each other with their teeth, take turns tail-swishing flies from each other's faces, and even play horsy games together, such as tag and I-dare-you-to-try-and-bite-me.

Follow the leader

Horses are very social creatures, and they even have their own rules of society. In any given herd of horses, some horses are dominant and others are submissive. Horses follow a precise pecking order, with one big kahuna at the top of the heap who lords over all the other horses. The individual personalities of various herd members, along with factors such as age and physical ability, determine which horses take on which roles within the herd. All in all, horse society doesn't operate that much differently than human society.

Human beings have benefited greatly from the horse's intrinsic need for leadership. The horse's penchant for dutifully submitting to authority is what ultimately allowed humankind to domesticate the horse thousands of years ago. After a human earns a horse's respect (just as a leader horse must earn his fellow horses' respect), the horse views the human as an authority figure to be respected and followed, just as he would view the leader horse.

When a human fails to gain a horse's respect early on in the relationship, the horse automatically takes charge. From the horse's perspective, every herd — even one made up of only two members — must have a leader. Although first impressions are important to horses, over-run humans can make up lost ground by becoming more assertive and telling the horse (in so many words) "I'm the one in charge now."

Just as horses test the leader horses in a herd, they also periodically test their human companions to make sure that the humans are still worthy of leadership. Horses who misbehave often do so to challenge the authority of whomever is handling them, and they are incredibly astute at determining the qualifications of those giving them orders. For a horse to feel secure, he must have strong leadership. If you don't measure up in this department or if the horse has a history of dealing with humans that don't measure up as leaders, the horse will take the leadership position from you — and we promise you won't like the results!

For example, in horse/human relationships where the horse has taken charge, you often see horses leading humans around the stable instead of vice versa. Leader horses who are being ridden make the decisions about where and when to go, despite their riders' pleas.

Equine followers feel safest when they have a strong leader making decisions for them and helping them determine what is and isn't dangerous. Human leadership accounts for why many horses find comfort in their associations with human beings. If we humans do things right, they see us as leaders. And if we say things are okay, then they must *be* okay.

The role of leader places a great responsibility on human shoulders, of course. We must convince the horse that we are confident and knowledgeable, and worthy of their invaluable equine trust.

Equine senses

To see things from the horse's perspective, you need to know — literally — how the horse takes in the world. Humans evolved to be hunters and gatherers, chasing down prey and finding appropriate plants to eat. Horses, on the other hand, are built to avoid hunters and eat nearly everything that grows around them. Given these fundamental distinctions, the horse's senses are bound to have nuances that are somewhat different from those of a human.

Sight

Sight is the most important equine sense. For a prey animal like the horse, in the wild, good eyesight means the difference between life and death. Literally seeing trouble coming is the best way the horse has to make it to safety before a predator gets too close.

Because horses have long, narrow heads with eyes on either side, they have the ability to take in more of the view than humans do. When their heads are facing forward, horses have a nearly 180-degree field of vision (as shown in Figure 2-1). They can see in front of and almost all the way around their bodies, though they do have some blind spots.

One of a horse's blind spots is directly behind, so you should never approach a horse from the back unless the horse already knows you're there.

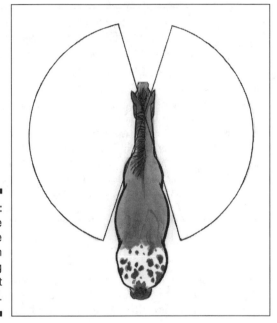

Figure 2-1:
A horse can see this much when facing straight ahead.

No one knows for sure how far horses can see, mainly because horses have trouble pronouncing the letters on eye tests. Scientists who have done experiments in this field have made some educated guesses that horses can see pretty darn far, in the realm of at least hundreds of yards away. Horses can distinguish patterns, which means they're able to take in fine details. They can also perceive depth well.

Horses also have much better night vision than humans. Many a rider has been out on a dark, moonless trail, dumbfounded by his or her horses' ability to see where the pair are going despite the incredibly dim light.

Scientists know far less about horses' color vision than about other areas of equine sight, but they are certain that horses can see some colors. Red and blue seem to be particularly distinct to the equine eye, but beyond this, we don't know. Researchers need to do more tests to find out whether horses can see the full spectrum of the rainbow.

Lost sight

Few things in the horse world are as tragic as a horse who has lost his sight. The horse's status as a prey animal makes him profoundly dependent on the sense of sight for both his physical and emotional well-being. In nature, a horse who loses his sight to an equine eye disease is a vulnerable horse — and the horse knows it.

Although some domestic horses can cope with life in a sightless world, most can't. Those who can't endure the darkness are destroyed. This problem strikes more often than you may think: Equine eye problems are the fourth most common ailment among domestic horses in the United States. In fact, one particular ailment, *equine recurrent uveitis,* actually affects 20 percent of the country's horses. This disease is painful, incurable, and always results in blindness.

Veterinary researchers are working hard to find cures and new treatments for equine eye ailments like ERU and other optic diseases. One such researcher is veterinary ophthalmologist Dennis E. Brooks, D.V.M., Ph.D. Working with a team of researchers at the University of Florida College of Veterinary Medicine, Dr. Brooks is making significant headway in discovering new treatments for ERU, corneal ulcers, and other equine eye diseases.

If you are interested in learning how to support the efforts of Dr. Brooks and his group at the University of Florida, please contact the University of Florida Foundation, College of Veterinary Medicine, P.O. Box 100125, Gainesville, FL 32610-0125, (352) 392-4700, ext. 5200. If you would like to make a gift today, make your check payable to the University of Florida Foundation/Equine Eye Disease.

Hearing

A species that survives by getting a head start on marauding predators needs a pretty good sense of hearing. The fact that horses have survived all the way to modern times is testimony to their incredible hearing, which is considerably better than a human's.

If you look at the shape of the horse's ear, you can see that it's built sort of like a funnel. With this design, the ear can capture sound in its outer part and channel it down into the ear canal. The broad outer part of the horse's ear very adequately takes in the slightest sound in the horse's environment.

The horse's ear also has an amazing ability to swivel. Just watch a horse's ears sometime while the horse is busy eating or just hanging out. You'll see one ear turn forward, while the other swings to the back. Sometimes both ears go forward at the same time, while at other times, both are poised to the rear. The purpose of all this twisting is simple — to take in as much information as possible at one time.

Using these very mobile ears, horses constantly monitor the world around them. Just imagine trying to pay complete attention to different sounds coming in to either ear at the same time. Impossible for a human, yet the horse does this on a steady basis. A horse can take in the sounds of a car driving by, children playing, a bird chirping and a human approaching, all at once, from different places in the environment. The horse then processes that information and makes split second decisions about whether to react — all while picking out the best blades of pasture grass or meandering down a rocky trail. The process really is mind-blowing.

Loud, unfamiliar noises can send a relaxed horse into a tizzy. On the other hand, a placid, reassuring sound can ease a horse's worries. It's amazing to see how a frightened horse can be comforted by a soft, gentle voice from a calm and confident human. Keep this fact in mind when handling your horse in a particularly noisy or frightening environment.

Smell

Like most non-human animals, horses have an acute sense of smell that they regularly employ to provide them with information on what is going on around them. Horses use their sense of smell in a number of different and important ways.

People talk about smelling danger, but when it comes to the horse, this metaphor is literally the case. Nature equipped the equine with a strong olfactory sense that can tell the animal whether a predator is near. All it takes is a strong upwind breeze to bring a dangerous scent to the attention of a wild herd. After getting a whiff of the predator, the herd literally high-tails — their tails stick way up in the air as they flee — it out of there in a flash.

Horses also use smell as part of their complicated social structure. Horses typically greet each other nose to nose, each taking in the odor of the other. Horses also come to recognize each other by scent as well as by sight. Mares and foals quickly memorize each other's scents and use this information to help locate each other in a crowd of horses.

Most horses also greet humans in the same way. When you introduce yourself to a horse for the first time, notice how the horse reaches out his muzzle to sniff you. Given this, the most polite way to approach a horse is with the back of your hand extended so the horse may take in your personal scent. Letting a horse breathe in your scent tells the animal that you are a fellow herdmate (not a predator), and usually makes the horse more agreeable to being handled.

The equine sense of smell also comes in handy when it's time to eat. Although horses also use their eyes and muzzles to ferret out the tastiest morsels out in a pasture, sense of smell plays a part as well. One plant may look just like another to you, but a horse can get a sense of whether or not foliage will taste good by getting a whiff of it first.

Touch

The equine sense of touch is an important (although often overlooked) element to the horse. Although many people think that horses have a tough hide, they really don't. Their skin is tougher than our human epidermis, but it is still rich with nerve endings. If it weren't, how could a horse possibly feel a tiny little fly landing on his body? Trust us, he can!

If you sit on a pasture fence and watch a herd of horses for a few hours, you'll see plenty of evidence of how horses use touch to communicate with each other. Mothers reassure their babies with a brush of the muzzle; comrades scratch each other's itches with their teeth. Whenever a message needs to be sent from one horse to another, visual cues and touch — or the threat of it — are nearly always used.

Humans can also use touch to convey messages to the horse. A gentle rub down, a pat on the shoulder, a vigorous massage in just the right place — these are all ways of saying "I'm your friend" to a horse. Sometimes, if you're lucky, you'll get a similar tactile message in return.

Horse talk

Because horses are such highly social creatures, they do quite a bit of talking to one another. Of course the equine way of communicating is nothing like what Mr. Ed did. Horses have their own exclusive language, and traditional nouns and verbs aren't part of the picture.

Humans primarily use verbal language to express thoughts and emotions to one another. Horses do the same thing within their species, only they mostly use their bodies to get their points across. This clear way of expressing a variety of attitudes, intents, and emotions is universal among all members of the equine family.

To truly understand horses, you absolutely have to know how to read equine body language. Trying to get by without this crucial skill is like trying to conduct business in a foreign country without comprehending the native tongue. You just can't do it.

Facial expressions

One of the most obvious ways that horses talk to each other — and to humans also — is by using facial expressions. Horses send out at least four distinct messages by using their faces (as shown in Figure 2-2): "I'm afraid and I'm about to bolt," "I'm alert and wondering what's next," "Get away or else!" and "I'm relaxed and secure." Each message has a distinct look. (Subtle variations of these expressions vary from horse to horse: Getting to know the individual expressions of your particular horse helps you understand him even better.)

✔ **I'm afraid and I'm about to bolt.** Horses who are on the verge of panic often warn you with this expression before they take off (although they may act in a matter of seconds). The ears are pointed toward whatever is the source of fear. The head is held high and the whites of the eye are showing. You can sometimes actually see the muscles in the neck tense up.

✔ **I'm alert and wondering what's next.** This welcome expression indicates that the horse is content and curious about his surroundings. The ears are pricked forward, the eyes are focused on the object of wonder. The head is held at medium height.

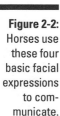

✔ **Get away or else!** This expression immediately precedes a bite or a kick. The horse usually directs the aggression at other horses, but occasionally, ill-tempered horses can direct this aggression at humans as well. The ears are laid back flat against the head, the nostrils take on an oblong shape and the mouth is open with teeth exposed.

✔ **I'm relaxed and secure.** The sign of a happy, healthy horse, you may see this expression while you are grooming, while your horse is dozing in the pasture or even while you are riding together along a familiar trail. The ears are in a relaxed state, usually pointing backward. The eye has a calm look, and the head is at medium height.

Figure 2-2: Horses use these four basic facial expressions to communicate.

Relaxed

Afraid

Threatening

Alert

The equine voice

Although body language is the primary means of equine communication, horses also use a range of sounds to talk to each other. The most prominent among these are the nicker, neigh, snort, and squeal. Each sound serves a particular purpose in a herd situation, and horses often use the sounds as a way of communicating with human beings, too. Although scientists aren't completely sure what each of these vocalizations means in a literal sense, each one seems to take place under certain circumstances, giving us a clue as to its intent.

- **Nicker:** The nicker is a soft, gentle call that is usually heard when horses with a close bond greet one another. Mares nicker to their foals, and herdmates nicker to each other. Horses who are very attached to their human caretakers sometimes nicker to them as well. You can also hear nickering at feeding time as the food-deliverer approaches.

- **Neigh:** A neigh, or whinny, is the loud call that most people associate with the horse. You hear it as a sound effect in Hollywood westerns all the time (usually used incorrectly — see Chapter 20 for more details). The neigh seems to be used most often by horses who have been separated from their herd or from a very close companion. Neighs have a sense of urgency to them that seem to be saying "Hey, I'm over here!"

- **Snort:** The snort, made by a rapid blowing of air from the nostrils, is most often heard when a horse is alarmed in some way. If a horse comes upon something that scares him, he may bolt, then spin around and snort at the offending object.

- **Squeal:** One of the more amusing equine vocalizations is the squeal. The squeal is usually reserved for other horses, and seems to be a message of controlled aggression. Strange horses often approach one another with heads up and necks arched. After a short muzzle sniffing session, one horse squeals. The other horse often reacts with an aggressive facial expression or a return squeal. The horses almost seem to be testing each other to see who backs down first. A mare who's not quite ready to breed may squeal to tell a frisky stallion to back off.

Another type of squeal comes from horses who are really frightened. These *fear squeals* are higher pitched and shorter in length than their more assertive cousins.

Horses in a Human World

The very instincts that have served the horse well in dealing with life as a prey animal are often in direct conflict with life in the human world. Domesticated horses need no longer fear ferocious carnivores because the horse's safety is guarded by his human companions, and his needs are (hopefully) always met. This new way of being, however, conflicts with everything the horse has become throughout its long history.

To make things even odder for the horse is the fact that humankind itself was one of the very predators that preyed upon horses thousands of years ago. Scientists are certain that primitive man actively hunted horses for food. In fact, many believe that human overhunting may be partially to blame for the horse's extinction in North America some 10,000 years ago.

This reality creates a conundrum for both horse and human. The human creature that horses once feared is now the very same one asking the horse for trust and companionship. These same human beings have also placed the horse in a human world where much of its natural survival behaviors are unnecessary. This paradox creates a weird scenario for both the horse and human, no matter how you look at it.

The dilemma that humans and horses face boils down to a couple of questions. How do humans deal with the horse's penchant for fear and flight? And how do horses deal with this strange world so alien to anything they would have ever encountered in the wild?

Because of mankind's greater brain capacity, the burden of bridging the gap between the reality of the domesticated horse's world and what a horse's instincts tells it falls on the human. Communicating to the horse that everything's really okay, however, requires the human to understand the equine mind and to pay close attention to the horse's modes of communication.

Developing a trusting relationship between horse and human can achieve miraculous results. Many, many horses trust their human caretakers so much that they tolerate all kinds of bizarre situations with minimal fear. Go to any horse show and you can see what we mean. The constant commotion and chaos that is a regular part of many horse shows should make every horse at the show go nuts. But this is rarely the case. Instead, you'll see scores of horses calmly lounging around, quietly munching their hay and performing beautifully in the show ring when it's their time in the spotlight. These horses have grown accustomed to the human-dominated world in which they live and have developed a basic trust in the humans who guide their lives.

Other examples of how horse-loving humans have helped horses transcend the gap between primitive equine instinct and the modern human world can be seen everyday in stables and pastures around the globe. Here you will find horses that greet their caretakers with an obvious joy. Some horses become incredibly attached to just one special person. Even more horses truly love their jobs and are eager to come out of their stalls or pastures and do whatever work is asked of them.

If you want to achieve a profound bond with your horse, always put yourself in your horse's place and try to comprehend the equine experience. Not only will you come to understand and appreciate your horse, but your horse will come to view you as a protector, and will ultimately grow to trust you with his very life.

Stable vice advice

Horses who are kept by humans in a way that is very unnatural to how they evolved (cooped up, unable to eat with frequency, lacking mental stimulation) sometimes develop neurotic behaviors. These *stable vices*, as they are known, are the equine equivalent to nail-biting and hair-twisting. Horse with these problems need more stimulation in the forms of more frequent feeding, more exercise, more companionship with other horses, and/or more room to move around. Once a horse develops one of these habits, it's hard to break, even with a change in environment, so prevention is key:

✔ **Cribbing:** Cribbing is a bizarre but all-too-common habit. The cribbing horse grabs a fence post or barn door in between his teeth, arches his neck, and sucks air into his stomach. This air sucking creates a head rush that becomes addictive. Cribbing is not only a sign of extreme boredom, it can be harmful to the horse's digestive system. Devices exist that are meant to curb this behavior, but in our opinion, you're better off addressing the source of the problem, which is a lack of stimulation. When it comes to cribbing, prevention is more effective than a cure. *Provide your horse with enough exercise and stimulation so he doesn't get into the cribbing habit.*

✔ **Weaving:** A horse who weaves stands in one place, shifting the weight from one front foot to the other in a rhythmic motion, back and forth, his head swaying from side to side. Weaving horses are pitiful to watch. Weaving is not only a sign of extreme boredom, but can also be a symptom of anxiety. *Weaving is almost always a stall problem that usually goes away when the horse is moved to a pasture or a bigger stall.*

✔ **Pacing:** A pacing horse walks endlessly around his stall. Horses who exhibit this behavior are usually showing discomfort with confinement. In most cases, the horses who pace are the ones kept in box stalls. Horses in paddocks will occasionally pace, too, especially if they have a neighboring horse they don't get along with. Pacing is a horse's way of saying "Get me out of here!" *Move the horse to a more open environment if possible.*

✔ **Bolting feed:** *Bolting feed* means eating too quickly, something that horses sometimes do when they are feeling overly hungry, anxious about the security of their food, or simply anxious in general. It's not healthy for a horse to bolt his feed because the food isn't thoroughly chewed or moistened. This situation can cause a blockage in the esophagus, or in the intestines where it can lead to colic. *Feed the horse more often, put medium-sized stones in the feeder along with the feed, and create a more secure environment for the horse*

Equine Company

The horse is a herd animal, and you can't get around this fact. Just like humans, horses need to have regular interaction with members of their own species to maintain a healthy sense of well-being. For a horse, being alone means being vulnerable — so vulnerable that it could be a matter of life or death.

Depriving a horse of regular companionship is inhumane, tantamount to keeping a person in solitary confinement. Some horses can tolerate the situation better than others, depending on the individual personality of the horse. But none enjoy isolation. In fact, a horse deprived of companionship often becomes neurotic and develops stable vices, the equine equivalent to human nail-biting (see the sidebar entitled "Stable vice advice"). Every horse needs to have some company, whether it be on two or four legs.

One or more horses for a friend is the best scenario, but many horses can also find solace in the companionship of a goat, sheep, donkey, or other hoofed animal. Human companionship also means a great deal to horses. Some horses — usually ones who were imprinted on humans at birth — actually prefer human companionship to that of other horses. But with most horses, human companionship alone doesn't fit the bill. Human companionship is better than nothing, however, and should be provided often to a horse who has no other comrades.

Horses Must Eat

Horses evolved on grassy plains, and in nature, horses spend most of their time grazing. The equine digestive system supports almost constant consumption of low-grade grasses.

The equine brain is also designed for lots of foraging and chewing. Grazing for a horse is the human equivalent to working, reading, or watching TV. For a horse, grazing provides not only nutrition, but mental stimulation, too.

The ideal situation for a horse is to be in a pasture, where he can munch on grass for nearly 18 hours a day. A horse who can do so is going to be a happy, well-adjusted critter who can give in to the natural urge to chew, chew, chew.

Unfortunately, for a number of reasons, providing a horse with pasture isn't always possible. Many horses — especially those in more urban areas — live in small dirt paddocks or tidy box stalls, without access to grass. Sometimes, these grazing-deprived horses develop stable vices because they are bored and frustrated by their inability to express their natural urge to graze (see the sidebar entitled "Stable vice advice").

For horses who can't graze in a field of grass, the next best thing is frequent feeding of roughage, like hay. You must feed horses a minimum of twice a day for basic nutrition. More frequent feedings are even better for their brains and help keep their digestive tracts working properly.

Horses Must Move

Just as Mother Nature designed the horse to eat on a nearly constant basis, she also built the horse for nearly constant movement.

If you watch a horse grazing out in a pasture, you'll see that with just about every bite of grass, the horse takes a step. In a 15-minute period, the horse moves quite a few feet from where he originally started nibbling.

This regular movement provides exercise for both the horse's body and mind. Energy is slowly released as the horse moves steadily around the pasture. Take this same horse and put him in a box stall or small paddock, and you have a horse who feels cooped up.

For the horse who must live in small quarters without the freedom to move about and graze, daily exercise is of vital importance. Every day, your confined equine needs to be taken out of the stall and walked for at least half an hour, turned out into a larger paddock to run around, or be ridden at least 45 minutes. If the horse doesn't receive adequate exercise, not only will he be prone to developing leg problems, but he'll also have plenty of pent up energy. The horse often expresses his overabundance of energy through stable vices (see the sidebar "Stable vice advice") or through misbehavior when he finally does get out of his stall.

Part II
Choosing a Horse

The 5th Wave By Rich Tennant

" I told you they were very social animals."

In this part . . .

The chapters in Part II tell you how to select and purchase a horse of your own. Before you take the
plunge, you should look deeply into yourself and make
sure that horse ownership is a commitment that you're
ready to make. Chapter 3 provides the information you
need to ensure that you're entering horse ownership with
your eyes open. In Chapter 4, we take you through the various breeds of horses so that you can choose a breed that
suits you. Finally, Chapter 5 takes you through the buying
process itself, from evaluating the horse to signing the
contract.

Chapter 3

Before You Buy

*B*ecoming a horse owner is a serious decision. Unlike skiing or golf or tennis, horseback riding is a hobby that involves *a living, breathing creature*. When you don't feel like playing golf or aren't in the mood to ski, you can just toss your equipment into the garage and forget about it until the urge strikes again. But owning a horse is a whole different ballgame.

When you own a horse, you're taking responsibility for another living being. You have to feed, groom, and even ride the horse on days when you just don't feel like it. A horse can't sit in a corner while you decide to do something that more suits your mood. Horses need regular care, attention, and TLC.

For these reasons, you need to consider some very serious points before you embark on the journey of horse ownership. In this chapter, we take a look at these important considerations, and give you some advice about preparing for the day when a horse ultimately calls you "mom" or "dad."

Asking Yourself the Right Questions

When you find yourself developing the urge to own a horse, you need to do some soul searching. We want you to ask yourself some profound and difficult questions. Not only does your happiness and enjoyment depend on the answers you give, but so does a horse's well-being.

We've heard too many stories of people coming into the horse world on a whim, casually entering into horse ownership without realizing the commitment involved. The final result is that the newcomer becomes unhappy, and the horse ends up paying the price for it. The owner loses interest, and the horse winds up standing in his stall for weeks or months at a time with little or no attention other than the most minimal amount of care. Or the animal ends up being sold for a quick buck and marked for the slaughterhouse. In extreme cases, the owner abandons the horse, leaving him to slowly starve to death in a grassless pasture because no one cares anymore.

These scenarios sound very dramatic, but this stuff does happen. We know that *you* don't want to be guilty of inflicting any such unfair treatment on a horse, the most noble and beautiful of all domestic creatures. That's why you need to probe deeply into your psyche to make sure that owning a horse is really something you want to do. And we're going to help you do that.

Why do you want a horse?

People are drawn to horse ownership for a number of reasons. Some of these reasons are good, some not so good.

Maybe you've wanted a horse your whole life, but couldn't afford one until now. If so, you are part of a fascinating, primarily female trend in the horse world. As little girls, many women longed to have a horse of their own. In fact, a horse obsession is almost a prerequisite to *being* a little girl, it seems. This little-girl passion for horses apparently reached an all-time high in the 1950s and 1960s. And now these once-obsessed little girls are all grown up and have the disposable income to fulfill their dream.

However, men are not exempt from this phenomenon. More than one little boy grew up wanting to be a cowboy, riding on a swift steed and galloping off into the sunset. For many men, that John Wayne fantasy never went away, and horse ownership makes that fantasy a reality (well, sort of).

Wanting a horse to fulfill your life's dream is fine as long as you realize all the real life responsibilities that come along with horse ownership. Here's a list of the not-so-glamorous things you'll be dealing with after you take the ownership plunge:

✓ **Unappealing jobs:** You won't only be riding the horse you own — you'll also be feeding him, grooming him, and cleaning up after him. The feeding and cleaning part is especially true if you'll be keeping the horse on your own property. Mucking stalls is hardly one of the more romantic aspects of horse ownership, yet the task is inevitable and just about every horse owner does it at some point in his or her life. Although horse manure doesn't smell anywhere near as bad as dog doo, you still won't relish the job!

- **Total responsibility:** The horse is completely dependent on you for food, water, exercise, and attention, so you must be willing to make the horse's needs a priority in your life. That means no going out to the karaoke bar with your friends after a hard day at the office until *after* you feed your horse. It also means braving any kind of weather Mother Nature throws at you — and she can have a pretty wicked aim — to get your horse out for grooming and exercise — whether you feel like doing it or not. The horse is standing there waiting for you to show up and take care of him, and doing so is your responsibility. Period.

- **Financial enslavement:** Owning a horse is downright expensive. Many horse people sport a bumper sticker on their cars that reads "Poverty is owning a horse," which is not that much of an exaggeration.

  If you get lucky and end up with a horse who never gets sick, at no time injures himself, and doesn't need shoes or supplements, that bumper sticker may not be for you. But we've yet to meet anyone who owns such a creature, so odds are that you'll be regularly coughing up cold hard cash to tend to your horse's special needs.

Fulfilling a dream isn't the reason that everyone is drawn to horse ownership. Some people just love animals and find the idea of spending time and bonding with a horse appealing. Some see other people riding and think it looks like great fun. These are both legitimate reasons to delve into horse ownership as long as you understand the responsibilities and drawbacks of owning a horse that we outline in the preceding bulleted list.

Don't fall prey to some of the not so good reasons for wanting a horse. Here are a few:

- **Zoning ordinances:** You just bought a house in the country that happens to be zoned for horses, and even though you've never had an interest in horses before and aren't terribly interested in them now, you feel like you should have one, well, because you can.

- **Lawn ornaments:** You think that horses are very attractive creatures, and even though you don't have any great urge to care for or ride one, having a horse on your property would make your yard look nicer.

- **Junior wants one:** You don't have much interest in horses, but your child wants a horse. Your child has never ridden a horse before, but rather than giving him lessons first, you'd rather just buy a horse straight away.

- **Romance:** You have absolutely no experience with horses but think that the whole notion of riding is very romantic. Rather than take lessons first to see whether you actually enjoy riding, you decide to buy a horse instead.

- **Spare change:** You just inherited a little bit of money and want to spend it all on buying a horse. You think that the biggest expense in horse ownership is the purchase price, so you aren't worried about maintenance costs.

If any of these scenarios sound like you, *stop* before you buy a horse and *think*. None of the above are good reasons to take on the huge commitment and responsibility that is horse ownership. You need to do much more research into what owning a horse is all about first. And most importantly, you have to develop a genuine interest in horses before taking the plunge into owning one. Horses require a huge commitment of time, money, and energy, and if you aren't sincerely dedicated to your equine charge, the responsibility will soon feel like a burden. Ultimately, both you and the horse will suffer.

Are you ready for a horse?

Before you delve into the challenging endeavor of horse ownership, you must prepare yourself for the experience by developing a basic knowledge of horses and what owning one is all about.

The money factor

Money — and how much of it you have — is a big thing to consider when you are debating whether to buy a horse. Horses are expensive animals to have around, and knowing exactly *how* expensive before you go out and buy one is imperative.

Find out the costs of the various aspects of horse ownership in your area and make sure that the total amount fits in your budget. Following is a rundown of what costs you can expect to incur.

Initial outlay

Buying a decent horse means shelling out some decent money. The cost of horses varies considerably from one place to another, but expect to spend at least $1,000 for a pleasure horse and much more for an animal you want to show.

In addition to the expense of getting the horse, you need to buy equipment and supplies, including a saddle, saddle pad, bridle, halter, grooming tools, and so on. Plus, you need riding clothes for yourself and possibly your family (see Part III, "Stuff You're Gonna Need" for details). All these things can really add up.

If you plan to keep your horse on your own property, you also need enough money to create the appropriate housing for the animal. This sum can be substantial, depending on the amount of work you have to do (see Chapter 7 for details).

Maintenance

One of the biggest mistakes that newcomers to the horse world make is underestimating the cost of maintaining a horse. In most cases, the purchase sum is minimal when compared to the amount of money that keeping the horse requires.

Here is a list of the regular expenses you can expect with horse ownership. The costs of each item or service vary considerably depending on where you live, so we advise calling commercial stables, veterinarians, *farriers* (the people who trim and put shoes on the horse's feet), and tack and feed stores in your area to get a sense of how much each of these items runs:

- **Boarding:** If you plan to keep your horse at a commercial boarding facility rather than on your own property, you'll be paying monthly for a stall, pasture, or *paddock* (a fenced enclosure). This fee usually includes food and stall maintenance; it may or may not include bedding.

- **Feed:** If you're keeping the horse on your own property, feed includes hay and/or pasture maintenance. If you plan to give grain or another special diet food to your horse, figure in that cost as well.

- **Supplements:** Many horses benefit from the inclusion of feed supplements. If your horse is one of these, add this cost to your monthly expenses.

- **Bedding:** If your horse is kept in a stall that you are responsible for maintaining, you have to provide shavings or another type of bedding, which you must clean and freshen daily (see Chapter 7 for more details on bedding).

- **Preventative veterinary care:** Regular health maintenance for most adult horses includes vaccinations and deworming several times a year. It also includes teeth floating once or twice a year — which, by the way, doesn't mean your horse's teeth will be set adrift in a bucket of Efferdent. Floating is another term for *filing down*. We discuss this topic in more detail in Chapter 10.

- **Veterinary treatment:** When a horse gets sick, the problem can be anything from a minor illness to a situation that requires major surgery. As an owner, you must be prepared to spend money on veterinary treatment if your horse becomes ill.

- **Shoes:** Most horses require new shoes every 6 to 8 weeks. A farrier still needs to trim horses who don't need shoes — because they're not doing much work or have tough feet — every 6 to 8 weeks. (Chapter 10 has more information about shoeing and other aspects of hoof care.)

- **Insurance:** If you insure your horse for major medical, mortality, loss of use and/or liability, add the premiums to your list of expenses. (See Chapter 5 for more information on insuring your horse.)

- **Training/lessons:** New horse owners with little riding experience need to continue their own and their horse's education with a trainer or riding instructor. (Training is a must if you intend to show your horse.) Weekly training or lessons for horse and/or rider are another expense.

- **Show expenses:** If you plan to show your horse, you'll be spending money on show clothes and tack, entry fees, and transportation. (See Chapter 18 for details on showing.)

Time

Owning a horse is much more time consuming than people usually think. The daily care of a 1,000-pound animal that can't be housebroken is pretty involved.

If you're keeping the horse at home, and the horse is going to be in a stall, you're going to have to find time to feed two to three times a day. You also need to make time to clean the stall (remove the manure and soiled bedding) at least once a day. Add this time to the amount of time you must spend grooming and exercising the horse, and you're going to spend a noteworthy chunk of your day on horse care.

Although a horse can be an ideal family companion, don't expect your kids to take on too much of the time responsibility. Sure, they can help out, but as the adult, *you* are the one ultimately responsible for the horse's care and well-being. And considering how most kids are about such things, you'll probably end up having to make time to do the work yourself.

Commitment

You have to be willing to be there for your horse every day, rain or shine, time or no time. Ask yourself the following questions to help determine whether you are really ready and willing to make this commitment:

- ✔ Am I willing to give up some of my other activities to spend time caring for my horse?
- ✔ Am I willing to drop everything and run to my horse's side should he get sick?
- ✔ Am I willing to spend time giving my horse medicine or treatment if he becomes ill?
- ✔ Am I willing to take time out of my busy day, each and every day, to groom and exercise my horse?
- ✔ Am I willing to work with my horse to solve any problems the two of us may encounter?
- ✔ Am I willing to perform the sometimes hard physical labor that horse care calls for?
- ✔ Am I willing to think of my horse as a partner, one who deserves the best care and treatment, regardless of the inconvenience I may experience?
- ✔ If I am buying this horse primarily for my children, am I willing to continue to care for him even if my children lose interest?

If you answered yes to all of these questions, then you are ready to make the commitment to horse ownership.

What's your discipline?

The first thing you have to do is figure out which discipline you want to ride in. The discipline you choose determines what kind of horse you buy because most horses are trained in only one or two disciplines.

If you haven't yet figured out how you want to ride, flip to Chapter 14 to decide which discipline interests you the most. Then take some riding lessons in that discipline to make sure that you really do like it before you commit to buying a horse you can only ride in that style.

Taking lessons

One of the smartest things you can do before you go out and buy a horse is to take riding lessons first. This statement may sound obvious, but if you don't know that much about riding, you may not realize how difficult it is, and how much work proper riding involves. After all, you need to know much more about riding than just hopping up on the critter's back!

Here are some of the benefits of learning to ride *before* you get your own horse:

  ✔ You'll know for certain that riding is something you truly enjoy because you have already been doing it.

  ✔ You'll have a good sense of what type of horse is best for you, based on your riding style and skill level.

  ✔ You'll be better able to evaluate horses for purchase because you will be able to ride them competently.

  ✔ You won't be risking *ruining* your new horse with poor riding skills that can disrupt his previous training.

  ✔ You'll be able to start enjoying your new horse right away, instead of spending precious bonding time just trying to learn the basics of riding.

Regular lessons

Formal riding lessons are the best way to learn how to ride a horse. In most areas of the civilized world, riding lessons are relatively easy to come by. Nearly every commercial boarding facility has trainers and instructors on staff that give lessons by the hour. In the United States, both western and English lessons are staples at commercial riding facilities. (For details on the differences between western and English riding, see Chapter 14.)

You can start looking for lessons by cracking open the telephone book and searching under the heading "Riding Academies." If several riding facilities are accessible to you, you can choose a good one by contacting an equine veterinarian in your area. Tell the veterinarian's staff that you're looking for beginner riding lessons and ask whether they can recommend a good facility in the area.

After locating a facility, we recommend that you take an initial riding lesson in the discipline of your choice, and if you like the instructor and the quality of the experience, sign up for a series of lessons. Most facilities offer discount packages of four or more lessons.

If you are arranging riding lessons for your child, make sure that the facility you call offers lessons for young riders in your child's age group.

The number of lessons you ultimately take depends on what you can afford and how much you still need to learn. We suggest that you take as many lessons as fits your budget. Some people continue to take lessons for years, gradually moving up in their individual training level just as any athlete does. You can never educate yourself enough about riding. In fact, even Olympic equestrian team members continue to take lessons after winning gold medals!

Horse camps

A horse camp is another way that you can start riding. By attending a horse camp, you can combine a vacation with an intensive riding experience.

Horse camps are resorts that specialize in equine activities. Most offer lessons for beginners, and will allow you to spend a concentrated amount of time with and around horses. The camps do provide access to other activities — tennis and hiking, typically — but you have the option of spending all your time studying horses. (See Chapter 21 for a handful of riding vacations to consider.)

Horse camps are a great way for beginners to start riding. However, plan to continue your riding education when you return home from your vacation. True, you'll get a good foundation in the week or two that you are at horse camp, but this short amount of time isn't enough for you to completely develop your riding skills. Sign up for ongoing lessons at a local riding academy to give yourself more time learning in the saddle.

Adult education programs

More and more community colleges and private learning centers are offering introductory courses in riding for adults. These classes can be a great way to have a first experience on a horse because they almost always include riding lessons. Basic information on equine anatomy, care and feeding, grooming, and other aspects of horsemanship are often a part of these courses, too.

Breed club programs

A number of national breed clubs sponsor programs that introduce people to the world of horses, particularly that association's breed. These programs match up beginning riders and experienced professionals within the given breed. The goal is to give new riders more information about horses and to assist them when they're ready to purchase that breed of horse (for a list of breed clubs, see Appendix B).

Nightmare experiences in rental stables

Most rental stables offer nothing in the way of instruction and plenty in the way of potential disaster. Stay away from them while trying to acquire basic horsemanship skills.

Rental stables are places where you can rent a horse in increments of one hour and take the horse out on a trail ride, usually with a group. Instead of offering riding lessons, these facilities stick you up on a horse and send you on your way.

Although you can find a few good rental stables, they are few and far between. At most rental stables, the horses are poorly treated and make terrible mounts. Because they're ridden day in and day out by people who don't even know the basics of riding, they lose whatever training they may have had when they first came to the place. The end result are horses who are uncooperative and sometimes even dangerous.

The sad truth is that most first riding experiences occur at these kinds of stables. Consequently, most first riding experiences are unpleasant ones. Ask your non-horsy friends about the first time they ever rode a horse, and you'll see what we mean. Tales of horses trying to rub riders off on trees, horses rolling on the ground with the riders still in the saddle, horses running back to barn while the riders hold on for dear life — these are all common rental stable stories.

Who is going to ride the horse?

Before you go out and start looking for a horse, figure out exactly who is going to ride it. Is the horse just for you? Will your spouse also be riding the animal? How about your children?

If more than one person in your family is going to ride the horse, then you must consider that person or persons when you're figuring out which horse to buy. The horse should be suitable for the family member with the least amount of riding experience. If you've been riding for years, but your spouse has never been on a horse before, get a horse who can take care of a rank beginner. (Meanwhile, sign your spouse up for some riding lessons!)

If your children are the only ones who plan to ride the horse, then you had better be very sure that they are committed to riding (as committed as a child can be anyway). After all, if your kids can't even sit still through *The Lion King,* they may not be ready for the concentration required in horseback riding. Make them take riding lessons for at least a year before you actually buy a horse. If they're still enthusiastic about riding after taking instruction for that long, then they'll probably stick with it once you purchase a horse.

Lease or buy?

Most people who want a horse have the impulse to buy one. But we heartily recommend another option: leasing.

Leasing a horse instead of or before you buy one is a great opportunity to find out what horse ownership is all about before committing to it. When you lease, you function pretty much as a horse owner but without the same financial and long-term pledge.

There never seems to be a shortage of horses available for lease. Leasing is a perfect arrangement for an owner who doesn't have time to ride the horse, doesn't have the money to care for him, or no longer has the desire or ability to ride. Why don't people in these situation just sell their horses? Because leasing allows them to stay in control of what happens to the horse while eliminating some or all of the ownership responsibilities.

Although leasing can be a great way to test out your commitment to horse ownership, one pitfall does exist: You can find yourself getting very attached to the horse you are leasing, only to discover that the owner refuses to sell the animal or that the owner wants to sell, but you can't afford to buy.

Deciphering leases

Leases, which are often flexible, can work in a number of different ways. The one you ultimately choose should be the one best suited to your own needs and wants. Following are some examples of common lease arrangements:

- ✔ **Full lease:** The owner leases the horse out completely, allowing the lessee to keep the horse in the lessee's facility of choice. The lessee pays a flat fee up front on the lease for a given amount of time (usually a year), and assumes all of the horse's maintenance costs, including food, shoes, and routine veterinary care. In most cases, if the horse becomes seriously ill or injured, the owner is responsible for the horse's medical bills. These types of leases sometimes come with an option to buy the horse at the end of the lease term. Consider this option if you want to get a very realistic taste of horse ownership before you make the commitment, or if you don't have the cash up front to actually purchase a horse.

- ✔ **Full lease with stipulations:** The owner leases out the horse but requires that the horse stay at the owner's facility (or another approved facility). The lessee can ride the horse each and every day, but must request permission to trailer the horse off the property or do anything out of the ordinary with the animal. Payment arrangements tend to vary considerably with this type of lease. Owners sometimes charge a monthly fee for the lease, which may or may not include the horse's vet care and shoeing. This lease arrangement is good if you want to get a sense of horse ownership without the total commitment of buying. Because of the stipulations involved, these kinds of leases are often cheaper than straightforward, full leases.

> ✔ **Partial lease:** With a partial lease, or half-lease, the owner leases the horse out to a lessee for riding only a few days a week. Often times, the owner rides the horse on the other days. Sometimes, the owner gives two half-leases to two different people, who end up sharing the horse. In a partial lease situation, the lessee rarely pays for any costs other than the leasing fee. This option is great if time and/or money is limited.

Finding a lease

Locating a good horse to lease is much easier than finding a good horse to buy, in most cases. Here are some methods:

> ✔ **Word of mouth:** Asking around at boarding stables is one way to find horses for lease. This method seems to work particularly well — undoubtedly due to the strength of the horse-owner grapevine.
>
> ✔ **Trainers:** Horse trainers often have clients who are looking to lease out their horses. Asking the trainers in your area will probably turn up several options.
>
> ✔ **Advertisements:** If your area has a horse-oriented publication, check the classified section for "for lease" ads. Tack and feed stores almost always have bulletin boards with notices featuring horses for lease.

Choosing a lease horse

The way you choose a horse to lease depends largely on what kind of lease agreement you will have with the horse's owner.

When you are considering leasing a horse, evaluate the animal the same as though you were buying it. Because your commitment is limited in a leasing situation, you don't need to be quite as certain of your choice, but you still want to make sure that the horse you choose will be good for you.

If you are going for a full lease where you'll be responsible for all the horse's veterinary care, you may want to pay for a basic veterinary pre-purchase exam to ensure that the horse is healthy. People often don't take this step because of the costs involved, but you may want to consider it.

Getting a written agreement

A lease is a business transaction, so put the details of the arrangement in writing and have both parties sign the agreement. Having the agreement looked over by an attorney before signing and then notarized upon signing is also a good idea.

If the owner doesn't offer a contract, draw one up yourself. If the horse's owner does provide a contract, make sure that the document includes the following details:

✔ **Names:** Your name and address and that of the horse's owner.

✔ **Description:** The horse's name and description of the horse, including age, color, height, and registration number, if any.

✔ **Purpose or intent:** How you intend to use the horse — trail riding only, showing in hunter classes, and so on. Write out all intended uses you have for the horse (after discussing them with the owner).

✔ **Equipment:** Whether the lease includes use of the horse's tack.

✔ **Restrictions:** What you *won't* be doing with the horse. If the owner does not want you to trailer the horse off the property, for example, she needs to stipulate this information in the lease.

✔ **Care requirements:** Any physical care the horse needs, including grooming, exercise, feeding, and so on (include any regular medications or treatments the horse is receiving).

✔ **Riders:** Who is allowed to ride the horse.

✔ **Lease terms:** How long the lease is for, and whether it is renewable.

✔ **Options:** If you hope to buy the horse at the end of the lease, make sure that the contract includes an option to buy.

✔ **Price:** The price you're paying for the lease and how you're going to make the payments.

✔ **Insurance coverage:** Details on what kind of insurance covers the horse, particularly who is responsible for maintaining the premiums. If no insurance covers the horse, indicate who is responsible if the horse is injured, becomes ill, or dies.

✔ **Medical care:** Who is responsible for paying the horse's medical bills.

✔ **Cancellation policy:** Whether the lease can be canceled, by whom, and under what circumstances.

✔ **Availability:** If yours is a partial lease, spell out which days you will be riding and which days the owner or other lessee will be using the horse.

Finding the Horse for You

Okay, you're certain that you really do want a horse, can afford it, have the time for it, and are ready for the commitment. Now you need to start thinking about what kind of horse you should have.

Why age matters

Age is an important factor when considering a horse. The idea of a young horse may be very appealing because of the animal's potential life span, but you can't go in a worse direction when purchasing a first horse. Young horses are typically inexperienced and full of "bugs." They don't have much confidence or knowledge, and their training is usually only cursory. Combine these elements with an inexperienced horse owner or rider, and you have a recipe for disaster.

The notion that a young, untrained horse and an inexperienced rider can "learn together" is a romantic one that doesn't cut it in the real world. Generally in these situations, the horse becomes unmanageable, the rider becomes miserable, and the relationship dissolves into disaster.

When you're learning to ride and care for a horse, your best teacher is an older, wizened horse who forgives your mistakes and helps show you the right way to do things. Horses over the age of six years are considered adults, and capable of the kind of equine maturity and experience that you need in a first horse.

For example, Audrey got her first horse at the age of 13. She'd been riding for a couple of years, but was definitely a neophyte when it came to horse ownership and serious riding. The horse her parents chose for her was a quiet, affectionate, older mare named Peggy, who was about 15 years old. Peggy had seen it all — including little kids who didn't really know how to ride — and she patiently taught Audrey much of what your humble author now knows about horses.

The age breakdown

The horse world has standardized ways of evaluating horses by their age. In humans, we think of babies, teenagers, adults, and senior citizens. Well, equine equivalents to these exist, too. You may be surprised to see how horse age groups are somewhat similar to human age groups.

Although horses tend to age somewhat differently based on breed (the larger draft and warmblood breeds take longer to mature than the smaller, lighter breeds), what follows is a generalization of how you can categorize horses by age. Looking at horses' ages in this way helps you get a sense of who they are at any given point in their lives:

- **Foals:** Foals are baby horses, anywhere from newborn to the age when they are weaned from their mothers (four to six months, usually). Foals are physically awkward and very curious about their surroundings, not unlike human infants and toddlers.

- **Weanlings:** Weanlings are usually anywhere from four to six months in age. As the term suggests, they are babies who have been removed from their mothers. In human terms, weanlings are equivalent to pre-teens.

- **Yearlings:** Yearlings are young horses that have reached their first year of life. They are the equine version of a teeny bopper.

- **Young horses:** Horses in this category are 2 to 3 years old and are just starting to be trained for riding. These are formative years for a horse, and equivalent to the older teenage years for a human. These horses tend to be harder to work with because they are not yet mentally mature. Physically, they're pretty much grown, but they still have lots of mental growth to go.

- **Young adult horses:** Horses in the age of range of 3 to 6 years old are in their peak learning phase. The majority of a horse's basic training takes place during this stage of life. As the horse slowly matures both physically and mentally, he becomes ready to take on the role of serious worker and companion. The human equivalent to this age group is the late teens to early 20s.

- **Adult horses:** This category is for horses between the ages of 6 and 14 years. Horses in this age group have matured both physically and mentally. Most of their training is complete and they're ready to do their jobs happily. Adult horses are similar to humans in their late-20s to late 40s.

- **Senior horses:** Horses 15 years old and over are seniors. Just like humans in this age bracket, 15-year-old horses start to become arthritic and may have other health problems. When a horse reaches the age of 20, it moves into the upper reaches of the senior range (the human equivalent of the mid-60s and 70s age bracket).

Confirming conformation

Horses who have the best build, or *conformation*, are the ones most capable of doing the work humans ask of them. If you take time to study the horse's structure and anatomy, you will develop an eye for what horse people call *good conformation*. Horses with good conformation are the ideal for most horse people.

No horse is perfect. Every horse — just like every human — has some physical characteristic that is less than pleasing to the eye. In horses, these *conformation faults* can not only affect the appearance of the horse, but also the horse's ability to function properly in his work.

Just because a horse has some conformation faults doesn't make him a bad horse. But being aware of those faults can help you know your horse's limitations (see the sidebar called "Faulty conformation").

Leg faults are a common problem for horses, and can cause performance troubles. Spotting conformation faults in horses helps you anticipate a horse's potential troubles.

Before you can spot the abnormal, you need an idea of how normal looks. When viewing the legs from the front, drop an imaginary line from the top center of the leg down to the ground. A horse with good conformation has a center line that splits the leg in half all the way to the ground.

Telling a horse's age

Ever hear the term "long in the tooth?" This horse-related expression has to do with the way horses' teeth change as they age.

As a horse gets older the length, color, shape, and markings of his teeth transform. If you come to recognize these changes and the ages they are associated with, you'll be able to tell pretty much how old any horse is just by looking in his mouth.

The older a horse gets, the longer his teeth grow. While the teeth are growing, the surfaces are also wearing down and changing their shape. Dark marks in the surface of the teeth called *dental cups* slowly appear and then disappear with age. The number and condition of dental cups visible in a horse's mouth are dead giveaways to the horse's age.

Another mark, this one in the horse's upper incisors, also helps determine age. Called the *Galvayne's groove,* this mark appears on the surface of the upper incisors once a horse hits 10 years of age. As the horse ages, the groove continues to expand downward. By age 20, the groove extends all the way to the end of the tooth.

It takes a bit of practice to learn how to age a horse by his teeth. Start by looking at horses whose ages you know to get a feel for how it works.

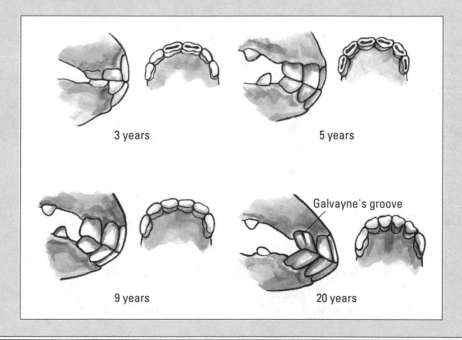

3 years

5 years

Galvayne's groove

9 years

20 years

Do the same thing when looking at the foreleg from the side. In your mind, draw a line from the top center of the leg all the way to the ground. A horse with good conformation has a center line that splits the leg to the level of the fetlock, and then falls to the ground just behind the heel.

When you view the hind leg from the side, imagine a line from the back of the hindquarters to the ground. In a horse with good conformation, this line runs along the back of the cannon bone to the bulbs of the heels (see Figure 3-1 for front and side views of straight legs).

Figure 3-1:
A horse with good conformation has a well-balanced appearance, and you can draw straight lines on the legs from the point of the chest down through the hoof.

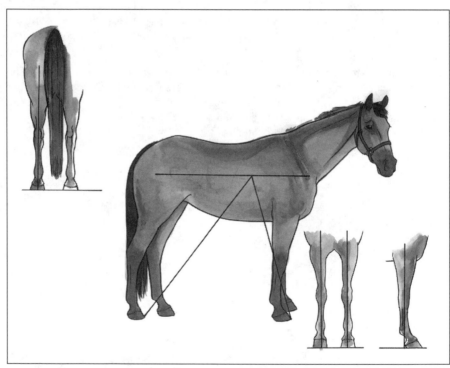

Distinguishing gender differences

We humans have among us boys and girls, men and women. Horses, however, have a whole slew of genders, as we show you in the following list:

- ✔ **Colts:** Young male horses under the age of 4 years old. Colts are typically full of energy and the older ones are looking for females under every rock.

- ✔ **Fillies:** Females under the age of 4, fillies are the female horses that hormone-enraged colts most eagerly seek. Like colts, fillies also have considerable energy, but they aren't as hormone driven as their male counterparts.

- **Geldings:** Geldings are castrated males. Many horse people think that geldings make the best mounts because they aren't plagued by hormones and the various distractions that often accompany surges of these organic chemicals.

- **Mares:** Mares are female horse ages 4 or over. We think that mares make wonderful companions, although many people find some mares difficult to handle whenever the mare comes into season (heat). Hormones, you see.

- **Stallions:** Colts who grow up to be 4 years old or older with their reproductive organs intact are called stallions. Because stallions' strong interest in breeding can drive them to distraction, they aren't recommended for beginning riders. In fact, many boarding stables don't permit stallions on the premises because stallions can sometimes be unruly. Only very experienced horse handlers have what it takes to train and manage most stallions.

Realistically, your choice of horse is limited to either mares or geldings. If you are thinking about a stallion, forget it. Few stallions are suitable for beginning riders and owners, no matter how romantic the notion of riding one is. And all stallions come with logistical problems. For instance, most boarding stables won't allow stallions on the premises, and if a stallion gets out of a pasture and impregnates a neighbor's mare, the situation is ripe for a lawsuit.

The question of whether to get a mare or a gelding is a big one to some horse people, and not something that not everyone agrees upon. Many people will only own geldings, while others swear by mares. Some people don't have a preference one way or another. The decision on whether to get a mare or a gelding ultimately rests on you. If you don't have a preference — most people don't — then just look for the best horse regardless of gender.

That time of the season

Many horse people prefer geldings for the following reason: Mares can be moody. Many female horses experience the equine version of PMS during the heavy estrus (ovulation) months of early spring. Some have this hormone problem year round. As a result of these raging hormones, the mare becomes nervous, irritable, and at times, irrational.

Most mares, if they experience this at all, have just a touch of moodiness as a result. They may be a bit spookier during their estrus time, or less cooperative with riders. Mares with serious equine PMS problems, however, can be helped with a daily dose of orally administered hormone or an implant in the uterus. Mares can also be spayed, although this procedure is not a common or easy surgery as it is for dogs and cats.

On the other hand, many mares do _not_ experience any kind of equine PMS. In fact, Audrey has had nothing but mares her whole life and has never had a horse with this condition.

Conformation faults

Here is a list of some typical leg conformation faults that can affect a horse's health or ability, and that you can learn to recognize by sight. To spot these, view the horse when he's standing still and alert:

✔ **Base narrow:** Base narrow is the exact opposite of base wide. When viewed from the front, the distance between the imaginary center lines of the hooves is less than the distance between the center lines of the chest. This construction occurs in wide-chested horses and tends to go with toed-in or toed-out hoof conformation. Horses with base narrow legs carry more weight on the outside of their legs, which means that bruising, sidebone, and arthritis commonly occur in these horses, affecting the outside of the leg regardless of whether the horse is toed-in or toed-out.

✔ **Base wide:** In base wide horses, when looking at the legs from the front, the distance between the center lines of the hooves is wider than the distance between the center lines at the top of the legs at the chest. This fault tends to show up in narrow-chested horses and usually goes hand-in-hand with toed-out hooves. As a result of this construction, the horse carries more weight on the inside of the leg, and so the hooves tend to land on the inside first, creating more strain on the inside of the leg. Horses with this conformation are more prone to problems on the inside of the leg such as bruising, sidebone, and arthritis.

✔ **Bowlegged:** When looking at a horse with bowed legs from the front, the legs arc outward at the knees. If the "bow" is severe, the horse may be more prone to developing arthritis in the knees.

✔ **Calf knee:** Calf-kneed horses have forelegs that, when viewed from the side, appear to bend backward at the knee.

✔ **Knee-sprung:** Horses who are knee-sprung are also described as being *over at the knee.* When viewed from the side, the forelegs of these horses appear to bend forward at the knee.

✔ **Knock-kneed:** When looking at the legs from the front, the knees come together. If this construction is severe enough, it can cause arthritis in the knees.

✔ **Sickle hocks:** With sickle hock construction, the horse has too much angulation of the hock and stifle. Sickle hocks are the opposite of being straight behind, and can result in arthritis of the hock if severe enough.

✔ **Straight behind:** Straight-behind build means the horse has very little angle to its hock and stifle. Horses who are straight behind are much more prone to hock arthritis and locking knee caps.

✔ **Toed-in:** Also called pigeon-toed, this conformation fault results in hooves that point toward each other. Usually, the leg starts to turn inward at the level of the fetlock but may start as high as the point where the leg meets the chest. This conformation causes the hooves to *paddle,* or swing outward while moving, creating interference between the legs and possible injury.

✔ **Toed-out:** Also known as *splayfooted*, toed-out hooves point away from each other. Similar to toed-in conformation, the toeing out may start at the fetlock or higher up the leg. Horses with this problem tend to "wing," or swing inward while they are moving. Sometimes the hooves can "wing in" to the point where the hooves hit each other.

Thinking about Insurance

Before you buy your horse, think about the possibility of getting insurance coverage on the animal. Your horse represents an investment in money, time, and emotion, which makes insurance a good idea. Companies that specialize in insuring horses offer many different kinds of equine insurance. Explore all of the different types of insurance to see which ones you want to purchase for your new horse:

- **Major medical:** Major medical policies for horses are similar to those for humans. The policy covers medical costs such as diagnostic procedures, surgery, medication, and visits by a veterinarian. A deductible for each incident is common with major medical policies. You must supply a veterinary health certificate to assure that your horse has no pre-existing conditions. Age restrictions often apply to older horses. Most insurance companies require that you also cover the horse for full mortality if you want to insure for major medical.

  We highly recommend major medical insurance. If your horse develops a serious illness, veterinary bills can mount up very quickly.

- **Surgical:** Surgical coverage is a medical policy that only applies to situations where surgery is required. You must also carry a full mortality policy on the horse.

  If you can get or can't afford major medical insurance, surgical is the next best thing. It can protect you and your horse if the animal requires colic surgery or another operation.

- **Full mortality:** Full mortality insurance covers the horse if he dies due to illness or accident, and usually pays the estimated value of the horse. If the horse is stolen and not recovered, full mortality is effective, too. The insurance company requires a veterinary health certificate indicating that the horse is healthy. If your horse is older than 14, you may have trouble finding coverage.

  If you paid a substantial sum of money for your horse, full mortality insurance is a must. Even if your horse didn't cost that much, realize that without this insurance, your horse's unexpected death could result in a loss of your investment.

- **Limited mortality:** Limited mortality usually only covers death as a result of accident or other specified cause. Because the policy doesn't cover illness, the insurance company doesn't require a health certificate.

  You are unlikely to need this insurance on your horse unless you have special circumstances that place your horse at risk for an accident. A typical example of special circumstances is shipping your horse cross-country. If you insure your horse with a limited mortality policy, and your horse dies in a trailer accident during the trip, the insurance company will pay out the value of the horse.

✔ **Loss of use:** If the horse is injured or ill to the point where he can no longer be ridden, loss of use insurance compensates you. You'll be paid a predetermined sum, which is based on an amount of money agreed to by both you and the insurance company. Loss of use policies require that you also carry some type of medical coverage.

Some horse owners like to have this option. Some policies allow the owner to euthanize the horse and still collect loss of use, while others allow the owner to keep the horse even though he can't be used for the specific purpose that the policy indicates.

✔ **Personal liability:** This type of insurance protects you if your horse injures a person or damages property. Your home owner's insurance may already provide you with this coverage.

Carrying personal liability on your horse is always a good idea, if you can afford it. You never know when your horse could accidentally hurt someone or cause damage to another person's possessions.

The cost of insurance varies depending on where you live and the type of insurance you purchase. If you plan to cover your horse for major medical and full mortality — which are the most common insurance coverages used by the average pleasure horse owner — expect to spend several hundred dollars a year.

To find an equine insurer, ask your veterinarian for a reference. You can also peruse the advertisements of most any equine publication. Most insurers take out ads regularly, both large ads and classified listings.

Getting Help with Your Hayburner

You can never educate yourself enough when it comes to horses. Even the most experienced, savvy horse people strive to gain more equine knowledge.

As a first-time horse owner, a whole world of information and experience awaits you. And the best place to garner that knowledge is from those whose professions revolve around horses: your trainer (or other equine expert), your veterinarian, and your farrier. These are the people who can guide you and help you with your new horse, so selecting them carefully is important. Take the time to get to know each of these individuals in your and your horse's life.

Before you go out and start horse shopping, you need to line up some very solid people to help you with the task. Finding the right horse isn't easy, but you have a good chance of making it happen if you have a decent trainer (or other such expert) and veterinarian to hold your hand through the process.

A good trainer or expert

For beginning horse people, we can't stress enough the importance of getting help from someone more experienced and knowledgeable about horses, both before you buy your horse and afterwards. Owning a horse for the first time can be very challenging, and few things are more terrible than the feeling you'll have if something goes wrong and you have no one to turn to for help. Having someone to call when you have a question, someone to show you the ropes and actually teach you, hands on, how to handle, ride, and care for your horse can make all the difference in the world.

Find a trainer

You have a number of options when looking for a good trainer:

- ✔ **Contact the American Riding Instructor Certification Program:** Listed in Appendix B of this book, they may be able to provide you with the names of certified instructors in your area.

- ✔ **Attend a few horse shows in your area:** As you watch the classes, you will notice trainers working with their students on the sidelines. The trainer is the one functioning as a coach of sorts, giving advice before the student enters the ring, and constructive criticism or congratulations after the class is over.

   Find a good moment and approach a trainer who seems to be working with students who are in your age range. Tell the trainer that you're a new rider, ask for a card, and get basic information about the trainer's program to make sure that the person works with beginners. The trainer may not have time to talk to you at length at the show, but should be happy to discuss his or her program with you over the phone at a later date.

- ✔ **Look in your phone book:** Check under "Riding Academies." Call a few trainers and talk to them about their riding programs. Let them know you are a beginning rider and are interested in learning horsemanship so you can eventually purchase your own horse. Take note of the trainer's personality, and get a sense of whether you think you will work well with the person.

- ✔ **Ask around for a referral:** Call a nearby tack and feed store, a local equine veterinarian, or just talk to some horse owners in the area. Ask for the name of a trainer who works with beginning riders.

After you meet a trainer or two whom you're interested in working with, take a few private riding lessons with that person (as opposed to group lessons, where other students are included). The trainer should begin and end your lesson on time, and should pay complete attention to you during the session. You should be comfortable with the trainer's teaching style and feel that it's compatible with your way of learning.

Be sure to choose a trainer who incorporates different aspects of horsemanship in his or her program. You should not only learn to ride, but also to groom a horse, put his tack on, lead him, and care for him after riding.

If you can't find a trainer

If you live in a small town or very rural area, you won't have a lot of choices when it comes to picking a trainer. In fact, you may not be able to find a trainer you like, or any trainer at all, for that matter. If that's the case, your next best thing is another equine expert of some kind.

The expert you find may be an equine veterinarian. Or she may be a horse breeder. She could even be a shoer. Or she could just be another horse owner who has been working with horses for a long time and really knows her way around a stable.

When you don't have access to a professional horse trainer, you have to be creative in finding someone to help you with your horse. Go to a local horse show and introduce yourself to the competitors. Call a veterinarian or farrier from the phone book. Do whatever is necessary to make contact with people who are experienced with horses and are willing to lend you a hand.

If the expert you come up with is an equine professional, you may have to pay that person a fee to help you buy a horse and give you lessons or teach you other aspects of horsemanship. If the person is a stranger to you, you should at least offer to pay. Many horse people are more than willing to help a new horse owner, and some will provide you with free guidance out of the kindness of their hearts.

Several breed associations now offer mentor programs to help beginning riders hook up with experienced horse professionals. See Appendix B, "Equine Resources" for a list of breed associations.

An equine veterinarian

A very important person in both your and your horse's life is your veterinarian. The veterinarian you choose ultimately provides your horse with regular preventative care. He or she is also the one who shows up in the middle of the night when your horse is colicking or when your horse has seriously injured himself. In emergency situations like these, your veterinarian appears as a guardian angel coming to Earth to rescue you from whatever trouble you and your horse have gotten into.

You won't need a regular veterinarian until after you purchase your horse. But you should start searching now, because you will need one for your pre-purchase examination (see Chapter 5 for details).

Before you actually start shopping for a horse, locate the veterinarian you want to hire to do the examination. Begin your homework on this subject long before you find a horse for the vet to look at. The night before you want someone to conduct the exam is not the time to start shopping for a vet!

If you like the pre-purchase veterinarian, you may want to consider keeping him or her as your regular vet after you purchase a horse. If that's your plan, make sure that you evaluate the veterinarian per our advice in Chapter 10.

A qualified farrier

Before you buy your horse, you're wise to start looking around for a qualified farrier. The *farrier* is the person who trims and shoes your new horse.

Finding a really good farrier is incredibly important. A good farrier helps keep your horse's legs and feet healthy and sound. A poor farrier, on the other hand, can make your horse lame and even permanently destroy his soundness.

Obviously, given the effect that your farrier has on your horse's well-being, the selection you make regarding this equine professional is rather important. For details on how to make the best possible choice in farriers, see Chapter 10.

Chapter 4

Breeds of Horses (The Big Ten and Beyond)

In This Chapter

▶ Choosing a breed

▶ Looking at the top ten breeds

▶ Looking at other breeds

▶ Recognizing other equines

Horses have been domesticated for thousands of years, and in that time scores of breeds have developed. Plenty of these breeds still exist today, giving newcomers to the equine world a swarm of choices to contemplate. Given this vast plethora of breeds, how in the world are you supposed to pick just one breed to ride or own? That's where we come in.

Figuring out which breed is for you is the main objective of this chapter. Feel free to turn to the color insert, too, to take a peek at what these breeds look like.

All Things Considered: Making Your Choice

You may not need to settle on just one breed. Many horse owners have absolutely no preference for a particular breed. Instead, they simply look for individual horses who possess the character traits they prefer. If that horse turns out to be a Quarter Horse, fine. If the horse turns out to be a Paint, that's fine, too. Basically, it doesn't matter. You can go this route if you choose. You sure won't be the only one out there who has.

In our humble opinion, however, one of the neatest things about the horse world is that you can choose from so many different breeds. We *like* the fact that the horse world is so diverse, and that each and every breed has a small subculture that surrounds it. That's why we encourage you to find a few breeds that really strike your fancy. You may not end up buying a horse of one of these breeds, but at least you'll have formed a strong opinion on the subject — and strong opinions are mandatory for all horse people!

We can't tell you which breed would be best for you because every person is an individual with different wants and needs. But we can give you some advice on how to go about making your decision:

- **Research, research, research:** Do as much reading as you can on the different breeds. Narrow your likes down to a few breeds, based on the way the breed looks, its history — whatever strikes you. Then, write to the breed associations and get more information, or visit their Web sites on the Internet (see Appendix B for addresses and URLs).

- **Meet the horses:** Find a horse show for the breeds you like and spend the day watching real horses in action. Go "backstage" and visit with the horses and their owners. (Always ask permission before petting any horse and never feed treats without a go-ahead from the owner.) This kind of close contact gives you a real sense of what the horses — and the people who care about them — are all about.

- **Spend some time:** If you find yourself getting serious about a breed and are thinking about buying a horse to show, spend real time with a few representatives of the breed, both equine and human. Lease a horse of the breed for a while, or ask a breeder whether you can come over and spend time riding and handling the horses so you can get to know the breed. Meanwhile, start hanging around at breed shows and becoming acquainted with people involved with the breed. Horse people love to talk about their horses, so all you have to do to get a conversation going is ask questions and let people know you're a fan of the breed. The purpose of all this socializing is to make sure that you really are in love with this breed *before* you make a commitment.

The Top Ten Breeds Hit Parade

Hundreds of horse breeds exist in the world today, but only a handful of them are among the top ten most popular breeds in the United States. The reasons for these breeds' popularity can be narrowed down to a couple of factors: Each breed has a strong registering organization promoting it with the horse-owning public, and each breed has redeeming qualities that a large number of horse people have come to appreciate.

Owning or riding one of the top ten breeds has its benefits. Plenty of information and support is available on the breed. Horse shows for the breed are also common, as are a vast array of sources from which you can learn more about the breed. And if you want to buy a horse of one of these breeds, you won't have too much trouble locating one. The fans of lesser-known breeds of horses do not have all these advantages, and must fend for themselves in many respects.

As you read our breed descriptions, keep in mind that we speak in generalities when it comes to the personalities of different horse breeds. For example, we say that Arabians are friendly horses. However, you may meet one or two Arabians in your travels who are complete grouches. Remember that each horse is an individual, and as you get to know different horses, you will find horses that simply don't match the personalities typically attributed to their breed.

That said, we're going to take a look at the top ten most popular breeds in the United States. (Their popularity has been determined by how many horses are registered each year.)

Appaloosa

The Appaloosa horse was first selectively bred by the Nez Percé Indians of northern Idaho in the 1700 and 1800s. When the Nez Percé were forced onto reservations, the Appaloosa breed nearly died out. In the 1930s, a concerned group of horsemen gathered together to start a registry to save the breed. Since that time, the Appaloosa horse has grown to considerable popularity.

The Appaloosa horse's most distinguishing characteristic is its spotted coat. Represented in several different patterns including the popular *leopard* (white with dark spots over the body) and *blanket with spots* (dark body color with white over the rump, which is covered with dark spots), this characteristic sets the breed apart. Other physical traits include white *sclera* (the tissue that surrounds the pupil), giving the eye an almost human appearance; striped hooves; and mottled skin. Some Appaloosas also have thin manes and tails. The height range for an Appaloosa is 14.3 to 16 hands (see Chapter 1 for information on horse measurements).

Appaloosas are known for their quiet and willing temperament. They excel in western events, three-day eventing, and trail riding, and are known for being athletic and versatile. Because of their gentle dispositions, Appaloosas make excellent companions.

Arabian

The Arabian is one of the oldest breeds of horse still in existence. Developed in the Middle East several hundred years ago, many experts consider the Arabian horse to be one of the finest and purest breeds of horse alive. The Arabian is also the most influential: Throughout equine history, humans have used Arabians to improve the quality of other breeds.

Arabian horses are known for their elegant and graceful beauty. The Arabian has a small head and a concave, or *dished,* face. The Arabian's ears are small and curve inward, and his neck is long and arched. Most Arabian horses have only five spinal vertebrae opposed to the six vertebrae typically found in most other breeds. This one less vertebrae gives Arabians a shorter back than many other breeds.

Arabians are small horses that rarely measure much over 15 hands in height. You can find them in a number of different colors, particularly gray, chestnut, bay, and black. Arabians are friendly and inquisitive horses, but can also be high spirited. They perform especially well in endurance competitions, and are also shown in western, hunt-seat, and saddle-seat classes (see Chapter 18 for details on equine competitions).

Arabians are often crossed with other breeds. Some examples of these are the Anglo-Arab (half Thoroughbred, half Arab), the Quarab (half Quarter Horse, half Arab), and the Ara-Appaloosa (half Appaloosa, half Arab). The purpose of these matings is to create half-Arabs who possess the refinement of the Arabian breed with the traits of another breed. Half-Arabians usually make excellent pleasure and show horses.

Morgan horse

The Morgan horse is a quintessential American breed, developed in Vermont during the 1700s from one horse, a little stallion named Justin Morgan. Justin Morgan achieved considerable fame for his astounding strength and willing disposition. The Morgan breed was developed by breeding a variety of different mares to Justin Morgan. These mares produced foals that looked almost exactly like Justin Morgan, and so the breed was born.

Morgans today have small, elegant heads and strong, highly arched necks. Just like their founding sire, Morgans tend to be smaller horses and rarely reach more than 15.2 hands in height. They are typically seen mostly in bay, black, and chestnut (see the color insert in the middle of the book for photos and descriptions of these colors). Also like their founding sire, Morgans are eager to please and willing to do whatever is asked of them.

Most Morgans are ridden simply for pleasure, although a good many are shown in saddle-seat, western, and hunt-seat classes. The breed is also popular as a light-carriage horse.

American Paint Horse

The Paint Horse used to be considered an anomaly — a colorful but unwanted result of many Quarter Horse to Quarter Horse breedings. Rejected by the Quarter Horse registry because of their coat markings, these patterned horses had no official recognition in the horse world. Finally, in the early 1960s, a group of horse lovers who appreciated the Paint for its unusual appearance created a registry for the breed that helped it survive and grow.

Paint Horse coats come in a variety of different patterns, most of which fall under the heading of *tobiano* (a white base with dark patches) or *overo* (a dark base with white patches). The breed's conformation is identical to that of the Quarter Horse, with a height range of 15 to 16 hands. Its temperament is very much like the Quarter Horse's too: mellow, easy going, and eager to please.

The Paint Horse has become wildly popular over the last two decades, and can be readily seen in stables and show arenas throughout the country. Most Paint Horses are shown in western classes, although an occasional Paint is seen in dressage, hunt seat, and other English events. Paints also make excellent companions and trail horses.

American Quarter Horse

In America in the 1600s, colonists bred horses kept by the Chickasaw Indian nation to horses they had imported from England. The result was the beginnings of the American Quarter Horse, a breed that later developed to its present state in the American West. Used to herd cattle and carry cowboys across the arid desert in the 1800s, the Quarter Horse has a rich and glamorous history. The breed earned its name as a result of its ability to run a quarter of a mile distance faster than any other breed, a feat it can still accomplish today.

The Quarter Horse is a sturdy horse with a small head and muscular neck. The breed's hindquarters are powerful, and the legs are straight and solid. Quarter Horses come in a number of different colors, including sorrel, chestnut, bay, black, dun, grulla, palomino, roan, and gray. They have a big height range, standing anywhere from 14.3 to 16 hands tall.

One of the Quarter Horse's most outstanding features is his disposition. This quiet temperament is a big reason behind the Quarter Horse's huge popularity. Well-known for his steady, easygoing personality, the Quarter Horse makes a good mount for beginning riders, who need a quiet and forgiving horse to help them learn.

In the show ring, Quarter Horses prevail in western events; you see them most often in cattle-working competitions, western pleasure classes, and gymkhana events.

Racking Horse

The Racking Horse is not as easy to define as most breeds of horses. He shared his history with the Tennessee Walking Horse until 1971, when a group of Alabama horsemen broke off from the Tennessee Walking Horse breed for political and economic reasons, and started a registry for what they dubbed The Racking Horse. A few years later, in 1975, the House and Senate of the Alabama state legislature named the Racking Horse the official state horse of Alabama.

What makes the Racking Horse so special is that it is a *gaited* breed, able to perform a four-beat racking gait, in addition to a walk and a canter (see Chapter 1 for details on equine gaits).

Racking Horses have a graceful build, with a long, sloping neck. Their legs are smooth and their hair finely textured. The typical Racking Horse averages around 15.2 hands, and comes in a number of colors including sorrel, chestnut, black, roan, white, bay, brown, gray, yellow, dun, and palomino. You may also see a pinto coloration, known within the breed as *spotted.* These horses are willing to work and eager to please their handlers.

Riders exhibit Racking Horses in saddle-seat and driving classes meant to show off their racking gait, but they also show less flashy individuals in more traditional pleasure classes. Racking horses make good trail horses and are popular for simple pleasure riding.

American Saddlebred

The American Saddlebred horse was developed in Kentucky in the early part of America's history, using Morgans, Canadian horses, Narragansett Pacers (now extinct), and horses of Spanish breeding. The goal of those who created the Saddlebred breed was to develop a horse who could comfortably carry riders over Eastern terrain.

The Saddlebred is a *gaited* horse, capable of performing a four-beat gait called a *rack,* and *stepping pace* (where the legs on each side move nearly in unison with each other), in addition to an animated walk, trot, and canter. Saddlebreds with these two extra gaits are called five-gaited Saddlebreds, and are used in the show ring. Not all Saddlebreds are born with the ability to move at the rack and stepping pace. Those who move only in the breed's high-stepping walk, trot, and canter are referred to as three-gaited.

Saddlebreds typically have long, arched necks and fine heads that they carry rather high. The Saddlebred's body is lithe and lean, almost like that of a human ballet dancer. Saddlebreds range in height from 15 hands to 17 hands high. The most common colors for this breed are bay, black, brown, chestnut, sorrel, and gray (see the color insert for photos showing various horse colors). Known for having a spirited, but willing temperament, Saddlebreds are easily trained, according to those who ride them.

In the breed show ring, Saddlebreds are exhibited as either five-gaited or three-gaited, usually in saddle seat. Driving classes are also popular for this breed. Despite their innate penchant for being flashy, Saddlebreds also make good pleasure horses, and are even shown in open-breed events like dressage and gymkhana.

Standardbred

If you've ever seen harness racing, then you've seen a Standardbred horse. Standardbreds originated during the early part of American history and were created specifically to race under harness at either the trot or the pace.

Standardbreds have an inborn ability to move at great speeds without galloping. Some members of the breed are natural born trotters, and can trot at nearly 30 miles per hour. Others are born *pacers* (where the legs on one side move in unison), and can attain these same speeds. The early training of prospective Standardbred race horses fine-tunes these skills while also discouraging the urge to gallop. However, Standardbreds *are* physically capable of galloping, as is evidenced by the many Standardbred pleasure horses who do so every day.

The Standardbred is closely related to the Thoroughbred, although the Standardbred is considerably more muscular. Standardbreds have rather large heads and powerful thighs. They usually measure anywhere from 15 to 16 hands, and come in bay, chestnut, brown, gray, and black. The Standardbred's disposition is typically gentle and trainable.

Although the majority of Standardbreds are used for harness racing, many retired race horses are also used as show horses and pleasure mounts. You can see them competing in a variety of different events including western classes and even dressage (see Chapter 18 for descriptions of various riding events).

Tennessee Walking Horse

A group of American breeds was used to create the Tennessee Walking Horse in the early part of the 18th century. Southern plantation owners needed a mount who could cover quite a bit of ground and do so comfortably. Early Tennessee Walking Horses worked in the fields, carried their owners long distances, and pulled the family wagon on weekends.

The Tennessee Walking Horse is a *gaited* horse, and can perform, in addition to the walk, trot, and canter, a four-beat running walk, for which it is famous.

Tennessee Walking Horses have a straight head with larger-than-usual ears. The breed has a gracefully arched neck, prominent withers, and large hooves. They come in just about any horse color. Ranging in height from 15 to 16 hands, Tennessee Walking Horses tend to be easygoing in personality.

Breed shows for the Tennessee Walking Horse emphasize the breed's gaited aspects. However, in open shows where many breeds compete together, you find Tennessee Walking Horses in all kinds of varied events. Many Tennessee Walking Horses are used as trail horses, too.

Thoroughbred

The Thoroughbred was developed in England in the 1700s strictly for the purpose of racing. The breed was later imported to the American colonies, where it ultimately influenced other breeds such as the Standardbred and Quarter Horse.

Thoroughbreds are the fastest horses in the world, and can reach speeds of 40 miles per hour on the racetrack. But racing isn't their only talent. You typically see Thoroughbreds in the show ring, where they make terrific jumpers and dressage mounts.

The typical Thoroughbred has a straight head, high withers, and long, fine legs. Standing anywhere from 15 to 17 hands high, Thoroughbreds have a lean, lanky appearance that sets them apart from other breeds. The colors

Breed clubbing

Breeds of horses don't exist by themselves. Each and every one was created by human beings, and to this day, human beings continue to manage the breeds.

Working together in clubs known as *breed associations,* these groups serve as watchdogs for their breeds, and perform a number of important functions, the most vital of which is to *register* horses. When a horse is registered with a breed association, his name along with his parentage and other vital information are recorded with the group. (If you buy a purebred horse, chances are the animal is already registered with a breed association.) By registering every horse that's born in the breed — and thereby establishing each individual horse's genetic purity — the associations are ensuring the continuation of their breed.

Breed associations also work to *promote* the breeds they represent by offering information about their breed to the public, sponsoring shows that encourage people to own a specific breed, and performing other services that increase their breed's visibility.

Breed associations are valuable resources for information on horse breeds, and can be a huge help to you if you want to learn even more about a breed than we tell you here. Write to the breed association of your choice, or visit their Web site for more information. (The addresses and URLs for all the major breed associations are listed in Appendix B.)

Making the grade horse

Oh sure, everyone wants a purebred. But what about *grade horses*, those mutts of the equine world whose parentage is unknown? Does horseland hold a place for them?

You'd better believe it. Although everyone makes a fuss about purebred horses, the fact of the matter is that most companion horses are grade horses. These horses make wonderful, loyal, and loving equine companions despite the fact that their individual heritages are one of life's great mysteries.

Experienced horse people can usually spot a breed type in any grade horse, and can tell you whether a particular grade has a Quarter Horse, Thoroughbred, Arabian, or Morgan horse type. But regardless of the breed type evident in any grade horse, what's most important is the horse's health and personality.

Although the purebred world sometimes looks down on grade horses, grade horses perform the role of companion as well — if not better — than any purebred. Some of the best trail and pleasure horses in the world are grade horses. Those people who love these special horses don't mind living with the mystery of the horse's parentage.

you most often see in this breed are bay, chestnut, black, brown, and gray. Thoroughbreds are willing horses but can be somewhat complicated in temperament, meaning that they can be hard for some people to figure out. Beginning riders sometimes have trouble handling Thoroughbreds because of the breed's spunky personality.

The Thoroughbreds you most commonly see in stables and backyard pastures are retired racehorses and horses bred specifically for the show world. Most of the horses shown in hunt-seat competitions are Thoroughbreds, although this breed does very well in other English events, too, such as dressage and show jumping.

There's More Than One Breed in This Town

Not all breeds have substantial numbers of horses in their ranks. Plenty of smaller, lesser-known breeds exist, and are popular among certain factions in the horse world. These types of horses have characteristics that set them apart and make them attractive to people who want something very specific from their horses.

Warmbloods

In the 1980s, a European type of horse called the warmblood became popular in the United States. Seen for years in international jumping and dressage competitions, the warmblood suddenly became the horse of choice for Americans who wanted to seriously compete in the Olympic disciplines of dressage, jumping, combined training (or three-day eventing), and driving.

Several different warmblood breeds exist, each with its own distinct characteristics. What they all have in common is a large stature, profound athletic ability, and a high price tag. Some of these breeds are more common in the United States and Canada, while others are only really available in Europe.

Here's a list of the warmblood breeds you see most often in North America:

- Belgian Warmblood
- Dutch Warmblood
- Hanoverian
- Holstein
- Oldenberg
- Swedish Warmblood
- Trakehner

Pony breeds

By definition, a *pony* is a small type of horse standing less than 14.2 hands at the withers. There is a distinction between a true pony and a horse who is simply on the short side, however. Not every horse under 14.2 is considered a pony, and not every pony over 14.1 is considered a horse. Ponies are members of distinctive pony breeds. In other words, you can't breed two Thoroughbreds or two Arabians and get a pony. Breeders produce a pony by breeding two ponies.

Ponies tend to be hardy little creatures. Most pony breeds developed in harsh European climates with rugged terrain; they had to become durable and levelheaded to survive.

Most adults are too big to comfortably ride a pony (neither the pony nor the adult will be happy), although a smaller adult can do fine with a larger pony. If you want a mount for your child, however, a pony can certainly do the job.

The following pony breeds are popular in North America:

✔ **Shetland:** The Shetland pony is the creature people most often think about when they hear the word *pony*. This breed is one of the smaller ponies around. Shetlands make excellent mounts for young children as long as the ponies — and the kids — are properly trained. American Shetlands are usually around 11 hands high and come in a wide variety of horse colors.

✔ **Welsh ponies:** These ponies come in four different types: the Welsh Mountain pony, the Welsh pony, the Welsh Pony of Cob Type and the Welsh Cob. Each of these four names represents different heights and conformation types within the Welsh breed. Okay, we know it's confusing, but stay with us. If you think of each type in terms of its height, it gets a little better: The Welsh Mountain is 12.2 hands or shorter; the Welsh Pony 12.2 to 13.2 hands high; the Welsh Pony of Cob Type is 13.2 hands high or less; and the Cob Type is actually horse-sized at 14 to 15.1 hands tall. All versions of Welsh ponies make excellent equine companions for children. The taller ones are even big enough for some smaller adults.

✔ **Connemara:** The Connemara is a refined-looking pony who excels in jumping. Measuring on the tall side (13 to 14.2 hands), Connemaras make suitable mounts for small adults as well as for children.

✔ **Pony of the Americas:** The Pony of the Americas, or POA as it is commonly called, originated from crossings with the Appaloosa horse and the Shetland pony. POAs typically have Appaloosa markings, and are good ponies for kids. In fact, the American POA breed association has one of the most extensive youth show programs in the country. POAs typically stand anywhere from 11.2 to 14 hands high.

Miniature horses

Miniature horses are the dwarfs of the equine world, and number one in the "adorable" category. The Miniature horse has all the physical and psychological characteristics of a regular horse in a very small package.

Miniature horses were developed in the United States in the 1800s to pull carts in and out of coal mines. This job required a tiny horse because mine tunnels could rarely accommodate a normal-sized equine.

The Miniature horse of today, which stands anywhere from 6 to 7 hands high, is kept primarily as a pet. Tiny tots can ride Miniature horses, but anyone over the age of 4 years old is probably too big to ride a Miniature horse.

Despite their small size, Miniature horses can easily pull a fully grown human in a light cart. Many Miniature horses are used for pleasure driving, and you can see them at special Miniature horse shows pulling light rigs in competition. They are also shown in halter classes and other special events.

Gaited horses

Gaited horses are those breeds possessing one or more additional gaits in addition to or instead of the usual walk, trot, and gallop found in so-called non-gaited horses. These unusual gaits were developed in these breeds by humans in order to make long-distance riding more comfortable. Equestrians who love gaited horses claim these horses are the most enjoyable mounts to ride.

Three gaited breeds are among the most popular horses in the United States: the Tennessee Walking Horse, the Racking Horse, and the American Saddlebred. Other, less-popular gaited breeds are found in the United States, each with its own fascinating history and characteristics. Although the breeds highlighted in the following sections aren't as common as the ones that made it to the top ten, they are nonetheless available in many parts of the country.

Peruvian Paso

Peruvian Pasos have found a devoted following in the United States. Developed in Peru in the 1800s to carry landowners across vast areas of the country, the breed contains the blood of Spanish Andalusians, Arabians, and Thoroughbreds.

Peruvian Pasos possess three gaits: the *paso llano,* the *sobreandando,* and the *huachano*. Each of these gaits is designed to be comfortable while covering considerable ground. Peruvian Paso horses who are in top condition can maintain these gaits for hours on end.

Peruvian Pasos are on the small to medium side, measuring 14.1 to 15.1 hands in height. They have well-muscled necks and long, thick manes and tails. They make excellent trail horses, and are shown under saddle in their natural gaits.

Paso Fino

You most often see the Paso Fino breed in Cuba, Puerto Rico, and Columbia, although it has quite a few fans in the United States, too. Paso Finos were originally created by crossing Spanish Andalusians with the now extinct Spanish Jennets a couple of centuries ago.

The Paso Fino gaits include the *paso fino, paso corto,* and the *paso largo.* Each gait is extremely comfortable to ride, and covers considerable ground. Some Paso Finos can also canter.

Paso Finos typically measure around 14 to 15 hands in height, and have a very pleasing and distinctive conformation. Paso Finos possess a personality trait known as *brio,* which means "controlled spirit." Horses with *brio* are full of energy, but are completely under the rider's control. Superb on the trail, Paso Finos are also shown extensively in their special gaits.

Missouri Fox Trotter

The Missouri Fox Trotter was created by Missouri cattlemen in the 1800s to carry riders across long distances of rough terrain and to work cattle.

Because the Missouri Fox Trotter was intended to be ridden for long periods of time, a comfortable gaited aspect was bred into this willing horse. As a result, the Missouri Fox Trotter has a special trot exemplified by a four-beat gait instead of the usual two beats found in a typical trot (see Chapter 1 for more about equine gaits).

Missouri Fox Trotters are handsome horses, measuring between 14 and 16 hands. They have easy going personalities and are considered a good beginner horse.

Icelandic Horse

The Icelandic Horse is a small, but sturdy creature with its roots in Viking history. The breed developed in complete isolation for more than 1,000 years and was the horse the Vikings used in their mounted exploits.

The Icelandic Horse is known for having either four or five gaits. In addition to the walk, trot, and gallop, all Icelandic Horses possess a gait called the *tolt,* which is similar to the Tennessee Walker's running walk. Some Icelandics also have a gait called the *flying pace,* where the legs on one side of the horse move in unison.

The Icelandic looks somewhat like a pony and measures only 12.3 to 14 hands in height. However, despite its small size, the Icelandic is considered a horse breed and not a pony breed. Full-grown men can easily ride this rugged little animal.

National Show Horse

The National Show Horse is a relatively new breed created in the 1980s by crossing Arabians to American Saddlebreds. The resulting horse turned out to be a flashy and refined animal perfect for the show ring.

As a result of its Saddlebred heritage, the National Show Horse possesses two other gaits besides the walk, trot, and gallop. National Show Horses are capable of performing the *slow gait* and the *rack,* both four beat gaits that are very comfortable to ride.

National Show Horses are on the taller side, standing 15 to 16 hands in height. They come in a variety of horse colors, and tend to be spirited. Their primary use is in the show ring (hence the name), where they can show off their high-stepping gaits.

Draft breeds

Draft horses are living relics of humanity's agricultural past. Originally bred for hundreds of years to pull heavy loads, draft breeds were used only until recently to work farms around the globe. When motorized tractors replaced draft horses in agricultural society, these magnificent creatures nearly died out. The work and dedication of those who loved these horses saved draft horses from sure extinction.

Today, draft horses are used mostly for showing and exhibition, although some are still used to work small farms and perform other hauling jobs not suited to trucks and tractors. Draft horses are also occasionally ridden, and because of their docile temperaments, make wonderful — if not rather large — companions.

You can find several breeds of draft horses in North America. Each of the breeds in the following sections has an American registry and a good number of devotees in various countries, although draft horses are still considered somewhat rare.

Clydesdale

The Clydesdale is probably the most well-known of all the draft breeds, thanks to Anheuser-Busch. Clydesdale horses have been pulling the Budweiser beer wagon for decades, and are regularly seen in the company's TV commercials and in exhibitions around the country.

Clydesdales usually come in a bay coloration, although they can also be seen in chestnut, black, brown, and roan. These horses can be anywhere from 16.1 to 18 hands in height. They have wonderful dispositions and are often used for riding as well as pulling.

Belgian

American Belgians differ somewhat from their European counterparts. Belgians in the United States are larger, heavier horses than those seen in the breed's native country. American Belgians stand around 18 hands, and are mostly seen in one coloration: sorrel with a flaxen (blonde) mane and tail.

These days, Belgians are used primarily in the show ring and for pulling contests. Some Midwestern American farmers still use Belgian teams to work their fields, as do many of the Amish in the United States.

Percheron

Percherons are seen only in gray or black, and average around 16 hands in height — a little on the short side for a draft horse. What they lack in height they make up for in bulk. They are strong and stocky horses.

You can ride Percherons or use them to pull carts and wagons; this breed is shown extensively in the United States. They're known for having very calm personalities and being very trainable.

Shire

Shires are attractive horses with heavy feathering around their fetlocks (see Chapter 1 for a diagram on parts of the horse) and long fuzzy beards on their jaws. They are medium height for a draft breed, measuring anywhere from 16 to 17.2 hands.

Shires are shown in harness and at halter in the United States and in other countries. The breed is often seen pulling beer wagons at events in Great Britain, and some people still use Shires to haul goods in parts of the world.

Suffolk Punch

The Suffolk Punch, or simply Suffolk, is a smaller draft horse, measuring in at around 16 hands. An unusual aspect to the breed is its single color; Suffolks only come in chestnut (which devotees of the breed spell *chesnut* in the archaic way).

Suffolks are still used to do field work and pull wagons for exhibitions. They are also shown and ridden.

Rare breeds

The world is full of horse breeds, many of them rather rare. Despite their small numbers, a handful of these breeds have managed to capture the hearts of horse lovers everywhere. You frequently see horses of these breeds in motion pictures or at equine fairs and exhibitions around the world. Though their numbers are scarce, they're important members of the horse community and worth taking a look at.

Andalusian

The Andalusian horse, also known as the Pure Spanish Horse, is one of the most spectacular studies in horse flesh on the planet. You see this horse in museum pieces and paintings from the Middle Ages: Leonardo da Vinci sculpted this horse, and the winged Pegasus was based on this breed. Because Andalusians have been around for so long, they have been instrumental in the development of other breeds such as the Peruvian Paso, Spanish Mustang, and Lipizzan.

Andalusians (called Lusitanos in Portugal) have a very distinctive look. Their necks are heavy and arched, their manes and tails are long and wavy. With a regalness about them that's hard to equal, even a relatively untrained eye can easily spot this breed.

Andalusians are spirited horses and are used for showing and pleasure riding. The majority of individual Andalusians in the United States are located in California, although a number of other states have small populations of this beautiful horse.

Friesian

The Friesian horse is hard to miss in a crowd. This regal, all-black equine has been around for centuries, developed first in Holland. The Friesian has had a great influence in the horse world, having been used to create a number of European breeds.

Friesians usually stand around 15 to 16 hands in height, although their proud carriage gives the impression that they are taller. Their manes and tails are long and flowing, and they have heavy feathering on their fetlocks. The high-stepping movement of the Friesian is a sight to behold.

Although only a few hundred Friesians live in the United States, this horse has managed to gain considerable visibility. The breed is being used successfully in dressage as well as in carriage work.

Lipizzaners

Lipizzaners are among the most well-known of all breeds, thanks to the famous Lipizzaner stallions of Vienna. These highly trained stallions have gained notoriety the world over for their skill at performing classical dressage movements also known as *airs above the ground.*

Lipizzaners originated in Austria as war horses, and are now seen mostly in Europe. A handful of Lipizzaners exist in the United States where they are shown and used for exhibitions.

Lipizzaner foals are born dark brown or black and mature to a light gray (nearly white). Adult Lipizzaners typically have thick, wavy manes and tails and heavy, arched necks.

Wild horse

One of the most romantic histories in horsedom belongs to the American wild horse, a creature that still inhabits certain parts of the United States. Believed by many to be escaped descendants of those horses used to build the American West, wild horses are protected by federal law. Consequently, horse wranglers can no longer capture the wild ones and sell them for pet food, a deplorable action that was rampant until the 1970s, when the Wild Horse Protection Act was passed.

Despite their official protection, wild horses are still at the center of political controversy. Ranchers who use public lands to graze livestock want wild horse herds kept to a minimum to allow more cattle to be grazed on the land, while many horse lovers believe the wild horse has first rights to the land.

Ranching interests usually win out of late, and the Bureau of Land Management periodically reduces the number of horses present on the land by rounding them up and putting them up for public adoption. Anyone who can prove they have access to proper horsekeeping facilities can pay a small fee to adopt a wild horse.

Although very young wild horses can be trained in much the same way as domestically born horses, adult wild horses need special handling to adapt to captivity. For this reason, fully grown wild horses are not recommended for beginning equestrians.

Spanish Mustang

In the 1500s, the Spaniards entered what is now the United States through New Mexico, bringing with them a number of their horses to populate the New World. The descendants of these original Spanish mounts are believed to be a breed now known as the Spanish Mustang.

Spanish Mustangs once roamed wild in the American West and have come to be exceptionally hardy and intelligent. They tend to be on the small side, measuring around 14 to 15 hands. Known for their incredible endurance, Spanish Mustangs make great trail horses and companions.

Not a Horse, but Equines All the Same

Horses are by far the most popular members of the equine family, but not the only members. Two other creatures that fall under the scientific category of *Equus* make good mounts and companions:

- ✔ **Donkey:** Donkeys, or burros, originally came from North Africa and spread throughout the world over the past thousand years or so. Donkeys were originally used to carry packs and riders, and even to haul small loads.

    Today, donkeys are kept as pets in North America, and can be shown in donkey shows and exhibitions. Donkeys are ridden in all sorts of classes similar to those found at horse shows, and are especially popular in driving classes.

    Donkeys are smaller than horses, with most measuring about 11 hands. Donkey ears are much bigger than horse ears, and donkeys bray rather than neigh when they want to express themselves vocally. They come mostly in a dun coloration, although other colors are possible. All donkeys have a vertical stripe down their backs and a cross-stripe along the withers.

    Wild burros, thought to be escapees from the Gold Rush period, still roam undeveloped parts of the West, and are under the management of the Bureau of Land Management. The Bureau periodically rounds up wild burros and puts them up for adoption to the public.

✔ **Mule:** Mules are sterile hybrids, the result of a breeding between a female horse and a male donkey. Mules retain the large ears and sturdy constitution of the donkey and the size and coloration of the horse. Another rarer variation of this cross breeding is an animal called a *Hinny,* which is the offspring of a female donkey and a male horse.

Mules come in many different sizes, depending on the breed of horse used in the crossing. Miniature mules who reach only about 9 hands exist, as do very tall mules up to 17 hands, the result of donkey crosses with draft horse breeds.

Mules can do the same type of riding work as horses, although mules are said to have greater stamina than horses and can carry more weight. Mules are shown in special mule shows, but also compete against horses in open shows and in endurance events.

Chapter 5

Ponying Up for a Horse

· ·

· ·

*B*efore you make the big decision to buy a horse, do some soul-searching regarding horse ownership and be sure that buying a horse is what you really want. You should also have a good idea of which discipline you and your family want to ride in, what you want to do with your horse, and how you are going to house and care for him. (Chapters 3 and 8 give you the background information you need to know before you go horse shopping.)

After you're sure that you want to progress into horse ownership, your next step is finding the right horse. Doing so, however, may not be as easy as you think; in fact, it can be downright difficult. Getting a horse with the disposition and physical capabilities to suit *your* needs and personality is almost as challenging as trying to find the right spouse (although much less stressful).

No need to fret, though! We're going to walk you through the horse-buying process, and if you follow our advice, you should end up with a wonderful equine companion who is just right for you.

Where to Get a Horse

Unfortunately, buying a horse is more complicated than going to the mall to pick out a new china pattern. One of the things that complicates the process is the fact that you can shop in more than one type of place.

The best sources of horses for sale are individual sellers, horse dealers, and breeding and training operations. If you prefer to adopt a horse rather than buy one, rescue groups usually have horses available, as do occasional private individuals. In the end, your horse comes from just one of these types of places, but that doesn't mean that you have to limit your search to only one. Check out each of the following horse sources as you conduct your quest, and then settle on the one who feels right for you.

Individual sellers

Buying a horse from an individual seller rather than from a trainer, breeder, or horse dealer can be a good way to save money. Individual sellers often advertise in the classified section of your daily newspaper, local horse publications, and on the bulletin board at your area tack and feed store.

Here are some of the advantages to buying a horse directly from an individual:

- **Possible bargain:** Under the right circumstances, you can get a really good horse for a really good price. For example, if the seller is attached to the horse yet desperate to sell him, she may charge you much less than the horse is worth if you are going to provide the animal with a good home.

- **No middle man:** You'll probably already be paying a fee to a trainer or other expert to help you find the right horse. However, if you buy from an individual, you also don't pay a middle man, which ultimately cuts down on the cost of the horse.

- **A history:** Horses who come from individual sellers often come with a known history. The seller can probably tell you who owned the horse before, what type of work the horse did, whether she produced any foals, and more. This information is important for a couple of reasons: It helps you get a feeling for what the horse is all about, and if you end up buying the horse, you'll know something about your new charge. When you know absolutely nothing about your horse's background, any problems that come up can be very frustrating.

Buying from an individual isn't always the best way to go, however. Here are some possible disadvantages:

- **Time:** Calling around and visiting horses for sale one at a time is very time consuming.

- **Personalities:** If you deal directly with individuals, you may find yourself face-to-face with personalities that are less than appealing to you. You may even run across people who are downright dishonest and try to pull the wool over your eyes. This uncertainty can add to the frustration of horse shopping.

- **Price:** Although you may find a great bargain when looking to buy from an individual, you also stand to pay more for a horse you buy this way than through a horse dealer, especially if the individual is in no hurry to sell the horse.

Individual horse owners put horses up for sale for any number of reasons. Some of the better reasons include a teenage daughter who's gone off to college leaving no one to ride the horse, a change in financial situation such that the seller can no longer afford to keep a horse, the desire to replace a beginner horse with a seasoned show animal, or just losing interest in the hobby. If you purchase a horse made available by one of these situations, you could end up with a wonderful animal at a reasonable price.

Unfortunately, individuals also sell horses for less positive reasons. Some examples include a horse who's difficult or dangerous to ride, a horse who won't load into a trailer, a horse with medical problems, and a mean horse who dislikes people. Exercise caution!

When you're considering purchasing a horse from an individual, be sure to bring an experienced horseperson with you to see the animal. A person with experience can ascertain any behavioral problems the horse may have. If the horse passes muster in the behavior department, a veterinarian can determine any medical problems during a check-up (see "Veterinary help" later in this chapter).

Horse dealers

You can find horse dealers in most areas that have an active horse industry. Horse dealers typically purchase horses at auctions or from individuals and then sell those horses to others at a higher price. In essence, they are the middlemen of the horse-buying world.

You can get a good horse from an honest horse dealer. Most horse dealers are experienced horse people who know how to judge a horse's disposition, quality of training, and athletic ability.

If a trainer or horse expert is helping you with your search, ask whether he or she can recommend a reputable horse dealer. Don't go to a horse dealer without the recommendation of someone you know well and trust. Horse dealers are much like used car dealers: Some are ethical; others aren't.

Some horse dealers will sell a horse with a guarantee that states you can return the horse within one year for another one if the horse develops medical or behavioral problems. The trouble with this type of guarantee is that, understandably, most people become attached to the horse and don't want to return him to the dealer for fear the horse will end up going to the slaughterhouse (see Chapter 12 for more information on horse slaughter).

Breeding and training operations

Horse breeders and trainers routinely sell horses to individual buyers. In fact, doing so is usually a large part of their business.

Breeders typically deal in purebred horses and sell very young stock. The weanlings and yearlings most often available from breeders aren't suitable for a first time horse owner because they're so young. However, a breeder does occasionally offer an older horse for sale, possibly a retired show horse or a broodmare who has been trained for riding.

Trainers are often a good source of older, trained horses — the kind you should be looking for. The horse for sale may be one who the trainer purchased with only basic training and then schooled to a higher level. Or the horse may belong to a trainer's client; the client has outgrown the horse and the trainer has taken on the task of selling him. Sometimes, a trainer is looking to sell off a lesson horse to a private owner. When healthy and *sound* (free from lameness), former lesson horses can make good mounts for beginning riders and you should consider them when you shop.

If you've been taking lessons from a trainer and intend to keep working with this person after you have your own horse, consider buying a horse directly from that person. The trainer you've been working with knows your skill level and personality, and may have a horse for sale who is perfectly suited to you.

As with anything else that you buy, the seller's reputation is very important — especially when dealing with breeders and trainers. If you don't know the breeder or trainer, ask for referrals, or inquire about them from other horse people in the area. Make sure that the business or the individual has a good reputation before you get involved in any business dealings.

A word about auctions

Although many people buy horses from public auctions because they find good bargains, we don't recommend this route for first-time horse owners. At an auction, you won't have the opportunity to spend much time — if any — with the horse you're considering. In many cases, you won't be able to ride the horse, and you won't have the opportunity to have a veterinarian examine the horse either. Because many public horse auctions sell horses without any kind of guarantee, you could be setting yourself up for a fall if you buy a horse this way.

Adoptions

You don't necessarily have to purchase a horse in order to acquire one. You can adopt a horse for nothing or for a minimal fee through several avenues.

Although we like the idea of horse adoption, we want to caution you that it's not always the best way to go if you're a first-time horse owner looking for a horse to ride. Some horses who are available for adoption make great beginner riding horses, but others are not suited to inexperienced riders. If you'd like to pursue this option, do so with your horse-shopping expert in tow. Remember to be rational and critical, just as you would if you were buying. Don't take a horse home who isn't right for you just because he's free or because you feel sorry for him. If the relationship doesn't work out (and chances are that it won't), the results can be disastrous for both you and the horse you are trying to help.

The following sections take you through the different kinds of horse adoptions that are available.

Rescue groups

Horses are beautiful, noble creatures, but sadly, life sometimes deals them a bad turn. Neglect, abuse, and death at the slaughterhouse are problems that plague horses in today's society.

Many people around the world are sensitive to the suffering of horses, and have come together to help remedy these horses' plight. The result is a bevy of private rescue and adoption groups that save horses from unfortunate situations. Many of these groups rehabilitate these horses and then place them up for adoption. Some rescue groups simply give the horse a quiet place where he can live out his life.

Rescue groups that rehabilitate horses and place them up for adoption are the ones you should explore if you are looking to adopt a horse. Some of these groups take former racehorses (usually Thoroughbreds and Standardbreds), retrain them for riding, and then adopt them out or sell them for a reduced fee. Others simply rehabilitate rescued saddle horses and try to find new homes for them.

Before you consider adopting a horse from a rescue group, research the organization. Go to the facilities for a visit and find out as much as you can about the group's work. If the people who run the organization seem responsible, organized, and professional, then pursue the adoption process in the same way as you would when buying a horse.

As always, be sure to have an equine trainer or other horse expert with you when deciding to take on a horse — whether you're buying or adopting the horse. And have a vet check the horse, too.

You should also ask to take the rescue horse on a trial basis. Because most responsible rescue groups have an open return policy on any horse they adopt out, you should have no problem with this request. In fact, many rescue groups insist that you take the horse for a trial period while they retain ownership of the horse. Some groups also send inspectors to spot check your property to make sure that you're properly caring for the horse. In many cases, the rescue group also asks you to sign a contract stating that you must return the horse to them when you decide you no longer want the animal.

To get you started in your search, a list of equine rescue groups appears in Appendix B.

Wild horse adoption

Every so often, the U.S. Bureau of Land Management (BLM) rounds up wild horses living in undeveloped regions of the country and places them in holding pens. These horses are put up for adoption at BLM facilities in several states; just about anyone can be take one of these horses home for a nominal fee.

Formerly wild horses are beautiful animals with a wonderful, historical past. However, because these animals have lived their lives with virtually no human contact, they're generally not suitable for first-time horse owners. Adult wild horses need extensive training before you can even handle them. Young foals are easier to work with, but they're years away from being ridden and are too much for a beginning horse person to handle.

If your dream is to adopt a wild mustang, don't fret. After you gain considerable experience riding and handling horses, you can always pursue that goal. (See Chapter 4 for more information on wild horses.)

Free horses

Once in a while, people find themselves in a situation where someone wants to give them a free horse. Horse giveaways occur for a few common reasons: an owner who doesn't want the hassle of selling the horse, an owner who is primarily interested in the horse going to a good home, and a horse who's such a big pain in the neck that no one will buy him.

Unfortunately, the last reason is the most common when it comes to free horses. And any beginning rider who takes on a horse who is so difficult or so unsound that no one will buy him is looking for serious trouble.

Just because a horse is free doesn't mean that he doesn't need to fit all the same qualifications as a horse you would buy. If someone is offering you a free horse and you want to consider him, take all the same steps you would if you were buying: bring a trainer/expert with you to help evaluate the horse; have a veterinarian examine the horse, and take the horse out on trial.

You may be wondering why you need to go through all this trouble for a free horse. Seems like you have nothing to lose because you aren't paying for him, right? Wrong. After you take possession of the horse, all of his problems become your problems. And if you're like most people, you'll become emotionally attached to the animal and will suddenly face some very difficult decisions should the horse turn out to have serious behavioral or medical problems.

If you're hoping to save a few bucks by taking any old free horse that someone offers, you are being penny-wise and pound foolish, as the saying goes. Remember that the initial cost of purchase is not what creates the greatest expense in horse ownership; the training, housing, and veterinary bills make up the larger part of the cost. If you end up with a problem horse, those expenses become even greater.

Finding the Right Horse

If your horse-owning experience is to be a successful one, you must find the right horse for you. We can't stress this point enough. If you get the wrong horse, you will be miserable, the horse will be unhappy, and your venture into horse ownership will be disastrous. That's why heeding the advice that we give you in the following sections is so important.

Your discipline

You can't know what kind of horse to buy until you know how you want to ride. If you haven't already looked at the section on riding disciplines in Chapter 3, you need to do so before making any buying decisions.

Perhaps western riding is the discipline that is most appealing to you. Or maybe you like the idea of riding hunt seat. Maybe you want a horse whom you can do both with, or maybe you want a horse you can ride English, while your spouse and the kids ride western.

Whatever discipline you choose, make sure that the horse you buy has been trained in that discipline. The only exception is if you want to have the horse trained in a new discipline after you buy him. However, don't make this judgment call on your own. Ask your trainer/expert to evaluate whether the horse is suited to your chosen discipline.

You can't ride every horse in every discipline, nor should you try. Specialization in the horse world has dictated that you ride some horses western, some hunt seat, some saddle seat. Some horses are versatile and can do two or more disciplines, but they still need to be trained in each. If your only plan is tool around the trail, then it probably doesn't matter too much if you put a western saddle on a big, rangy Thoroughbred (if you don't care how odd it may look). But if you plan to show your horse at all, having the right horse for your discipline of choice is a big issue.

Purebred versus non-purebred

Whether to buy a purebred horse or a *grade horse* (a horse of unknown parentage) depends on several factors. Each has its advantages and disadvantages. Personal taste comes into play, as well. Some people couldn't care less about their horse's genetic background, while others are fanatical about it. Read on to discover which camp *you* are in.

Purebreds

In our opinion, purebred horses are really wonderful. Each and every breed has a fascinating and unique history, and every horse of that breed is a living, breathing relic of that amazing past (see Chapter 4 for a rundown of some of the more well-known horse breeds).

Purebred horses have been bred over time to fit into a certain niche, each breed with its own specialties. Quarter Horses, for instance, are renowned for their abilities in western sports, just as Paso Finos are famous the world over for their *paso* gait. Clydesdales are known for their massive size and strength, while Shetland Ponies have found acclaim as durable and reliable children's mounts.

The show angle

If you are planning to show your horse, and a particular breed dominates the sport you choose, then you should seriously consider buying a purebred horse. If you want to show in open western pleasure shows at your local stable, for example, you would do best to purchase a Quarter Horse or Paint. These are the breeds you most often see winning in these events.

Owning a purebred also provides you with an opportunity to show in breed-specific events, too. Nearly every breed has regional shows where owners can present their animals in a variety of classes.

Getting involved in breed showing is a good way to meet other horse people, too. By making contact with your local breed club, you have a whole slew of opportunities to meet horse owners with the same goals and interests.

The prestige angle

For some people, owning a purebred horse is a status thing. Purebred horses typically cost more than non-purebreds, have a pedigree behind them, and are recognizable to most horse people as purebreds. If you care about this kind of stuff, then you'll probably want to own a purebred horse.

For other people, purebreds are simply more beautiful and more interesting than non-purebreds. These individuals are willing to spend more money on a purebred horse just so they can have a magnificent horse in their stable. In fact, Janice owns a purebred Miniature Horse and enjoys the prestige that ownership brings her!

A disadvantage

The one distinct disadvantage to purebred horses is their tendency toward inherited diseases or weakness. Some Quarter Horses carry a gene for *hyperkalemic periodic paralysis (HYPP),* a severe muscle disorder; Appaloosas are inclined toward *uveitis* (a serious eye condition); Arabians have a tendency to develop *enteroliths* (stones in the intestines); Thoroughbreds are known for poor hooves, and the list goes on.

You can screen horses for HYPP, but not for most other breed-associated diseases. Buying a purebred comes with the risk that your horse could develop one of the conditions associated with his breed.

Non-purebreds

A non-purebred can be a horse who is the result of the crossing of two breeds (called a *cross-breed*), or a horse whose parentage is simply unknown (called a grade horse). Many breed crosses have names for the cross, as well as associations that register them. The Morab, which is a breeding between a Morgan and an Arabian, is one. The Anglo-Arab, a cross between a Thoroughbred and an Arabian, is another.

Cross-bred horses are usually the result of a deliberate breeding between horses of differing breeds, orchestrated by people who are looking to combine the qualities found in each.

Grade horses, on the other hand, are the mutts of the horse world. In most cases, little thought goes into their breeding. They're simply the product of a stallion and a mare, put together for the purpose of creating a generic horse. Some grade horses may actually be purebreds, but due to circumstances, their registration papers and pedigrees are lost somewhere along the way.

The reality of the horse world is that non-purebreds are more plentiful than purebreds, which is just fine. Non-purebreds can make wonderful mounts and excellent companions, just like purebreds can. The horse world differs from the dog world in that sense: Pedigree just isn't that important to the average horse person. For these people, good behavior and a sound body has much more value than pure breeding.

Purebreds and non-purebreds do have several differences, however. For one thing, non-purebreds are typically less expensive than purebreds. They're also easier to come by. If you open your equine search to non-purebreds, you have many more horses to choose from. You're also less at risk of purchasing a horse with an inherited disease if you get a grade horse because the horse comes from a larger gene pool.

The disadvantages to owning a non-purebred are primarily show related. In many show rings, you compete against purebreds who have been carefully bred to perform in the discipline in which you are showing. Your non-purebred may be at a disadvantage. (Some of the more performance-oriented sports like endurance riding and show jumping are exceptions because the events place more emphasis on athletic ability than form and general appearance. You commonly see cross-breeds and even grade horses in such events.)

If all you want in your first horse is an equine friend to take you out on the trail and spend time with you around the barn, then a non-purebred is more than qualified for the job. Audrey's very first horse, a little bay mare named Peggy, was a non-purebred and an excellent child's mount and companion. No one knew a thing about Peggy's ancestry, but it didn't matter. She was simply a wonderful horse.

Choosing wisely

Successful horse selection requires you to compartmentalize your brain. On the one hand, you want a horse who is emotionally appealing; on the other hand, you need a horse who also makes sense for you from an unemotional standpoint. You find a particular horse attractive, friendly, and interested in you, and you can hardly wait to ride such a beautiful creature. These are matters of the heart and so are important factors to consider in your decision. But you can't base your decision solely on how you *feel* about the horse.

You need to balance your heart's reaction with your rational side. Is the horse well-trained and suitable for a beginning rider? How about for children, if your kids are going to ride him? Is easy to handle from the ground and from the saddle? Is the animal free of any health problems? Truly *liking* the horse you're going to buy is important, as is having a good feeling about the animal, but the practical answers to these and other questions must take precedence over things like how you good you think you'll look riding the horse.

The decision to buy a particular horse should be a combination of intellectual and emotional thinking. Your intellect should stoically compute the practical information on any horse you are considering, while your emotional side should provide you with that very important "gut feeling" so necessary when trying to decide such important matters. The key is to balance the two sides of your mind, using a good measure of intellect and a good measure of emotion.

Getting help

If you're like most people, you'll be nervous the first time you go out to a stable to look at a horse you are considering for purchase. As the seller shows you the horse, you'll be wracked with indecision and possibly a great deal of angst. How do I know whether this horse is the right one? Will the horse and I get along? How do I know whether the horse is healthy? If you aren't thinking all these things, then you *should* be. These are all legitimate and important concerns when shopping for a horse.

Don't panic — you don't have to find the answers to these questions alone and off the top of your head. You can get help with the decision and take your time making it. You can have a trainer or experienced horseperson with you to help you decide whether the horse has the right disposition; you can have a veterinarian examine the horse to determine whether the animal is healthy; and in many cases, you can try the horse out for a period of time before buying him.

The following sections take a closer look at each of these options.

Expert help from a horse trainer

Horse trainers are horse experts. As such, a big part of their job is evaluating horses and matching them with the right riders.

Enlisting the services of a knowledgeable, experienced, and reliable horse trainer is imperative as you begin your horse-buying quest. Without the help of someone with this kind of expertise, you are unlikely to find the best animal for you. (For details on finding the right trainer, see Chapter 3.)

If you live in a rural area, finding a professional trainer to help you with your search may be next to impossible. In this situation, get help with your search from an experienced horseperson. A local breeder or show competitor may be happy to provide you with assistance. (Chapter 3 contains information on finding an alternative equine expert.)

The best person to take with you when you horse shop is the trainer who has been giving you lessons, or who will give you lessons on your new horse. This person has a relationship with you and will be most motivated to help you find the very best horse. (If you have been taking lessons with a riding instructor rather than a trainer, talk to the instructor about his or her experience in purchasing horses. If the individual is lacking experience in this area, try to find a horse trainer to help you instead.)

The trainer/expert you hire accompanies you to see horses for sale, watches you ride and handle the horse, and rides the horse him- or herself. The trainer/expert then gives you an opinion as to whether or not the horse is a good match for you. Sometimes, a potential buyer falls in love with a horse, but the trainer/expert advises against buying him. The decision is ultimately up to you, but we advise you to weigh heavily on the recommendation of your trainer/expert. Trainers and experts are sometimes wrong, but usually not. If your trainer/expert doesn't like the horse, he or she is seeing something that your untrained eye isn't, and you would be wise to move on to the next prospect.

Veterinary help

After you find a horse that both you and your trainer/expert agree upon, you need to call in the veterinarian.

Most equine veterinarians offer a service known as a pre-purchase exam, or a *vet check* in casual terms. If you hire a vet to perform such an exam, the doctor comes out to where the horse resides and thoroughly examines the animal.

If you're working with a reputable trainer to find a horse, your veterinarian may recommend that you take the horse you're considering to a training facility and keep him there on a one-week trial period before conducting the pre-purchase exam. This way, you have a chance to spend time with the horse, and you can ensure that the horse is drug-free before the exam. *Note:* Trainers and breeders usually extend this courtesy to other trainers and breeders, but not usually to individuals looking to a buy a horse on their own (another good reason to have a trainer helping you with your purchase).

Make sure that you select an independent veterinarian to perform the pre-purchase exam — not one the seller suggests or who considers the seller a client. If you are unable to locate an independent veterinarian on your own, contact the American Association of Equine Practitioners for a referral (see Appendix B for this organization's address and telephone number).

Some aspects of the pre-purchase exam are included in the basic price, while other services will cost you extra. The more tests you can have the vet perform, the more you'll learn about your prospective horse — and the more you'll pay for the exam.

The results of the examination give you a good idea as to any health problems the horse may have. Keep in mind that the pre-purchase exam is not foolproof, however. A disease or condition can evade discovery during a vet check.

Following are just a few of the things the vet examines:

- ✔ **Vital signs:** The vet checks the horse for normal temperature, respiration, and pulse while at rest. After some light exercise, the vet checks these vital signs again. Abnormal readings are sometimes a way to detect illness.

- ✔ **Heart and lungs:** The vet listens to the horse's heart and lungs with a stethoscope to determine whether any problems are present.

- **Gut sounds:** Using a stethoscope, the vet listens to the sounds coming from the horse's gastrointestinal system. Normal gut sounds indicate a healthy digestive system.

- **Teeth:** The vet examines the horse's mouth for problems with missing teeth, overgrown molars, poor alignment, and the wear from the habit of cribbing (see Chapter 2 for information on cribbing).

- **Eyes:** Using a light source, the vet checks the health of the horse's eyes, looking for corneal scarring, cataracts, inflammation, and other signs of disease.

- **Blood:** At your request, the vet will draw blood from the horse and have it tested for *equine infectious anemia (EIA)* — see Appendix A for a description of this illness — thyroid function, and other possible problems.

- **Lameness:** The veterinarian evaluates the horse's conformation for any faults that may affect the animal's ability to perform in the job you intend for him (see Chapter 1 for more information on conformation). The horse then undergoes something called a *flexion test,* where he is gaited in front of the veterinarian on hard and soft ground and in circles so the doctor can determine any problems in movement. Also during the lameness part of the examination, the vet palpates the lower limbs in search of abnormalities, and examines the hooves visually and with a device called a *hoof tester.*

- **X ray:** At your request, the veterinarian may take X rays to further evaluate soundness and health.

You should also ask your veterinarian to do a blood or urine test for drug detection. We have heard stories of sellers tranquilizing or otherwise drugging a horse before selling him, leaving the unfortunate buyer to discover the truth after the drug wears off and the horse's true personality comes out.

The veterinarian who is conducting the pre-purchase exam should ask the seller about the horse's medical history and current use. The vet will also question you about what you intend to do with the horse if you buy him. The reason for these questions is so the veterinarian can determine whether the horse is physically capable of performing the job you want him to do.

The veterinarian doesn't give the horse a pass or fail on the exam: he or she simply alerts you to the horse's condition at the time of the exam. The vet may tell you whether the horse seems suitable for certain disciplines or sports depending on the correctness of his conformation, although most veterinarians aren't willing to give an opinion on this subject for liability reasons. If the horse is suffering from a serious illness, the vet will indicate the abnormal finding on the horse's report.

You can discuss the results of the pre-purchase exam with your trainer/ expert to get his or her input as well, but the decision on whether or not to purchase the animal is ultimately yours.

Trial period

If the horse you're interested in has passed the muster with your trainer/expert and turned up healthy in the pre-purchase exam, you can move forward to the trial period. Most sellers will allow you to take the horse for a try-out period. We recommend negotiating for a 30-day trial period, which allows you the greatest amount of time to get to know the horse. However, a week or two is better than nothing if that's all the seller will let you have.

When negotiating the trial period, put all the terms of the trial in writing and have both parties sign the agreement. You, as the potential buyer, customarily pay for the horse's board and feed during the time he's in your possession. The seller usually pays any medical costs that come up.

If the seller doesn't agree to a trial period, suggest a lease agreement instead. You can opt to lease the horse for several months at an agreed fee with the goal of getting to know the animal. At the end of your lease, you can purchase the horse or return him to the seller (see Chapter 3 for more about leasing a horse). The seller may agree to this arrangement because it generates monthly income for the seller — with a good chance that you'll buy the animal as a result of the lease.

Before you take a horse on trial, make sure that seller has insurance on the horse to cover any accidents or death that could result while the horse is in your possession. If the horse isn't insured, take out a temporary policy on the animal yourself (the cost is $100 or so), and make sure that you stipulate the terms of your liability in writing (like who is responsible for the horse's medical care during the trial, who will be liable should the horse suddenly die — whatever your insurance stipulates). Before you agree to be personally responsible for the horse's medical care when he is in your possession, be aware that equine medical bills can be very high. In most cases, the seller is willing to assume this responsibility.

If a trial period or lease are out of the question (some sellers don't feel comfortable allowing the horse off their property), try to spend as much time with the horse as you possibly can before you buy him. Ask the seller whether you can come and see the horse more than once, and when you are with the animal, tie him, lead and groom him, and by all means ride him, to get a sense of what the horse is really like.

During your trial period or lease, spend a lot of time with the horse so the two of you can get acquainted. Perform the same tasks with the horse that you plan to do once you buy him — or at least as much as you can. If you want to trail ride, take the trial horse out on the trail. If you plan to jump, do some jumping with the horse. If your children or spouse will be involved with the horse once you buy him, have them spend time with the horse now so they can see how they feel about him.

The horse's ground manners are extremely important yet often overlooked when people are evaluating a horse for purchase. Use this time to see what kind of ground manners the horse has by spending time tying the horse, grooming him, and leading him around the barn.

The point of all this evaluation is to make sure that you and your family are truly compatible with the horse. If the horse hates being on the trail, constantly refuses jumps, or is so ill-mannered he drags you around when you lead him, you're better off finding out now than before you actually buy him.

Goin' shopping

Okay, your ready to roll up your sleeves and start really looking for that horse. This part of the process can be both fun and scary. But if you take our advice and have someone with you who is experienced in horse shopping and knows her way around a barn, the process is much less stressful.

Getting initial information

Before you even go look at a horse who is for sale, you need to get some basic information on the animal. Start by contacting the seller and asking the following questions (if the advertisement doesn't already give you the answers):

- ✔ How much are you asking for the horse? Is this price negotiable?
- ✔ How old is the horse?
- ✔ What is the horse's gender and size?
- ✔ In which discipline is the horse ridden?
- ✔ Is the horse suitable for a beginning rider?
- ✔ Is the horse suitable for children (if you have kids who will ride the horse)?
- ✔ Does the horse have any bad habits?
- ✔ Does the horse have any medical problems or a history of medical problems like colic, lameness, or allergies?
- ✔ Why are you selling the horse?

These questions help you determine whether the horse meets your basic requirements of price range, age, gender, size, discipline, disposition, and health. If you sense a problem or incompatibility at this stage of the game, don't waste your time. Say "no thanks" and go on to the next prospect. If the horse sounds great, set up a mutually acceptable time for you to see the horse. Make sure that your trainer/expert is available at that time, too.

Paying a visit

Okay, you've found a horse you want to look at and possibly buy. You've lined up a time when you and your trainer or other equine expert can go visit the horse, and have on hand the name and phone number of a veterinarian who can do the pre-purchase exam if you like the animal.

Bringing your trainer or equine expert with you the first time you go see the horse is important. You need that person's opinion on the horse immediately. If your trainer/expert gives the horse a thumbs up, then you can pursue a pre-purchase veterinary exam and possible trial period. If your trainer/expert gives the horse a thumbs down, then you shouldn't waste any more of your or the seller's time.

In most cases, you do ride the horse on that first visit, so be sure to wear your riding clothes when you go — and don't forget your helmet!

Start the evaluation process once you drive out to see the horse. Your trainer/expert will guide you through this process.

Just because you have a trainer/expert with you when you go to evaluate a horse for purchase doesn't mean that you should sit back and let this person do all the work! Take this opportunity to learn about horses and how to look at them. Be involved, and after the evaluation, when the two of you are alone, ask plenty of questions.

Follow these steps as you evaluate the horse in question:

1. **Take in the whole horse.**

   Take a long, hard look at the horse. The horse should be wearing only a halter so you can see his conformation (see Chapter 1 for details on equine conformation). Your trainer/expert will help you evaluate the horse's conformation both visually and with a hands-on exam, where you feel the horse's legs and pick up his feet to look at the underside of his hooves. The two of you are looking for overall balance, blemishes, and conformation pluses and minuses in the horse. (If the horse has already been tacked up in anticipation of your arrival, ask to see the horse without tack after you ride him.)

2. **Watch the horse move.**

   Ask the seller to walk and trot the horse away from you and toward you on a loose lead. The seller should also walk and trot the horse so that you can view him from the side, and the seller should have the horse lunge on hard and soft ground. Your trainer/expert watches the horse's movement to judge whether the horse is sound.

3. **Watch the horse as someone rides him.**

   Ask the seller to ride (or have someone else ride) the horse so you and your trainer/expert can watch the horse work under saddle. The rider should ask the horse to walk, trot, and canter. If you're buying a horse who is intended for jumping, ask the rider to take the horse over a few jumps, if intended for barrel racing, negotiate a few barrels, and so on. Observe the horse during this time to get a sense of what he's like when someone is riding him.

4. **Have your trainer/expert ride.**

   This crucial step allows your trainer/expert to get a real feel for the horse's disposition under saddle and his suitability as a beginner's horse.

5. **Ride the horse yourself.**

   If your trainer/expert likes the horse, he or she will suggest that you ride him. Work the horse in a walk, trot, and canter. Pay attention to the way the horse feels for you. Ask yourself whether you're comfortable on the horse and whether you like the way horse responds to you. For this part of the process, you can rely heavily on gut feeling. Tune into yourself and see whether the horse *feels* right. If the horse is meant for your child to ride, have him or her get up on the horse, too, assuming the animal appears safe to both you and your trainer/expert.

6. **Observe the horse.**

   If you and your trainer/expert both really like the horse, ask the seller whether you can spend some time handling the horse from the ground and observing him in his stall or pasture. Lead him around, groom him, pick up his feet. Get a sense of what the horse's personality is like.

   The horse should exhibit gentle, easygoing behavior. If he is difficult to handle or tries to bite or kick, this horse isn't for you.

   When the horse is in his stall or pasture, notice whether he has any stable vices like cribbing or weaving (see Chapter 2 for more information).

7. **Find out whether the horse loads into a trailer.**

   Ask the seller whether the horse willingly loads into a trailer. If the answer is yes, ask for a demonstration. Any horse who won't load into a trailer is not a good choice as a purchase. Even if you don't plan to trailer the horse on a regular basis, you may someday need to take him to the hospital or transport him from one area to another. In these and other situations, horses who won't load cause enormous problems for their owners.

Questions to ask yourself on the ground

As a new rider and horse owner, your first horse should be one who will be your guide as you're learning the ropes. For this task, you need a gentle, kind, and willing horse, one who will become your best friend and your greatest teacher — as opposed to a difficult horse who will make your first experience unpleasant (and possibly even dangerous). Ask yourself these questions:

✔ When I handle the horse from the ground, is he gentle and obedient?

✔ Does he allow me to groom him without moving away from me or trying to kick or bite me?

✔ Does he lift his feet for cleaning when I ask him to and hold them up until I finish?

✔ When I lead him, does he walk and trot along beside me quietly, waiting for my cue on which direction and at what speed he should move?

✔ When I take him out of his stall or pasture, does he stand still and allow me to place the halter on his head, rather than running away or turning his hindquarters to me?

✔ When I tie him to a post or cross tie, does he stand quietly without pawing, neighing, pulling back, or jumping around?

✔ When I attempt to clip his face and legs with a clipper, does he stand quietly and allow it? (You may want to have the horse's owner demonstrate the horse's tolerance for clipping — many horses won't allow a stranger to clip them but are fine for a person they know and trust.)

✔ Does the horse allow me to touch his head and ears without jerking his head up and showing fear or discomfort?

✔ When I put a pad and saddle on the horse, does he stand still and behave, even when I'm tightening the girth?

✔ When I put the bridle on the horse, does he willingly open his mouth for the bit when I ask him to, and does he allow me to slide the headstall over his ears?

✔ When my children handle the horse, does the horse behave as well for them as he does for me?

After the ride

After you evaluate the horse, thank the seller. Tell him or her that you are interested in the horse, and need some time to think about what you just saw and experienced. After you leave the premises, discuss the horse with your trainer/expert. If the two of you agree that the horse is a good match for you, pay another visit to the horse and ride him again (you may have to do so as early as the next day if other people are also interested in buying the horse.) If you still like the horse, contact a veterinarian and arrange for a pre-purchase exam.

Whatever you do, don't purchase a horse without completing the entire evaluation process outlined here simply because you're afraid someone else may buy the horse first. Better to let the horse go than to buy him without knowing what you are getting. You'll soon find another horse that you like just as much.

Questions to ask yourself when the horse is under saddle

You probably want to ride whatever horse you buy, so how the horse acts under saddle is very important to your purchase decision. Ask yourself these questions:

✔ Does the horse stand still when I mount him?

✔ Does the horse wait for me to cue him before he moves forward after I mount?

✔ Does the horse move from a walk to a trot to a canter smoothly and only when I ask him to?

✔ Does the horse behave well when riding near another horse, not trying to kick or bite the other animal?

✔ Is the horse willing to do the type of work I want him to do (such as jumping, barrel racing, dressage, and so on)?

✔ For a horse I plan to use for trail riding, does he seem comfortable on the trail (not spooking at every little thing)? Does he behave well, meaning he does not try to run back to the barn, roll on the ground with me on his back, or do anything that would be dangerous?

✔ Do I feel safe, comfortable, and in control when riding the horse?

✔ When my children ride the horse, do they seem comfortable? Do they seem to like the horse?

If you and your trainer/expert feel very positive about the horse, you may want to give the seller a small deposit (usually around 10 percent of the sale price) to hold the animal while you make your final evaluation. If you decide not to buy the horse, and the seller turns down another offer while you're still in the evaluation process, be prepared to lose your deposit. Some sellers keep your deposit even if they receive no other offers on the horse. Stipulate the terms of your deposit up front and in writing.

If the horse's health is acceptable based on the pre-purchase exam, ask your trainer/expert for advice on how to proceed. We strongly recommend taking the horse on a trial period. If doing so is not possible, your trainer/expert may recommend that you contact the seller to discuss another visit or simply the possible purchase of the horse.

Closing the deal

You've consulted with your trainer/expert, spoken to your veterinarian, asked yourself some important questions (see the sidebars "Questions to ask yourself on the ground" and "Questions to ask yourself when the horse is under saddle") and made a decision that you want this horse. Now comes the business part of the deal.

Julie I. Fershtman, an attorney practicing equine law in Bingham Farms, Michigan, and author of the book *Equine Law & Horse Sense* (Horses & the Law Publishing, Franklin, Michigan) recommends that you draft a contract and present it to the seller to sign before the purchase. A contract spells out all the terms of the sale for both you and the seller, which significantly reduces the likelihood of any misunderstanding later on.

Julie suggests that the contract contain the following information:

- **Names:** Include the names of both parties, along with addresses and telephone numbers.

- **Legal rights:** Ask for a guarantee that the seller is indeed the horse's legal owner and has the right to sell the animal.

- **Description:** Include a description of the horse, including size, color, breed, and registration number, if any.

- **The price that you and the seller agree upon:** Indicate whether the seller has received full payment or whether you will pay the price in installments, how much each installment will be, and the due date of each. Also list where you will send the installments, and whether you will pay by check or money order. Include information on the recourses for both you and the seller should you be unable to make the payments.

- **The date the horse becomes yours:** If registration papers and pedigrees are involved, give the dates you'll receive each of these as well.

- **The terms of the warranty on the horse, if any:** If you want the seller to guarantee the horse in any way, you must spell it out on the contract. The seller must agree to the warranty, of course. You can include express conditions like "does not rear," "is free of any lameness," or whatever you determine is most important to you and whatever the seller will agree upon.

- **Signatures of both parties.**

If you want even greater protection than this brief contract can afford, consult an attorney experienced in equine law and ask him or her to draw up a detailed contract.

Bringing Home Baby

Okay, you've bought yourself a horse. Do you now just hop on his back and ride away?

No! You need to get the horse home first. The seller may be willing to deliver the horse to your stable. If not, you can hire someone with a trailer to pick your horse up and bring him to his new home.

We don't suggest you rent a trailer yourself and do the job yourself if you've never hitched up a trailer, loaded a horse, or driven a horse trailer before — unless you have an expert on hand to help you with these tasks. Your horse must have a good experience (as opposed to a traumatic one) traveling to his new home. Right now, concentrate on getting your horse to wherever you will keep him. You can always work on your trailering skills later.

When your horse arrives home, make him feel welcome by following these steps:

- ✔ **Feed your horse:** If your horse will be kept in a stall or paddock, have food waiting for him. Make sure that you give him the same food he's been eating at his previous home so he doesn't colic (see Chapter 8 for information on what to feed your horse).

- ✔ **Change food sources gradually:** If you're going to keep your horse in a pasture where grass is his primary food source (see Chapter 8 for information on maintaining your pasture), make sure that you gradually introduce him to the grass over a period of a two weeks. By gradually, we mean keep him in a stall or paddock and feed him what his previous owner fed him, while letting him graze for only one hour the first couple of days, two hours the next couple of days, three hours the next two days, an so on, until his system acclimates to his new diet.

- ✔ **Water your horse:** Have clean, fresh water available in his enclosure.

- ✔ **Stay with your horse for a while:** Horses are often nervous and uncertain when they move from familiar surroundings to a strange new place. Your company helps soothe his worries and allows you to keep an eye on him as he takes in his new environment.

- ✔ **Give your horse some adjustment time:** Don't ride him right away, and don't take him to a horse show two days after he's been in your possession! From the horse's perspective, he's just lost all that is familiar to him: his home, his routine, and most likely the person he was bonded to. He needs time to adjust to his new life, and the two of you need time get to know one another.

- ✔ **Give your horse attention:** Spend time grooming him, talking to him, and just hanging out with him. Deliver his food yourself, and stand by him as he eats. All these things help foster a bond between the two of you.

Part III
Stuff You're Gonna Need

The 5th Wave   By Rich Tennant

A HORSE CALLED MAN

In this part . . .

There's more to owning a horse than just buying the horse, believe us! In Part III, we guide you through the different types of equine equipment available. We sort out all the various saddles and bridles, grooming tools, and other items you'll need to ride and care for your horse. You'll also find plenty of advice on what to wear yourself, depending on the type of riding you plan to do.

And don't forget shelter for your horse. This is another huge concern for horse owners. In Chapter 7, we take you through the decision of where to house your horse.

Chapter 6

From Bridles to Grooming: Horse Equipment

In This Chapter
▶ Knowing saddle styles
▶ Understanding bits and bridles
▶ Dressing properly for riding

*I*f you like to shop, horsemanship is the right hobby! All kinds of horsy stuff is available in the retail world. Some of it is necessary to every horse owner; some of it you only need if you plan to spoil your horse.

Either way, if you're going to be a part of the horse world, you should have a handle on all this stuff. We don't want you to share the fate of Audrey's non-horsy husband who, after walking through a tack store in a foiled attempt to buy his wife a gift, exclaimed, "Everything just looks like belts!" All that leather has a purpose. And we explain it all to you in this chapter.

A Different Tack: Riding Equipment

There's more than one way to ride a horse.

Okay, that's not the original saying, but we're cat lovers and prefer it this way. Anyway, the modified statement is true: Riders have options in the style they choose.

Each particular riding discipline not only has its own associated style of riding, but also its own equipment. To function properly in the horse world — and to eventually shop intelligently for your own stuff — you need to know the differences.

Saddles

Most people know that a saddle is a big piece of wood or fiberglass covered with leather that goes on a horse's back. But there's more to it than that. Saddles come in different styles. The one you buy depends on the type of riding you plan to do. Pay close attention here, because the saddle represents one of your biggest investment in your new hobby.

Hunt seat

The hunt-seat saddle was originally designed for fox hunters, those members of the British aristocracy who found pleasure in chasing foxes through the countryside, leaping over fences, logs, and other obstacles in the process. In recent times, this type of saddle has undergone a few design changes to make it more comfortable for the rider.

If you plan to ride your horse in the hunt-seat discipline — eventually learning to jump — you need this saddle, which is designed to make going over jumps comfortable and secure for the rider. A *saddle tree,* the wooden or fiberglass frame on which the saddle is constructed, determines the fit of the saddle on the horse's back.

A hunt-seat saddle and its parts are shown in Figure 6-1. These same parts also apply to other English saddles.

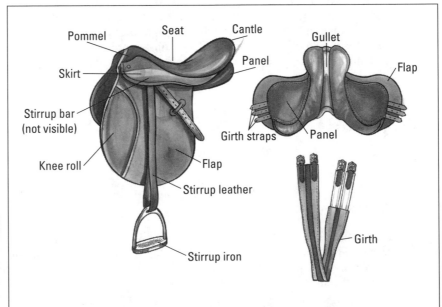

Figure 6-1:
The hunt-seat saddle and its parts.

Western saddle

The western saddle was created out of sheer necessity in the old American West. This quintessential working saddle hasn't changed very much in design over the past 100 years.

If you plan to compete in western events with your horse or if you are simply just attracted to western riding and want to participate in this discipline strictly for enjoyment, a western saddle is what you need.

The western saddle is designed to give a secure, comfortable ride. The deep seat, high pommel, and high cantle help keep the rider in the saddle while the horse makes sudden maneuvers, making this the saddle of choice for calf roping, reining, cutting, and other western working sports. The long stirrups are meant to make for greater comfort during long hours in the saddle (see Figure 6-2 for parts of the western saddle).

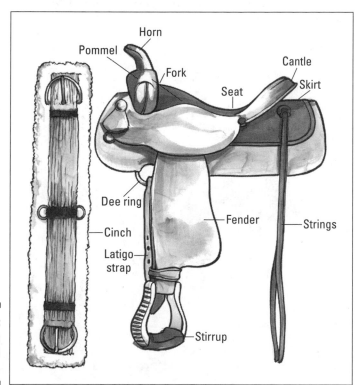

Figure 6-2:
A western saddle and its parts.

Horn

Pommel

Fork

Cantle

Seat

Skirt

Dee ring

Fender

Strings

Cinch

Latigo strap

Stirrup

Dressage

The *dressage saddle* is a type of English saddle that is specifically designed for use in the discipline of dressage. It differs from a hunt-seat saddle in that the cantle and pommel are a bit higher, the seat deeper, and the stirrup irons longer.

If you want to really learn dressage, you need a dressage saddle. You can learn dressage in an all-purpose hunt-seat saddle, but this difficult discipline is made easier by using a saddle designed specifically for it.

Dressage saddles are constructed to put the rider in a more upright position than you see in a hunt-seat saddle. The rider sits deep in the saddle with her legs underneath her body, providing more contact with the horse.

A drawing of a dressage saddle appears in Figure 6-3. The parts of the dressage saddle are identical to the parts of a hunt-seat saddle. The only difference is the design nuance of those parts (refer to Figure 6-1 for the parts of the hunt-seat saddle).

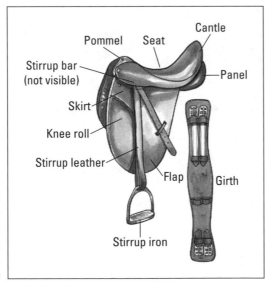

Figure 6-3:
The dressage saddle.

Show saddle

The *show saddle* is primarily used in American saddle-seat riding to show off flashy, high-stepping horses. Show saddles are designed to keep the rider's weight off the horse's front end so the animal can produce a lot of action in his forelegs. Consequently, the rider sits further back on the horse with his or her legs farther out in front than would be the case with a hunt-seat or dressage saddle.

If you ride a gaited horse, such as an American Saddlebred, Tennessee Walking Horse, or Racking Horse, and if you plan to show in gaited classes, you need a show saddle. You can also ride on the trail with a show saddle, although this activity is not the saddle's primary purpose.

To get an idea of what a show saddle looks like and how it differs from other English saddles, see Figure 6-4. The parts of the show saddle are the same as those of a hunt-seat saddle, except that the show saddle does not have a knee roll (refer to Figure 6-1 for the hunt-seat saddle).

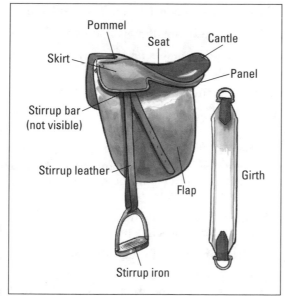

Figure 6-4:
The show saddle.

A saddle that fits

Saddle shopping is more than just finding a nice-looking saddle in your price range. You have to make sure that the saddle fits both you and your horse before you commit to its purchase.

Fitting the horse

As far as the horse is concerned, a saddle that doesn't fit correctly can result in all kinds of back problems. The horse's back muscles can become bruised if the saddle doesn't fit properly, often resulting in serious behavioral problems when the horse starts reacting to the pain.

Finding a saddle that fits your horse takes some work. When you buy a saddle, take it on a trial period so you can be sure that it fits. During that trial period, follow these steps to determine the saddle's fit. Also, enlist an experienced horseperson to help you determine the fit of the saddle.

English saddles

To determine whether the English saddle you're considering fits your horse, follow these steps:

1. **Put the saddle on the horse without using a saddle pad.**

   Tighten the girth so that the saddle is comfortably secure.

2. **Have someone sit in the saddle with his or her feet in the stirrups.**

3. **Using a flat hand, slide your fingers underneath the pommel, near the horse's withers.**

   (See Chapter 1 for a diagram showing the parts of the horse.)

   Your fingers should fit comfortably between the horse and saddle. Be certain that you can place at least three fingers between the horse's withers and the arch below the pommel.

4. **Have a helper lift the horse's left foreleg and pull it forward while your fingers are in between the top of the horse's shoulder blade and the pommel.**

   As the horse's shoulder moves, check that the saddle doesn't impede shoulder movement. Perform the same test on the horse's right side.

5. **Stand behind the horse and look through the saddle.**

   If the saddle fits, you should see a tunnel of light shining through. If you don't see any light, the saddle is too snug. Also, make sure that the saddle isn't too long for the horse. The seat panel shouldn't reach past the main part of the back onto the loins.

Western saddles

To make sure that a western saddle fits correctly, follow these steps:

1. **Place the saddle on the horse's back with a one-inch-or-so-thick saddle pad underneath it.**

   Tighten the cinch so that the cinch is snug but comfortable.

   When you attempt to tighten the cinch you may find that it's too short for the horse's barrel. Don't discard the saddle simply because the cinch is too short. If you really like the saddle, you can always buy a longer, replacement cinch. Meanwhile, borrow a cinch that fits so you can continue to try out the saddle.

2. **Have a rider sit in the saddle with his or her feet in the stirrups.**

   Be sure that you can fit at least three fingers between the arch of the pommel and the horse's withers.

3. **Examine the width of the saddle's tree, or frame, as it sits on the horse and compare it to the shape of the horse's back.**

   On a horse with a wide back and lower withers, the tree should be wide. On a narrower back with higher withers, the tree shouldn't be too wide. You can place your fingers sideways (on a flat hand) between the saddle and the top of the horse's shoulder to help determine the width of the tree. If the fit is so tight that you can't squeeze your fingers between the saddle and the top of the horse's shoulder, the tree is too wide for your horse. If you can put your entire hand between the saddle and the top of the horse's shoulder, the tree is too narrow.

Fitting the rider

The saddle has to fit the horse, sure, but it also needs to fit you. Otherwise, you'll be miserable when you ride. The good news is that finding a saddle that suits you is much easier than finding one that suits your horse.

The seats of English and western saddles are measured in inches. If you're taking lessons, or using a friend's saddle and you like the feel of it, find out the inch measurement on the seat. Armed with this information, you can rule out saddles that don't have the same seat measurement. You can also try sitting in different saddles in a tack shop and take note of which size suits you best.

If you're buying a saddle for a child, get a saddle that fits him or her *now* (because kids grow so rapidly, used saddles are the most economical purchase). Don't try to anticipate how big your child will be in six months and buy an oversized saddle. If your kid is forced to ride in a saddle that is too big, the child may be uncomfortable and may have trouble controlling the horse. Likewise, when your child grows out of a saddle, sell the old one and buy a bigger one. Don't make your child ride in a saddle that is too small. If you do, you'll end up with one unhappy kid who won't want to ride.

English saddles

To determine whether an English saddle fits you, try it out in the store or on the horse, whichever is easier. We think you should try the saddle out in the store first so that you don't find that it fits your horse perfectly but doesn't work for you.

Sit in the seat with your stirrups at the length you prefer (see Chapter 15 for information on determining the right stirrup length) and gauge how comfortable the saddle feels. You should have about four inches in front of your body and four inches behind it.

If you like the way the saddle feels and you take it home to try on your horse, check the fit on the horse's back first. If it fits your horse, then put a pad under the saddle and take it for a spin to see how it feels. Ask a trainer or other person experienced in English riding to watch you and point out any problems with the saddle that he or she may see.

Western saddles

Western saddles are usually easy to try out in the store because they're often displayed on wooden sawhorses. If for some reason you can't try the saddle on a sawhorse, take it home and try it on your real horse. Make sure that it fits your horse's back first.

Adjust your stirrups to the proper length (see Chapter 15 for information on how to do so). Sit in the saddle with your feet in the stirrups, and judge the comfort of the saddle. You should have about four inches in between the front of your body and the pommel. Your derriere needs to rest against the base of the cantle but not be squashed against the rise of the cantle.

If the saddle appears to fit you and your horse upon initial inspection, get on and ride in it. After half an hour of riding, it should still feel comfortable.

Saddle pads

Saddle pads help protect the horse's back from rubbing and chafing, and protect the saddle from sweat. Whether you're going English or western, you need to buy a good saddle pad or two to place underneath your saddle when you ride:

- **English pads:** The type of pad you need depends on the style of English riding you plan to do. Hunt-seat riders typically use white synthetic fleece pads underneath their saddles. Dressage riders usually use white square quilted cotton pads called *dressage pads*, while saddle-seat riders typically use no pad or a thin cotton pad.

- **Western pads:** For a western saddle, you need a western pad. Most western pads are about an inch thick or thicker, and are made from synthetic fleece or felt. Many of these pads come in decorative designs these days. You can also just get a plain white-foam western pad and put a thin Navajo-style blanket on top of it.

Buying a saddle

A saddle is a big-ticket item — at least as far as horse equipment goes. That's why you need to do some homework before you buy.

Here's our advice on buying a saddle:

✔ Be certain that you're comfortable with the discipline you choose before you invest in a saddle. Take some lessons in that type of saddle first to be sure that you like how it feels.

✔ Take an experienced horseperson with you when you go saddle shopping. You need that person's expertise to help you make a good decision.

✔ Buy your saddle only after you buy or lease your horse because the saddle needs to fit the horse you're riding.

✔ Because you're making a long-term investment, buy the best saddle you can afford. Spending money on a quality saddle now pays off later.

✔ Research the brand names of the saddles made for your discipline. Contact the manufacturers and ask them about the features of their products. Survey other riders in your discipline to see which brands they prefer.

✔ Only purchase a saddle with a return policy. You need time to try the saddle on the horse before you commit to keeping the equipment (see the section "A saddle that fits" for more information). This practice goes for used saddles as well as new ones.

✔ If you're buying a used saddle, have a trainer or independent saddlemaker inspect the tree during your trial period to make sure that the frame is not broken.

✔ The seats of saddles come in different sizes, measured in inches (a woman of average size and weight typically fits in a 15- to 16-inch seat). Try sitting in the saddle before you take it home to make sure that the saddle comfortably fits your rear end (see the section "A saddle that fits" for more information).

✔ If you can't find a saddle that fits both you and your horse, consider having a saddle custom-made. You'll spend more than if you buy a saddle off the rack, but it's worth the money. Contact a local tack store for a referral to a saddle-maker in your area.

English saddles do not include the stirrup leathers, stirrup irons, and girths. You need to purchase these items separately. The purchase of a western saddle always includes stirrups and usually includes cinches (although you may want to upgrade to a better cinch if the one that comes with your saddle is a cheapy).

Bridles

Bridle is the word that applies to the headgear used on the horse during riding. A bridle consists of a *headstall* (the part that goes over the ears and connects to the bit), *reins* (the leather straps that attach to the bit and are held by the rider), and *bit* (the usually metal piece that goes inside the horse's mouth) or a substitute for a bit.

Each riding discipline has its own style of bridle, and styles vary within those. The needs of your horse are the determining factors in what kind of bridle you ultimately buy.

Remember that bridles have buckles on them and are adjustable. Don't worry too much about matching your horse's head to a particular bridle — most bridles fit most horses. The exception to this rule is if you have a horse or pony with a very small head or a draft-type horse with a very large head. In either of these situations, you need to buy bridles that are specially suited to these head sizes. Sometimes, you may run across a bridle that is meant for an average-sized horse but turns out to be too small.

 Before you go bridle shopping, have an experienced horseperson help you determine the type of bridle your horse needs. Figure 6-5 shows a variety of English and western bridles. The remainder of the section explains the different bridles.

The English disciplines of hunt-seat, dressage, and saddle seat use several different types of bridle styles. The basic bridle is virtually the same, although you find the following variations (refer to Figure 6-5):

- **Hunt-seat bridle:** Hunt-seat riders typically use a standard *snaffle bridle* with a snaffle bit. This bridle consists of headstall strap, brow band (goes across the forehead), throatlatch (attaches under the horse's jowl), and noseband (goes across the nose and under the jaw).

- **Dressage bridle:** Although the aesthetics of the bridle are somewhat different, riders also use the snaffle bridle in dressage.

   Although many of the same bits and headstalls used in hunt seat are also used in dressage, some levels of dressage competition don't allow certain bits and nosebands. If you intend to show in dressage, contact the ruling dressage federation in your country to find out the latest rules.

- **Saddle-seat bridle:** Horses ridden saddle seat typically wear a double bridle, which is similar to a snaffle bridle but with an additional cheek piece to hold an additional bit.

Bridles for western riding come in a few styles. Each style has a headstall and reins. Some western bridles are *split ear* style, which means a piece of leather at the top of the headstall is attached for the horse's ear to fit through. Some western bridles have browbands instead. Other bridles have neither a browband nor a split ear design, and simply rest behind the horse's ears.

Within western styles, bridles differ mostly on whether or not you use a bit. Also, the material of western bridles varies of late, and western riders can find not only traditional leather bridles but brightly colored and elaborately patterned nylon bridles as well. The following list explains some of the types of western bridles (refer to Figure 6-5):

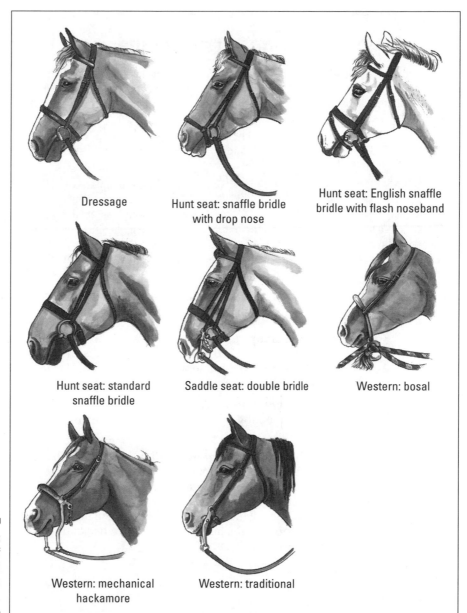

Dressage

Hunt seat: snaffle bridle with drop nose

Hunt seat: English snaffle bridle with flash noseband

Hunt seat: standard snaffle bridle

Saddle seat: double bridle

Western: bosal

Western: mechanical hackamore

Western: traditional

Figure 6-5:
Examples of English and western bridles.

✔ **Traditional western bridle:** The traditional western bridle consists of either a split ear, brow band, or plain headstall design with a bit attached. If the bit you use has a *curb shank* (a long, curved piece between the bit and the part where the reins attach), a curb chain or strap under the chin is included. A pair of reins finishes off the bridle.

Synthetic versus leather tack

Once upon a time, leather was the only material available for saddles, bridles, and their accessories. But this is the modern age, after all, so it shouldn't be surprising that horse people now have a choice between the traditional leather and synthetic materials. Just about every piece of horse equipment available in leather — including saddles, bridles, halters, breast collars, and saddle bags — can also be found in synthetic material these days.

Purists in the horse world tend to prefer leather instead of synthetic material for its aesthetic and historical value. Horse people tend to be conservative about their hobby, and leather has

been the material of choice for horse equipment for centuries. Plus, at many horse shows, leather is virtually the only material you see in the show ring. For example, it's considered somewhat tacky (so to speak) to show up in a western pleasure or equitation class in synthetic tack.

Other horse people swear by synthetic tack because it tends to be lighter in weight, easier to care for, and less expensive. If the quality of workmanship is good, synthetic tack can last even longer than leather. So buying your tack in leather, synthetic, or a combination of both is just a matter of personal preference.

✔ **Western hackamore bridle:** Not all western bridles have bits; some are fitted with a device called a *hackamore*, which is a nosepiece that allows the rider to control the horse without using a bit. Hackamore bridles can be split into two main types, as follows:

- *Bosal hackamore bridle:* A rolled leather training device, used to school young horses, that fits over the horse's head like a noseband.

- *Mechanical hackamore bridle:* You can use this device not only for training, but for general riding as well. The mechanical hackamore consists of a metal device that has a rolled leather noseband with metal parts beneath it. The reins attach to the metal piece, which helps you control the horse by putting pressure on the nose, chin, and poll. The entire hackamore piece is attached to a western headstall.

Bits

If you ever feel like being overwhelmed, go into any large tack store and look at the bits. There are easily as many bit styles as there are breeds of horses. Why the huge number? Horse people throughout the centuries have endeavored to invent a bit for every equine riding problem, and they have nearly succeeded.

The purpose of a bit (which is usually made of metal) is to apply pressure to the horse's mouth and thus send the message to stop, slow down, turn, and so on. The shape of the mouthpiece determines how that pressure is applied. Some bits are mild, meaning they apply minimal pressure. Others are harsh, demanding the horse's undivided attention by stricter means.

Western and English riding use different bits. The curb bit is the most common bit in western riding, while English riders typically use a bit called the loose ring snaffle. See Figure 6-6 for examples of some types of western and English bits.

Other things used for riding

The number of contraptions that have been invented over the years to aid in riding is almost mind-boggling. The following sections list some of the most common gear. Some of these things are necessities, but others are luxuries.

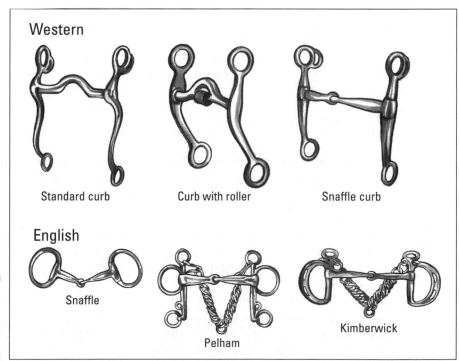

Figure 6-6: Western and English bits.

Buying the right-sized bit

When buying a bit for your horse, know the measurement of your horse's mouth, in inches. Figure this out by trying different bitted bridles on your horse. The average bit size for a horse is 5 inches.

Ask a friend with several horses or a trainer to loan you bits in different size ranges. Try the bridles on your horse and see which bit fits the best. The best fitting bit protrudes one fourth of an inch on each side of the horse's mouth.

Just to be sure of the size, measure the actual mouthpiece of the best fitting bit with a measuring tape. The measurement in inches is the bit size you need for your horse.

Girths/cinches

In English riding dialect, the piece of equipment that holds the saddle onto the horse's body is the *girth*. In western lingo, it is known as the *cinch*. You obviously need one of these if you plan to ride your horse.

When you buy an English saddle, you have to buy a girth, too, because the two rarely come together as a package. You can purchase a leather girth or one made from a man-made material — either is fine (see sidebar "Synthetic versus leather tack," earlier in this chapter, for more information). Before you buy, be sure to measure your horse's girth area (underneath the horse) from each side of the saddle. The resulting number in inches is the size girth you need.

When you purchase a western saddle, you normally get a cinch with it. If not, you can buy one in leather or nylon. Measure the area of your horse's girth from the right side of the saddle to about ⅓ of the way up the left side past the horse's elbow. Buy a cinch that is closest to that length.

For your horse's comfort, consider buying a fleece (or synthetic fleece) girth cover for your English girth or western cinch strap. This fuzzy covering keeps the strap from rubbing on your horse's skin.

Stirrup irons and leathers

Only English riders need to worry about buying stirrup irons and leathers, because western saddles come with the stirrups and leathers attached. In case you're wondering, stirrip irons are those metal doohickeys you keep your foot in while you ride. Stirrup leathers are what hold the irons on to the saddle.

Find stirrup leathers that match the leather of your saddle so the entire saddle looks like one unit. If your saddle is brown, don't get black stirrup leathers!

Stirrup irons (usually made of stainless steel, despite the name) are relatively standard items. Make sure that you buy a pair that fit your feet (while you're wearing riding boots or shoes, of course), and invest in some rubber pads to go on the stirrups. They help your foot stay securely in the stirrup. (Be sure to get the right size pads for your stirrup irons. If you aren't sure of the size, take an iron with you to a tack store and ask a store employee to help you.)

Artificial aids

In riding, the legs, hands, and voice are *natural aids* you use to communicate with the horse. Any external device that you use to send a message (other than the bridle) is an *artificial aid:*

- **Spurs:** Both English and western riders wear spurs on occasion. English spurs are blunt tipped, and come in either short or long lengths. Western spurs come in a variety of styles, nearly all with something called a *rowel,* a star-like wheel.

   You use spurs to prompt a horse forward. Horses who aren't responsive to leg aids usually respond to the prodding of spurs. If you use them properly, spurs are not inhumane but merely send a stronger message to the horse than does a leg squeeze.

   In the wrong hands, spurs can be cruel and dangerous devices. Before you strap on a pair of spurs, make sure that you understand the proper way to use them. Only riders who have considerable training in the saddle should attempt to use spurs.

- **Whips:** Each discipline of riding has its own design of whip. Hunt-seat riders use a *crop,* a short stick with a leather bat on the end of it. Dressage riders use a *dressage whip,* which is longer than a crop, with a tiny tassel on the end. Western riders traditionally use something called a *switch,* which is, in essence, a big tassel (plenty of western riders also use crops as these are more readily available). For lungeing a horse, a long *lunge whip* is used to keep the horse moving in a forward direction. (For more information on lungeing, see Chapter 13.)

   Although whips are typically thought of as instruments of brutality, riders shouldn't use them this way. Whips usually serve as visual aids for riders who want to send any number of messages to a horse. In some cases, the whip actually makes contact with the horse, but merely as a tap, and never to deliver a beating.

   Beating a horse is inhumane, and even illegal in many places. Never use your whip to punish your horse, and don't stand by and allow other people to do it either. A whip should never be used in anger.

Bareback pad

A bareback pad is not a necessity, but just a fun item to have around. If you ever have a day that you don't feel like throwing on the saddle, but would rather just have a relaxing stroll around the barn or countryside, a bareback pad helps make your ride more comfortable for both you and your horse.

Bareback pads are usually brightly colored and made from synthetic fleece. Most have a nylon hand strap sown on near the horse's withers specifically for the rider to grab when security is needed. The pad attaches to the horse via a nylon girth that buckles on either side of the horse.

Most bareback pads don't have stirrups, although some do. We don't recommend you ride your horse extensively in a bareback pad with stirrups because this practice can result in a sore back for your horse.

Training gear

A few of the items used in training — or at least management of the horse — are worthy of your attention:

- **Lunge line:** To exercise your horse from the ground by lungeing him (see Chapter 13 for more about lungeing), you need a lunge whip, mentioned earlier in this chapter, and a lunge line as well.

  A lunge line is a cotton or nylon rope ranging anywhere from 15 to 30 feet in length. One end of the line attaches to the horse's halter, *cavesson* (a headpiece made just for the purpose of lungeing), or bridle, the other end is held in your hand. We prefer cotton lunge lines because they're less likely to give you rope burn should the horse pull it through your hands.

- **Lunge cavesson:** You can lunge your horse in a snaffle bridle or halter, but a lunge cavesson is actually preferable. This item fits on the horse's head like a halter but unlike a halter, features a series of rings on the top part of the noseband. The lunge line attaches to the center ring and gives the handler good control over the horse during lungeing.

- **Stud chain:** A stud chain is a steel, linked chain usually about a foot long, with a ring at one end and a clip at the other. The chain fits around the horse's muzzle in conjunction with a halter, and is used to apply pressure to help control the horse.

  Stud chains derive their names from being typically used on stallions during breeding. Ordinary horse people tend to use them on horses who have poor ground manners and problems leading. If you ever have to lead a horse who prefers to drag you rather than walk beside you, a stud chain is a literal lifesaver.

Stuff to Care for Your Horse

Riding is only one part of horsemanship. True horse people are just as dedicated to caring for their horses "on the ground." A trip to your local tack store or a flip through an equine mail order catalog shows that there's no shortage of horse care items. Making heads or tails out of all that stuff can be a challenge — unless you have this book to show you the way!

Halters

The halter is probably the piece of equine equipment you use most often. Just about everything you do with your horse involves a halter. In fact, halters are so important that wearing one is the very first thing a horse learns to do.

Halters differ from bridles in that halters have neither a bit nor reins. Instead, halters exist solely to provide control of the horse from the ground. When you take your horse out of his stall or pasture, groom your horse, bathe him, clip him, or tie him, you use a halter.

If you need to leave a halter on a horse who's loose in his stall or pasture, choose a breakaway model that snaps under pressure to avoid the halter snagging on something and trapping him.

Halters are available in both expensive leather designs and in inexpensive, yet colorful nylon versions. When you buy a halter, get one big enough to fit your horse's head. The halter should be comfortably loose, but not so loose that it falls way down on the horse's nose (see Figure 6-7 for a correct fit of a halter).

We recommend that you keep more than one halter on hand. You never know when you may need a second one in an emergency.

Lead ropes

You can't own a horse and not own a lead rope. Without one, you can't maneuver your horse while you're on the ground.

The lead rope attaches to the ring at the bottom of the halter's noseband, underneath the horse's jaw. You tie your horse with the lead rope and hold it as the horse walks beside you.

Lead ropes are available in cotton or synthetic material. Although synthetic lead ropes come in bright colors and in sets with matching synthetic halters, we recommend you purchase a cotton rope. Cotton is less likely to burn your hands should your horse pull back while you're holding the rope.

Figure 6-7:
A correctly
fitted
halter with
lead rope
attached.

Grooming tools

How do you keep a 1,000-pound horse clean? With specially-made equine grooming tools, of course. Scores of different kinds of brushes, combs and other doodads exist for the express purpose of horse grooming. If you like to spend money, go ahead and buy some of them. But the list that follows is all you really need to get started. See Figure 6-8 for illustrations of the different basic grooming tools.

Brushes

You need to have three types of brushes in your tack organizer to properly groom your horse. Each brush serves a different purpose:

- **Stiff brush:** Also known as a *dandy brush,* this handy tool helps you get the dirt out of your horse's coat — which is no easy task.

- **Soft brush:** A gentler version of the stiff brush, the soft brush gets that top layer of dust off your horse's coat and makes it shine. This brush is also perfect for grooming your horse's face.

- **Mane & tail brush:** Some people use a comb to groom their horse's mane and tail, but we think that a vented brush with plastic bristles is best for untangling hair without breaking it.

Stiff brush

Soft brush

Mane & tail brush

Sponge

Sweat scraper

Hoof pick

Rubber curry comb

Sweat scraper/Shedding blade

Figure 6-8:
Grooming
tools for
your horse.

Before using brushes that have been used on other horses, disinfect them first by soaking them in a solution of one part bleach to four parts water. This way, you'll be less likely to spread possible fungal infections between horses.

Other items

In addition to brushes and combs, you need a couple of other nifty items:

✔ **Hoof pick:** The standard hoof pick has a colored, rubber handle and a metal, V-shaped head for cleaning out the underside of the horse's hooves. You can also find hoof picks made of solid plastic with scrapers attached and picks with nylon brushes for cleaning feet.

✔ **Sweat scraper:** Sweat scrapers come in two styles: long, straight plastic wands; and metal bows with one straight ridge and one toothed ridge, with each end of the bow attached to a plastic handle (refer to Figure 6-8 to get an idea of what each of these scrapers looks like). The toothed side of the metal sweat scraper functions as a shedding blade for removing loose hair during the horse's springtime shed.

Maintaining your equine equipment

If you want your tack and other equipment to last a long time, you have to invest some time in caring for it.

Synthetic materials are easy to clean — just hose down saddles and bridles, and wash saddle pads and pseudo-fleece items in a washing machine. Soak other synthetic items in mild soap and rinse thoroughly with water.

Leather, on the other hand, is a different story. Properly caring for this natural material takes a concerted effort. Here's some advice on how to treat your leather tack:

✔ **Inspect it:** Every time you clean your tack, check to make sure that the straps are in good condition. If you see leather that is heavily worn, have a leathersmith replace it. One of the most disconcerting things that can happen is to have your tack break while you're riding, especially if you're out on the trail and far from home.

✔ **Wash it:** If your leather is to last a long time, you have to keep it clean by washing it as often as every day if you are using it daily. Wash it with saddle soap and water, using a special tack sponge available in tack stores. Be sure to get all of the soap residue off the leather with a wet sponge before the water dries. If you don't have time for a complete cleaning, at least wipe it down with a damp sponge after every use.

A few times a year, put oil or leather dressing on all the leather parts. It's especially important to perform this procedure on new tack to help break in the leather.

✔ **Store it:** Keep your leather tack in a cool, dry place out of the sunlight. Hang your saddle on a saddle rack with the stirrups hanging down if it's a western saddle and the stirrup irons run up the leathers if it's an English saddle. If you don't plan to use the saddle for awhile, cover it to protect it from dust.

Despite the name of this tool, we recommend it only be used for scraping water off a freshly bathed horse. Merely scraping off sweat isn't healthy for your horse's skin — water should be applied to remove the salts.

✔ **Sponges:** Sponges are good for giving baths and for wiping off sweat and other things that stick to your horse. Horse-friendly sponges are available in different sizes, shapes, and colors. The ones you buy are a matter of personal preference.

✔ **Tack organizer:** Rather than throwing all your grooming tools into a shoe box, keep your equipment in a tack organizer. A tack organizer is a plastic box with different compartments and a handle. You probably already have one for your gardening tools. Buy a tack organizer at a tack store, or get the same product at your local gardening center. Be sure to buy yourself an organizer in a really cool color!

Where to buy equipment

If you're new to horses, you probably aren't sure where to buy the equine equipment and riding apparel you need. Here's a list of the places we recommend for buying tack and other horse supplies:

✔ **Tack and feed stores:** Most communities that have horses also have at least one tack and feed store. These places not only sell food for horses, but equipment, too. If you have more than one tack and feed store in your area, be sure to comparison shop. Sometimes pricing differences are huge from one store to another in the same area. Also, keep an eye out for used equipment in these places. Many tack and feed stores sell used saddles and other items on consignment.

✔ **Mail-order catalogs:** The horse world has a number of quality mail-order companies that exclusively deal in equine equipment. You can buy everything from saddles to show apparel from these catalogs, often at a big discount from retail prices. The downside of buying from a catalog is that you can't try on the clothes or sit in the saddle before you make a purchase. This shouldn't stop you from buying from a catalog, however, because all good catalogs have a return policy allowing customers to send back whatever doesn't fit (see Appendix B, "Equine Resources," for a list of equine mail-order catalogs).

✔ **Consignment shops:** Less common than regular tack and feed stores, equine consignment shops deal almost exclusively in used tack. They are great places to shop if you have a limited budget (and who doesn't unless you are Donald Trump), and the reputable ones have return policies on saddles and other items that require a good fit. Keep these shops in mind when you're ready to upgrade and sell off your old tack, too.

✔ **Other horse owners:** Buying your equine equipment from another horse owner — or former horse owner — is a good way to get a good deal on tack. People who are getting out of horses, or simply have too much stuff (horse equipment is easy to accumulate, as you may soon find out) are often anxious to get rid of their horsy things and are willing to sell the items for low prices. You can find these people by looking at the bulletin boards of riding stables, the classified section of your local equine publication, or even your daily newspaper under "horses."

Remember: If you buy a saddle from a private seller, take the saddle on a trial basis so you can make sure that it fits both you and your horse. If the seller is a total stranger and doesn't like the idea of you taking the saddle out of sight, ask the seller to be present when you try the saddle on your horse. If the seller won't cooperate and expects you to buy the saddle outright without trying it on your horse, politely refuse the sale.

✔ **Buckets:** You can never own too many buckets when you own a horse. Buckets have many uses, including giving baths, serving grain and sweet feed, and providing water in an emergency or when on the road (to name just a few uses). Be sure to buy your buckets from a horsy source so you're sure that you're getting specially designed horse buckets. Regular buckets like the kind sold in grocery and hardware stores are not heavy duty enough for use with horses.

Clippers

If you want to keep your horse's errant hairs trimmed, you need to purchase a pair of horse clippers. Horse clippers look much like barber's clippers, although they're specially made for horses in that they tend to be quieter and smaller so as not to intimidate the horse.

Several manufacturers make horse clippers in a variety of styles. For regular maintenance, you only need a small pair. If you intend to do serious body clips on a regular basis, you may want to consider investing in a larger pair to use just for that purpose (see Chapter 9 for instructions on how to clip your horse).

When you buy your clippers, pick up a couple of extra blades, too. Nothing is worse than having to clip a horse with a dull clipper blade because it's the only one you have. When your blades become dull, have them sharpened by a clipper service, referred to you by your local tack and feed store.

Horse Clothing

People wear clothes, so why not horses, too? Actually, horse clothes exist for some very practical reasons. The following sections look at some common items of horse clothing and their functions.

Cover-ups

Horses somehow managed to survive for a long time before humans began dressing them in cover-ups. Now, it seems, they can't do without them!

When you go to most busy stables in either summer or winter, you see several different kinds of cover-ups in use. Although they may all look pretty much the same to your as-yet-untrained eye, each one has a unique purpose.

Blankets and sheets

The term *blanket* applies to cover-ups that are used specifically to keep the horse warm in cold weather. Blankets come in different styles and materials, but most fit over the horse's shoulders and reach to the horse's tail. The body is covered to midway down the legs. Straps sown into the blanket fit around the horse's girth and back legs to keep the blanket in place.

Blankets can be quilted and lined with wool. Or, they can be thin, breathable, and water-resistant. Whatever blanket need your horse has, a blanket exists to fill it (see Figure 6-9 for a couple of examples of horse blankets). Here are a few types of blankets on the market in the United States and Canada:

- ✔ **Stable blanket:** Horses in stalls and small paddocks wear stable blankets, which are thick and very warm, or very lightweight. A huge variety of different stable blanket designs are out there, suited to different weather needs and horse-owner tastes.

- ✔ **Turn-out blanket:** Turn-out blankets are for horses who spend most of their time outdoors at pasture. These blankets are usually warm, water resistant, and durable. They are fitted with special straps that prevent the blanket from getting twisted when the horse rolls.

Not every horse needs to wear a blanket in the wintertime. If your horse is very old or very young, sick or recovering from illness, has a very thin winter coat, or is body clipped, he may need a blanket. If your horse doesn't fit one of these descriptions, chances are that a blanket isn't necessary. The coat nature gave the horse gets the animal through the cold of winter.

Some cover-ups are to keep horses warm — others have a different purpose. Refer to Figure 6-9 for examples of these cover-ups:

- ✔ **Coolers:** You use coolers specifically to help a horse cool down after a workout without catching a chill. Coolers fit over the ears and stretch to the back of the horse, covering everything but the head and lower legs. Coolers are only worn when the horse is being handled, never when the horse is unattended in his stall or pasture.

- ✔ **Anti-sweat sheets:** The purpose of an anti-sweat sheet is to help a horse cool down after a workout. Woven in a pattern that encourages circulation, the sheet fits over the horse like a blanket and keeps the horse warm while allowing sweat to dry quickly.

- ✔ **Flysheets:** Flysheets are for use mostly in the summer to protect the horse's body from biting flies. The sheets are lightweight, breathable material woven tightly enough so flies cannot fit their mouth parts through the weave.

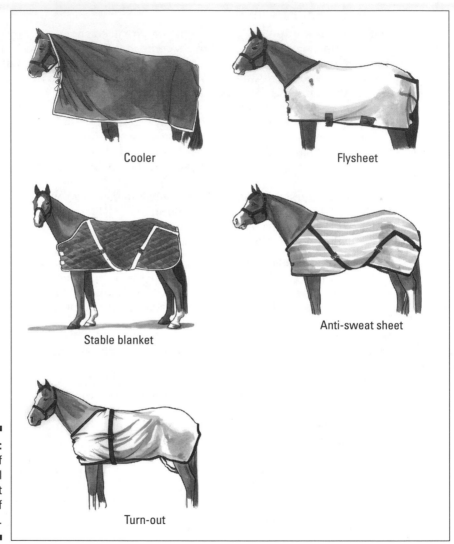

Cooler

Flysheet

Stable blanket

Anti-sweat sheet

Turn-out

Figure 6-9:
Examples of several different types of cover-ups.

Leg protectors

Considering how important a horse's legs are, it's no wonder so many leg protection devices exist. Our favorites include the following:

- ✔ **Bell boots:** Bell boots are to protect a horse from nicking his front pasterns with his back hooves during exercise, known as *overreaching*. Rubber bell boots fit over the horse's front hooves.

✓ **Splint boots:** Controversy rages over whether splint boots really do any good, but their purpose is to support the horse's tendons during workouts. Some people put them only on the front legs, while other riders dress all four legs with splint boots.

✓ **Polo wraps:** Dressage riders traditionally use polo wraps on their horses' legs as protection for the tendons during hard workouts. Riders in other disciplines use them, too. No concrete scientific evidence exists to prove that polo wraps do indeed help hard-working horses, but many riders swear by them.

Before you attempt to put splint boots or polo wraps on your horse's legs the first time, you need a trainer or experienced person to show you exactly how to do it. Improperly applied leg protection can actually harm your horse's legs.

Assorted things

So many items are available for horses to wear, describing them all in this book is impossible. Here are three of our favorites:

✓ **Fly mask:** Whoever invented the fly mask did a great service to the domestic horse. Fly masks are mesh hoods that fit over the center part of the head. They shield the horse's eyes from face flies that feed on the eyes' moisture. Some fly masks also have ear covers that protect the horse's ears from biting gnats while also protecting the horse's eyes.

✓ **Fly wraps:** These plastic mesh wraps keep flies from biting the horse's legs, the insects' favorite part of the horse. The wraps go on all four legs and fasten with hook-and-eye fasteners.

✓ **Tail bag:** They may look goofy, but tail bags are the answer to growing a long, luxurious tail. As the name implies, the tail bag is just that: a bag that holds a loosely braided tail. It serves as protection for fragile tail hairs, keeping them clean and unbroken. Usually made from nylon, tail bags often have a tassel or fringes at the end that helps the horse chase away flies when it swings the encased swisher.

What You Should Wear

The horse world has much tradition, and nowhere is this more obvious than in riding apparel. Unlike the ready-to-wear market where fashions change, equestrians have been wearing the same basic outfits for decades.

Just like with other sports, horseback riding has its own distinctive look. You wouldn't play tennis in jeans and a flannel shirt unless you wanted to give the impression that you didn't know what you were doing, right? Well, the same thing with riding. If you want to look like one of the gang, you'd better dress like the gang. This is especially true if you plan to show your horse.

The apparel in each discipline has its own look, of course, just like the tack. In this section, we describe the appropriate apparel for each riding style, both for the show ring and for *schooling* (regular riding). Although you may see riders donning variations of what we describe here, if you follow our advice, you won't find yourself in the horse-world equivalent of plaid golfing pants.

Riding apparel for children is virtually the same as it is for adults, just in miniature. When you buy riding clothes for kids, get a comfortable size that really fits. No one is more miserable than a kid trying to ride in boots or breeches that are too big or too small.

Hunt seat

Hunt-seat riding is based on British tradition and has a very formal appearance. The only thing that seems to change periodically is the color of jackets and breeches. We've seen green, rust, and beige come and go in popularity over the past 15 years or so:

- ✔ **Show:** Hunt-seat riders in the show ring wear a white or pinstriped cotton riding shirt, long-sleeved preferred. The women's shirt has a band collar that usually bears a monogram. Men wear shirts with a standard straight collar and a regular necktie. Both genders wear breeches and dress (riding) or field boots. (Although breech colors go in and out of style, avoiding white if you ride hunt seat is always a safe bet.) A dark-colored or gray pinstriped, tapered wool riding jacket tops off the ensemble for men and women, along with a black velvet hunt cap or riding helmet. See Figure 6-10 for a drawing of this apparel.

- ✔ **Schooling:** Male and female hunt-seat riders wear breeches for schooling, along with dress boots, field boots, or paddock boots and chaps. Tops are casual, and are anything from a T-shirt to a turtleneck. A schooling or velvet-covered show helmet is also worn.

Dressage

Everything about dressage is elegant, including the clothing. Very traditional in style, dressage apparel never seems to change much:

- ✔ **Show:** Most dressage riders wear white cotton shirts with long or short sleeves. Both sexes sport a stock tie, fastened with a gold horsy pin over a band collar. In the lower levels and at smaller shows, riders often wear light-colored breeches, black dress (riding) or field boots, a black or dark dressage or hunting jacket, and a hunt cap or regular black helmet.

In the upper levels and at bigger shows, male and female riders wear white breeches, black dress boots, a black derby, and a black dressage jacket or shadbelly coat. See Figure 6-11 to get a look at dressage show apparel.

✔ **Schooling:** Dressage riders dress more casually when schooling than they do in the show ring. Many wear any color breeches, dress boots, field boots, or paddock shoes with chaps or half-chaps, and T-shirts or mock turtlenecks. They also wear schooling or show helmets.

Figure 6-10:
Male and female hunt-seat show apparel.

Figure 6-11:
Male and female dressage riders in dressage show apparel.

Saddle seat

While hunt-seat and dressage apparel both have a distinct European look to them, saddle-seat apparel has old-fashioned, all-American appeal:

✔ **Show:** In the show ring, both male and female saddle-seat riders wear a white shirt, dark jodhpurs, and a riding derby. They both wear saddle-seat coats, day coats or saddle-seat suit jackets, and jodhpur boots under the jodhpurs. Women sometimes wear tuxedo shirts with feminine bow ties or rosettes, and both genders wear wingtip or straight collars with men's bow ties or neckties, respectively. A vest is sometimes worn under the coat. See Figure 6-12 for saddle-seat show attire.

✔ **Schooling:** Saddle-seat riders of both sexes usually wear jodhpurs for schooling, along with jodhpur boots. They sometimes wear regular breeches and paddock boots, too. Their tops are often casual T-shirts or mock turtlenecks. They also usually wear a schooling helmet or hunt-seat show helmet.

Figure 6-12:
Saddle-seat
show attire
for men and
women.

Western

Formal western attire is only required in the show ring, and then only in "rail" classes like western pleasure, horsemanship, and trail. Otherwise, the western look is casual and comfortable, and a favorite of male riders:

✔ **Show:** In classes calling for formal western attire, female riders wear tuxedo shirts with long-sleeved western jackets or western riding vests, and feminine bow ties or rosettes. They also wear jeans and fringed chaps, western paddock boots or riding boots, and broad-brimmed western felt hats. Male riders wear straight-collared western shirts with a western tie, along with jeans and fringed chaps. Both also wear paddock boots or western riding boots, and a broad-brimmed western felt hat tops off the outfit. Both wear leather belts with large silver, western belt buckles. See Figure 6-13 for formal western show ring apparel.

Riders showing in performance classes such as reining, barrel racing, and cutting need only to wear a western hat, jeans, fringed chaps, western boots or paddock boots, and a western shirt. A western tie is a nice touch.

REMEMBER

When buying western boots for riding, pick out a style designed specifically for riding. Most western boots for sale in regular shoe stores are for street wear and don't have the right style heel for safe riding. Boots designed for riding have soles that prevent the rider's foot from slipping through the stirrup and help keep the rider's foot in place. Shopping for your boots at a tack store is the best way to find appropriate riding boots.

✔ **Schooling:** Western riders usually wear loose-fitting jeans or special riding jeans that combine elastic with denim for a comfortable fit. They often ride in paddock boots, riding shoes, or western boots, and wear just about any kind of shirt including T-shirts, western shirts, or mock turtlenecks. Cautious western riders school their horses in helmets, usually the vented kind that endurance riders use.

Figure 6-13:
Formal western show attire for men and women.

Around the barn

For days when you aren't riding, but are instead doing equine-related chores like grooming, lungeing or simply mucking stalls, wear the following apparel for comfort and safety:

- **Pants:** Jeans or stretch tights are the most comfortable pants to work in around the stable.

- **Shirt:** Wear a T-shirt, sweatshirt, mock turtleneck, or flannel shirt. Make sure that the shirt is loose-fitting and comfortable. Make sure that it's something you don't care too much about, too, because your shirt is sure to get pretty dirty.

- **Shoes:** Riding shoes, barn shoes, or hiking boots are best around the stable when the weather is dry. Rubber barn boots are good if the ground is muddy or you plan to muck stalls. Never wear tennis shoes to work around horses because they don't provide your foot with much protection if a 1,000-pound klutz steps on your toe. Of course no functional footwear provides 100-percent protection if you get stepped on, but the heavier the shoe, the better off your toes are, should it happen.

Use your head: Wear a helmet

Riding can be a dangerous sport. Not because horses are vicious creatures, but because the laws of the universe dictate that falling off a horse is way too easy.

Falling off a horse usually results in nothing more than muscle soreness, but if you fall and hit your head, serious injury or even permanent brain damage can result. To prevent these dire consequences, most riders wear helmets. Some riders, however, don't wear helmets because they're hot during the summer. Helmets are also the cause of a female tragedy known as "helmet hair." Riders who don't wear helmets are risking the health and well-being of an often-ignored organ known as *the brain* every time they mount up on a horse.

Although fashion and peer pressure may dictate that you should not wear a helmet (western riders are notorious for not wearing them), we recommend that all riders wear a helmet whenever possible. If you are jumping on horseback, you really have no choice. When jumping, you absolutely *must* wear a helmet.

When you shop for a helmet, make sure you buy one for equestrians (bike helmets will not do) that provides significant protection to your skull. In the United States, the American Society for Testing and Materials (ASTM) sets standards for helmet construction. If a helmet meets these standards, it receives a seal of approval from the Safety Equipment Institute (SEI). Only buy an SEI-approved helmet.

Helmets are especially important for children, whose growing skulls are more fragile than the skulls of adults. Make sure your child always wears a safety helmet when he or she rides.

Chapter 7

A Stable Environment: Housing for Your Horse

In This Chapter
- Keeping your horse at home or away
- Providing equine accommodations
- Feeding your horse

*H*orses are pretty big creatures. Unlike a dog or cat, your horse can't just move in with you and start sleeping at the foot of the bed. No, you have to do a lot of thinking and planning on the subject of where and how to house your horse.

Ultimately, you need to attain the most convenient and economically feasible housing arrangement for your horse. You want your horse to be happy and healthy, and you want horse ownership to be both fun and manageable for you. Keep these points in mind when making your decisions about housing.

Where Should You Keep Your Horse?

People who own horses in today's world basically have two choices when it comes to equine housing: Keep the horse on their own property or board the animal elsewhere. These options are vastly different logistically, and your choice has a significant impact on your lifestyle.

If you bought this book because you own property that's zoned for horses and if you dream of a having a horse in your backyard, you may not need to ponder the question of where to keep your equine buddy. But, maybe you live in an urban or suburban area, have a small backyard barely suitable for your Labrador Retriever, and think that you have little choice other than to board your horse at your Uncle Jasper's house 70 miles outside the city limits.

Before you decide where your horse can call home, we urge you to read this chapter to get an idea of both backyard horsekeeping and boarding, along with details on how to correctly do both. After you discover the pros and cons of backyard horsekeeping and boarding, you'll be able to make a much more intelligent — and ultimately correct — decision.

Away from Home: The Boarding Stable

In case you don't already know, a boarding stable is a commercial establishment that provides housing and limited care for horses. Boarding stables earn their income by charging horse owners a monthly fee for boarding their horse. Some boarding stables also offer horse owners additional horse care, such as exercising or blanketing their horses.

Most people who utilize the services of boarding stables live in urban or suburban areas. They can't keep their horses on their own land, and so they board their horses at a nearby stable. Accommodations for horses vary greatly from stable to stable and region to region, with the more luxurious offerings costing more than the ordinary ones. Generally speaking, keeping your horse in a *box stall* (an indoor, barn-like enclosure) will cost you more than pasture boarding.

Even if you have your own horse property, you should still consider boarding. Boarding offers many benefits, particularly to first time horse owners. Even if your dream is to have your horse in your backyard, explore the possibility of boarding for at least the first year that you own your horse.

Benefits of boarding

Plenty of really good reasons exist to board your horse, especially if you are a first time horse owner:

- ✔ **Convenience:** When you board your horse, you are hiring someone else to do much of the daily upkeep needed to maintain a horse in good, healthy condition. This means the boarding stable staff is responsible for feeding your horse every day, providing water, and cleaning his stall. If you choose to board your horse, not only do you avoid these chores, but you also avoid worrying about things like buying and storing hay and bedding material as well as disposing of equine waste.

- ✔ **Help with your horse:** Boarding stables are places where horse owners of varying experience congregate. Most boarding stables also have trainers available for hire to boarders. First-time horse owners who board their animals often find they are surrounded by people who can help them with just about any equine problem that comes up. That's a big contrast to being alone at home with your horse.

✔ **A place to learn:** You can find out a great deal about horse care and handling just by being around other boarders. You may see others make mistakes that you can then avoid, and you can figure out the right way to do many things simply from observing.

✔ **Social atmosphere:** Boarding stables are wonderful places to meet and make new friends who share your interest in horses. Many stables even foster the inherent social aspect of the environment by holding events like barbecues, dances, and play days. Boarding stables are also good for your horse's social life, too. Your horse will find himself with plenty of built-in equine friends.

✔ **Riding facilities:** Most boarding stables have arenas for exercise, wash racks where you can bathe your horse, mechanical hot walkers for exercising your horse, and access to riding trails. These facilities are available to horse owners as part of their boarding fee. You may not have access to these amenities at home.

Disadvantages of boarding

Of course nothing is perfect, and boarding has its down side:

✔ **Expense:** If you figure out the day-to-day expense of keeping a horse, you discover that you spend more boarding your horse than you do keeping him at home. Of course, you're not only paying for the horse's feed when you board, but also for the services that the stable provides.

✔ **Inaccessibility:** Boarding your horse can be very convenient because you don't need to worry about feeding and cleaning up after it daily. However, you *do* have the chore of driving to and from the stable every time you want to see your horse (as opposed to merely stepping outside your back door).

✔ **Politics:** Just as in any situation that involves humans, boarding stables have their politics. Boarders get into squabbles, talk behind each other's backs, and even sometimes try to make trouble for one another with stable management. Of course, you can avoid much of this by keeping to yourself, but then you miss out on many opportunities for camaraderie.

✔ **Instability:** You may keep your horse at a wonderful boarding stable for years, only to wake up one morning to find out the place has been sold. The new owner could be someone who couldn't care less about the business, or even worse, a developer who wants to knock down your horse's stall and build condos instead. Both of these situations — and particularly the latter — occur in the boarding stable world more than you might think. If it happens to you, you have to start shopping for a new place to keep your horse.

Responsibilities

If you think that boarding sounds like a good idea, keep in mind that you also have certain responsibilities as a boarder:

- ✔ **Be considerate of other horse owners:** In this book, we provide you with all the information you need to be a responsible and considerate horse owner. If you board your horse, you have a significant obligation to follow the rules of safety and protocol. Handling your horse carelessly can jeopardize the safety of your fellow boarders and their horses.

- ✔ **Consider the community:** Boarding stables and horse property in general are becoming more and more scarce these days. Land developers are quickly gobbling up rural areas for housing and commercial buildings, minimizing the amount of places left where horses can live. Homeowners in many once-rural-now-suburban neighborhoods are also looking to push horses out of their communities.

  If you're boarding your horse in an urban or suburban area, remember that your stable's very presence in that area is tenuous. Be kind and considerate to the people who live in the surrounding community so that they maintain a positive opinion of the stable.

- ✔ **Pay your board**: Most boarding stable owners who run a clean, well-kept operation aren't making profits hand over fist; they put a significant amount money back into the stable's upkeep. So paying your board *in full, on time, every month* is very important. Don't expect the stable to carry you for a few months because you want to buy yourself a big-screen TV. If enough boarders pay late in any given month, the stable can experience serious cash flow problems.

- ✔ **Be courteous:** If you find a really nice boarding stable that you're happy with, count your blessings and be considerate to the staff. It's amazing how many boarders behave rudely to staffers whenever they want something done or have a problem. You get further with boarding stable staff by being nice rather than demanding.

Finding a good boarding stable

Boarding stables are just like any another type of business: Some are really good, and others are really bad. The good ones provide safe, comfortable accommodations for horses; have caring, conscientious, and knowledgeable staff; and offer excellent facilities for riders. The lousy ones are just the opposite: They sport unsafe conditions for horses, have staffers who couldn't care less, and have nothing to offer boarders in the way of conveniences or facilities.

Before you commit to keeping your horse at any commercial facility, we strongly recommend that you check the place out thoroughly. Go down to the stable and spend some time walking around and talking to other boarders. These are the things you are looking for:

✔ **Safe, sturdy accommodations:** Inspect the box stalls, paddocks, and pastures. Make sure that each of these enclosures is well constructed and well maintained. Check to see whether gate latches are secure and horse-proof (that is, they can't be opened with a flip of the nose).

Do not board your horse at a stable that uses barbed wire as an enclosure. A close encounter with barbed wire can seriously injure your horse. If you find a stable you really like that uses barbed wire, politely ask them to switch to a safer fencing. If they decline, consider boarding your horse elsewhere.

If you choose to board your horse in a pasture or paddock, look for accessibility to shelter from rain, snow, wind, and hot sun. If you plan to keep your horse in a box stall, check to make sure that the horses are given at least 8 inches of bedding in their stalls.

✔ **Clean, safe surroundings:** The stable property should appear well maintained and devoid of hazards. Be wary of a place that has junk lying around and an unkempt look. If they don't take care of their own property, they probably won't take very good care of your horse either.

✔ **Water:** Find out how water is provided to each enclosure, and scout around to make sure that each horse at the stable has a generous supply of water at all times. If you live in a cold climate, find out how the management keeps the water from freezing in the winter.

✔ **Security:** Find out whether a guard or caretaker is on duty at the stable 24 hours a day. Not all boarding stables provide this kind of protection, but we recommend that you hold out for it if you can.

✔ **Quality feed:** If quality pasture isn't available to your horse, then hay should make up the majority of his diet. Make sure that the stable you're considering offers hay as an option for feeding. Ask to take a look at the stored hay on the stable property, and inspect it for quality. (See Chapter 8 for information on determining hay quality.)

If the stable stores grain, be certain they keep it securely locked up so that the horses can't get to it. Any escaped horse who gets into the grain is in danger of colicking or foundering. (See Chapter 11 for more information on preventing and reacting to these maladies.)

Use caution with stables that only feed commercial pelleted feed with no other options because a diet consisting solely of pellets is unhealthy for your horse. If a stable that you like feeds only pelleted feed as part of your regular boarding agreement, make sure that they agree to feed your horse hay if you provide it.

✔ **Good care:** Have a talk with the stable manager and find out about the daily care the horses receive. Make sure that they clean your horse's stall at least once a day, every day, and that they feed your horse at least twice daily. Also, ask the manager about the stable's pest control program. Find out what steps they take to control flies, rodents, and internal parasites, and what method the stable uses to dispose of its waste.

If you want extra care options for your horse, such as daily exercise, blanketing, and supplemental feeding, find out whether these options are available at the stable and, if so, at what cost.

✔ **Health requirements:** Determine which, if any, inoculations the stable requires for horses to board. The more inoculations the stable requires, the less likely your horse will become ill. The stable you choose should require regular inoculations for influenza/rhinopneumonitis and equine encephalomyelitis, at the very minimum. Boarders should also show proof of regular dewormings.

✔ **Riding facilities:** Look for good-sized, well-maintained riding arenas, turn-out pens, wash racks, and hotwalkers. Look for good footing in all riding arenas, which means the dirt is soft — without being too deep — not hard. If you live in an area that gets a lot of rain or snow, consider holding out for a stable with a covered or indoor arena so you can ride all year long regardless of the weather.

If you plan to trail ride, ask the manager for a map of the local trails and find out how you can access them. Beware of trails that require you to spend too much time riding on busy roads before you can gain access.

✔ **Tack storage:** You need a place to store your saddle, bridles, halter, grooming equipment, and everything else you need to care for your horse (see Chapter 6). Find out whether the boarding stable rents on-site tack lockers or storage sheds to boarders. If not, you have to provide your own or keep your equipment at home and bring it with you every time you visit your horse.

✔ **A professional demeanor:** The boarding stable management should expect you to sign injury liability waivers and a boarding agreement, plus fill out other official papers stating the name of your veterinarian and a person to contact in case of an emergency. They should also provide you with written rules of the stable. Be wary of any boarding stable that has an overly casual attitude about your boarding agreement. They may also have an overly casual attitude about caring for your horse as well.

Be aware that the nicer the stable, the more you have to pay for board. Don't opt for a stable that isn't up to par just because the fees are low. When it comes to boarding stables, you really do get what you pay for.

Private boarding

Boarding your horse at a commercial facility isn't your only option. Plenty of people who own horse property rent out stalls, paddocks, and pasture to individual horse owners to help offset the costs of keeping their own horses.

If you decide to board at a friend or neighbor's house, remember to look for the same type of qualities you look for when considering boarding at a commercial facility. The quality of feed, care, and accommodations should be no less than they would be at a 200-horse facility.

Most people who offer private boarding don't have a riding arena on their property. If you are a beginning rider, you need access to a riding arena where you can safely develop your skills. Before you visit a property where you may decide to board, ask the owner whether you have access to an on-site riding arena or a nearby community riding arena.

If you decide to board with a private party, be sure to get an agreement in writing. The agreement should spell out the amount of your board, everything included in the boarding price, the length of prior notice you must give before vacating the property, and what your liabilities and responsibilities are as a boarder.

In Your Own Backyard: The Home Stable

If you are one of the many who dreams of seeing a horse every morning when you look out your kitchen window, a home stable may be the right housing option for you — providing that you live on property that has been zoned for horses. If you live in a suburban or even rural neighborhood that forbids the keeping of livestock, you have no other option than to board.

Double-check your zoning laws before you run out and buy a horse to put on your land. If it turns out that you can keep a horse or two on your property, then you can discover the joys of at-home horsekeeping. Knowing that your backyard horse is waiting for you whenever you get the urge to ride or simply share in some relaxing equine company is a wonderful feeling. Plus, something about the feel and smell of horses on the property makes even the most modest home feel very special indeed.

Although having a horse in your backyard is a great experience, don't overly romanticize the notion either. Keeping a horse on your property requires an investment of time and hard work.

Benefits of the at-home horse

Here are some really good reasons to keep a horse in your own home stable:

- ✔ **Easy access:** No driving to the stable when you want to ride! Your horse is right there in your yard, just outside the back door. And if your horse needs special care like a blanket put on every night, feeding of extra or special feed, or medicating, his close proximity is very convenient.

- ✔ **Security:** If you like to keep a close eye on your horse, a home stable provides a chance to watch your equine buddy nearly 24 hours a day.

- ✔ **Cost:** Keeping a horse on your own property is less expensive than boarding him. At a boarding stable, you pay for daily feeding and clean up, plus use of the facilities. With an at-home horse, you do the work yourself — your only cost is time.

Disadvantages of horsekeeping at home

If you determine that you want to keep your horse at home, you may find that the disadvantages can easily outweigh the benefits:

- ✔ **Hard work:** With an at-home horse, you are responsible for the daily chores of feeding and cleaning. If you work full-time, you may find that mucking your horse's stall is the last thing you want to do either before or after work.

- ✔ **Being tied down:** Because horses need to eat at regular times each day, you need to be home during these times to put out the feed. If you can't be home, you need to make arrangements with a responsible neighbor or a professional horse sitter.

- ✔ **Maintenance responsibilities:** Keeping a horse in your yard means storing hay on your property, and possibly maintaining a quality pasture. Add to that list storing and disposing of the waste your horse creates and building and maintaining proper facilities for your animal.

- ✔ **No support system:** New horse owners who keep their animals at boarding facilities have the benefit of asking other horse owners and professional trainers for help. If you keep your horse at home and you run into a problem, chances are you have no one to turn to for advice.

- ✔ **Limited riding facilities:** Most owners of single-family horse properties don't have the space, time, or money to build and maintain their own riding facilities. If you're one of these people, you may not have access to an arena you can ride in — a real problem if you are a beginning rider. And if your property isn't near riding trails, you won't be able to ride on those, either.

✔ **Liability:** All kinds of potential liabilities fall on the shoulders of horse owners. You need to have a talk with your insurance agent to determine exactly what kind of property insurance you need to have with a horse at home.

Your responsibilities

If you decide to keep your horse at home, you must uphold a number of responsibilities:

✔ **Cleanliness:** You have an obligation to your horse and to your neighbors to keep your property clean and well-maintained. If you don't, you may even get in trouble with the law.

✔ **Continuing education:** Because you and your horse are pretty much on your own, you need to learn as much about horses and horsekeeping as possible. If you don't continue to learn, your knowledge of all things equine won't advance, and you'll end up shortchanging both yourself and your horse. Read plenty of books and magazines on horses, check out responsible discussion groups on the Internet, and most importantly, join an equestrian group in your community.

✔ **A good image:** In urban and suburban areas everywhere, horse owners are facing a growing challenge to their hobby. Whereas horse property was commonplace at one time, it's becoming harder and harder for horse owners to find communities that are accepting of horses. You can do your part by being friendly and considerate toward your neighbors, and make every effort to resolve any horse-related problems that arise.

The financial commitment

Purchasing property that's zoned for horses is more costly than purchasing property that isn't zoned for horses. If you are lucky enough to get horse property that is already outfitted with safe and comfortable equine accommodations, consider yourself fortunate. If you buy a place that was zoned for horses but not set up to house them, you have expenses ahead of you. You have to install adequate shelters, enclosures, waterers, feeders, and other items will all have to be installed before your property is ready for a horse.

Upkeep on horse property is costly, too. You need to keep your property in good working order, the fences painted, and the grass trimmed (unless you have your horse do the lawn mowing for you). You should factor these upkeep fees into your annual budget.

Don't forget about the cost of owning a horse, which you have to consider whether you keep your companion at home or board him. Include veterinarian and shoer bills, feed, tack, and other equipment in your budget.

Shelter from the Storm: Living Arrangements at Home

Okay, suppose you decide to keep your horse at home, on your own property. Where do you keep him and what exactly are your housing options? Well, you have a few options, and we give you a close-up look at each in the following sections.

Keeping your equine buddy outdoors

In nature, horses live outdoors, where they constantly roam and graze. Outdoor enclosures, which confine horses in an open-air, outdoor area are popular places to keep horses because they are more natural. Most horses prefer to be outdoors and seem to do best there as long as you meet their needs for food, water, and shelter.

You need to keep the enclosure you choose for your horse free from debris. For your horse's safety, don't use the enclosure to store old pipes, car parts, or anything else.

Pasture

We define *pasture* as a substantial portion of fenced land where high-quality grass grows for equine consumption.

If you have the land, motivation, and ability to create and manage a high-quality pasture for your horse, this is the best way to go. Horses who live on pasture suffer the least from colic, leg problems, breathing disorders, stable vices (see Chapter 2 for a description of stable vices), and other maladies that tend to afflict horses confined in stalls. Pastures can usually accommodate more than one horse at a time, too, providing an opportunity for its occupants to live together in groups, as nature intended them to do.

Starting and maintaining a pasture is hard work and takes some know-how. We don't have room in this book to give you a crash course on how to grow a pasture, but we do have enough space to tell you to go to your local agriculture office and library for help. Find a good book with information on growing a pasture, and follow it. One such book is *Horsekeeping on a Small Acreage* by Cherry Hill, published by Garden Way Publishing.

Even if your horse is on pasture, you still may need to supplement the animal's diet with hay during times when the grass is not growing or is lacking in quality. Don't assume that the grass alone will provide enough sustenance to the horse. Overgrazing, drought, and other problems can render a quality pasture into a field of starvation for a horse.

Also, don't forget to provide your horse with shelter from hot sun and inclement weather (see the sidebar, "The run-in shed"). Add a shed to your horse's pasture so the animal can get out of the weather if he wants to.

Paddock

A *paddock,* by our definition, is a small outdoor enclosure that is void of viable pasture grass. In certain parts of the Eastern U.S., a paddock is typically thought of as a large pen with board fencing. In the Western U.S., most horses live in small 12 x 12 or 12 x 24 foot paddocks made of a pipe enclosure, called *pipe corrals.*

A paddock is the next best thing to pasture because it gives the horse room to move around. Because paddocks are outdoors, they also provide good ventilation and more opportunities for mental stimulation for your horse than a box stall does.

If you decide to keep your horse in a paddock, make sure that you provide him with a place where he can seek shelter from the rain, snow, wind, and hot sun. A three-sided, run-in shed is a good option (see the sidebar, "The run-in shed").

Fencing

A number of options exist regarding pasture and paddock fencing, including wood, pipe fencing, and polyvinylchloride, to name just a few. The best material to use, in our opinion, is polyvinylchloride, arranged in a post-and-rail design. Polyvinylchloride is attractive, durable, and easy to maintain. Wood, while traditional and charming, is expensive and very destructible (horses love to chew it). You also need to paint wood fencing on a regular basis, whereas polyvinylchloride never needs painting. Pipe fencing is certainly safe and affordable, although not as attractive as polyvinylchloride.

The run-in shed

An old standby in the way of equine shelter is something called a *run-in shed.* The run-in shed is a three-sided rectangular shelter with one open side that offers the horse a place to get out of the rain, snow, wind, and hot sun.

You can purchase a prefabricated run-in shed or build your own from scratch. Make sure that the shed is big enough to safely accommodate however many horses you keep together in your pasture or paddock. Occasionally, the "herd" will all want to crowd into the shed at the same time.

The best location for your run-in shed is the highest ground in your pasture or paddock, with the opening of the shed facing away from the direction that the winter winds typically blow.

Keep fresh bedding in your run-in shed to make it comfortable for your horse, and clean it every day.

Whatever type of fence you choose, we strongly suggest that you only use fencing material that is designed with equine safety in mind.

Don't enclose your pasture with barbed wire. Barbed wire is very dangerous to use around horses. If you have a large area that needs fencing and you can't afford the more expensive materials, consider using smooth wire instead.

Your pasture fence should be high enough to discourage your horse from jumping out. That means that the posts should stand at least 5 feet high, after they have been inserted in the ground. And don't forget to include a gate! Make the gate at least 4 feet wide to accommodate both you and your horse.

Housing your horse indoors

The majority of horse owners keep their horses in outdoor enclosures, but some owners keep them inside. Indoor accommodations for horses nearly always consist of a box stall, which is just what it sounds like: a stall in the shape of a box.

Keeping a horse in a box stall has a couple of advantages:

- ✓ **Stall-kept horses stay cleaner and neater:** They don't end up muddy when it rains, or dusty when it's dry.
- ✓ **Stall-kept horses avoid bites and other scars:** Horses kept outdoors in pastures or paddocks usually suffer more from such maladies.

The downside of keeping a horse in a box stall is that it is less healthy for the horse than living outdoors. A horse who stands in nearly the same place for hours on end is more prone to colic, leg problems, and boredom, which often results in stable vices (see Chapter 2 for stable vices). Also, because ventilation isn't as good in a stall as it is outdoors, stall-kept horses are more prone to respiratory disease.

If you choose to keep your horse in a box stall, make sure that the stall is at least 12 x 12 feet in size, larger if you can manage it. Provide the horse with at least one window to look out of, to give him something to do and to improve ventilation. If you have room on your property, attach a small outdoor paddock to the stall so the horse can go outside whenever he wants. Also, the stall's design should allow for plenty of cross-ventilation without being drafty.

Bedding options

Horses need bedding in their stalls or shelters to be comfortable. A thick layer of bedding material protects their legs and joints from the hard ground and their hooves from damaging moisture in wet weather. Plus, horses just love clean, fluffy bedding. Just watch them roll in it when you first put it down!

Two safe bedding options for horses are wood shavings and loose straw. You may find it easier to buy one type of bedding over another, depending on where you live. Wood shavings, available loose or packaged, offer a thick,

comfortable bed, and are easy to buy and store in bulk. Straw, sold in bales, isn't as absorbent as wood shavings but is less dusty, and very soft and warm. Stick with bedding that your horse seems less likely to eat since this habit is neither healthy for the equine digestive system nor your wallet. And make sure that whatever you use is specifically made with horses in mind.

Wood shavings made from black walnut are toxic to horses and you must avoid them for your horse's health!

When it comes to designing and building a box stall, we recommend you purchase a prefabricated box stall made from wood or aluminum, or hire a well-recommended professional to design and build the stall. Either of these methods ensures that your horse is housed in a stall that is appropriate in size, design, and material.

Don't forget to keep the stall floor covered with at least 8 inches of bedding to protect the horse's legs and resting body from the hard concrete floor (see the sidebar, "Bedding Options"). You can also use a rubber stall mat to soften the flooring for your horse. Clean the stall daily of manure and fouled bedding. You should also completely and thoroughly clean the stall by using a mild bleach and water solution at least once every six months.

Convenience for Work and Play

Whether you are keeping your horse at home or boarding your equine buddy, you should make sure that your horsy environment includes certain equipment that makes caring for and riding your horse safer and more enjoyable.

Tack room

You need a place to keep your saddle, bridle, grooming tools, horse blanket, and other items you use on or for your horse. This storage place can either be as luxurious as a shed equipped with a saddle rack and pegs for your bridle and halter, or as modest as a large trunk that you store inside a barn or other weatherproof building.

If you plan to board your horse, find out whether you can rent a tack room or locker for an added fee, or supply your own.

If you are keeping your horse at home, take advantage of the fact that you own the property and erect the nicest tack room that you can. A roomy, well-designed tack room can really enhance your enjoyment of your horse.

Work area

Horses' bodies take up a lot of room, so you need to have a decent amount of space in order to perform the tasks of grooming, bathing, and tacking up. You should also have things like hitching posts or cross-ties (see Chapter 13 for information on these means of restraining a horse), and a wash rack to bathe your horse in your designated work area.

If you plan to board your horse, select a facility for your horse that has safe, roomy work areas, complete with cross-ties or hitching posts. Look for a place that has a wash rack with a cement floor so you can bathe your horse when necessary. A sheltered work area is preferable so that you can attend to your horse even in inclement weather. The work area you choose shouldn't be too far from the area where you store your tack.

If you plan to keep your horse on your own property, make sure that you create a good work area and a wash rack with a cement floor so your newly bathed horse doesn't end up standing in the mud. A roof over your work area protects both of you when it's raining, snowing, or when the sun is blistering.

Riding arena

Having a safe, enclosed place to ride is extremely important if you are a beginning rider. In an arena, you can perfect your riding skills and gain the confidence you need to take your horse on the trail or anywhere beyond the stable.

Good riding arenas have well-constructed fencing at least 4–4 ½ feet in height, along with adequate footing to help cushion the shock to your horse's legs as you ride. Covered arenas are best because they shelter you and your horse from the sun, rain, and snow as you ride.

If you plan to board, make sure that the facility you choose has at least one good-sized and well-maintained riding arena. If the stable has more than one arena, all the better! Multiple arenas mean you rarely have to ride in crowded conditions.

If you plan to keep your horse at home, consider building your own arena, if you have the money and the room. If not, find out whether the neighborhood you live in has a community arena where you can ride.

Trails

Few things are as relaxing and soul-enhancing as a horseback ride on a wilderness trail. The soothing feel of your horse's rhythmic step and the singing of the birds helps to melt your stress away.

If trail riding is an activity that you want to enjoy with your horse, be sure to house your horse at a stable that has plenty of trail accessibility. Or make sure that trails are nearby when you think about keeping your horse at home.

Don't put yourself in a situation where you have to travel for any extended amount of time on busy streets via horseback before you reach a trailhead. Horses and traffic don't mix (ever see *The Horse Whisperer*?), so limiting the amount of riding you do on major thoroughfares is wise.

Part IV
Caring for Your Horse

"I read that horses are very good at picking out patterns."

In this part . . .

Part IV provides you with just about everything you need to know to take good care of your horse. You'll find information on what and how to feed your horse, how to groom your horse, and how to prevent maladies common to horses. In Chapter 11, we give you a list of common equine ailments and explain the symptoms of each so you'll know what to watch for.

Chapter 8

The Daily Routine

In This Chapter
▶ Feeding your horse
▶ Managing your horse's waste
▶ Controlling flies

*O*wning a horse means caring for him every single day. You may find that you actually look forward to that time you spend in the stable cleaning up after your horse and tending to his needs. Or, you may think of it as nothing more than a necessary chore. The truth of the matter is that whether you feel like it or not, you *have* to do it, even on those days when the rain is coming down like mad and the last thing you want to do is trudge through the mud to get to the barn.

As a horse owner with a horse on your own property, you have to deal with three major factors in your horse's care: feeding, exercising, and managing the horse's environment. If you handle all of these areas properly, you will not only be highly regarded by your neighbors and fellow horse owners, but your horse will love you for it, too.

If you're boarding your horse rather than keeping him on your own property, don't think you're completely off the hook! It's your responsibility to make sure that your horse's boarding facility adheres the standards we describe regarding feeding, watering, and stable management. While the boarding stable does this part of the job, you still have to provide the horse with daily exercise and hands-on care.

Handling Horse-Sized Hunger

Food is a very important thing to a horse, probably even more important than it is to humans. Nature designed the equine to spend the majority of their time chewing, swallowing, and digesting. The equine digestive system is meant to be constantly on the go and to process vast quantities of fibrous foods.

What you feed your horse and how often you feed it plays a big part in determining your horse's physical and psychological health.

What to feed

Much confusion exists in the horse world about the best food to feed a horse. The reason for this confusion probably lies in the fact that individual horses have different nutritional requirements. Factors in determining the best diet for a horse include where and how the horse lives, what kind of work the horse does, and the horse's own physiological makeup.

The best person to guide you when it comes to your horse's diet is your veterinarian. Your vet is familiar with your individual horse and therefore with his nutritional needs. Furthermore, your vet should also be up on the local availability of different kinds of hay. For example, alfalfa hay, popular and readily available in California, is often hard to come by in the Northeast. Here's some general information on horse feeds to get you started:

✔ **Hay:** Hay is basically a feedstuff composed of plants that have been cut, dried, and baled. Two different types of hays exist: legumes and grasses. Alfalfa, rich in protein, calcium, and other nutrients, is the legume horses most commonly eat, and timothy is the most commonly fed grass hay. Timothy and other grass hays have less nutrients than alfalfa, but are higher in fiber.

Hay is a good feed because it provides roughage in addition to proper nutrition. The roughage keeps the horse's digestive system working properly and also satisfies the horse's natural urge to chew.

If you keep your horse stabled, we recommend feeding at least two *flakes* (a flake is a section of a bale of hay, weighing around 4 pounds) of an alfalfa and timothy mix per day for a horse of average weight (1,100 pounds) who gets at least 30 minutes of solid exercise, two to three times per week. If an alfalfa/timothy mix is not available, then feed one flake of alfalfa and one flake of timothy per day. Provided your horse is an average-sized adult on a moderate exercise program, either of these types of hay should provide all of the energy and nutrients your horse needs to maintain his normal body weight. If your horse has trouble keeping weight on, you may need to provide two flakes of alfalfa and one flake of timothy each day. If your horse tends to be overweight, you can feed a little less alfalfa.

Generally speaking, legumes such as alfalfa are the best feed for horses who need to put on and maintain weight, and for horses who work on a regular basis. Timothy and other grass hays are good for horses who need to lose weight and don't work as hard.

✔ **Pasture:** Horses do best when they can graze in a pasture; however, providing your horse with lush pasture requires work and knowledge. If you happen to live on property where pasture has already been cultivated, your task is to carefully maintain it. If you want to start a pasture from scratch, you will need considerable help. Contact your local agricultural agency for assistance in starting and maintaining a quality horse pasture.

You can grow a number of different kinds of pasture grasses for equine consumption. Timothy, bromegrass, fescue, bluegrass, and orchard grass are among the types that horses enjoy. Talk to your veterinarian about which of the grasses that grow in your area best suit your horse.

Don't graze a pregnant mare on fescue! It can cause the mare to spontaneously abort the foal.

If your pasture does not yield a substantial amount of good-quality, nutritious grass, supplement your horse's diet with a daily ration of hay. If you don't, the horse may suffer from malnutrition. To verify that your pasture is of good quality, call your local agricultural office and ask an expert to inspect your pasture and help analyze its nutritional content.

Play close attention to weed control. Any number of toxic plants can invade your pasture, causing liver disease, neurological disorders, and abortions. Contact your agricultural office for a list of plants in your region that are toxic to horses.

✔ **Hay cubes:** You can feed your horse concentrated blocks of hay called *hay cubes.* Hay cubes tend to be cheaper than hay, and are good for older horses with worn-down teeth (cubes break apart quickly when chewed), horses with respiratory problems (cubes are less dusty than hay), and horses who have trouble keeping on weight. However, most horses prefer baled hay to cubes because baled hay satisfies their need to chew.

✔ **Pellets:** Another form of concentrated feed is pellets made from alfalfa. Pellets are even cheaper than cubes, but they're not at the top of our list of recommended feeds unless you have a horse who has respiratory problems or trouble keeping up his weight. Horses can easily choke on pellets, and pellets provide little in the way of chewing satisfaction for the horse.

✔ **Grain:** When it comes to horse food, people often think of grain as a staple of the equine diet. However, if your horse is receiving only moderate exercise, he probably doesn't need grain. Grain is a high-energy carbohydrate that does wonders for racehorses and other serious equine athletes but usually does little for the average horse other than leave him with too much energy. One exception to this rule is a horse pastured in extremely cold weather who needs the extra source of energy to stay warm.

If you want to give your horse an occasional treat of grain, do so in moderation, maybe once or twice a week. Oats, barley, corn, or a combination of these with molasses are healthy grains that you can feed every so often in small amounts. A serving of a one or two cups of grain makes a nice snack for your horse.

✔ **Bran:** Horse people love to give their horses warm bran mashes, and horses love eating them. Just remember not to give your horse too much too often (not more than once a week at the most). To feed bran (which you can buy in your local feed store, by the way), use a bucket to mix four to five cups of bran with some chopped up carrots or apples, and a small amount of grain. Add enough warm water to make the bran wet but not soupy.

✔ **Commercial feeds:** Horse owners today have access to a number of good-quality commercial horse feeds. Readily available in tack stores, these feeds range from simple mixes like alfalfa and molasses (great for mixing with vitamins, supplements, and medications) to complex *extruded* feeds, which get their name from the way they're made (many extruded feeds are designed for older horses, very active horses, horses who have trouble keeping weight on, and young horses).

We're big advocates of complex extruded feeds over grain because they're designed specifically with horses in mind, and are balanced with vitamins, minerals, carbohydrates, and fats. Talk to your veterinarian to find out whether your horse may benefit from a commercial feed.

✔ **Treats:** Few things rate as high on a horse's list as treats. All kinds of commercial horse treats are available at your local tack store. Or you can stick with two old favorites: carrots and red apples, both cut up in small pieces to prevent choking (especially important with ponies). The proverbial lump of sugar is okay only once in a while — it provides absolutely no nutritional value and isn't very good for the horse.

✔ **Fat:** Horses tend to get very little fat in their diets, even though this nutrient is required for basic equine function. Give your horse one cup of vegetable oil daily, mixed in with the grain or other supplemental feed (an alfalfa and molasses mix called A & M is good for this). If your horse tends to be overweight, reduce the oil to half a cup.

✔ **Vitamins:** Horses need plenty of vitamins and minerals for good health. Lots of small problems ranging from lameness to colic to infection can result from vitamin and mineral deficiencies. We recommend that you give your horse a dose of equine multivitamin supplement every day or every other day.

✔ **Minerals:** Provide your horse with access to a mineral salt block in his feeder or paddock, available at your local feed store. Your horse will lick the block to obtain salt and other minerals he needs.

How fat is my horse?

Horses tend to go one of two ways: They either have trouble keeping weight on or they have trouble keeping it off. To tell which one of these types you have at home, take a close look at your horse's rib cage. If you can see the ribs or your horse has a sunken-in appearance, the animal is underweight and needs to be fed more hay and a complex commercial feed. If you can neither see nor feel your horse's ribs, and notice excess fat around the head, tail, and neck, your horse is on the chubby side. Reduce the amount of alfalfa and grain in his diet and replace it with grass hay, which is lower in calories. If you can feel your horse's ribs but not see them, and don't notice any fat pockets around his head, neck, or tail, your horse is at just the right weight.

The quality of what you feed is just as important as the feed itself. If you buy cheap, poor-quality hay, your horse will suffer for it. Don't scrimp on this most important aspect of your horse's care.

Look for the following factors in any hay you buy to ensure its quality:

- **Plenty of leaves or blades:** Make sure that 60 percent or more of the hay consists of leaves or blades as opposed to stems. Leaves and blades contain most of the hay's nutrients.

- **Good scent:** Good quality hay has a pleasant smell. Moldy hay has a foul odor and should be avoided at all costs.

- **Purity:** The bale should contain only hay. That means no sticks, dirt, weeds, rope, or other foreign objects.

How to feed

Although feeding your horse only once a day would be easier for you, a horse's digestive system isn't meant to handle only one large meal. Small, frequent meals are the way to go when feeding horses. Provide a minimum of two feedings of hay per day. Most horse owners feed once in the morning and once at night. Feed three times a day if you can but only if you can do so consistently.

Using a feeder

Always feed your horse out of a feeder. The feeder can be something as simple as a plastic barrel with a side cut out, or a commercial hay rack purchased at a tack and feed store.

The purpose of a feeder is to keep your horse from eating directly off the ground. A horse who eats off the ground can easily ingest sand with his feed, resulting in colic or poor absorption of food.

If you decide to feed your horse grain or a commercial feed, provide it to your horse in a shallow bucket or rubber pan. Many commercial feeders are also designed so you simply dump the grain or feed directly into them.

Feeding treats

When it comes to the how of feeding treats, horse people are divided. Some swear that feeding treats from your hand causes a horse to become bratty and obnoxious. Other people find that their horses don't misbehave when treats are fed and believe that feeding by hand helps foster the bond between horse and human.

Here's our position: If your horse acts like a spoiled kid when you hand feed treats to him (starts pushing and crowding you, demanding that you hand over all the goods), then your horse is not a candidate for hand feeding. Or, if you plan to show your horse at halter or another event where the horse needs to behave perfectly when standing at your side, we don't recommend hand feeding either. In these cases, give your horse his treats in a bucket or in his feeder. On the other hand, if your horse is gentle soul who politely waits for you to hand over delectables and doesn't have a job that requires him to behave a certain way, you can go ahead and feed your horse by hand.

Watering Your Thirsty Filly

We can't overemphasize the importance of providing plenty of water as part your horse's daily care. Your horse needs water — lots of it — to stay alive and to ensure a healthy digestive system. That's why it's vitally important that your horse have constant access to clean, fresh H_2O at all times.

Horse owners can provide water in a few different ways. You can install an automatic waterer that automatically refills by using a float system whenever the horse drinks. Or, you can provide your horse with a large water trough and fill it manually as necessary. If you opt for the second method, you have to be diligent in keeping the trough full. In either case, keep the waterer clean of algae and other debris.

If you live in a climate where temperatures fall below freezing, you also need to keep your horse's water supply from turning to ice. You can do so with a heating element made especially for horse waterers, or by manually breaking the ice whenever it forms. We recommend the heating element because it requires less work on your part and also keeps the water at a warmer temperature, which encourages your horse to drink it.

Taking Care of Business

Daily horsekeeping requires more than just feeding and watering. You also have to keep a close eye on your charge, exercise the critter, clean up after him, and work at keeping pests at bay. All these things are an integral part of maintaining a horse.

The daily once over

Horses may seem like rather independent creatures, but in reality, they're more like half-ton toddlers. They easily get themselves into trouble and sometimes develop problems through no fault of their own.

That's why your horse needs what we like to call *the daily once over*. Every day, you must take your horse out of his stall or pasture and examine him from head to toe. This task is easiest to do as you are grooming, because grooming calls for close contact between your hands and eyes and the horse's body. Plus, grooming is usually enjoyable for the horse and helps the two of you bond.

As you go over your horse, check for the following signs of trouble:

- Lumps or bumps
- Scabs or hair loss
- Swellings or hot spots, especially around backs of pasterns, lower legs and tendon areas
- Rocks in hooves
- Discharge from eyes or nose
- Foul smells, especially in the nose and mouth areas
- Limping, walking very stiff
- Lack of appetite, depression, unresponsiveness, or sleepiness

For more information on what to do if you discover a problem during your daily once over, see Chapter 11.

Exercise

Stabled horses need daily exercise to keep both their minds and bodies in good working order. Pastured horses don't need as much formal exercise as their stabled counterparts, but they still require consistent time under saddle if they are to stay in good physical shape.

A word about turning out

Taking a stabled horse and giving it *turn-out time* where he can exercise on his own in an arena is a common practice in the horse world. Advocates of this practice see it as a way for a confined horse to expend some of his pent-up energy by bucking, rearing, running, rolling, and basically just being a horse.

Although turn-out time sounds good in theory, we've seen plenty of problems arise from this practice. Leg injuries like bowed tendons and even irreparable fractures often occur during turn-outs. The reason is that horses who are cooped up all day tend to go berserk during turn-out time and end up hurting themselves.

If you need to turn a horse out for behavioral reasons, or want to turn him out so he can roll (rolling is good for horses because it helps them stretch out their spine and back muscles), take these precautions to help avoid injuries:

✔ Turn the horse out only after you have ridden so he will be less likely to jump around.

✔ Help limber up your horse's muscles and tendons with a ten-minute walk before turning him out if you can't ride beforehand.

✔ Dress the horse in protective leg wear.

✔ Never turn your horse out with another horse.

✔ Make sure that the arena is safe and has a high enough fence that your horse won't jump it.

✔ Use an arena small enough that the horse can't work up too much speed when he runs.

✔ Stay with your horse in the arena so you can keep an eye on him.

✔ Never chase your horse in the arena with a whip or other object.

✔ Never turn your horse out in an arena where someone is riding.

In situations where a horse has so much pent up energy that he poses a danger to his rider, turn-outs may be necessary. However, we recommend that you try giving the horse more controlled exercise, like lungeing, on a daily basis before you resort to turning the animal out. Or, if you are unable to give the horse controlled exercise, turn the horse out on a regular basis so that he won't be as inclined to go berserk.

Give your horse a minimum of 30 minutes of exercise per day — more if you have the time (although don't overdo if your horse isn't used to a lot of work). If you don't have time to tack up and ride, you should at least take the horse out and walk him for half an hour. On the other hand, 30 minutes of just walking every day isn't enough exercise for the average horse, so you have to find time to give your equine buddy a good work out at least a few days a week. If you don't, your horse will start getting a bit crazy from all that pent-up energy, and you'll pay for it with misbehavior on the rare days when you do ride.

Although riding is the best way to exercise your horse, you can also vary the routine by occasionally lungeing him (see Chapter 13 for information on lungeing). Don't overdo the lungeing, however. Too much of it can put severe stress on your horse's legs and result in lameness.

Manure management

One of the least fun things about owning a horse is cleaning up after him. Horses are virtual poop machines who never seem to stop evacuating their bowels. Of course if your horse is producing plenty of waste, that means his digestive system is in good working order. Try keeping that happy thought in mind every time you pick up your shovel.

Manure is not the only waste product your horse produces. Horses eliminate several gallons of urine per day, creating soiled bedding to clean up also.

We can give you a whole slew of really good reasons to pick up after your horse on a daily basis, whether he is pastured or stabled. Here are some of the biggies:

- Your property begins to smell pretty awful if you let manure and urine-soaked bedding pile up.
- Your horse's health suffers if he is forced to stand in his own waste.
- The accumulated manure and urine provides a breeding ground for bacteria, flies, and internal parasites.
- You can get in trouble with your neighbors and the law if you don't clean up.

Scooping manure is really not a difficult job to perform, provided you are in decent physical shape and have a reasonably healthy back. All you need to do is scoop the poop into a wheelbarrow by using a manure fork, a wonderful invention that separates the manure balls from the dirt or bedding.

Cleaning urine-soaked bedding is a little more difficult, although the shavings, straw, or whatever you chose for your horse's bed sticks together when it's wet and so isn't that hard to remove. You can use your manure fork for this part of the job or simply a shovel, being careful not to take too much clean bedding with you as you scoop. Remember to replace the removed bedding with clean, fresh stuff when you're done.

You can dispose of the gathered waste by either dumping it in a trash receptacle for pick up or keeping it to compost. Whatever you do, be sure to follow the regulations in your municipality regarding equine waste disposal. If you aren't sure what those rules are, contact your county or city government for information.

If you want to compost your horse's manure and soiled bedding to use in your garden or to spread on the surface of a riding arena, make sure that you age the waste for at least eight weeks. We also suggest that you get a good book on composting so you can find out all about this method of waste disposal. Keep a close eye on your manure pile. Compost piles filled with manure have been known to catch fire as a result of internal combustion caused by the heat of decay.

Pest control

Where you find horses, you also find bugs. Flies, gnats, and intestinal worms tend to congregate at stables, dining on the horses and making their lives a living hell. These pests are a cold, harsh reality of the horse world, and all owners can do is try their darnedest to control them.

If you follow the instructions regarding waste control in the previous section, you'll already be doing a great deal to control pests in your horse's environment. Many species of flies and intestinal parasites need access to horse manure to complete their life cycles. So, if you get rid of the manure quickly, the pests can't reproduce. This is especially true of internal parasites, many of which reinfect a horse when the horse accidentally ingests larvae in his environment.

You don't have to be terribly observant to notice that flies are a particular nuisance at stables. Not only are they annoying, but they also deliver painful bites to horses (and sometimes humans) and spread disease.

In addition to diligent waste removal, you can do a few other things to help control the number of flies on your property:

- ✔ **Hang fly strips or traps around the barn:** These products are good for snagging flies.

- ✔ **Consider purchasing biological controls from companies that specialize in this aspect of pest control:** A tiny species of predatory wasp in the *Chalcididae* family that feeds on fly larvae is a popular choice among horse owners.

- ✔ **Apply fly sprays or wipes to your horse on a regular basis:** Also, consider installing an automated insecticide system installed in your barn.

- ✔ **Dress your horse in a fly mask, fly sheet, and special fly-screen leg wraps to keep flies from biting him (see Chapter 6).**

The bad news is that you can never completely eliminate flies from a horse's environment. The good news is that, with hard work, you can keep their pesky numbers in check.

Chapter 9

Brushing Up on Grooming Skills

*F*ew things make a horse lover happier than being up on a horse who looks really good. Mane and tail flowing, coat glowing — you'll feel proud passing other riders on the trail as you sit astride such a glamorous beast.

Of course, your trusty steed isn't going to come out of the pasture looking like this — you have to make it happen. Although cleaning up a half-ton animal who's been milling around in the dirt for days may not sound like a picnic, we think grooming is one of the most enjoyable parts of horse ownership. And besides, most horses absolutely love the attention.

If you groom your horse every time you take him out for a ride, the effects are cumulative. His coat shines more every day, his tail is silkier. He looks pretty darn good, even when he's just standing there eating in his stall (provided he hasn't just rolled in the mud, that is). In this chapter, we give you the essential information for making your horse look his best.

Why Grooming Is Important

Take a look in any tack store or equine supply catalog and you'll see oodles of grooming tools for sale. That's because grooming is a very important activity in the horse world, as you will soon discover as you spend more and more time around horses. In fact, we can give you several really good reasons *right now* as to why you should groom your horse on a regular basis:

✔ To remove sweat and dirt from your horse's coat, helping keep his skin healthy.

✔ To prevent chafing and skin irritation to your horse by removing dirt, burrs, and other material before you put on the tack.

✔ To help build that all important bond with your horse.

✔ To give you a chance to inspect your horse for any unusual lumps, bumps or blemishes. You're more likely to notice changes or problems as they arise if you're familiar with your horse's body.

✔ To give your horse the attention he thrives on.

✔ To earn the high regard of other horse people, who will respect and admire your dedication to your horse.

✔ To help you (as well as your horse) relax, and reduce the daily stress in both your lives.

✔ To make your horse look handsome and well cared for.

If you still aren't convinced that you need to take time out as often as you can to groom your horse, then hear this: Regular grooming is important to your horse's health and welfare, and it's a requirement of every horse owner, pure and simple.

How to Groom

Grooming your horse isn't difficult. In fact, it's one of the easiest and most enjoyable aspects of horsemanship.

Grooming should be done as often as possible, but the optimum schedule is to groom once a day. Even if you can't spruce him up every day, grooming your horse before and after you ride him is imperative. When you groom after you ride, make sure that the horse is completely cooled down because trying to groom a sweaty coat is aggravating and nearly impossible.

Horse people all over the world use the grooming procedures described in the following sections, with slight variations for personal style and preference. If you hope to fit in with the horsy set, you have to practice proper grooming procedures and protocols. After you become familiar with the basics, you can vary the steps somewhat to suit your own personality. For example, some people prefer to clean the hooves before grooming the body, and others tend to the horse's head only after taking care of every other part of his anatomy.

Before you start

The first thing you need to do is assemble all of your grooming tools in a tack box or organizer. Make sure that everything is clean and in good working order. At the very minimum, your tools should include the following items:

- ✔ Rubber curry comb
- ✔ Stiff brush
- ✔ Soft brush
- ✔ Hoof pick
- ✔ Hoof brush
- ✔ Shedding blade
- ✔ Mane and tail brush
- ✔ Cloth (any old soft, clean rag will do)
- ✔ Cotton balls

You can find descriptions of these items and their uses in Chapter 6.

After you organize your tools, put a halter and lead rope on your horse, and lead him to a roomy area in the stable where you can tie him securely, either in cross-ties or at a post.

Never try to groom a horse who is loose in a stall or pasture. Also, if the weather is inclement, find a spot to shelter both you and your horse from wind and wetness. (To lead and tie your horse, follow the directions in Chapter 13.)

The body

Start with the biggest part of the horse: his body. The body includes the head, neck, legs, rump and everything in between.

Everyone knows that horses are covered in hair, but unless you've spent some time around horses, you may not realize horse hair is a trap for every speck of dirt, mud, and dust that the horse comes into contact with. Your job as a groomer is to get as much as that grunge off the horse's coat as you can, exposing the clean-looking, shimmering coat beneath.

If your horse is stabled indoors all the time, the amount of dirt in his coat will be minimal. Horses who live in pastures or paddocks, however, usually require a bit of elbow grease to get them clean.

To clean the body of your horse, you use a rubber curry comb, stiff brush, soft brush, and cloth. With these tools at your disposal, follow these steps:

1. **Use the curry comb to bring the dirt to the surface of the coat by rubbing in a circular motion. (If your horse has a very thin coat, proceed gently or skip this step altogether.)**

Start on your horse's left side with your curry comb in your right hand. Begin rubbing at the end of your horse's neck (where it joins the head) and work down toward the horse's body. (See Figure 9-1 for the correct way to stand and groom.) The order in which to groom is neck, chest, shoulders, back, belly, rump, and haunches.

Be very gentle when working around the horse's flanks and underbelly. Some horses are very sensitive in this area and may kick out at you.

If mud is caked on the horse's legs, use a very gentle circular motion to shake it loose from the coat. Only do so with dry mud because wet mud is impossible to remove, and with a rubber curry comb, not a metal one, because a metal comb can damage the skin on your horse's legs.

After finishing the left side, move over to the right side, switching the curry comb to your left hand, and repeat the process.

If your horse is the least bit dirty — and we're sure he is — the dust comes to the surface of his coat.

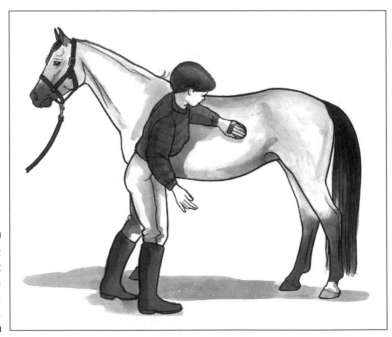

Figure 9-1:
The correct
way to
groom a
horse.

2. **Use the stiff brush to dissipate the dirt into the air by brushing in short strokes in the direction of the coat.**

Again, start on the horse's left side with the stiff brush in your right hand and start at the top of the neck, moving down the horse's neck, to his chest, shoulder, back, barrel, belly, rump, and haunches. You can also use the stiff brush to loosen the dirt from your horse's legs, but be sure to be gentle.

After you finish the left side of the horse, move over to the right side and repeat the process with the stiff brush in your right hand.

As you brush your horse with the stiff brush and soft brush, continuously clean the brushes by rubbing them against the rubber curry comb. Doing so helps to get rid of the dust that has accumulated in the brushes and keeps the dirt from going back on the horse.

3. **Use the soft brush to remove the remaining dust from the coat, brushing along the lay of the coat by using short strokes.**

   Again, start on the horse's left with the brush in your right hand and move from the horse's neck, to his chest, shoulder, back, barrel, belly, rump, and haunches. Move to the right side of the horse with the brush in your left hand, and repeat the brushing process.

   You should begin to see a shine on your horse's coat.

4. **Complete the body-grooming process by wiping down the horse's body with the cloth.**

   This step gives the coat even more shine.

5. **Use the cloth to clean out the insides of your horse's nostrils, where dirt and mucus tend to accumulate.**

6. **Use the soft brush to gently groom your horse's head with long, soft strokes.**

   Stand at the side and in front of your horse to do this step.

   Most horses enjoy having their heads groomed, but some don't. Be sure to calmly approach your horse's head with the brush, showing him the brush and letting him smell it before you use it on his head. Be careful when brushing his ears because some horses are funny about having their ears touched. If your horse objects to having his ears brushed, try grooming them with a soft towel.

When your horse is shedding (something that occurs in early spring), you can use your shedding blade to remove the loose hair from the coat. Use the blade before you groom, starting on the left side of the horse, moving down the body, and then starting again on the right.

Shedding blades work best on horses with thick winter coats. If your horse has a thin winter coat and is only shedding minimally, you can use a shedding stone or metal curry comb to remove the excess hair.

Safety in grooming

Although grooming is a relaxing activity for you and your horse, we don't want you to get too comfortable! Remember these safety tips when you are working on and around your horse:

- ✔ **Never duck under your horse's neck or belly.** If you want to get from one side of the horse to the other, walk around.

- ✔ **Never stand directly behind your horse when grooming him.** Stand off to the side in case he decides to kick.

- ✔ **Never kneel down or sit while you are working on your horse's legs.** Stay in a bending or squatting position so you can move out of the way quickly if necessary.

- ✔ **Never stand directly in front of your horse's legs when grooming.** Stay to the side of the legs to avoid being struck should the horse move forward or strike out.

- ✔ **Never groom a horse who is loose in a stall or pasture.** Always make sure that the horse is correctly secured before you begin grooming.

- ✔ **Never assume that a strange horse is open to grooming.** When grooming a new horse, use caution, especially when brushing the flanks and underbelly.

Use caution whenever you use the shedding blade. The sharp teeth on this tool can injure your horse's skin if not used carefully. Apply only minimal pressure, and *never* use this tool on your horse's legs.

Mane and tail

Your horse's mane and tail are made up of hair not unlike human hair. And as with human hair, regular cleaning and brushing helps keep it looking lovely and luxurious.

You need the body brush and tail brush to groom your horse's mane and tail. You may also want to use a mane and tail detangling solution — the kind you apply when the mane and tail is dry, not wet.

Follow these steps to groom your horse's mane and tail:

1. **Using your fingers, pick out any shavings, burrs, or other foreign material lodged in the mane, tail, or forelock.**

   The *forelock* is the area of the mane that hangs down onto the horse's forehead, between the horse's ears.

2. **Separate tangles in the mane and tail with your fingers, if you can.**

If the hair is badly tangled, use a human hair, dry-detangling solution. Put some of the detangler in the palm of your hand and work it into the mane and tail for later brushing.

3. **Using your soft brush, groom the base of the horse's tail, where the hairs are short.**

   Try to reach the skin when you do this step, because brushing helps stimulate the circulation.

4. **Using the soft brush, groom the base of the mane, where it joins the crest of the neck.**

   Again, let the brush reach the skin to help with circulation.

5. **Using the mane and tail brush, brush out the hair of the mane and tail, gently removing any tangles with your fingers first, until you get a silky look.**

The hooves

The health of your horse's hooves is extremely important, and you should try to clean them daily, if possible. Hooves that are not cleaned regularly can develop thrush, stone bruises, and other problems.

Luxurious manes and tails

Soft, silky manes and tails are both made *and* born. Although nature certainly has a lot to do with the quality and texture of your horse's lovely locks, you can do plenty to enhance what's already there:

✔ **Keep it clean.** Washing your horse's mane and tail once a month or so with a good shampoo keeps them looking really good and prevents their getting dirty, sticky, and stringy. Use a gentle shampoo, one made especially for horses.

✔ **Condition, condition, condition.** If you put a really good made-for-equines conditioner on your horse's mane and tail every time you wash them, your horse will sport some glorious tresses. Buy a premium conditioner, one that moisturizes. Be sure to rinse it all out after you apply it.

✔ **Brush it out.** Before every ride and after every washing, brush that mane and tail with a wide-toothed hair brush to keep snarls from getting out of control. Avoid using a comb or any other implement that can break and pull out the hairs.

✔ **Wrap it up.** Protect that magnificent hair when your horse is at pasture or in the stable with braids and bags. Large, loose braids in the mane keep the hair from getting dirty and tangled, and keeping a braided tail in a tail bag protects it from knots and mud.

If you want your horse's tail to grow, keep it loosely braided and in a tail bag.

To properly clean your horse's hooves, you need a hoof pick and a hoof brush. Your horse should be securely tied to a hitching post or cross-ties.

Picking up the feet

Before you can clean your horse's hooves, you have to be able to pick up his feet. Standing on the left side of your horse, facing toward the horse's back end, bend down and run your left hand along your horse's left front leg, starting above the knee and moving down toward the *pastern* (ankle). Some horses pick their feet up for you automatically. If yours doesn't, lean your shoulder against your horse's shoulder to shift his weight to the opposite leg, and squeeze the back of the leg you are hoping to lift. The horse should then pick up his foot, allowing you to cradle the left hoof with your hand. Be sure to bend the leg back at its natural angle and not off to the side. Support this uplifted foot in your hand and begin cleaning.

Some horses are trained to pick up their feet if you gently squeeze the horny growth on the inside of their elbows and hocks called the *chestnut*. Give this a try if you are having trouble getting a new horse to lift his feet.

Cleaning the hoof

To clean out the inside of the uplifted hoof, take the pick in your right hand, with the handle in your fist and the point of the pick facing away from you. Stand at the horse's left side at his shoulder, looking toward the back of the horse. You'll know you are in the right position if your left shoulder is next to your horse's left shoulder. Ask your horse for his hoof, then support this uplifted foot in your left hand and start scraping out the dirt with the tip of the hoof pick. (Figure 9-2 shows the correct way to hold the hoof and the hoof pick.) Be sure to clean out the areas around the triangular frog of the hoof, but don't scrape the frog itself. Look for rocks, nails, or other items that may be lodged around the frog. See Chapter 1 for a picture of the parts of the horse's foot.

Get to know the anatomy of a horse's foot so you can scrape in just the right areas. See Chapter 1 for details on what the underside of the hoof looks like under all that dirt.

After you dig out the dirt and debris from the hoof, use your hoof brush to wipe away any excess dirt in the foot. You get a good view of the foot after you do this, so you can spot any stones or other objects that may be lodged inside.

When you're satisfied that that first hoof is clean, move to the hind leg on the same (left) side. Facing the back of the horse, again run your hand down the horse's leg and lift the foot off the ground. If the horse doesn't lift his foot right away, push gently on his thigh so he shifts his weight to the other leg.

Figure 9-2:
The correct way to hold the hoof and hoof pick.

After you finish the hooves on the left side, move over to the right. Don't start with the front leg on the right side, though. Tradition dictates that you move from the left foreleg to the left hind leg to the right hind leg, then to the right foreleg.

After you clean out your horse's hooves, use your hoof brush to clean off any dirt clinging to the outside of the hoof.

Down at the Horse Wash

Bathing a horse isn't that much different from washing a car, except that with a horse, you don't need to wax. Both objects are large, however, and require a lot of soap, water, and elbow grease.

You can choose any number of ways to bathe your horse, but we show you one of the fastest and easiest methods.

Why and when to bathe?

Why wash a horse? In nature, horses don't get baths. In fact, the only time wild horses ever get wet is during a rainstorm.

Captivity is essentially the reason we wash horses. First of all, humans like to be around clean horses. Most horse owners see their horses as extensions of themselves and want their equine companions to look just as good as they do.

Secondly, the fact that we ride horses demands that we keep them clean. A dirty horse is prone for trouble after tack is placed on his body. Sweat and dirt underneath a saddle and girth can cause chafing, itching, and sheer misery. Tack is also a breeding ground for fungus.

That said, how do you know *when* to bathe your horse? There's no firm rule. Some horse owners bathe their horses once a month like clockwork, others do it just before a show. Some people wait until the horse is really, really dirty. Still others, by necessity, wait until the weather warms up or simply until they have time to do it.

How often should *you* bathe your horse? It depends on several factors, such as your climate, how dirty your horse is, and what you use him for. Because they're graded on their looks, show horses get more baths than non-competitive equines do. On the other hand, bathing a horse too often isn't good because the shampoo can strip the natural oils from the horse's skin and coat.

If your horse works hard and gets dirty and sweaty often, you can opt to simply rinse him all over with clear water, without the shampoo. Clear water doesn't hurt him and keeps his skin and coat free of irritating debris.

Because horses live outside, think about the weather before you give your horse a bath. If you live in a cold climate and it's the dead of winter, you should only bathe your horse if you can provide him with warm water, and a washing and drying place that is warm and free of drafts. Otherwise, only sunny warm days are good days for a bath.

Before you bathe

Don't start washing that horse unless you're prepared. Consider the following:

- **Be sure that your horse is amenable to being washed:** Most horses are fine when tied in a *wash rack* (a place specially made for bathing horses, complete with asphalt flooring and hitches for tying the horse) and when hosed or sponged down with water. However, until you know for sure that your horse won't panic in the confines of a wash rack or freak out at the sight of a garden hose, hold off on the bath. First, find out the horse's history with bathing if you can or try bringing him into the wash rack with the help of another person. Watch carefully for the horse's reaction.

- **Make sure that you have enough time to do the job right before you even get started:** Washing a horse is a big chore. It takes at least 20 minutes, maybe more, to thoroughly wash and rinse a horse and another 30–45 minutes to get him dry, depending on the weather.

✓ **Have a good place to bathe:** Use a specially designed wash rack, or a roomy, hard-floored area where you can securely tie the horse to a hitching post or cross-ties (see Chapter 13 for information about tying your horse).

✓ **Ensure that the running water reaches all the way to your horse:** Garden hoses are the most convenient way of bringing water from the faucet directly to your horse's body.

✓ **Have at least 72 gallons of lukewarm water on hand:** Warm the water in buckets using an electrical device called a *bucket warmer,* if you don't have access to warm running water.

✓ **Use a nylon halter and lead rope if you can:** These can best withstand the rigors of being soaked with water.

✓ **Wear clothes and shoes that you don't mind getting wet:** Bathing a horse is messy business.

Get your tools

Assemble your bathing tools before you bring your horse to the washing area. You should have the following on hand:

✓ **Shampoo:** Plenty of equine shampoos are available at tack and feed stores. You can also use human shampoo on your horse if you prefer.

✓ **Conditioner:** Some equine (and human) shampoos have a conditioner built in. Or, you can add one later as a second step. Many horse owners use conditioner only on the horse's mane and tail. This decision is strictly a matter of personal preference.

✓ **Body sponge:** For sale in tack and feed stores, these large sponges are good for working the shampoo into your horse's coat.

✓ **Face sponge:** You use this sponge, usually a natural sea sponge, to clean the delicate areas of your horse's face.

✓ **Sweat scraper:** The sweat scraper is great for removing excess water from your horse's coat once the bath is over.

✓ **Towels:** Use these to dry the horse's face (and probably your own) and to clean up any other wet areas. Also, use your towel to dry the back of your horse's pasterns to prevent the growth of fungus in this area of the leg.

✓ **Cooler or sweat sheet:** If you are bathing your horse on a hot summer day, you won't need this piece of horse clothing. However, if there is any chance your horse will be exposed to drafts while you are walking him to dry him off, a cooler or sweat sheet is necessary.

How to Bathe

Your horse is securely tied in a wash area, your tools are assembled and you're ready to start scrubbing. Follow these steps to give your horse a bath:

1. **Starting on the left side of your horse (you wash and rinse one side of the horse at a time), run lukewarm water from the garden hose on the horse's legs if your wash rack has a hot water faucet. If not, you'll have to use warm water in a bucket for this step.**

   Doing so allows your horse to get used to the water and the idea that he's about to be bathed.

2. **After the horse has had a bit of time to adjust to the water, slowly move the hose up to where the neck joins the head and wet the body all the way to the rear end of the horse.**

3. **Apply shampoo to your sponge and begin lathering your horse's coat, starting where the neck joins the head and working your way down across the body.**

   Be sure to scrub underneath your horse, where the girth lies, as well as along the back where the saddle sits because sweat and dirt tend to accumulate in these areas. Wash your horse's legs too, as well as the outsides of his hooves.

4. **After you're confident that you've loosened the dirt and sweat from your horse's coat, take the hose or a bucket of water and begin rinsing the shampoo from your horse's coat.**

   Rinse very thoroughly; you don't want to leave behind any soap residue that may irritate your horse's skin.

5. **Shampoo, condition, and rinse the horse's mane.**

   If the mane is on the right side of the horse, move over to that side.

6. **Repeat Steps 1–4 for the right side of the horse.**

7. **Wash the horse's tail.**

   Wet the tail with water and apply shampoo. Be sure to work the lather into the tail so that you get all of the hair. Rinse, condition, and rinse again. Be sure to get all the soap residue out of the base of the tail. Soap residue can irritate the horse's skin and he'll probably rub his tail on whatever he can find, dirtying those luxurious locks.

8. **Wash the horse's head.**

   This step can be tricky, depending on the horse. Most horses are very cooperative when having their faces cleaned. Others have had bad experiences or are simply wary of the process and will give you trouble. In either case, be gentle and considerate when washing your horse's face.

Bathing do's and don'ts

There is a right way to bathe a horse and a wrong way. Your horse wants you to do it the right way:

✔ **Do have patience with your horse when bathing him.** Bathing makes no sense to horses; they only put up with it because we ask them to.

✔ **Do have consideration for your horse during the bath.** Use a comfortable water temperature and appropriate water pressure.

✔ **Do talk to your horse when bathing him.** Constantly reassure him and tell him what a good horse he is.

✔ **Don't spray your horse in the face with water.** How would you like it if someone did that to you?

✔ **Don't get water in your horse's eyes, ears, or nostrils.** This not only causes the horse fear and discomfort, but it can result in medical problems too.

✔ **Don't put your horse back in his pasture or stall while he's dripping wet.**

Wet the horse's face with a sponge and warm water. Don't forget to wet the forelock, because you wash this when you do the head. We recommend that you just rinse the face with a clean sponge and water and avoid using shampoo on your horse's face. Shampoo is difficult to rinse off thoroughly, and it can get in the horse's eyes. Also, avoid the temptation to wash your horse's face by squirting his face with the garden hose. Some horses will tolerate it, but all clearly hate it.

After-bath care

After you give your horse a bath, it's time to dry him off. How fast your horse dries depends on the thickness of his coat, the air temperature, and the humidity. Here's some advice to help you get that 1,000-pound, dripping animal dry in the shortest time and safest manner possible:

✔ Whisk away as much excess water on the body as you can by using your sweat scraper.

✔ Walk your horse around in the sun, if the weather is hot and sunny, preferably on a hard surface or on grass so dust doesn't stick to his newly washed legs and hooves. If your horse is amenable to going on a hotwalker (a mechanical merry-go-round of sorts), you can put him on one of these contraptions as long as you stay there to supervise.

✔ Cover your horse with a cooler or sweat sheet before walking him if the air temperature feels cool to you.

Never put your horse back in his stall, paddock, or pasture while he is still soaking wet. Not only is this unhealthy for the horse, but all your hard work goes down the drain when he gets down and rolls!

Grooming for Show

If you're planning to show your horse, you may have your work cut out for you in the grooming department, depending on the discipline you've chosen. Although some events like reining and cross-country jumping don't call for special grooming, some of the more popular types of showing require that your horse look a certain way.

We're not going to try to explain every aspect of how to groom a show horse for every possible discipline. You can find out this information from your trainer or from your fellow equestrians after you become immersed in the show world. But we can give you some general advice on how to make your horse look good in the ring:

Mane pulling

Some horse owners like their horses to have long, flowing manes. Others prefer a shorter, thinner look. In fact, people who show their horses in western "rail" classes like western pleasure, equitation, trail, and horsemanship must keep their horse's manes short and trim. The same goes for those who show in English events like dressage and hunt seat, where manes are often braided for competition and so need to be kept short and manageable.

Keeping your horse's mane short and thinned out is not as simple as you may think. You can't just take a pair of scissors and cut it. If you do, it will look thick and chopped up. Instead, what you need to do is "pull" the mane, using a mane comb (which we describe in Chapter 6).

Here is how you pull a horse's mane:

1. **Start with a clean, dry mane, all on one side of the horse's neck.**

2. **Begin at the center of the horse's neck. Hold your mane comb in your right hand, and take a 1-inch wide section of mane in** your left hand, between your forefinger and your thumb.

3. **Stretch down the mane hairs you are holding. Then, using the same fingers that are holding the hairs, push up some of the hairs that you are holding. This leaves you with several hairs still between your forefingers.**

4. **Wrap these remaining hairs in the metal mane comb and yank down in a short, quick pull.**

5. **Perform this step over the length of the entire mane until you have a nice, neat look.**

If you use short, quick pulls, mane pulling shouldn't bother your horse. If it does, ask an experienced horse person to help you get the hang of it. If your horse is extremely sensitive when it comes to having his mane pulled, you may have to have a veterinarian come out and give the horse a sedative before you can proceed.

Private parts

Like it or not, the private areas of the horse need to be washed on a regular basis. In the wild, the normal course of equine reproduction keeps these areas clean, healthy, and in working order. But unbred horses in captivity need help keeping tidy.

To clean your mare or gelding's private areas, use a mild soap or a gel product made specifically for this purpose, available in tack stores. You also want to have a supply of latex gloves on hand.

If your horse is a mare, your job is relatively easy. All you need to do for her is to clean out the waxy substance that builds up between the teats, located underneath her body between her back legs. Wet the area with warm water and apply shampoo between the teats. Manually remove the wax that builds up there (this is where the latex glove comes in). Rinse thoroughly to remove all the soap. Be aware that your mare may not like all this attention and may try to kick out at you. Be cautious until you know how she reacts to this process.

If your horse is a gelding, you need to clean his sheath at least once a year. A lovely little item affectionately known as "the bean" can result from a build-up of secretions in the pocket at the end of the penis, and result in irritation and swelling. The bean needs to be removed annually, sometimes more often.

If you've never cleaned your gelding's sheath, we recommend that you have a veterinarian do it the first time. Some geldings react violently to interference in this very delicate area, and it's best to have a trained professional deal with this situation.

If your vet tells you that your gelding is amenable to having his sheath cleaned, you can try doing it yourself. Start out by putting on a latex glove and covering your hand with a very small amount of soap. Wet the area with warm water and loosen and remove the built-up material inside the sheath. If your horse is very cooperative, he will "drop" his penis and allow you to wash that too.

After you finish cleaning, rinse the entire area thoroughly with cool water, making sure to remove all the soap. Any residue left on the horse's private parts will irritate him.

Although you can try to clean your own horse's sheath, the truth of the matter is that most geldings are uncooperative when sheath-cleaning time comes and need a sedative before they allow their genitals to be handled. Don't feel that you're cheating if you opt to skip performing this aspect of horse care yourself. It's perfectly reasonable to have your vet do the cleaning each and every time.

✔ **A good trim.** All show disciplines have one thing in common, and that's the requirement for a neatly clipped horse. Ears, muzzle, and fetlock must be properly trimmed. In some breeds, the bridle path (the area of the mane just behind the ears) needs to be clipped too. To find out how to clip these areas, see the "Maintenance Clipping" section later in this chapter.

✔ **Winning sheen.** No matter what type of showing you plan to do, your horse stands a better chance of winning if his coat is clean and shiny. Bathe your horse a day or so before the show to give his coat time to regain some of its natural oils. On the day of the event, you can apply any number of commercial coat polishing products meant to add sheen to a horse's coat.

✔ **Beautiful braids.** A number of disciplines — including dressage and hunt seat — call for the horse's mane (and sometimes the tail) to be braided. We could describe these procedures for you here, but we don't think a written description can help you all that much. The best way to find out the proper braids for your discipline is to have a trainer or fellow competitor show you how. Don't be shy about asking for help. Everyone has to learn sometime, and most knowledgeable horse people are happy to teach newcomers the braiding ropes.

✔ **Proper manes and tails.** Some disciplines, such as western pleasure and saddle seat, require trimmed mane and tail styles. Learn the particulars of your discipline and make it your business to acquire the skills needed to make your horse look like it should for the show ring.

The Joys of Clipping

You've seen those before-and-after make-over photos, right? Well, the equine equivalent to those images would be before-and-after clipping photos. *Clipping* is the practice of shaving a horse's hair, or sections of his hair, so the hair is close to the skin. If you take a horse who hasn't been clipped in a few months and then clip him, chances are you won't recognize the beast. And just like in the make-over pictures, the *after* photo looks a whole lot better than the *before* shot.

Clipping is a simple and easy way to make your horse look good. Even a less-than-beautiful horse can be made to look much more handsome with a simple head and leg trim.

Several types of clipping exist. Basic maintenance clipping involves trimming the head and legs. More extensive clipping is necessary in body clips, where large amounts of hair are removed from the horse's coat to help him cool down after a workout.

The type of clippers you use depends on what you plan to clip. Maintenance clips require nothing more than a good pair of small horse clippers. Body clips, on the other hand, call for heavy duty equipment: body clippers. (See Chapter 6 for more information on clippers.)

Clipping your horse is a relatively simple chore, provided your horse cooperates. A simple maintenance clip shouldn't take more than 15 or 20 minutes at most. Body clips can take anywhere from half an hour to all day, depending on the extent of the clip.

Maintenance clipping

To keep your horse looking nice and neat, perform a maintenance clip on him at least twice a month. This means trimming the whiskers off the nose, clipping the excess hair from his ears, and removing the overgrown hair on his fetlocks. Unless you show your horse in a discipline that forbids it, you should also trim your horse's bridle path as part of this routine.

Follow these steps to perform a maintenance clip on your horse. Remember to move the clippers along the hair in the opposite direction that it grows:

1. **Make sure that your clipper blades are sharp and well oiled (see the sidebar "Clipper care").**

2. **Tie your horse securely at a hitching post or at cross-ties (see Chapter 13).**

   If you're not sure whether your horse is amenable to clippers, instead of tying your horse, ask someone to hold the lead rope while you do your clipping. If your horse is cooperative, you can tie him up next time.

3. **Start clipping your horse's head at the jaw line, lightly trimming the hair that extends beyond the horse's jaw line.**

   Clip up to the level of the jaw, removing that shaggy look. Many horses are frightened of having their heads trimmed. If your horse gets panicky when you try to clip his head, recondition him to tolerate the clippers (see the sidebar "Clipping: One horse's story" in this chapter.

   If you have a clipper-phobic horse and you haven't been able to recondition him, try trimming his fetlocks, bridle path, and whiskers with scissors. Most horses afraid of clippers don't mind being trimmed this way.

4. **Trim the whiskers from your horse's muzzle very gently, one whisker at a time.**

   Although a muzzle full of whiskers isn't pretty, some equine experts believe that horses use their whiskers as feelers in the dark. If you prefer that your horse keep his whiskers, simply skip this part of the process. Also, be sure to leave the long whisker-type hairs around the horse's eyes intact. Experts believe these hairs help keep horses from injuring their eyes on objects in the dark.

5. **Move up to the horse's ears and trim the hair protruding around the edges.**

   Don't trim the inside of the horse's ears because the horse needs that interior hair to protect the inner ear from insects, dirt, and other intrusions.

6. **Shave a bridle path for your horse, just behind the ears.**

   The length of the bridle path depends on the discipline in which you ride your horse, and/or your horse's breed. If you plan to show your horse, this detail is important. Talk to other equestrians who ride in your discipline to find out the proper length of bridle path for your horse. If you aren't showing but just want to create a comfortable landing strip for the top of your horse's headstall so his mane doesn't get tangled in the bridle (this is, after all, the actual purpose of a bridle path) clip back about three inches of mane from behind the ears.

7. **Check the back of your horse's fetlocks to see whether your horse has *ergots*, soft, horny growths at the point of the fetlock joints.**

   If so, take scissors and cut down the ergots so they are only about half an inch long.

8. **Trim your horse's fetlocks.**

   Before you start clipping, use your hand to feel the shape of the bone at your horse's ankle. The object here is to clip short the hair around the ankle bone.

9. **Trim the long hair that hangs over the coronet onto the top of the hoof (see Chapter 1 for a diagram indicating the exact location of the coronet).**

   Clip the hair gently until the line between the top of the hoof and the coronet is straight and void of shaggy hairs.

Clipper care

If you take good care of your clippers, they'll take good care of your horse. Follow these rules of clipper care:

✔ **Keep your clippers well lubricated.** Buy quality clipper lubricator and lubricate the clippers before, while, and after you use them.

✔ **Use only sharp blades on your clippers.** Ensure that you use blades made specifically for your model.

✔ **Don't let your clippers overheat when you are using them.** Check them often while you're clipping. If they get hot, turn them off and let them cool.

✔ **Keep your horse from stepping on the clipper cord.** If the cord breaks, the horse can get shocked or even electrocuted.

✔ **Check the cord and plug regularly.** Make sure that they aren't frayed or broken.

✔ **Dismantle your clippers periodically.** Clean the various parts.

✔ **Store your clippers in a dry place.**

When clipping your horse, don't ever put your head in front of or behind your horse's legs or under his belly. Doing so puts you at risk for getting kicked in the head.

Body clipping

One of the banes of the busy horse owner's existence is the equine winter coat. If you live in a very cold climate where you don't ride much in the winter and if your horse is out in a pasture, this wad of fuzzy hair is a blessing to your horse, who needs it to keep warm. But if you live in a temperate — or worse, a mild climate — and if you ride in the wintertime, then that long shaggy coat can be a real pain in the you-know-what.

Here's the dilemma with winter coats: Nature designed this shaggy hair to keep the horse warm in the coldest of winter months. In the wild, this works great. Wild horses do little in the winter besides forage for food and huddle together for warmth. But the domestic horse has a whole other lifestyle. He is usually ridden in the winter, and is often kept indoors in a stall, where a thick winter coat is unnecessary.

When a horse in full winter coat is ridden, he sweats profusely, and it's no wonder. Imagine moving furniture all day dressed in a down coat! After the horse's workout, the thick hair is filled with sweat, and it can take hours to dry out. In the meantime, the horse is subject to draft, chill, and ultimately illness, while you, the poor horse's owner, spend half the day desperately trying to get the horse to dry.

Humans have found a way out of this predicament: body clipping. By removing some or all of the horse's body hair in the wintertime, you can avoid having to deal with the time and trouble it takes to properly cool out a hot and hairy horse. And another perk: Clipped horses are easier to keep clean.

Of course, body clipping does have its down side. In cases where horses receive substantial body clips, you must keep the horse constantly blanketed. This is only logical because the clip removes the horse's natural means of staying warm in winter. If you choose to clip your horse, you need to make sure your horse wears a blanket in cold weather and that the blanket comes off when the weather heats up.

Types of body clips

If you plan to ride your horse often in the wintertime, you may want to consider body clipping. Depending on your horse's living conditions, work schedule, and your personal preference, you can choose from several different types of clips, shown in Figure 9-3.

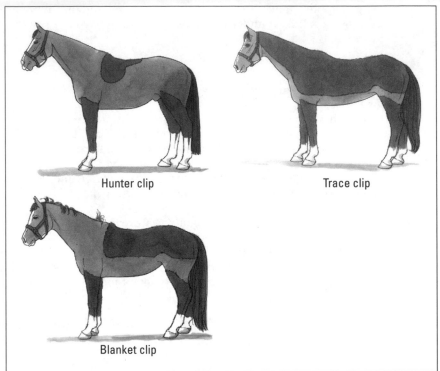

Figure 9-3:
Different
types of
body clips.

The following list explains the uses of the different clip styles:

- **Trace clip:** The trace clip is a good choice for horses who live outdoors and do moderate work in the winter. With the trace clip, only the bottom third of the horse's coat is removed. The underside of the neck and belly are trimmed, as is the chest. With this clip, the horse sweats less during workouts, but still retains enough coat to stay warm outdoors in temperate weather. In cold weather climates, a horse with a trace clip must be blanketed on cold days and every night.

- **Blanket clip:** This clip requires removal of the hair on the horse's head, neck, chest, shoulders, and the lower portion of the abdomen and hindquarters. The blanket clip is good for horses who work hard in the winter but still need some protection from the cold on their legs, back, and hips. Horses with blanket clips must be blanketed on cold days and every night.

- **Hunter clip**: The hunter clip is helpful to horses who work hard out on the field, such as foxhunters, cross-country event horses and endurance horses. This clip leaves a patch of hair on the back where the saddle lays and a patch of hair on the legs. The rest of the horse is completely clipped. Horses with hunter clips must be blanketed on cold days and every night.

- **Full clip:** With the full clip, the entire winter coat is removed from the horse's body. This is the clip of choice for many riders who compete with their horses in events year-round or who work them very hard. It is best to use this clip on a horse who is stabled indoors. A blanket is required for cold days and every night.

How to body clip

Body clipping is an art and takes a bit of practice. You may want to find an experienced horse person to help you do the clipping the first time around — or at least to get you started, anyway.

Before you start clipping, assemble everything you need to do the job:

- **Body clippers:** If you plan to do a full clip, blanket clip, or hunter clip, you need a good pair of body clippers. (You can usually do a trace clip using regular horse clippers.) If you don't want to invest in a pair of body clippers, you can usually rent them from a local tack and feed store. Make sure the blades are sharp before you begin your task.

- **Clipper lubricant:** To keep your clippers from getting jammed or overheated, keep lubricating them as you clip. You can purchase clipper lubricant at a tack and feed store.

- **White chalk:** For any clip other than a full clip, use a piece of white chalk to draw the outline of the clip before you start trimming. You're better off with grooming chalk purchased at a tack and feed store rather than blackboard chalk simply because grooming chalk draws better on horse hair.

- **Towels:** Wipe the oil and hair from your clipper periodically with a towel. You can also use a towel to wipe the hair from yourself. Clipping is messy business, especially on a windy day!

- **Work goggles:** You'll need these to protect your eyes from flying horse hair if clipping on a windy day.

When you're ready to do the actual clipping, keep these pointers in mind:

- **Wear work clothes.** You'll be covered with horse hair by the time you finish! Consider wearing a windbreaker suit that you can just strip off before you get in your car or go back into your house.

- **Feed your horse.** Give your horse a hay net filled with hay to occupy him as you clip.

✔ **Make sure that your horse is clean and dry before you start clipping.** A dirty coat is nearly impossible to clip.

✔ **Lubricate your running clipper blades frequently.** Lubricate before you start trimming and frequently as you go along; remove hair fragments with a brush.

✔ **Start at the front of your horse and work backward.**

✔ **Clip against the lay of the hair.**

✔ **Hold the clipper so the blades lay flat against the horse.** This keeps you from cutting too deep.

✔ **Give your horse frequent breaks.** Clipping is not only tiring for you, but for the horse who has to stand still for long periods of time. Consider doing your clipping in segments over two or three days.

✔ **Check the temperature of the blades frequently.** If they start to feel hot, let them cool down before you continue.

✔ **Sweep up the clipped hair after you finish.** If you're boarding your horse, sweep up as a courtesy to others who use the facilities. If you keep your horse at home, clean the hair up before the wind scatters it around.

If you clip your horse in the early spring, consider leaving some of the hair on the ground. Birds love to use it as nesting material.

Clipping: One horse's story

Although clipping seems like no big deal to us humans, it can be a downright terrifying experience for some horses. Horses don't understand the point of clippers. They simply see them as noisy, vibrating objects, usually aimed at their heads.

Take Rosie, for example, Audrey's now deceased Appaloosa mare. Rosie was the kindest, most cooperative horse you'd ever meet. But show Rosie a pair of clippers, and you had a maniac on your hands.

Horses can be taught not to fear the clippers, and Rosie is proof of that. At the time that Audrey bought her, the only way to clip her was to have the vet sedate her. If she wasn't sedated, she'd drag whoever tried to clip her, rear up — do anything possible to escape.

After owning her for six months, Audrey began the following program, based in large part on the advice of an animal behaviorist. After three months of working with Rosie by using this method, she eventually stood quietly as Audrey clipped her head, legs, and any other part of her body. Here's how it worked:

1. **Associate the clippers with something good.** Rosie was so afraid of clippers that even the sight of an unplugged pair left her trembling. So, Audrey began to help Rosie associate something pleasant with the clippers. Every time Audrey took out the clippers and showed them to Rosie, Audrey gave her a handful of carrots and told her she was a good girl. After about two weeks, Rosie looked for carrots whenever Audrey brought out the clippers.

2. **Give rewards for reaching for clippers.** The next step was to get Rosie to permit Audrey to touch her with the unplugged clippers. She learned that if she reached her muzzle in the clippers' direction, she would get carrots and praise. She caught on to this quickly.

Eventually, Audrey only gave her carrots and praise if she reached out and actually touched the clippers. This soon turned into a game — Rosie would tap the clippers with her nose and then look expectantly for carrots.

3. **Give rewards for allowing clippers to touch her.** Audrey began approaching Rosie with the clippers, touching them to Rosie's cheek, and giving her a handful of carrots and praise immediately afterwards. The first few times, Rosie looked alarmed, but was soon distracted by the offer of food.

Gradually, Audrey began touching Rosie all around the head with the clippers, rewarding her with carrots and praise.

4. **Associate the noise with something good.** The time came to turn on the clippers. At this point, Audrey had to go back to step one and stand at a distance with the clippers. Audrey rewarded Rosie with carrots and praise as she had done in the beginning just for being in the presence of the humming device. After Rosie seemed comfortable, Audrey began the touching process again, this time with the clippers turned on.

5. **Give rewards for allowing herself to be trimmed.** When Rosie seemed comfortable with being touched with the running clippers, Audrey began to trim small areas of her muzzle, giving her handfuls of carrots and praise with each whisker trimmed. Only once did Rosie suddenly panic. Audrey responded by simply putting the clippers and carrots away. The next day, Audrey approached Rosie with the clippers again, going back to the previous step.

After several months of this program, Rosie showed no fear of the clippers, and in fact, acted excited whenever Audrey took them out, anticipating carrots and TLC. In a relatively short time, she went from a fear-filled maniac to an easy horse to clip.

Chapter 10

Keeping Your Horse Healthy

● ●

● ●

Despite their size and physical strength, horses are actually rather delicate creatures when it comes to their health. They need regular preventative care to keep them healthy and able to perform the tasks asked of them.

The Importance of Preventative Care

When a horse gets sick, he can be a real pain in the neck to his owner: vet bills can add up quickly, a sick horse means time lost in the saddle, and horses can be notoriously difficult to medicate. For these reasons and more, horse owners should work hard at preventing equine illness.

The best way to take care of your horse's health is to find a good veterinarian and work with him or her to establish a preventative care plan for your horse. Although the cost of preventative care may tweak your wallet a bit, anteing up is well worth the money. In return, you'll have a happy, healthy horse who can do whatever you ask, and lower vet bills in the long run.

Finding a Veterinarian

One of the most important things you can do for your horse's health is to find a good veterinarian. Just like human doctors, veterinarians vary in skill, knowledge, dedication, and bedside manner. Finding a horse doctor who can provide you with all of these elements ensures that both you and your horse feel well taken care of.

Choose a veterinarian *before* your find yourself in an emergency situation. A veterinarian already familiar with your horse can be a huge plus during an emergency. Also, if you're a regular client, your request for an emergency barn call will receive priority treatment over a similar request from a non-regular client.

Locating a good equine veterinarian usually takes a bit of research. You shouldn't settle on the first name you see in the telephone book or use the vet your next-door neighbor is using without doing some investigation first.

The best choice for your horse's health care provider (preventative, regular, and emergency care) is a veterinarian who *specializes* in horses. Equine veterinarians are specially trained to diagnose and treat equine illnesses, and they have more knowledge of horse issues than their small animal counterparts. If you can't find a veterinarian in your area who deals exclusively with horses, make sure that the vet you choose has at least moderate experience in equine medicine.

Follow these steps to find yourself a vet who really knows his or her stuff:

1. **Get referrals.**

   Unlike cat and dog owners, horse owners religiously share veterinary information with each other — and that includes opinions on local vets. Identifying the veterinarians in your area who have the best reputations among horse owners should be easy. Listen in on conversations around the stable concerning veterinarians, and go so far as to ask your fellow horse owners which veterinarians they prefer. Make note of the names you hear over again in a positive light, and put these on the top of your list.

   If horse owners are few and far between where you live — or if equine veterinarians are scarce — you may be limited to only one or two names when it comes to referrals.

2. **Ask questions.**

   After you're armed with a couple of names of equine veterinarians, call each one to get more information. Because most equine vets have very limited or nonexistent office staff, you may be asking your questions of the actual veterinarian. Find out whether more than one doctor works in the practice and whether the vet or vets are available 24 hours a day for emergencies. (The answer should be "yes.") Also, ask about the qualifications of the doctors in the practice. Look for a specialization in equine medicine and several years of experience.

3. **Make an appointment.**

Based on what you hear from other horse owners and over the phone from the veterinarian or practice staff, decide which vet or practice is your first choice. Then schedule an appointment for your horse's next inoculation or deworming. Note how long it takes to get an appointment. You don't want to settle on a veterinarian who is very hard to reach.

You can also try to observe the vet at work on your horse during a vaccination clinic at a local boarding stable.

4. **Meet the vet.**

When the vet comes out to see your horse, talk to him or her and try to get a feeling for the vet's bedside manner. The vet should be willing to answer all your questions in a clear and understandable fashion. Also, pay attention to the way the vet behaves with your horse. You're looking for someone who feels comfortable around horses and knows how to handle them.

At this point in the process, you can pretty much go on gut instinct. If you like the veterinarian and you feel comfortable with this person, make him or her your permanent vet. If not, call the vet who came in second on your list and perform the same evaluation.

If you already went through an evaluation process when choosing the veterinarian who performed the prepurchase exam on your horse and were happy with the service you received, consider this individual as your horse's regular veterinarian.

Equine versus small animal vets

Horse vets are different from small animal vets — the doctors who take care of your dog and cat. Unlike small animal vets, horse vets are always on the go. They usually operate from the back of a pick-up truck, where they keep nearly everything they need to make a diagnosis, provide preventative care, and administer emergency treatment. Although most horse vets have actual offices where they do their paperwork, horse owners rarely see these places, because the vet nearly always comes to them.

Equine vets often work alone, but they may team up with other horse vets in a multi-person practice. The benefits of going with a vet who works alone is that you always get the same doctor when your horse needs care, as opposed to a larger practice where you most likely get whomever is available. The downside is that vets who work alone can't be in more than one place at a time, and so can be harder to reach in an emergency situation.

Unlike small animal vets, horse vets do not have a large office staff covering their phones and schedules. Instead, they tend to rely heavily on a receptionist or answering service that pages them during emergencies and takes messages from owners who need their calls returned.

Finding a Farrier

Nearly as important as finding a veterinarian for your horse is finding a skilled and qualified *farrier,* a specialist in trimming and shoeing your horse's hooves. Choose your farrier wisely: The health of your horse's hooves and legs depends on it.

The best way to locate a good farrier is through a referral, and the first person you should ask for a referral is your veterinarian. Most equine veterinarians are well acquainted with the farriers in their area and can recommend one or two good ones.

You can ask other horse owners for farrier referrals as well. If you go this route, be sure to take a consensus and see which farriers get the most thumbs up. Don't base your decision on the comments of only one owner — you want to get a feeling for which farriers are able to successfully handle horses with different shoeing needs.

Before you settle on a farrier, find out where the person was educated and how long he or she has been in business. You want to select a farrier who has a strong background in the trade, through both education and hands-on experience. Pick someone you're comfortable with who seems willing to discuss your horse's needs in a friendly and articulate manner.

Major Points in Preventative Care

In addition to having a good veterinarian and farrier, two other factors play a large part in determining the general well-being of your horse: food and exercise. You can have the best veterinarian and farrier in the world, but if you don't feed and exercise your horse properly, you won't have a healthy horse.

Feeding

The quality of the feed you provide and the frequency with which you feed it is a big factor in your horse's health:

✔ **Quality:** Good feed is of vital importance when it comes to your horse's general well being. Poor hay or pasture lacks nutrients and may cause vitamin and mineral deficiencies. Moldy or diseased hay can make your horse very sick. Don't scrimp on your horse's feed. Buying poor quality hay, or grazing your horse on poor pasture just to save a few bucks will come back to haunt you in the form of poor health for your horse. (See Chapter 8 for details on determining the quality of hay.)

✓ **Frequency:** Horses evolved as grazing animals, and so they need to eat often. Their digestive systems can't tolerate long periods of time with no activity. If you force your horse to go too long between meals, you're asking for trouble in the form of colic and other problems. Feed your horse at least twice a day at regular times, with three times a day the ideal. Or, you can supplement your horse's regular feedings with low-calorie grass hay to keep it occupied. Even better is keeping your horse in a pasture that provides access to quality grass at all times.

 ✓ **Consistency:** The equine digestive system is such that any sudden change in feed can cause considerable disruption and even serious illness. If you want to change your horse's feed from one type to another, do so gradually over a period of at least two weeks.

Exercise

Nature designed horses to be on the go all the time. Wild horses walk constantly as they graze, and stand still only for a few hours a day to sleep. Contrast this reality with the life of a typical stabled horse, who spends most of his time standing around and moving only a few hours a day! The result of this sedentary life can be a host of leg and digestive problems for your horse.

If you keep your horse in a stable, you need to make special efforts to keep his body in good working order. Provide a minimum of 30 minutes of exercise a day to increase circulation, loosen muscles, and provide mental stimulation. Be sure to warm up and cool down with at least 10 minutes of walking before and after a workout to help your horse's body stay healthy.

The right amount of exercise is not only necessary for your horse's physical well-being, but for his mental well-being, too. If you spent most of your time standing around inside a box with nothing to do, you'd get pretty bored. Horses are no different, and need time and exercise outside their stalls to keep from developing neurotic habits (known as stable vices; see Chapter 2) and other assorted misbehaviors.

If your horse lives in a pasture and can graze at will, the need for formal exercise is less important than for a stabled horse.

Vaccinating

A number of dangerous infectious diseases plague the horse world, but the good news is that vaccines exist for many of these. To keep your horse in his optimal state of health, you need to commit to a regular vaccination program, developed with your veterinarian, to protect your horse from serious illness.

Although a host of other vaccines exist, the three following represent the absolute minimum your horse should receive:

- ✔ **Influenza/rhinopneumonitis:** These two respiratory illnesses strike with the same kind of regularity as human flu viruses, and with similar symptoms. Your veterinarian may recommend that your horse be inoculated with flu/rhino vaccine as frequently as every three months, or only twice a year if the horse is at minimal risk of exposure.

- ✔ **Equine encephalomyelitis:** Three strains of the same encephalomyelitis illnesses — Western equine encephalomyelitis (WEE), Eastern equine encephalomyelitis (EEE) and Venezuelan equine encephalomyelitis (VEE) — can infect horses through mosquito bites. Encephalomyelitis attacks the central nervous system and can cause severe neurological symptoms and even death. Your veterinarian will recommend inoculation against one or more of these diseases at least once a year.

- ✔ **Tetanus:** Tetanus is not contagious but can be contracted through open wounds. This bacterial disease can result in serious symptoms, and ultimately death in many cases. Because horses are particularly susceptible to tetanus, veterinarians recommend an inoculation of tetanus toxoid for your horse at least once a year.

Reputable boarding stables require that all horses on the property be kept up-to-date on inoculations against contagious disease. If your horse is boarded, maintaining a consistent schedule of inoculations is imperative.

Deworming

Horses, like most other animals, are quite susceptible to a number of internal parasites. These parasites, more commonly known as worms, can cause serious damage to your horse's internal organs. When left uncontrolled, they can result in chronic colic and even death.

Although keeping worms from infecting your horse is nearly impossible, controling their numbers is very possible. Regular deworming with a chemical agent kills parasites in their various stages of growth, and is a necessary part of your horse's preventative care.

Although several over-the-counter dewormers are available to horse owners, we recommend you have a veterinarian deworm your horse. Veterinarians have access to the highest potency deworming agents and also have the most effective means of administering these drugs. If you opt to give your horse over-the-counter dewormers, we suggest you at least discuss your plans with your veterinarian so he or she can help you develop the most effective self-administration program.

Deworm your horse on a regular basis, the frequency depending on the climate and environment where you reside. Discuss your horse's deworming needs with your veterinarian so the two of you can come up with an effective program.

Hoof Care

If you want your horse to do more than just look good, you have to take care of his feet. A horse with poorly treated feet can be plagued with chronic lameness and may eventually end up unrideable. The best way to care for your horse's feet is to find a good farrier (see the previous section "Finding a Farrier") and to keep regular appointments with him or her. Regular trimming and shoeing by a qualified farrier are the keys to good hoof care.

Trimming

Horses's hooves are always growing, just like human fingernails. In order for your horse to stay sound, his feet must be kept neatly trimmed at an angle parallel to the slope of his pastern. No one is better qualified to perform this trimming accurately than a professional farrier.

Each horse's feet grow at a different pace, so the frequency between trimmings varies from horse to horse. The time range for trims can be anywhere from four to eight weeks. No horse should ever go longer than eight weeks without a trim.

Shoeing

The vast majority of horses ridden for pleasure and show have to wear metal shoes for protection. Shoes guard a horse's hoof from cracking and splitting, two problems that can result with normal riding on pavement, on trails, and in riding arenas.

You can opt to have your horse shod on all four feet or on just the front hooves where the majority of pressure exists during exercise, depending on the strength of your horse's hooves and what you're using him for. Some horses who are ridden lightly or have very tough hooves don't need shoes at all; horses who spend all their time at pasture rarely need shoes. Because each individual horse is different, discuss your particular shoeing needs with your farrier. Horses need new shoes every four to eight weeks, depending on how fast the hoof grows and how quickly the shoes wear out. Your farrier can help you determine the frequency of shoeing for your horse.

Every now and then, a horse will throw a shoe. Never ride your horse with a shoe missing from his hoof. Doing so can result in damage to the bare hoof and possibly to the other legs. If you're riding when the shoe comes off, dismount, retrieve the shoe, walk your horse back to the stable, and call your farrier to have it nailed back on. You can also keep an item known as a *hoof boot* with you when you ride, and use this as a substitute for a shoe until you make it back to the barn. If you find your horse in his stall with a shoe missing, skip riding until the farrier replaces the shoe.

Teeth

Horses depend on their teeth. Because the food they eat is so difficult to chew and digest (try downing a sprig of alfalfa hay sometime and you'll see what we mean), the health of their teeth is vitally important.

To combat the normal wear that occurs from chewing such tough, fibrous foods, nature has equipped the horse with teeth that slowly erupt from the gum as the top layer wears off. However, the horse's upper jaw is wider than his lower jaw, so the upper outside teeth and lower inside teeth have nothing to wear against as they erupt, and ridges and sharp points result. These ridges and points restrict the horse's normal side-to-side rotary chewing motion, resulting in poor and painful chewing and the dropping of food. Horses with this condition tend to chew up and down instead of side to side, making horses with neglected teeth prone to problems like choking and colic. These sharp points also hurt the horse when the noseband is tightened and when the bit hits the horse's teeth.

In order to keep sharp points from interfering with your horse's ability to chew and subsequently digest his food, have your veterinarian file down those pointy teeth as often as once or twice a year, depending on how fast they grow. Called *floating,* this procedure is an absolute must in preventative care.

Have your veterinarian examine your horse's teeth on a regular basis to determine when his teeth need floating. During these exams, the vet can also spot any other dental problems that may be developing, such as infected teeth or abnormal wear patterns.

Signs that your horse needs his teeth floated include discomfort when wearing a bit; *quidding,* where pieces of unchewed food fall from the horse's mouth while he's eating; and recurrent colic.

Chapter 11

The Most Common Health Problems

*P*eople who have spent a significant amount of time around horses often wonder about the sanity of the guy who coined the phrase "Healthy as a horse." Horses are notorious for getting sick — whether a self-inflicted injury, a bout of colic that requires surgery, or simply the arthritis that comes with old age, horses seem to require more veterinary attention than do cats or dogs. In fact, a vet has to treat the average horse about twice a year — not including preventative care.

Okay, now we've scared you. But really, you don't need to panic. The majority of vet calls are for fairly common problems that the vet resolves with short-term treatment — so long as you address the problem right away.

In this chapter, we show you some of the more common ailments and conditions that can affect your equine friend during his lifetime. Armed with this knowledge, you'll be able to recognize early symptoms of these ailments and get help for your horse in a timely manner.

When to Call the Vet

Not every equine ailment requires a frantic phone call to the nearest veterinarian. You can deal with some problems at home, or at least monitor them *before* making that call. Here are signs to look for when your horse seems under the weather. If your horse has one or more of these symptoms, the condition is an emergency that warrants a call to — and a possible visit from the vet:

- ✔ **Bleeding:** If your horse is bleeding heavily from any place on his body, try applying pressure to stop the flow. Even if you can stop the bleeding, call the vet.

- ✔ **Blood in urine:** If you see your horse urinating blood, a severe infection or bladder injury is a possibility.

- ✔ **Choking:** A horse is choking if he coughs and salivates with his head down while watery food exits his nose and mouth, backs away from his food, acts anxious, and/or swallows repeatedly. A horse chokes when food is trapped in the esophagus. The food doesn't block the airway, so the horse can still breathe, but you still must call the vet right away. The trapped food can cause damage that will result in scarring and subsequent narrowing of the diameter of the esophagus. This narrowing causes the horse to be more prone to choking in the future.

- ✔ **Colic:** If your horse is sweating profusely, lying down and getting up, pawing the ground, standing with his legs outstretched, rolling, and/or biting at his abdomen, the animal is suffering from colic. Remove the horse's food and lead the horse around at a walk until the vet arrives (for more information on colic, see section titled "Colic" in this chapter).

  Not all colic symptoms are severe. If you see your horse behaving in any way that indicates he may be having even slight stomach pain, you should still call a veterinarian.

  If you see some signs of colic but aren't sure whether your horse is actually sick, a good way to tell is to offer him a carrot. No healthy horse *ever* turns down a carrot. If your horse refuses it, he is suffering from abdominal distress or some other health problem and needs to see a vet right away.

- ✔ **Diarrhea:** Severe, very liquid, foul-smelling diarrhea can be life-threatening.

- ✔ **Fever:** A horse's normal body temperature ranges between 99˚F (37.7˚C) and 101.5˚F (38.6˚C). If your horse's temperature is significantly above or below the normal range, you have an emergency (see the sidebar "Taking your horse's temperature").

- ✔ **Inability to stand:** A horse who will not or cannot stand up is a very sick horse. A horse who staggers or has trouble staying on his feet is also in an emergency situation.

- ✔ **Injury:** Wounds that are deep or that expose the bone are emergencies, as are puncture wounds, which can easily become infected. You should also contact your vet if a less serious injury that doesn't require sutures begins to look infected.

- ✔ **Labored breathing:** Rapid breathing, raspy breath, or heavy coughing can be life-threatening for a horse.

- ✔ **Painful eye:** Call the vet if one or both of your horse's eyes suddenly becomes teary, the horse holds the lids partially or completely closed, the white part of the eye is red, or the surface of the eye is cloudy.

✓ **Refusal to eat:** When a horse won't eat, you're often seeing a sign of serious illness or possibly mild colic.

✓ **Severe pain:** A veterinarian should immediately examine any horse who appears to have severe pain in any part of his body.

✓ **Straining:** If your horse is straining to defecate or urinate and nothing or very little passes out, an intestinal or urethral blockage is likely.

✓ **Swelling:** Any part of the body is swollen and hot to the touch.

Taking your horse's temperature

Okay, taking your horse's temperature is not the most fun part of owning a horse, but you still need to know how to do it. If your horse ever appears sick, you should take his temperature before you call the veterinarian. The horse's temperature helps the vet decide whether the situation is an emergency or can wait until later or the next day.

Before you can take your horse's temperature, you need to purchase a veterinary thermometer from a pet supply or tack store, or you can simply buy a human rectal thermometer. Veterinary thermometers are better because they have a loop at the end; you can tie some string or yarn onto the device, making it easier to hold onto while taking the horse's temperature.

You need lubricant, too. K-Y Jelly or another human-grade lubricant is sufficient. Stay away from petroleum jelly because it can irritate the sensitive lining of the rectum. In a pinch, you can use your own saliva as a lubricant.

Here's how you actually do the deed:

1. **Shake the instrument down.**

   Holding the meter tip away from you, shake the thermometer until the temperature reads 96°F (35.5°C) or below.

2. **Lubricate the thermometer.**

   Apply a good amount of lubricant to the thermometer's tip so it slides in easily.

3. **Prepare your horse.**

Some horses are very calm when you take their temperature; others freak out. If you have the kind of horse who doesn't appreciate the procedures, ask someone to hold the horse's head before you insert the thermometer and position the horse against a wall so he can't move away from you. Be patient and try to reassure the horse that nothing terrible is about to happen to him.

4. **Insert the thermometer.**

   Hold the thermometer at an angle parallel to the horse's back, lift the tail, and slowly insert the thermometer about 3 inches into the horse's rectum. The thermometer should slide in gently. If the thermometer stops part way in and won't move forward, do *not* force it. Instead, pull it out and reinsert it again, angling it slightly up or down until it gently slides in.

5. **Wait three minutes.**

   Keep the thermometer inside the horse's rectum for three minutes, holding onto the end or the string the entire time.

6. **Read the thermometer.**

   After three minutes, you can remove the thermometer and read it. Normal adult equine body temperature ranges from 99–101°F (37–38°C). Foals are 100–102°F (37.5–39°C). If your horse's temperature is above normal, call a veterinarian immediately.

The Usual Troubles

Although horses are susceptible to a wide variety of ailments, the same handful of problems routinely crop up. Some of these illnesses have the potential to be serious, while others are simply annoyances to both the horse and the human. In each situation, prompt treatment by a veterinarian is important to keep the problem from getting out of hand.

This section outlines the most common equine health problems, along with their symptoms, usual treatment, and general prognosis. Your veterinarian can give you even more information — specific to your individual horse — on any one of these conditions.

Azoturia

Azoturia, or *tying up* as it is commonly called, is a problem that affects a horse's muscles. A high amount of lactic acid in the body causes the condition, which results in severe muscle breakdown. Veterinarians don't know why the lactic acid becomes so high, but they do know that the result is muscle and kidney damage.

The symptoms of azoturia — anxiety, abnormally heavy perspiration, and unusually fast pulse — usually come on 15 minutes to an hour into exercise. Soon, the horse is experiencing severe stiffness and a lack of coordination. Some horses ultimately collapse.

If you suspect that your horse has azoturia, do not force the animal to move. Instead, call a veterinarian immediately.

Prevention: To prevent your horse from ever having to experience the anguish of azoturia, follow these guidelines:

- ✔ **Provide regular exercise:** Provide your horse with exercise on a daily basis. Regular exercise helps him to eliminate any lactic acid that is building up in his body, reducing the risk of azoturia. (Pastured horses tend to exercise themselves and so are less prone to azoturia.)

- ✔ **Cut feed rations:** During times of long inactivity for your horse (bad weather, lameness, and so on), reduce his intake of alfalfa (a particularly high-protein hay) and grain. If the lay-up is short (only a day or two), stop the grain only. Too much in the way of protein and carbohydrates while inactive can result in azoturia when the horse returns to work. Supplement the diet with low-protein timothy hay or orchard grass and a fat source such as vegetable oil or rice bran so your horse still has enough hay and energy in his diet.

✔ **Warm up, cool down:** You must spend at least 10 minutes warming up your horse by walking and trotting. When your ride is over, walk the horse for at least 10 minutes to help him cool down. Horses who are properly warmed up and cooled down are less susceptible to azoturia.

✔ **Provide supplements:** If your horse has repeated attacks of azoturia, talk to your vet about supplementing the horse's feed with vitamin E, selenium, and fat sources such as rice bran. These additives can help protect the horse from a recurrent attack.

Colic

Colic is actually a symptom, not a disease. The term *colic* refers to abdominal pain, which can have any number of sources. Because horses are designed to be grazers, they're meant to ingest plant material at a slow and constant rate. The equine digestive system is often upset when humans confine horses and give them concentrated feeds.

Colic is a rather common problem among horses. It can be serious or it can be mild, but it's always a cause for concern, and *always* warrants a call to the vet.

Horses suffering from colic are usually in a great deal of pain. They express their discomfort by doing some or all of the following:

✔ Biting at the flanks or abdomen

✔ Kicking at the belly

✔ Laying down

✔ Pacing

✔ Pawing

✔ Rolling

✔ Standing with legs stretched out

✔ Straining

✔ Sweating profusely

✔ Swishing the tail violently

These bouts of pain often come in waves, so the horse may seem all right one minute but frantic the next. The pain can also start out mild and get progressively worse, or simply remain mild.

If you suspect that your horse has colic, call a veterinarian immediately. Take away the horse's food and walk him while you wait for the vet to arrive.

Colic classifications

Colic has two classifications: medical or surgical. Here's a look at each and the problems that usually cause them.

✔ **Medical colic:** Colics that can be fixed with simple medical treatment, usually without having to transport the horse to a hospital, are considered medical colics. Medical colics are the most common classification of colic, and are usually caused by gas or *impactions* (blockages). Each one of these causes has its own symptoms and treatments:

  • *Gas colic:* This type of colic is the result of gas that has built up inside the large intestine. Common causes of gas colic is the eating of spoiled food, along with eating too much of a new food. The horse's digestive system becomes dominated with gas-producing organisms, resulting in excessive gas.

    Gas colic is usually not life threatening, but is extremely painful and requires immediate veterinary attention.

  • *Impaction colic:* This colic is caused by an impaction in the large intestine. Any number of things can cause an impaction in the intestine, but lack of sufficient water intake is often to blame, resulting in manure that is dry, hard, and difficult to pass. Horses with teeth problems often develop impaction colic due to their inability to properly chew their food. The ingestion of sand — which can happen when horses are fed hay directly off the ground, graze at pasture, or deliberately eat sand in a turn-out arena — as well as dehydration, can also cause impaction colic.

✔ **Surgical colic:** Surgical colic refers to a colic that requires surgery for repair. In most cases of surgical colic, the horse will die without the surgery.

Preventing colic

The good news about colic is that in many cases, it is preventable. Follow these guidelines to keep your horse's digestive system working properly:

✔ **Feed often:** Feeding your horse as frequently as possible is a good way to ward off colic. The equine digestive system seems to function best when it is constantly working to digest fibrous foods. Keep your horse at pasture if possible, or if he's stabled, try to give him three meals a day. Two is the absolute minimum.

✔ **Feed hay:** Veterinarians have discovered that fibrous particles inside the intestine tend to stimulate the horse's gut and therefore reduce the incidence of colic. Give your horse a diet of primarily hay, rather than pellets, because the fiber particles in pellets aren't large enough to adequately stimulate the intestine. (Avoid feeding the hay off the ground so the horse doesn't ingest sand particles that can cause colic.) Don't feed too much grain either, because it provides little fiber content. (See Chapter 8 for information on what to feed your horse.)

✔ **Provide high-quality feed:** When you feed your horse, give him only the highest quality hay and/or grain. Don't try to save a buck by purchasing cheaper (and therefore lower-quality) feed, because lousy feed contributes to colic.

✔ **Give plenty of water:** Another way to prevent colic is to ensure that your horse has access to plenty of fresh water. Be sure to keep waterers and troughs clean. Also, in the wintertime, be certain that the horse's water supply is not frozen over. A water heater is a good investment for horse owners who live in frigid climates.

Keeping your water in liquid form isn't the only service a water heater can provide; it can also keep the water at a comfortable temperature. Horses are less likely to drink water that is very cold, so keeping water lukewarm even in winter encourages your horse to drink.

✔ **Use electrolytes:** In any situation where your horse may not be drinking enough water (like on cold winter days) or may be losing a good deal of body fluids and salts (during the hot summer or when exercising heavily), supplement his feed with an electrolyte mixture. Electrolytes increase the salt level in the horse's body, thus stimulating his thirst. Several commercial electrolyte products for horses are available through tack and feed stores; you can mix them with the horse's grain or administer them directly into the mouth in paste form. (Although some manufacturers' labeling on electrolyte products suggest adding the product to the horse's water, we don't recommend that you do because the taste can discourage the animal from drinking.)

✔ **Provide exercise:** Regular exercise is another way to help prevent colic, because it stimulates gut motility. Given this fact, your horse should receive some kind of exercise daily — especially if your horse is stabled. Even if you only have time for a half hour walk around the property, the exercise helps keep your horse's digestive system in working order.

✔ **Warm up and cool down:** When you ride your horse, be sure to make time for gradual warm-ups and cool downs before and after exercise. Don't work your horse hard without at least a 10 minute walk/trot warm up first, and be sure to finish up your ride with at least 10 minutes of walking.

Be certain that your horse is completely cooled down before you let him have anything to eat or drink. Eating or drinking immediately after strenuous exercise can bring on a bout of colic.

✔ **Care for those teeth:** Horses who have problems chewing do not properly masticate their food before swallowing it, making them more susceptible to impaction colic. Have a veterinarian check your horse's teeth at least twice a year to determine whether they are healthy. (See Chapter 10 for details on tooth care.)

Equine influenza/Rhinopneumonitis

People aren't the only ones who get the flu. Horses have their own versions of the virus, known as equine influenza and *rhinopneumonitis* (the latter caused by the equine herpes virus). Like the human version of the flu, these viruses spread across the country every fall and winter. They're just as contagious as the human version of the virus (not to humans, however!), and result in a respiratory infection that attacks both the upper and lower respiratory tracts.

Although equine influenza and rhinopneumonitis are two different viruses, they both cause the same symptoms. Veterinarians handle the two infections identically. If your horse has a mild case, he may just have a runny nose and seem a bit lethargic for a few days. If his case is moderate to serious, he will run a high fever, have runny eyes and nose, be coughing, and appear stiff. He may also lose his appetite.

Prevention: You can reduce your horse's chances of contracting equine influenza or rhinopneumonitis in two ways:

- ✔ **Vaccinate:** Just as with the human flu vaccine, the equine version is not foolproof. However, it can go a long way toward keeping your horse from contracting the diseases. The number of times per year you need to vaccinate your horse depends on how much exposure he receives to other horses. Follow your veterinarian's recommendations regarding the frequency of flu/rhino vaccine.

- ✔ **Practice equine hygiene:** During flu/rhino season, try to minimize your horse's contact with other horses who may be carrying the virus. Don't allow him to sniff muzzles or drink from the same trough as other horses, even those who appear healthy, because horses can shed the virus before showing any symptoms of the disease. If you board your horse, make sure that the stable management requires all boarders to be current on their flu/rhino vaccines.

Equine protozoal myeloencephalitis (EPM)

In recent years, a disease called equine protozoal myeloencephalitis, or EPM, began affecting a small but still significant number of the U.S. equine population. Veterinarians now understand EPM fairly well (although it was rather mysterious when it first appeared).

A protozoa called *Sarcocystis nerona* causes EPM, and is believed to be present in the feces of affected opussums. The protozoa affects the spinal cord and brain, resulting in a variety of possible symptoms, including uncoordinated movement of some or all of the horse's limbs, spastic movements of one or more legs, tilted head, muscles that waste away in the face or one of the hind legs, and seizures.

Diagnosing EPM is not easy. Sometimes a horse seems only slightly lame, or may just perform poorly. Most often, a horse with EPM suffers from an obvious lack of coordination, looking almost as if he is drunk when he walks. The only way to definitively diagnose EPM is through laboratory tests.

Prevention: To prevent EPM you have to keep opossums far away from your horse — no easy feat because opossums are common wildlife in most suburban and rural areas. You can do much to keep opossums from contaminating your horse's feed, though. Follow these simple horsekeeping rules to prevent opossums from soiling your horse's food:

- **Close it:** Keep grain and other supplements in tightly lidded containers.

- **Lift it:** Feed your horse in a trough or bucket — never on the ground.

- **Clean it:** Wash feeders with soap and water on a regular basis.

- **Toss it:** Throw out feed that falls on the ground.

Heaves

Heaves is the common term for *chronic obstructive pulmonary disease (COPD).* The illness is similar to asthma in humans in that the horse has difficulty breathing in, and even more difficulty breathing out. Heaves causes inflammation and spasm within the lungs, and is usually brought on by airborne allergies to mold, dust, and pollen, or by poor air quality.

Horses suffering from heaves may experience shortness of breath during exercise, chronic coughing, and wheezing. Because heaves is chronic by definition, these symptoms persist over a period of time. Horse with heaves often have something called a *heave line,* which is a line of developed muscle along the belly that forms as a result of the horse's struggle to push air out of his lungs. Presence of a heave line is a good way of telling whether a horse suffers from heaves.

Prevention: Horses are born with a predisposition to heaves, but you can still do plenty to help keep your horse from developing the condition:

- **Supply good air:** Horses need quality air to breathe, just like humans do. Try to give your horse as much ventilation as possible. If you are stabling him in a box stall, choose one that has ample windows so fresh air can enter. Buy bedding and hay that is low in dust, and change the bedding often to avoid ammonia build up. Avoid using straw bedding because allergy-inducing mold spores flourish in it.

- **Feed low:** Provide your horse with a feeder that requires him to keep his head down when eating, which encourages nasal drainage.

Although you want to keep your horse's head down while he eats, don't feed your horse directly off the ground because he may ingest sand and develop colic.

✔ **Move the horse:** When cleaning your horse's stall, move your horse out of the immediate area so he doesn't breathe in an excessive amount of dust and other particles.

✔ **Keep him outside:** If your horse has a tendency toward heaves, keep him outdoors in a pasture instead of in a stall (see Chapter 7 for information on housing your horse outdoors).

Skin problems

A number of different skin problems plague horses. Allergic reactions bring on some of them, while others are the result of parasitic infections and various other biological reactions. Five of the most common skin ailments are fly allergies, hives, sarcoids, melanomas, and fungal infections. Each of these problems has its own unique symptoms, causes, and treatments.

Fly allergies

For horses, flies are probably the worst thing in the world to be allergic to, because where you have horses, you have flies. Sure, you can and should do plenty to keep flies under control, but getting rid of them completely is impossible. A fact of equine life is that flies are here to stay.

Flies are annoying enough to horses, but when a horse is allergic to these obnoxious insects, the situation becomes unbearable. If your horse has areas of skin that are scabby and itchy, and the flies are out in force, he probably has a fly allergy. Your veterinarian will recommend that you bathe your horse a couple of times a week to remove the itchy scabs and apply a steroidal ointment (safe because it's applied topically) — possibly containing an antibiotic if the sores are infected — on a daily basis.

Prevention: The only way to prevent your horse from developing a fly allergy is to keep him from ever being bitten by a fly — a virtually impossible task. So, all you can do is implement a strict pest control program in an effort to keep the fly population under control (see Chapter 7 for tips) and minimize your horse's exposure to bites.

You should also use a fly mask, fly sheet, and fly-screen leg wraps to minimize fly contact with your horse (see Chapter 6 for information on these items.)

Fungal infections

Several different kinds of fungal organisms can affect a horse's skin. Among these culprits are ringworm and rain scalds. Each of these infections has different symptoms and treatments.

Feeding horse pills

The first time your horse gets sick and the vet hands you a bottle of pills with instructions of how many to give, you may not realize that your horse may choose not to cooperate. This realization usually dawns as you are trying to convince your horse to swallow the darn thing. No way is he just going to open his mouth and let you pop the pill in.

The secret to getting your horse to swallow a horse pill (you'll see why people call big pills "horse pills" once you view one of these things) is to disguise it. You have to grind it up with a pestle and mortar, or dissolve it in a little bit of water. Then you have to find the right horse-pleasing ingredient to cover up the pill's smell and taste.

Every horse has different tastes and preferences (just like people do), so you need to experiment to find the masking ingredient that is most palatable to your beast. Also, some pills taste worse than others. Try some of these proven, tried-and-true pill disguisers — you may have to experiment with different ingredients, depending on how bad the pill tastes:

✔ **Grain:** Horses adore grain, and the ones who get it as part of their regular feed ration come to expect it. Grain is a great pill cover up, especially if the two are mixed well. If your horse gets grain, try this one first.

✔ **Applesauce:** Not too many horses can resist apples, and many of them will settle for applesauce when the actual apple isn't available. The great thing about applesauce is that it mixes well with most ground-up pills.

✔ **Molasses:** Pure molasses tastes pretty gross to most humans, but horses seem to love it. Try mixing a ground-up pill with a couple of cupfuls of molasses. If the horse won't eat it, you may have to pour the mixture into a large syringe and force it into the horse's mouth. Enlist the aid of another person who can hold the horse's head while you patiently insert the syringe into the side of the horse's mouth.

✔ **Pancake syrup.** If molasses doesn't cut it for your horse, try pancake syrup. Boysenberry flavor seems to be particularly effective.

✔ **Powdered drink or gelatin mix:** Believe it or not, if you mix some sweet feed (a commercially prepared alfalfa and molasses blend for example) with half a packet of strawberry powdered drink mix (*not* the artificially sweetened kind) or fruit-flavored, naturally sweetened gelatin mix powder, you can get a horse to wolf down just about any crushed pill. Add a little water to the mixture to help the powder blend with the sweet feed.

✔ **Cake frosting:** Some horse owners swear by cake frosting when it comes to disguising a bitter pill. Grind the pill up, mix it with the frosting, and then offer it straight to your horse. You may have to experiment with flavors. Strawberry is usually a good bet; lemon and orange rarely work.

Rain Scalds

Rain scalds (technically called *dermatophilosis*) is a genetic anomaly that's sort of a cross between a fungus and a bacteria. The organism comes to life in damp weather, and often shows up on horses when weather conditions are very wet, such as during rainy seasons or in tropical regions.

Although often present in the horse's environment, the organism that causes rain scalds can only enter the skin at a break. An insect bite or minor scratch that is invisible to your eye is all the organism needs to gain entry. After the condition takes hold, you see areas of matted hair on your horse's coat that look like paintbrush strokes. These patches are mostly around the back area where the saddle lies, on the hindquarters, and on the thighs. Crusty scabs accompany the matted coat.

Prevention: Keeping your horse dry in wet weather helps keep rain scalds away. Give your horse adequate shelter to escape from rainy weather. If you can't keep him completely dry, provide him with a waterproof blanket to wear during rainstorms.

Ringworm

Horses with ringworm have one or more round lesions on the skin, often found near areas of the abdomen where the girth sits or on the back. The center of the lesion is hairless, and can be raw or covered with a scab. Ringworm is highly contagious to humans and other horses. The disease usually occurs in the winter when the conditions are dark and damp and horses are being kept indoors.

Ringworm actually goes away by itself in six to eight weeks, but to keep it from spreading to other areas of the horse — and to other people and animals — wash the lesion with Betadine scrub, which contains iodine and is available from your local tack store. Aside from being sensitive to iodine, ringworm is also sensitive to sunlight and dry conditions. You can also treat the area with an over-the-counter ringworm medicine meant for humans.

Prevention: To prevent ringworm, keep your horse clean and dry. Sweat is a good food source for the organism that causes ringworm, so wash or sponge your horse down after every workout. Turn your horse out in the sun frequently, because the organism is also sensitive to sunlight.

Another way to prevent ringworm is to avoid using tack and grooming equipment that has been used on other horses. If you have to borrow equipment, at least disinfect brushes, saddle pads, and other washable items with a solution of mild bleach (one part bleach to four parts water). Leave the solution on the item for eight minutes and then be sure to rinse thoroughly, because bleach residue will irritate your horse's skin.

Hives

Plenty of humans get hives, and they know how unpleasant these little lumps can be. On horses, hives usually cover the entire body or a section of the body, are anywhere from half an inch to a few inches in diameter, and uniform in shape. When you touch the hive, it gives to the pressure. Hives can be itchy or not itchy, and swelling of the face and eyelids sometimes occurs with them.

In horses, just as in people, hives are the result of an allergic reaction to a substance, either airborne or eaten. Horses prone to hives typically get them from inhaling certain pollens and eating some feeds.

Because hives are the result of an allergy, you can't do much to prevent their onset. Pay close attention to your horse and notice any possible outbreaks right away. The sooner you address the problem, the less your horse will suffer.

Melanomas

Melanomas are rather common tumors in horses. A predisposition to developing these tumors seems to exist in certain individual horses, as well as in certain breeds (Arabians and Percherons in particular). Horses who are gray in coloring also tend to develop melanomas as they age. In fact, 80 percent of gray horses over the age of 15 develop melanomas.

Melanomas take on the form of black growths on or under the skin, usually about an inch in diameter, and are sometimes hairless and ulcerated. They can be single or clustered in groups, and can grow rather large in size. These tumors typically appear on the horse's genitals (both male and female), under the tail, near the anus, and on the eyelids, throat, and mouth, but they can be found anywhere on the horse's body.

In gray horses, melanomas are usually non-threatening, slow-growing tumors. You only need to remove them if they are interfering with the horse's function (tumors on the anus can interfere with defecation, for example). *Note:* Gray horses are the only mammals known to science who can host a cancer that is not life-threatening.

In horses who are not gray, melanomas can be much more serious because they can *metastasize* (spread to other areas of the body) through the blood stream and affect the major organs. A melanoma in a horse who isn't gray is usually serious.

Veterinarians have yet to discover a way to prevent melanomas.

Sarcoids

Sarcoids are very common, benign skin tumors. You typically see them on the horse's head, stomach area, or legs. Sarcoids sometimes come in groups and are usually about an inch to a few inches in size. They occasionally appear in wounds that are healing.

Sarcoids are most commonly seen in two forms: flat sarcoids and proliferative sarcoids. Veterinary researchers believe that sarcoids are the result of a virus, although no conclusive evidence exists to prove this theory.

Veterinary science has yet to discover the exact cause of sarcoid tumors, leaving horse owners with no way to prevent the problem.

Strangles

Strangles, a condition caused by a bacteria known as *Streptococcus equi.,* takes hold around a horse's neck and upper respiratory tract, forming abscesses within the lymph nodes. The illness results in fever, lack of appetite, runny eyes and nose, and a dry cough. The horse sometimes acts very depressed and anorexic, and stands with his head down. In more severe cases, the lymph nodes enlarge (about two weeks after the disease hits) as the abscesses develop. You can see these abscesses as big lumps under the horse's throatlatch (see Chapter 1 for a diagram indicating exactly where the throatlatch is). Often, these lumps break open and drain externally.

Strangles is a contagious disease, spread from one horse to another through direct contact, by secretions from the mouth and respiratory tract that are left behind on food and water troughs or other objects, and by flies.

The only way to know for sure whether your horse has strangles is to have a veterinarian examine him.

Prevention: A strangles vaccine exists, and many veterinarians recommend yearly inoculations to guard against the disease, especially if your horse is exposed to a number of other horses.

To keep your horse from contracting strangles and other infectious diseases, don't allow him to drink from community water troughs at horse shows and other places where strange horses gather. Instead, bring your own bucket and fill it with water when you horse needs a drink. Keep him from making nose-to-nose contact with the other horses because any horse he meets is a potential carrier of the disease.

Thrush

Thrush, a bacterial infection of the foot, is one of the most common problems afflicting horses today. Horses who don't undergo regular feet cleaning are prone to this disease; the bacteria can only take hold if the foot is routinely packed with mud, soiled bedding, and manure for long periods of time.

Horses with thrush have a foul-smelling black discharge on the bottom of the hoof surrounding the frog (see Chapter 1 for a diagram of the hoof). When you scrape the bottom of the hoof with a hoof pick, a clay-like material comes off, leaving deep grooves in the hoof.

If thrush is left untreated, it can result in a more severe foot infection. The bacteria can also damage the horse's tendons. In serious cases, thrush can cause lameness.

If you suspect that your horse has a mild case of thrush (odor and some discharge, but no lameness), you can try treating the condition yourself with an over-the-counter thrush medication. If this treatment isn't effective or if thrush seems to be severe and causing your horse pain when he stands or walks, call your veterinarian.

Prevention: If you provide your horse with good foot care, thrush is easy to keep at bay. Follow these guidelines for healthy hooves:

- ✔ **Clean 'em:** Using a hoof pick, clean out your horse's hooves every day (see Chapter 9 for instructions).

- ✔ **Keep 'em dry:** The bacteria that causes thrush loves moisture. Keep your horse's feet dry by providing clean, dry bedding. Don't let your horse stand around in urine-soaked bedding or accumulated manure. Avoid keeping your horse in a muddy paddock or pasture.

Lots of Lameness

Many of the ailments that plague horses are related to their legs, which probably has much to do with the way people keep and ride horses in today's world. In the wild, horses walk almost constantly as they graze, keeping their muscles loose and flexible and their circulation up. Wild horses also trod on nicely cushioned, plant-covered soil. Compare these scenarios to the life of stabled horses who stand for hours on end as their muscles tighten and their joints become stiff. Look, too, at the riding horses who regularly walk on tightly packed trails and even asphalt and concrete. These same horses are asked to perform rather unnatural maneuvers like trotting or cantering in tight collected circles, jumping, and other discipline-specific maneuvers.

Another part of the problem is that rather delicate bones, tendons, and ligaments make up the equine leg. A horse's legs are expected to not only support the animal's weight, but also the rider's — on less-than-ideal footing and during strenuous activity. Considering all these factors, you can easily see why leg problems are so common.

The following sections take a look at the five most common leg ailments affecting horses, and we tell you how you can help manage and prevent them.

Arthritis

People are not the only ones who get arthritis. Horses do, too — and often. Simply put, *arthritis* is the inflammation of a joint. It's the most common form of lameness in horses. Several different forms of arthritis exist, ranging from infections to severe, crippling fusion of joints.

The key symptom of arthritis is lameness. Horses with arthritis limp — some very mildly, others dramatically. (To find out how to determine whether your horse is lame, see the sidebar "Finding lameness.")

Degenerative joint disease

The most common type of arthritis is what is collectively known as degenerative joint disease, or DJD. This disease starts out mildly with an inflamed joint capsule and can progress into erosion of the cartilage and fusion of the joint.

Degenerative joint disease can affect both young and old horses, and the causes vary. Fifty to sixty percent of the time, the hocks are the affected joints. The knees are the next most common site. Other joints such as the fetlocks and stifles can be affected, too, although DJD in these joints tend to result in less lameness (see Chapter 1 for a diagram showing the parts of the horse). Poor conformation, hard work, trauma, and old age are other main causes of arthritis (see Chapter 1 for information on conformation).

Several treatments exist for DJD, and their uses depend on the severity of the problem. All are aimed at stopping the cycle of inflammation and restoring the health of the joint fluid and joint surface cartilage.

Prevention: You can't always prevent arthritis, especially when it strikes a young horse or when poor conformation is the cause. Sometimes, just the wear and tear of carrying people around takes its toll on a horse's joints. Honestly, nature didn't intend horses to carry humans around on their backs while doing dressage, jumping, reining, and other equine sports. But shoeing your horse properly, riding him on surfaces that provide good footing, and refraining from working him too hard can help keep arthritis at bay.

You can also opt to give your horse intravenous hylauronic acid, Adequan, yucca, chondrotin sulfates, and glucosamine as preventatives against degenerative joint disease. The use of these supplements are aimed at keeping the joint healthy before arthritis sets in.

Ringbone

Ringbone is another type of arthritis that affects the pastern and coffin joints. Extra bone development occurs around the joint or in the joint itself. When the coffin joint is affected, the condition is termed *low ringbone*; when the pastern joint is affected it's called *high ringbone*.

In the early stages of ringbone, bone development is usually mild and lameness tends to be present but not severe. As the disease progresses, more of the joint becomes affected and the lameness increases. In high ringbone, the joint may actually fuse completely, which can be quite painful — most horses with this problem are very lame.

Researchers don't fully understand why horses develop this condition, but they think that part of the problem is genetic and part has to do with uneven trimming of the hooves. When the hooves are not trimmed completely level, they land on the ground unevenly, causing trauma to the joint.

Treatment usually involves *therapeutic shoeing,* special trimming and shoeing techniques, that ensure a balanced foot. Shortening the toe during trimming also helps to ease stress on the joint. All of the other arthritis treatments apply to this disease as well.

Prevention: Because uneven trimming of the hooves can bring on ringbone, make sure that you use a skilled and reputable farrier.

Bowed tendons

Also known in the veterinary world as *tendonitis,* bowed tendons are a lower-leg problem. Bowed tendons occur when the tendons at the back of the leg become over-stretched and strained or torn. The back of the leg becomes very swollen, hot and painful to the touch, and lameness usually results. Overexertion of the tendons either through jumping, galloping, or galloping in deep footing causes bowed tendons.

A veterinarian usually uses an ultrasound of the affected tendons to diagnose and determine the severity of the problem. Severely bowed tendons have tears in the tendons, while mildly bowed tendons have swelling and enlargement.

Treatment is aimed at reducing the swelling by using icing, anti-inflammatory drugs (such as phenylbutazone), and stall rest. All tendon injuries require long periods — six months to a year — of rest and controlled exercise in order to heal. You can treat tendons that have tears in them with a drug called Bapten that helps the tendon heal to be stronger.

Prevention: You can help prevent bowed tendons by providing proper shoeing and riding sensibly in good footing that isn't too deep, slippery, or muddy. Despite precautions, however, bowed tendons are sometimes unavoidable.

Hoof abscesses

When an abscess forms in a horse's hoof, it can cause severe lameness. The abscess is an infection that starts at the bottom of the hoof or the sole and travels up the lamina (also called the white line), and often breaks open at the coronary band, where it drains. A puncture wound to the bottom of the hoof usually causes the abscess. Horses with this problem appear fine one day and suddenly very lame on one leg the next.

Vets base their diagnosis of hoof abscesses on symptoms of severe and sudden lameness on one leg, increased pulse in the leg, and sensitivity to hoof testers. Your veterinarian will make a final diagnosis when she finds the abscess.

Treatment involves opening up the abscess on the sole of the hoof with a hoof knife and allowing the abscess to drain. The vet soaks the foot in Epsom salts to help draw out the inflammation and pus from the abscess. Your horse also receives anti-inflammatory drugs and pain killers. Most horses recover fully from this problem in three to five days and return to full, regular work without any problems.

Finding lameness

Determining whether your horse is lame, and on which leg, can be tricky business. Although some lamenesses are painfully obvious to even the most casual observer, you need a trained eye to detect the more subtle limps.

If you suspect your horse is limping, or if someone else tells you horse appears to be lame — a common occurrence in the horse world because lamenesses are most obvious while the horse is being ridden — take these steps to help figure out whether your horse does indeed have a problem. (If he does, a call to your veterinarian is in order.)

✔ **Examine the legs:** Do a visual inspection of your horse's legs, shoulders, and hips, searching for swelling.

✔ **Check the feet:** Lift each of your horse's feet up one at a time and examine the frog and the sole of the foot for bruises or foreign objects (see Chapter 1 for a diagram showing parts of the hoof). If the frog is filled with dirt, get a hoof pick and clean it out so you can clearly see around the frog. Check the outside of the hoof for cracks.

✔ **Feel around:** Run your hand down each of your horse's legs, feeling for heat, swelling, cuts, or unusual bumps.

✔ **Step back:** Tie your horse up or ask someone to hold him. As your horse is standing, check to see whether he is putting his weight evenly on all four feet. If one leg is raised or cocked, it could be causing him pain.

✔ **View from the front:** Most lamenesses are visible when the horse is moving. If you've been unable to locate any swelling or injury, try watching your horse gait. Ask someone to walk and trot your horse on a loose lead rope. As the horse comes toward you, notice whether his head bobs up as he lands on one of his forelegs. The leg his head bobs up on is the lame leg. You can also judge which leg is hurting by watching the horse's stride. The lame leg will move faster with a shorter stride.

✔ **View from the back:** Have someone walk and trot the horse on a loose line as you view from behind. If the horse's hip rises higher on one side as he moves, his hind leg is lame on that side. The horse's stride on that leg is also faster and shorter.

Prevention: Help prevent hoof abcesses by cleaning your horse's feet daily and by getting regular hoof trimmings from a competent farrier. Keep your horse's bedding clean and try to discourage bacterial growth.

Laminitis

Laminitis, also known as *founder,* is a devastating disease that affects an area within the hoof known as the *sensitive lamina,* the connective layer between the hoof and the coffin bone that holds the coffin bone in place. Laminitis occurs when the lamina becomes inflamed and the coffin bone begins to separate from the hoof. With severe laminitis, the coffin bone may actually come out of the bottom of the hoof.

In the mildest forms of laminitis, the horse appears to be *walking on eggshells,* moving tenderly on his feet. As the disease progresses, the horse feels greater pain and adopts a *rocked back* stance, with his weight shifted toward his rear, in an attempt to take weight off the hooves. The horse also resists walking. As more damage occurs and subsequent pain develops, the horse starts lying down often in order to take the weight off his feet.

Causes of this disease are plentiful and include trimming the feet too short, galloping on hard ground, absorbing toxins from the gut during colic, eating too much grain, keeping the horse on black walnut shavings, and sometimes, receiving steroid medications.

If your horse demonstrates sensitive hooves (particularly at the toe) and an increased pulse in the leg, he may have laminitis. Consult your vet, who should x-ray the affected hoof. *Rotation,* the separation of the bone from the hoof, shows up on X rays.

Treatment of this disease varies depending on the severity of the problem. The basics include complete stall rest on very soft footing (preferably soft sand or very deep shavings), therapeutic shoeing, changes in the diet, administration of anti-inflammatory drugs such as phenylbutazone, Banamine, and DMSO, and drugs that increase the blood flow to the foot (acepromazine and nitroglycerine are two).

Laminitis can become so severe that the horse can die. If the horse survives, he is prone to relapses. Each relapse means more damage, with chances of recovery lessening with each episode. Many horses who survive are also are lame for life. If you find yourself in this situation, discuss your horse's condition with your veterinarian to determine whether the horse's quality of life is such that euthanasia may be warranted (see the section entitled "Euthanasia" later in this chapter for more information).

Prevention: Provide proper shoeing; feed balanced diets that are not too rich in carbohydrates; and ride and stable your horse on good footing.

Navicular disease

This disease involves a small bone called the navicular bone that acts as a fulcrum between something called the *deep flexor tendon* and the coffin bone. Researchers are still debating over exactly what causes the disease, but the traditional belief is that it occurs when the bone undergoes degeneration and — as a result of decreased circulation to the bone itself — forms cysts and large channels inside its center. Horses with this problem are typically lame in both front legs, and their pain tends to be isolated at the heel area.

A vet usually diagnoses this disease through the use of nerve blocks and X rays of the navicular area. This disease has no cure, but the condition can be managed. Treatment usually involves therapeutic shoeing (usually in the form of a bar shoe), drugs to help increase the blood flow to the navicular bone, and anti- inflammatory and pain killing drugs. In the most severe of cases, where the horse stops improving with medication and shoeing, nerves to the heels are cut so that the horse no longer feels the pain from the disease.

Prevention: Prevention of this disease is very difficult because researchers don't fully know how it develops. Veterinarians suspect a genetic link, so not breeding horses with this problem may be a way of preventing of the disease.

Equine First Aid

If you spend much time around horses, you soon discover that first aid knowledge is a godsend. Horse are big animals, and they sometimes get hurt. Knowing just what to do when an accident occurs not only helps your horse, but also makes you a hero around the barn, too. You may just save your horse's life — or another's — as you wait for the vet to arrive.

If your horse is injured, let him quiet down before attempting to release him from any situation where he may be trapped. Injured horses often thrash about, sometimes causing injury to themselves and others. Horses who are hurt often have trouble recognizing their owners and tend to not respond to humans the way they normally do.

Stopping bleeding

With serious equine wounds comes heavy bleeding. Take these steps if your horse is bleeding freely:

- ✔ **Know the bleeding:** Understanding the type of bleeding helps you gauge the seriousness of it. If blood is spurting from your horse, chances are that an artery is involved, and you should take immediate action to stop the flow. If the blood is dark and oozing, it's coming from a vein and isn't immediately life threatening.

- ✔ **Keep the horse still:** Calm your horse by talking to him softly, and make him stand in one place. Keep other people (especially children) and dogs quiet. Hysterical people make for hysterical horses. The more the horse moves around because he's upset, the more the wound will bleed.

- ✔ **Apply pressure:** Whether the bleeding is coming from an artery or a vein, bandage the wound securely. The pressure reduces the blood flow. If the bleeding is coming from an area that is too large to bandage, use a piece of gauze or other clean, absorbent material and hold it firmly against the wound. If the blood is coming from an artery and you don't have a bandage or cloth, use your bare hand to create pressure. (Wear a latex glove if you can, in order to avoid infecting the wound.)

- ✔ **Make a tourniquet:** When an artery is spurting blood and regular pressure won't stop the flow, make a tourniquet. Tourniquets are most practical for leg wounds. Wrap a clean towel or a piece of cloth around the leg above the wound (between the heart and the point of bleeding). Tighten the tourniquet with your hands and tie it firmly until the blood flow stops. Call a veterinarian immediately, explain the situation, and get advice as to whether the tourniquet will cause any harm. Your phone call also helps the veterinarian determine the seriousness of the situation and how fast he or she needs to get there. While waiting for the vet to arrive, loosen the tourniquet every 15 minutes for a few minutes at a time to allow blood to temporarily flow back into the leg.

Here are some important things to keep in mind when your horse is injured:

- ✔ **Stay calm and call for help:** Hysterics only frighten the horse further and aggravate the situation.

- ✔ **Make human safety first and foremost:** If a human gets hurt trying to help an injured horse, the human becomes the priority.

- ✔ **Avoid contaminating a wound with bacteria:** Before you handle any wound on your horse, wash your hands first and wear latex gloves.

Your first-aid kit

Every good horseperson has a first-aid kit on hand to deal with any possible emergencies that come up. What's great about having an equine first-aid kit is that many of the items in the kit also come in handy for humans as well.

Store your first-aid kit in an easily accessible place near your horse's tack. Make sure that you can get to it quickly in case of an emergency. The last thing you need when you're frantic is a first-aid kit that you can't find.

You can go out and buy yourself a pre-assembled equine first-aid kit at a tack and feed store. Or, you can put together your own. Most items for your kit are available at your local drug store.

If you opt to create your own kit, you need the following:

- **Antibiotic ointment:** Triple antibiotic ointments or Betadine provide the best protection against infection on minor wounds.

- **Antiseptic cleanser:** Betadine scrub is your best choice and a staple for every equine first-aid kit.

- **Container:** Use one of those medium-sized plastic bins that sell for a few dollars to hold all your first aid supplies. You can easily take this type of container with you if you travel to a horse show or other event.

- **Bandages:** Leg bandages made specifically for horses are best. You have to purchase these at a tack store or through a mail-order catalog.

- **Disposable diapers:** You can use disposable diapers, which are very absorbent and thick, to apply pressure to lacerations.

- **Gauze pads:** Sterile gauze pads are useful when dealing with wounds, abscesses, and other breaks in the skin. You can get a few different sizes for use with varying types of wounds.

- **Jagged-edged knife:** Because horses sometimes get tangled in ropes and other equipment, a jagged knife is a good item to have in your kit. You can use it to cut away an entrapping strap or rope.

- **Lubricant:** A product such as K-Y jelly is useful for lubricating the thermometer. Don't use petroleum jelly, which can irritate the sensitive lining of the rectum.

- **Rubbing alcohol:** You can use rubbing alcohol to disinfect the thermometer between uses.

- **Scissors:** A pair of scissors is useful for cutting bandages and clothes in an emergency.

- **Tweezers:** In the event your horse gets a splinter or other object lodged in his skin, a pair of tweezers can come in handy.

- **Veterinary or human rectal thermometer:** A thermometer is good to have around. If your horse seems ill, taking his temperature before calling the vet helps give the doctor a better idea of what's wrong (see sidebar "Taking your horse's temperature").

The first thing you need to do when your horse hurts himself is determine what kind of wound your horse has suffered, and then act accordingly. Table 11-1 tells you about the most common horse wounds and what to do about them.

Table 11-1		Horse Wounds and What to Do about Them
Wound	*What It Is*	*What to Do*
Abrasion	The most superficial of wounds, abrasions tend to result when a horse scrapes himself against something with a rough surface. Abrasions can also happen when saddles or blankets fit poorly and rub the skin away. As long as a fall doesn't cause the abrasion, they're not usually critical, but they are among the most painful of wounds.	Stop the bleeding (see the sidebar "Stopping bleeding") and cleanse the area with Betadine scrub and apply scrub and apply an antibiotic ointment. You may occasionally need a veterinarian-prescribed, anti-inflammatory ointment. Do not bandage the area. If the cause of the abrasion is a fall, call your veterinarian.
Animal bites	Horses frequently bite each other, and on occasion, these bites can be severe. Sometimes, horses also suffer bites from other animals like dogs, cats, and wildlife.	If your horse receives a deep bite from either another horse or another animal, call your veterinarian right away. Bites tend to become easily infected, and an injection of an antibiotic can ward off this possibility. If your horse gets bitten by another horse but the wound is superficial and isn't bleeding, you can leave it to heal on its own. Horse bites are susceptible to tetanus, so get your horse a tetanus toxoid shot if he hasn't been vaccinated within six months prior to the bite.
Laceration	A cut anywhere on the horse's body that can be large or small, superficial or serious, depending on the size and amount of bleeding.	If the wound seems minor, flush it out by using water from a garden hose to get rid of any foreign objects that may be inside. If dirt and other materials continue to adhere to the skin, use water and Betadine scrub on a sponge to gently clean it. Apply antibiotic ointment to the wound and let it heal on its own. If the laceration is large and deep, do not apply any ointments or sprays and call your veterinarian immediately. Work to control the bleeding (see the sidebar "Stopping bleeding"). **Note:** When lacerations heal (both the major and minor kind), they can develop something called *proud flesh*. Proud flesh

(continued)

Table 11-1 *(Continued)*

Wound	What It Is	What to Do
		is the normal first layer of healing tissue that occurs in a wound. In horses, this first layer of tissue tends to overproduce. If this condition applies to your horse, you need to have the vet come out and remove the proud flesh. The vet then treats the area with a special ointment so the proud flesh won't grow back.
Puncture wound	Potentially the most serious of wounds because they tend to penetrate far into the horse's flesh, deeply implanting bacteria into the horse's body. Nails and other sharp objects that plunge straight into the skin usually cause puncture wounds. Puncture wounds in hooves result from stepping on protruding objects such as nails. If the wound is in the back third of the hoof, bacteria may get into an area called the *navicular bursa*. If such is the case, infection can travel up the entire leg and the horse can lose his life.	Don't attempt to stop the bleeding, unless it's very profuse, but call a veterinarian right away — especially if the wound is in the hoof. The vet will probably opt to give the horse a series of antibiotic injections.

Euthanasia

Euthanasia is a fact of horse ownership that no horse owner likes to think about. At some point in your horse experience, you may have to cope with this unfortunate reality.

Sometimes, a horse's illness is incurable. The horse may simply be too old to fight off whatever it is that's plaguing him. Or, the horse may be gravely ill and veterinary science may be unable to provide any hope for the animal. In many situations, care and treatment for a horse can be so costly that the owner simply can't afford to pursue it. In a number of these cases, a poor prognosis makes trying at all unfeasible.

What it is

Euthanasia is the humane process of taking an animal's life. Veterinarians use a barbiturate, which they inject in large quantities into a horse's bloodstream. The drug stops brain function almost instantly, and the horse loses consciousness. The horse then stops breathing, and his heartbeat ceases.

Making the decision

The decision to put your horse down is incredibly hard. You will probably feel all kinds of emotions, the strongest of which is doubt. We humans are not often put in the position of playing God, and when we suddenly find ourselves forced to make a life and death decision over an animal we love, the experience can be confusing and extremely upsetting.

Should you find yourself struggling with this terrible dilemma, remember that the act of euthanasia can be a gift to a horse who is suffering. Without you to make that decision and allow him a painless, dignified end, your horse will undoubtedly suffer. Think about your horse's quality of life and put yourself in his place. Would you prefer to stay alive in his condition, or would a peaceful death be a welcome relief? Thinking of the subject in these terms and seeking your veterinarian's advice can help you decide what's best for your horse.

The grieving process

Losing a beloved horse can be an incredibly painful experience. As your horse's caretaker, you will feel profound loss, sadness, and even guilt. Your thinking process at this time won't be very rational, and even though you may feel as if you did something terrible by having your horse euthanized, in time you will probably come to see that you made the right choice.

Sometimes, horse lovers can have difficulty finding a sympathetic ear when they're grieving. People who don't care much for animals will tell you to just "get over it," or ask you what the big deal is. At this time of grieving, try to surround yourself with other animal lovers who will understand what you are going through.

Over the past several years, a number of veterinary schools have set up grief counseling hotlines for horse people and other pet owners who have lost a beloved animal. A listing of these hotlines is in Appendix B of this book. Make use of these services. They will help you work through the grieving process and help you recover from your loss.

Your horse's remains

You may be wondering what will happen to your horse's remains after euthanasia. The sad reality is the disposal of equine remains is not as easy as it is with smaller animal companions, such as dogs or cats.

If you are fortunate enough to own a large amount of property and your zoning laws allow it, consider burying your horse on your land. If you don't have land but can afford a burial in a commercially run pet cemetery, this is another option to consider. It will cost you upwards of $1,000 to bury your horse in a pet cemetery, depending on where you live.

Because most horse owners have neither the land nor the money to bury their horses, they are faced with the unpleasant reality of sending their horse's body to a rendering plant. This is the least expensive and most convenient method of disposal. This method usually costs well under $200 for both removal and disposal of the body.

Chapter 12

Options for Old Faithful

● ●

● ●

*U*nfortunately, nothing lasts forever, including human/horse relationships. Your horse may get so old that you can no longer ride him. Perhaps lifestyle changes prevent your having time for your horse. Maybe you've learned so much from your first horse that you've outgrown him. You may find yourself wanting a horse who can provide a new challenge and an opportunity to learn even more.

When these situations arise, do the right thing by your horse. A horse is not an object to be discarded when he has outlived his usefulness. Horses are feeling creatures capable of suffering, and so are deserving of consideration.

What Happens to Horses?

The equine version of the county animal shelter is the slaughterhouse. Every year, hundreds of thousands of horses are slaughtered and the meat sold for human consumption in parts of Europe and Asia. This fate befalls not only to old, lame animals, but young, rideable horses in their prime. How can this be? A perfectly rideable horse can land at a slaughterhouse merely because the horse was sold at an auction and purchased by a *killer buyer*. The killer buyer gets the horse at a price below meat market value, making the animal worth more dead than alive.

In the United States, few regulations govern the transportation of slaughter-bound horses. Consequently, the animals are crowded into double-decker cattle trucks and sent on several-day journeys to slaughterhouses with no food or water for the duration of the trip. All the horses suffer under these conditions, but the infirm, the very old, and the very young suffer the most.

Debate rages in the horse world over the issue of slaughter. Some people believe that slaughter is a practical solution for the disposal of thousands of unwanted horses, and argue that once the horse arrives at the slaughter-house, his death is quick and painless. Others offer proof that the end does not always come swiftly and feel that this is no way for an animal to end up after serving his life as a companion to humankind.

We aren't telling you this to bum you out, but rather to make you aware. We think you should know what happens to horses who are casually sold or given away after they've outlived their usefulness. The reality of the horse world is this: If you don't give much thought to what happens to your horse after you sell him, he'll likely end up at a public auction, where he may be purchased by a killer buyer and shipped to slaughter.

We assume that you love your horse too much to see him end up this way. With this fact in mind, we tell you how you can protect your horse so he doesn't find himself in this situation, while at the same time meeting your own needs to get a different horse or get out of horse ownership altogether.

Movin' On

You may have trouble imagining a time when you may not want to or be able to ride your companion anymore. Yet it happens to horse owners all the time. If you lose interest in riding or if your horse can't be ridden, your decision not to ride your horse anymore is pretty cut-and-dried. But if you simply outgrow your horse, the decision to stop riding him is not so easy. This is a gray area, where the question of whether your skills have surpassed those of your horse is a bit subjective. Emotions can muddle the situation even more, making the decision an agonizing one.

Showing signs of outgrowing your horse

One day, you may look at your horse and realize that you've learned more from him than you ever would have imagined. He served as your guide to an exciting but uncertain world. But now you feel both comfortable and confi-dent in that world, and life with your horse is beginning to get a bit stagnant. If you suspect you're outgrowing your horse, certain signs can help you determine the truth. Examine yourself for these feelings and situations:

✔ You used to love riding your horse, but you're getting bored. You've tried varying your riding routine and pursuing different riding activities, but nothing makes riding your horse fun. You're certain the problem isn't riding itself because whenever you ride someone else's horse, you find the experience exhilarating.

✔ You enjoyed learning to ride on your horse, but now that you're more competent, you want to get involved in a competitive activity. Your horse is a great beginner's horse but he's not a show horse. You have no hope of moving into the show world if you keep him as your mount.

✔ You feel you've mastered the basics of horsemanship and now want to move up to the next level within your discipline so you can become a better rider. Or, maybe you want to change to a different discipline. Your horse is holding you back because he doesn't possess the athletic ability to help you get to the next level or to work in another discipline.

If any of these scenarios apply to you and your horse, talk with your trainer or another equine expert who is familiar with both your riding ability and your horse to see whether that person agrees that you're outgrowing your horse.

Making the decision

When you're certain that you've outgrown your horse, you must decide what you're going to do about it. If moving on in your riding is very important to you, then you obviously need to get a new horse. You can either keep your first horse and care for him in addition to your new horse, or you can find a new life for your first horse and replace him with another horse. (See "Options for Old Faithful" for information on what to do with your first horse.)

If your urges to learn more aren't more important than your relationship with your horse, consider keeping him and continuing to ride him while taking lessons on other horses, or put your desires to grow aside. Although many horse people believe that you may be doing a disservice to yourself by following this latter option, there's something to be said for loyalty, dedication, and commitment to your old friend.

Options for Old Faithful

Once you make the decision to stop riding your first horse in favor of getting another one (or even leaving the hobby completely), think long and hard about what you're going to do with Old Faithful. You can protect your horse from the slaughterhouse, and we tell you how in the following sections.

Selling him

Selling your horse outright is the riskiest option for your horse in terms of his long-term future, especially if he's in the upper age range. Yet this is the most common way of divesting oneself of an unwanted horse.

If you're determined to sell your horse and recover your investment but are concerned about where the horse ends up, follow these guidelines:

- ✓ **Find out the meat market price for horses in your area (usually around $1.00 per pound, and price your horse considerably higher than what he would sell for at slaughter.**

- ✓ **Don't consign your horse to a public auction:** The majority of horses purchased for slaughter come from public auctions.

- ✓ **Don't sell your horse to a horse dealer who ships horses to slaughter (ask him if you aren't sure):** Your horse may end up on a truck to the slaughterhouse instead of being purchased by someone who wants to ride him.

- ✓ **Sell your horse only to a good home:** Screen potential buyers by asking them questions such as whether they've owned a horse before (and if so, what happened to him), their intended uses for the horse, the type of housing the horse will receive, and what they plan to do with your horse when they no longer want him.

- ✓ **Be cautious about potential buyers:** Unscrupulous people in the horse world sometimes pretend to be buying a horse to ride when in reality they intend the animal for slaughter. Combat this problem by asking potential buyers lots of questions about themselves and their intent for the horse, and don't hesitate to say no if you get a bad feeling. Keeping your horse's price tag well above meat value helps keep these buyers away.

- ✓ **Offer a buy-back option on the horse:** Tell the buyer you would like to buy the horse back at the purchase price at any time in the horse's life should the owner decide he or she no longer wants the horse.

Leasing him

If your horse is still healthy and sound, the best alternative to selling him is to lease him. When you lease your horse, you still maintain control over his ultimate destiny while divesting yourself of the time and financial responsibilities of ownership. In a lease situation, the lessee pays you a sum for use of the horse, in addition to whatever other costs you wish to charge (board, shoes, and preventative veterinary care are the norm in full leases). The lessee does the work of caring for and riding the horse while you collect the fee.

The three typical types of leases are: A *full lease,* where someone rides and cares for your horse off your premises; a *full lease with stipulations,* where the lessee rides and cares for your horse on your property or approved facility; and *a partial lease,* where the lessee shares use of the horse with you or another partial lessee.

Some headaches come along with leasing. If the horse develops a major health or training problem, you need to get involved. If your lessee stops making payments to you or backs out of the lease, you have to deal with the problem. But if you truly care about your horse's future, leasing is surely the best way to go (see Chapter 3 "Before You Buy" for more details on leasing).

Retiring him

Probably the kindest option for an older horse is to retire him. Retirement is also practical because older horses tend to be harder to sell. After years of service, older horses often need and deserve a break from regular work.

Retiring a horse doesn't mean just putting him out to pasture and ignoring him, though. Although a pasture is the best place for a retired horse, you can't just put him out there and forget about him. He still needs daily care as well as grooming, veterinary care, and TLC.

Retiring a horse to pasture is a good idea, but retiring a horse to a stall or a small, grassless paddock is *not* the best route to take. If your horse has nothing to graze on and is confined in a small space, he will deteriorate due to the lack of exercise and mental stimulation. If you don't have your own pasture, you can rent one, either at a boarding facility or a private equine property. The most convenient arrangement is to board your horse in a pasture where daily care is part of the boarding agreement. Even with this arrangement, try to find a pasture that isn't too far from where you live so you can check on your horse on regular basis (see Chapter 7 for information on providing a pasture for your horse).

If you can't find a pasture where your horse receives daily care from the pasture's owner or management, you need to do the work yourself. This means grooming the horse, checking him for illness or injury, and providing him with whatever medication or supplements he's on.

Donating him

Donating your outgrown horse to a special riding program is another humane option. If he's healthy and sound, donation is an excellent alternative to selling him because most centers for therapeutic riding accept donations of horses. The centers typically look for horses who are quiet, gentle, and forgiving to inexperienced riders. In turn, the horse receives excellent care.

If you contact a therapeutic riding center and offer your horse for donation, center personnel will want to evaluate the horse to make sure that he has the right disposition for the job. If the horse passes muster, you can grant the center legal possession and receive a charitable tax write-off for your trouble.

Although this option can be great for an older horse, we want to caution you about two things regarding donating your horse:

✔ **Make sure that you donate your horse to a legitimate organization:** Con artists often present themselves as representing a therapeutic riding program when they're really procuring free horses to sell for slaughter. Ask for proof of the group's nonprofit status, and pay a visit their stables. If in doubt, contact your state government to determine whether the group is registered as a nonprofit therapeutic riding program.

✔ **Find out the therapeutic riding program's policy on disposing of horses who are no longer needed:** Most therapeutic riding organizations euthanize horses who are too old or ill to perform their duties. However, some organizations sell the horses for slaughter. Get the group's policy in writing. If the group sells horses to slaughter, decline to donate your horse or stipulate in writing that you're donating your horse only if you're allowed to take the horse back or buy him back at meat price when he's no longer needed in the program. The horse may be returned to you when he is very old and sick, but at least with this arrangement, you can have the horse humanely euthanized instead of sending him off to slaughter.

Passing him down within the family

If your horse is rideable but you've outgrown him, consider passing him along to someone in your immediately family. Perhaps your oldest child is getting more interested in riding and wants his or her own horse. Maybe your spouse hasn't been riding much but wants to learn and could benefit from the teachings of your old veteran.

Of course, this option only works if your family can afford to keep two horses. If not, consider passing Old Faithful along to a relative who has a genuine interest in horses and seriously wants to get into riding. You can sell the horse to your relative for a nominal fee or even give the horse away, but only under one condition: that the relative won't eventually resell the horse, but will instead sell or give the horse back to you. Be sure to get this agreement in writing so the relative feels obligated to stick to it.

Euthanizing him

If you're no longer riding your horse because he's old and lame, and you can't afford to retire him, consider euthanasia. Although losing a companion after all he's done for you is painful, euthanizing him is a much kinder end than being shipped off to slaughter. You can think of the minimal cost of the euthanasia and disposal of the body (either by burial on your own property or livestock removal service to a rendering plant) as your final gift to your old friend. See Chapter 11 for more information on euthanasia.

Horses by Color

CLiX Photography

White

White horses are solid white with pink muzzles and light-colored hooves. Don't confuse white horses with gray horses, though. Gray horses have some colored hairs in their coats — whites do not. White horses are sometimes seen with pink eyes (albinos) or blue eyes (perlinos). Others have brown eyes.

Gray

Gray horses come in a variety of shades, and can range from nearly white to a darker, dappled coloration. White hairs are mixed with darker hairs of any other color to produce a gray coloration. Gray horses are often born solid colored and lighten as they get older. One variety, called *flea-bitten gray*, is usually seen on older horses.

Gemma Giannini

Pinto
Pinto markings consist of patches of dark color against white. Only certain breeds have pinto coloration.

Buckskin
The true buckskin has a yellow or gold body coloration with a black mane and tail. The lower legs are usually black, and can also have white markings. Many horse lovers believe a horse must have a dark stripe down its back to be considered a buckskin, but in reality, true buckskins have no dorsal stripe.

Grullo

Grullo horses have a dark, smoky-gray body coloration with a black mane and tail. Grullos usually have a dark stripe down their backs and dark legs.

Palomino

Palominos have a golden yellow body coloration, with white manes and tails.

Dun

Dun horses have a gold body color and a black or brown mane and tail. The most distinctive indication of a dun coloration is a dark stripe running down the length of the horse's back. Sometimes, you may see a transverse stripe across the withers, as well as horizontal stripes on the legs. (The dun coloration is considered the closest thing to a natural "wild" color in the horse.)

Red dun

Red duns are a type of dun that have a reddish tint to their coats. They have a dark stripe running down the back, and have a white, red, or flaxen mane and tail.

Sorrel
The body color of a sorrel horse is copper-red. Sorrels are sometimes hard to distinguish from chestnuts. The main difference between the two is that sorrels usually have more of a yellow tint to their coats than do chestnuts. Sorrels tend to have a mane and tail color that matches the body color, although sorrel horses sometimes have *flaxen,* or blonde, manes and tails.

Chestnut (light)
Chestnut-colored horses have a distinct reddish color on their bodies, and usually have the same color in the mane and tail. Chestnut colorations come in a variety of shades, from dark to light. A light chestnut horse is shown here.

Chestnut (dark)
Chestnut horses can be
a dark reddish color, as
in this classic liver
chestnut.

Bay
Bay horses have bodies
that are anywhere from
dark tan to reddish brown.
Their manes and tails are
always black, and they
often have black on the
lower parts of their legs.

Brown

Horses that are described as brown have brown or light black body coloration with a lighter color around the muzzle, flank, and inside upper legs. The mane and tail are always black.

Gemma Giannini

Red roan

The bodies of red roans are covered with a uniform mixture of white hairs mixed with red hairs. The head and lower legs are usually darker than the rest of the body because these areas have a proliferation of red hairs. The manes and tails of red roans can be black, red, or flaxen.

CLiX Photography

Blue roan

Blue roans have a uniform mixture of white hairs mixed with black hairs, which gives the body a bluish appearance — hence the name. The heads and lower legs of blue roans are usually darker than the bodies. The mane and tail are nearly always black.

Black

For a horse to be considered a true black, his body color must be a solid black with no light areas anywhere on his body. The mane and tail are black as well.

Horses by Breed

CLiX Photography

Andalusian

The Andalusian horse, also known as the Pure Spanish Horse, is one of the most spectacular studies in horse flesh on the planet. You see this horse in museum pieces and paintings from the Middle Ages. Leonardo da Vinci sculpted this horse, and the winged Pegasus was based on this breed. Their necks are heavy and arched, their manes and tails are long and wavy. With a regalness about them that is hard to equal, even a relatively untrained eye can easily spot this breed.

Appaloosa

The Appaloosa horse's most distinguishing characteristic is its spotted coat. Represented in several different patterns including the popular *leopard* (shown) and *blanket with spots* (dark body color with white over the rump, which is covered with dark spots), this characteristic sets the breed apart. Other physical traits include white sclera in the eye, striped hooves and mottled skin. Some Appaloosas also have thin manes and tails. The height range for an Appaloosa is 14.3 to 16 hands.

Gemma Giannini

Arabian

Arabian horses are known for their elegant and graceful beauty. The head of the Arabian is small and has a concave, or dished, face. The Arabian's ears are small and curve inward, and its neck is long and arched. Most Arabian horses have only five spinal vertebrae as opposed to the six vertebrae typically found in most other breeds. This one less vertebrae gives Arabians a shorter back than a lot of other breeds. Arabians are small horses that rarely measure much over 15 hands in height.

Clydesdale

Clydesdale horses have been pulling the Budweiser beer wagon for decades and are regularly seen in the company's TV commercials and in exhibitions around the country. The Clydesdale originated in Scotland where it was originally used to haul heavy loads in the coal fields and on the roads of that country during the 1700s. These horses can be anywhere from 16.1 to 18 hands in height. They have wonderful dispositions and are often used for riding as well as pulling.

Dutch Warmblood
The result of Trakehner, Gelderland, and Thoroughbred crossings, the Dutch Warmblood was developed to be the consummate performance horse. Standing 16 to 17 hands high, Dutch Warm-bloods are especially known for their skills in jumping, dressage (shown), and carriage driving.

Miniature Horse
Miniature horses are the dwarfs of the equine world, and number one in the "adorable" category. The Miniature horse has all the physical and psychological characteristics of a regular horse in a very small package. The Miniature horse, which stands anywhere from 6 to 7 hands high, is kept primarily as a pet. Tiny tots can ride Miniature horses, but anyone over the age of four years old is probably too big to ride a Miniature horse.

Morgan

Morgans have small, elegant heads and strong, highly arched necks. They also have very deep chests, which gives them considerable endurance. Just like their founding sire, Justin Morgan, Morgans tend to be smaller horses and rarely reach more than 15.2 hands in height. They are eager to please and willing to do whatever is asked of them.

Paint Horse

Paint horse coats come in a variety of different patterns, most of which fall under the heading of tobiano (a white base with dark patches, shown) or overo (a dark base with white patches). The breed's conformation is identical to that of the Quarter Horse, with a height range of 15 to 16 hands. Its temperament is very much like the Quarter Horse's too: mellow, easygoing, and eager to please.

Peruvian Paso

Developed in Peru in the 1800s to carry plantation owners across vast areas of land, the Peruvian Paso possess three gaits: the *paso llano,* the *sobreandando,* and the *huachano.* Each of these gaits is designed to be comfortable while covering considerable ground. Peruvian Paso horses that are in top condition can maintain these gaits for hours on end. Peruvian Pasos are on the small to medium size, measuring 14.1 to 15.1 hands in height. They have well muscled necks and long, thick manes and tails.

Quarter Horse

The Quarter Horse is a sturdy horse with a small head and muscular neck. The breed's hindquarters are powerful, and the legs are straight and solid. Quarter Horses have a big height range, standing anywhere from 14.3 to 16 hands tall. One of the Quarter Horse's most outstanding features is its disposition. This quiet temperament is a big reason behind the Quarter Horse's huge popularity.

Sandra Hall

Racking Horse

Racking Horses have a graceful build, with a long, sloping neck. Their legs are smooth and their hair finely textured. The typical Racking Horse averages around 15.2 hands. What makes the Racking Horse so special is that it is a *gaited* breed, able to perform a four-beat racking gait, in addition to a walk and a canter. These horses are willing to work and eager to please their handlers.

Saddlebred

The Saddlebred is a *gaited* horse, capable of performing a rack and stepping pace, in addition to an animated walk, trot, and canter. Saddlebreds typically have long, arched necks and fine heads that they carry rather high. The Saddlebred's body is rather lithe and lean, almost like that of a human ballet dancer. Saddlebreds range in height from 15 hands to 17 hands high.

Gemma Giannini

Standardbred

Standardbreds have an inborn ability to move at great speeds without galloping. Some members of the breed are natural born trotters and can trot at nearly 30 mph. Others are born *pacers* (where the legs on one side move in unison), and can attain these same speeds. Standardbreds can also gallop. The Standardbred is closely related to the Thorough-bred, although the Standardbred is considerably heavier in muscle. Standardbreds have rather large heads and powerful thighs. They usually measure anywhere from 15 to 16 hands.

Tennessee Walking Horse

The Tennessee Walking Horse is a *gaited* horse, and can perform, in addition to the walk, trot, and canter, a four-beat running walk, for which it is famous. Tennessee Walking Horses have a straight head with larger-than-usual ears. The breed has a gracefully arched neck, prominent withers and large hooves. Ranging in height from 15 to 16 hands, Tennessee Walking Horses have very tractable temperaments.

Thoroughbred

The typical Thoroughbred has a straight head, high withers, and long, fine legs. Standing anywhere from 15 to 17 hands high, Thoroughbreds have a lean, lanky appearance that sets them apart from other breeds. Thoroughbreds are willing horses but can be somewhat complicated in temperament, meaning that they can be hard for some people to figure out. Beginning riders sometimes have trouble handling Thoroughbreds because of the breed's spunky personality.

Welsh Pony

Welsh Ponies come in four different types: Mountain pony, Welsh pony, Welsh Pony of Cob Type and Welsh Cob. Each of these four names represents different heights and conformation types within the Welsh breed. It's easiest to think of each type in terms of its height: The Welsh Mountain is 12.2 hands or shorter; the Welsh Pony 12.2 to 13.2 hands high; the Welsh Pony of Cob Type is 13.2 hands high or less; and the Cob Type is actually horse-sized at 14 to 15.1 hands tall.

Part V
Horsin' Around

In this part . . .

Part V shows you all the different ways you can ride a horse. Along with descriptions of the different riding disciplines, you'll find details on handling your horse before you get on, putting on the saddle and bridle, and tips for actual riding. You'll also find out about the many fun things you can do on horseback.

Chapter 13

Handling Your Horse When You're On the Ground

. . . .

In This Chapter

▶ Knowing how horses should act

▶ Putting on the halter

▶ Dealing with naughty horses

▶ Lungeing a horse

. . . .

Most people associate horses with riding, and understandably so. Nearly every equine image they're exposed to depicts a human sitting on a horse. But what most people don't think about is that before you can get up on the horse, you have to handle him from the ground.

Because horses are such large creatures — weighing nearly 10 times as much as most humans — you need both skill and tact (not to mention the tack!) to handle them from the ground. The fact that most horses are gentle and enjoy human company makes the job easier, but accidents can still occur if humans are careless. Even though most people worry about falling off when they ride, humans are actually more vulnerable to horse-related injury on the ground.

In this chapter, we give you a crash course in horse handling from the ground up. You'll find out the safest and most effective ways to deal with your horse before you get up on his back. As you learn to handle your horse, you'll also discover the deep bond that develops between a human and a horse just from hanging out together.

Handling Your Horse on Terra Firma

Horses are herd animals, which means that they are genetically programmed to be social. A big part of being social for a horse is fitting into the herd hierarchy.

In horse-herd politics, a self-appointed leader pretty much tells all the other horses what to do. When you handle your horse on the ground, you become the self-appointed leader. If you get your horse's buy-in, he listens to you and you have the basis for a good relationship on the ground — one that translates into good rapport in the saddle.

Human responsibilities

Before you begin handling your horse from the ground, know that you have certain responsibilities to your horse. As the leader of your small herd, you must hold up your end of the bargain by being firm and confident. If you aren't, your horse will dismiss you as leader and take over the job himself. Or, if you're too rough, your horse may come to think of you as a predator rather than a benevolent leader.

To help you establish the right tone with your horse, do the following:

- ✔ **Be firm:** When you handle your horse from the ground, remember that you're the one in charge, not the horse. Don't allow your horse to push you around — literally or figuratively. Don't ever let the horse think that he is the one making the decisions. If he ever tries to boss you around, a firm jerk on the lead rope and a loud "Quit!" should get the message across.

- ✔ **Be fair:** Require the horse to do your bidding, but do so in a way that shows compassion and understanding. For example, if you're leading your horse and he's walking obediently beside you until a bale of hay falls from a nearby rafter and scares the heck out of him, making him pull away and nearly knocking you off your feet, don't punish the horse for reacting in a normal way to something out of his control. Instead, understand the circumstances of his misbehavior.

- ✔ **Be patient:** Think of your horse as a 1,000-pound toddler. Sometimes he knows what he should do but doesn't feel like doing it. Sometimes he's at a total loss and can't figure out what you want. Have some compassion for your horse, who would much rather be out in a pasture eating with other horses instead of doing things that make no sense to him. Think before you react, make sure that he understands what you want before you assume he doesn't, and above all, be patient.

- ✔ **Be anger-free:** Unfortunately, taking anger out on those who can't defend themselves is an all-too-human trait. Despite the horse's large size, he's a rather gentle creature who is quite vulnerable to the abuses of human kind. (If you ever saw or read *Black Beauty,* you know what we mean.) Never lose your temper with your horse and never take out your daily frustrations on him.

If you're particularly angry with your horse in a situation and feel you might lose control, put the horse back in his stall, go home, and punch a pillow. Taking your anger out on the horse may damage the fragile trust that has been painstakingly built between you, and you may have to spend a considerable amount of time to earn it back again.

✔ **Be calm:** Because horses are prey animals, they tend to be nervous sorts. Whenever you're around your horse, move slowly and speak quietly. Loud voices and quick movements make horses nervous. And whatever you do, avoid waving your arms over your head when you're around a horse. For some reason, waving arms scare the daylights out of some horses and make them want to head for the hills.

Horse responsibilities

Humans aren't the only ones expected to act a certain way during on-the-ground interactions. Horses should have "good ground manners," which means they should behave themselves when a human is handling them on the ground. Horses who do *not* have good ground manners are a hazard and a liability, and they need training.

These are the good ground manners you should expect your horse to follow:

✔ **Stand still:** When your horse is being haltered or tacked up, he should stand quietly until you signal him that it's time for him to move.

✔ **Be nice:** While you're working around your horse, he should have a pleasant attitude, meaning no attempts at biting or kicking, and no threatening facial expressions.

✔ **Walk alongside:** As you lead your horse, he should walk quietly beside you, taking your cue as to speed and which direction to turn.

✔ **Respect your space:** Your horse should always respect your physical space, never intruding on it, and responding immediately for your requests for more space (see section titled "Crowding" in this chapter for details on how to ask your horse for space).

In the Stall or Pasture

Before you can do anything with your horse, you have to "catch" him. This expression means approaching him in his stall or pasture and placing a halter over his head, securing it, and leading him out.

If your horse is well-behaved in this regard, this part is pretty easy. If he's not well-behaved, you have a real job on your hands. Either way, handle the situation with safety first and foremost in your mind.

The stall

Horses are much easier to catch when they're in a stall or small paddock. The horse realizes he has nowhere to go, and rarely puts up a fight. The exception to the rule is a horse who fears his handlers or simply hates to be handled, both of which are the result of mistreatment.

Assuming that your horse likes you and doesn't mind being caught, follow these steps when you go to retrieve him from his stall:

1. **Have your halter with you with the lead rope attached.**

   See Figure 13-1 for a diagram of how the lead rope attaches to the halter.

2. **Speak to your horse to let him know you're there before you enter the stall or paddock.**

3. **Enter the stall or paddock.**

4. **Approach the horse at his left shoulder rather than directly at his face.**

   Horses can't see directly under their noses or directly behind them. If the horse's hindquarters are facing you as you enter the stall or paddock, make sure that the horse knows you're there before you get too close.

5. **As you get close to the horse, extend your hand, palm down, and let the horse sniff you.**

   This greeting assures the horse that you're friend, not foe. Loop the lead rope around the horse's neck and slip the halter over his head.

6. **Loop the lead rope around the horse's neck and slip the halter over his head.**

Figure 13-1:
The correct way to put on a halter.

The pasture

Catching a horse in a pasture can be tricky if the horse doesn't want to be caught. Fortunately, most horses don't mind it and will cooperate provided the human handler approaches the horse in the right way.

Catching a horse in a pasture is different from catching him in a stall because in a pasture, the horse has a lot more room to move away from you. Following is the best way to approach a horse who is loose in a pasture with other horses:

1. **Walk quietly toward the horse with your hands at your side and your halter and lead rope in hand, making sure he sees you.**

2. **Approach the horse at his left shoulder, never directly from the front or back.**

   As you make contact with the horse, gently pat or scratch his neck, speaking softly.

3. **Place the lead rope around the horse's neck in a loop as you continue speaking to him.**

   Holding the noosed lead rope, proceed to put on the halter as we describe in the section "Putting on the halter."

Whatever you do, don't let your horse get away without being caught. After you make an attempt to catch the horse, keep trying until you succeed. If you don't, the horse quickly learns that capture can be easily foiled.

Some people take treats out in a pasture to help catch a horse. We don't recommend doing so if other horses are in the pasture. The group may get nasty and competitive with one another over the treats, leaving you vulnerable to a misplaced bite or kick.

Turning your horse loose in the pasture after you're finished with him requires some finesse, too, so that he doesn't develop the habit of bolting away after you remove his halter:

- Noose the lead rope around the horse's neck before you take the halter off.
- Secure the horse with the lead rope with your hand; then slip the halter off the horse's head.
- Release the noose and allow the horse to walk away.

Putting on the Halter

The fundamental tool for controlling a horse on the ground is the halter. Most horses are very amenable to having a halter placed on their heads because they've been wearing one since foalhood.

The hardest thing about learning to halter a horse is visualizing where all those straps are supposed to go. Study horses wearing halters before you attempt to put one on. Become familiar with the way the straps sit on a horse, and then hold a halter in your hand, imagining the horse's head inside it.

Your horse should stand quietly as you halter him. If he doesn't, you have a behavior problem on your hands, one that a professional trainer or experienced horseperson needs to deal with.

To halter your horse, follow these steps:

1. **Face the same direction that your horse is facing as you stand at the horse's left shoulder.**

   Place the lead rope in a loose loop around the middle of the horse's neck. Don't tie the rope, but hold it together with your right hand. Doing so secures the horse and keeps him from walking away from you.

2. **Check to make sure that the crown strap of the halter is unbuckled.**

3. **With the buckle side of the strap in your left hand and the crown strap in your right hand, slip the horse's nose through the noseband of the halter by reaching your right hand underneath the horse's neck, as shown in Figure 13-1.**

4. **When the horse's nose is through the halter, bring the crown piece up behind the horse's ears and buckle it so the halter fits comfortably — not too tight and not too loose.**

5. **Take the lead rope from around the horse's neck and fold it in your left hand, with your right hand holding the attached rope just below the halter.**

   You're now ready to lead your horse out of his stall or paddock.

Leading

Your role as your horse's leader is never more literal than when you're actually, physically leading him. Providing your horse is well-trained and well behaved, and you are confident and adept, leading a horse can be fun and easy.

Leading right

For safety reasons, you need to lead a horse the right way:

- Stand on the horse's left side.

- Hold the end of the lead rope closest to the horse's head in your right hand, with your thumb pointing up toward the horse's head. Your hand should be about 6 inches from the halter. If your lead rope has a chain at the end, hold the rope just below the chain so your hand doesn't get injured if the horse pulls back.

TIP

If you find you need more control when leading your horse, gain it by moving your hand closer to the halter.

✔ In your left hand, hold the remainder of the lead rope folded up. Don't coil the remainder of the rope around your hand. If you do and the horse pulls back, the coil can tighten, trapping your hand.

✔ Before you ask the horse to move, stand at his left shoulder, facing forward, your hands holding the lead rope as described above. See Figure 13-2 for the correct position to stand when leading a horse.

✔ As you begin to walk forward, give the lead rope a gentle pull with your right hand. The horse should begin walking, keeping pace with you so you remain at his shoulder.

✔ To turn your horse while leading him, turn the wrist on your right hand either left or right (depending on which way you want to turn). Your horse should follow your lead.

✔ To stop your horse, say "Ho!" and stop walking, giving a backward tug on the rope with your right hand.

Figure 13-2:
The correct way to lead a horse.

Leading don'ts

It's important not to forget how big your horse really is when you're leading him. Should something happen — like your horse spooks or starts to misbehave — you could be in serious physical danger if you aren't leading the proper way.

Avoid these bad habits when leading your horse:

- ✔ Don't lead a horse by anything other than a halter and lead rope, or the reins of a bridle. If leading by the reins, don't loop them over the horse's neck while leading but hold them free instead.

- ✔ Don't lead your horse by putting your hand in the halter instead of using a lead rope. If the horse bolts and your hand gets caught in the halter you may be dragged.

- ✔ Don't walk in front of your horse with him trailing behind you. If your horse suddenly bolts forward, you could be trampled.

- ✔ Don't trot your horse when you are leading him unless someone is evaluating the animal for lameness. Leading a trotting horse is difficult.

- ✔ Don't coil or wrap the lead rope in your hand. If the horse pulls back or runs off, the rope may tighten around your hand and you can be dragged.

- ✔ Don't wrap your hand around the chain part of a lead rope (if your lead rope has a chain that is — not all do). If the horse pulls back, your hand can be injured.

Tying

To tie up a horse, you just take a rope and tie him to a post. Right? Wrong. Tying a horse, though seemingly simple, is anything but. Horses have to be secured in just the right way or they can get themselves into all kinds of trouble.

Pulling back when frightened is one of the most common and dangerous problems that arise when a horse is tied. Another problem involves the horse getting tangled up in the lead rope.

When tying a horse, follow these rules to ensure safety:

- ✔ Whenever possible, tie a horse in *cross-ties*, which are two ropes on either side of the horse that attach to the sides of the horse's halter. Cross-ties should be about the same height as the top of the horse's shoulders . (See Figure 13-3 to see what cross-ties look like.) Tying a horse in cross-ties is much safer than tying a horse to a hitching post or other object.

Make sure that your horse is familiar with the feeling of being cross-tied before you tie him this way. To gradually get him used to the idea, attach one cross-tie to his halter first, and your lead rope to the other. This way, he can get used to the pull that comes from the cross-tie without being completely confined in it.

Also, make sure that the cross-ties have a breakaway feature so the horse won't get hung up in the ties should he panic and thrash around. Quick release snaps are also a good item to have on cross-ties so a frightened horse can be turned loose if he's in danger of hurting himself or someone else.

✔ Tie a horse only by a halter and lead rope, or halter and cross-ties. *Never* tie a horse by the reins of a bridle. If the horse pulls back, the reins can break and the bit may damage the horse's jaw.

✔ Tie a horse only to an immovable object. Horses should be tied to solid fence posts, hitching posts made for this purpose, horse trailers hooked to a truck, cross-ties, or, if on the trail, to strong, secure tree trunks. The rope should be tied so that its height is stable and won't slip down toward the ground. Horses are big and strong, and if they spook and pull back when tied to something that isn't secure, they can drag the object or pull it right out of the ground.

Figure 13-3:
A horse
secured
with
cross-ties.

✔ When tying a horse with a lead rope, use a safety, or quick release, knot. The knot can be released in an emergency by pulling on the loose end. Practice tying a safety knot and make sure that you have it down pat before you actually use it to secure a horse. See Figure 13-4 for instructions on how to tie a safety knot.

✔ Always tie a horse with the knot about level to the horse's withers, with no more than 3 feet of rope from the post to the halter. Doing so keeps the horse from getting the rope over his head or from getting a leg caught in it. See Figure 13-5 for a drawing of a horse safely tied to a hitching post.

✔ Don't ever tie a horse with a chain shank run through his halter. If the horse pulls back, the chain can injure him.

✔ Consider buying a cotton lead rope affixed with something called a panic or quick release snap that you can release if a horse is pulling back or tangled up. This rope is the safest kind for tying.

✔ Never leave a horse alone and unsupervised when tied up. You'd be amazed at how quickly a tied horse can get into trouble.

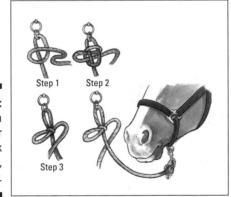

Figure 13-4:
How to tie a safety, or quick release, knot.

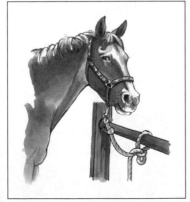

Figure 13-5:
A horse safely tied to a hitching post.

Naughty Things Horses Do

Sometimes, no matter how hard you try to do things right, your horse may make handling from the ground difficult for you. Horses are a lot like small children — they easily develop bad habits and often test you to see what they can get away with. At times, their misbehavior comes from fear; other times, it stems from sheer boredom or lack of training.

The way you handle problem behaviors on the ground is important. If your horse learns that he can get away with naughty behavior, he'll keep doing it. Eventually, you'll have a serious problem on your hands. Conversely, if you let your horse know that you're wise to these shenanigans and are consistent in correcting the bad behaviors, he'll soon give it up.

Below are some typical stunts that horses pull when you are handling them on the ground, and ways you can combat these behaviors.

Evading capture

Refusal to be caught is a much bigger problem with horses who live out in a pasture with other horses. Horses who have been worked very hard or don't enjoy being around humans all that much because they've been mistreated in the past may come to associate being caught with something unpleasant. If a horse discovers that he can evade capture, watch out. You may find yourself spending vast amounts of time trying to capture the recalcitrant beast.

If your horse refuses to be caught — or at least gives you a good run for your money before allowing you to get close (even though you have tried catching him by using the method we describe earlier in the "In the pasture" section), the horse needs to be reconditioned to associate being caught with something pleasant. Practice catching him alone in a small enclosure (not his pasture) by using this method:

1. **Arm yourself with a favorite treat like a carrot or slice of apple.**

2. **Attempt to approach the horse by using the method described in the section titled "In the pasture" above.**

   Don't bring a halter with you because you're only practicing right now. Be nonchalant about your approach, and don't look the horse right in the eye.

3. **As you get closer to the horse, extend your hand so the horse sees the treat.**

   The horse will probably let you approach or may even walk toward you to get the treat.

Jailbreak! Catching a runaway horse

Nothing can disrupt the quiet atmosphere of a stable like a horse who's gotten loose from his handler. The cry "Loose horse!" makes human heads go up in a flash.

Something strange happens when a horse gets loose at a stable. Once they realize what's going on, the other horses present get excited and start bucking, whinnying, and dancing around. It's much like those prison escapes you see in the movies, where all the inmates start banging their tin cups on the cell bars, yelling "Run for it!" When this jailbreak attitude takes hold at a stable, the pandemonium can cause havoc for everyone within earshot.

Here are some pointers on how to cope when an errant horse makes a bid for freedom:

- **Don't panic:** Stay calm and shout "Loose horse!" at the top of your lungs to warn other people that an escapee is on the premises.

- **If the escapee is not your charge, but you are leading, riding, or standing next to your own horse when the culprit gets loose, be aware that your horse is probably going to react with excitement when he discovers what's happening:** Stop in your tracks and dismount or untie your horse quickly. Hold on to your horse tightly and be prepared for some dancing around.

- **If a horse you were handling has gotten away from you, do not chase him:** Chasing the horse only makes him run away from you with increasing speed.

- **Walk slowly in the direction your horse ran to see where he's gone:** Most horses who escape from a handler in a familiar setting don't go far — usually to the nearest food storage area. If you find that he has stopped somewhere to eat, speak softly and walk up to him slowly, placing a lead rope around his neck to secure him. Remember not to give off any vibes that you are angry — if you do, the horse won't let you get close.

- **If your loose horse is not eating but just milling around, get a handful of hay or a carrot and slowly walk in his direction:** After the horse sees you, stand still and offer him the food in an outstretched hand as you speak to him softly. Most horses are more than happy to exchange their new-found freedom for a bite of something tasty. While the sell-out is happily munching away, slowly place a lead rope around his neck.

- **If your loose horse has stopped to eat, but takes off again when he sees you approaching, you'll need the help of one or two other people to catch him:** Arm yourselves with halters, and walk in different directions with the idea of surrounding him by blocking all his exits. Most horses will realize their defeat and allow themselves to be caught.

4. **When you make contact with the horse, give him the treat, scratch him on the withers or in his favorite spot, and then walk away before he has a chance to leave.**

    Practice this a number of times over a period of a few days until the horse seems comfortable with your approach.

5. **Begin placing the halter on the horse after you give him the treat.**

Don't take him out of the enclosure, though. Simply halter him, give him his treat, scratch him where he likes it, then remove the halter and leave.

When you get the feeling that the horse is comfortable with this routine, move the horse to a larger enclosure and practice the same method for a couple of weeks, alternating times that you take him out of his enclosure to ride him, and times that you just halter him and remove the halter and leave him alone.

Make sure that you don't overwork or mistreat the horse after you take him out of the enclosure. Many horses don't like to be caught because they're unhappy about what happens to them after they leave their pasture.

6. **After several weeks of practice, you can move your horse back to the original pasture and try this method in this larger area.**

If other horses share the pasture, you'll have to skip the treats as things can get dangerous if the other horses start fighting over the food. Instead of treats, give lots of scratches and kind words instead.

If, after a month or so of working on this problem, you're not getting anywhere with your difficult-to-catch horse, you need to call in a professional trainer for help.

Pulling back

The habit of pulling back when tied creates terrible problems for owners. Some horses are so bad about this that they can't be tied at all and must be held by hand whenever they need to be secured.

Occasionally, a horse pulls back when something frightens him at the tie rack. You can't miss it when this happens: The horse gets a terrified look in his eye and throws all of his weight on his haunches, practically sitting down as he pulls with all his might against his halter. If the horse breaks loose one or two times during such an incident, it can be the beginning of a bad habit — the horse has discovered that pulling back means freedom.

Follow these steps to ensure that your horse doesn't develop the terrible habit of pulling back:

✔ **Always tie your horse to something secure, using a lead rope or cross-ties:** See the preceding section "Tying."

✔ **Be careful about how you approach your horse when he's tied:** Don't come at the horse suddenly with a strange object, spray the horse in the face or upper body with water or fly spray, or do anything else that may spook him and make him pull to get away.

✔ **Anticipate what may scare your horse:** If you have to do something to the horse's head that frighten or upset him — applying eye medicine, for example — untie the rope first and hold the horse yourself so he doesn't have the opportunity to pull back when tied.

✔ **Tie your horse securely with a safety knot, using an unbreakable halter and lead rope.**

✔ **Don't tie the horse with too little rope:** If the horse feels he can't move his head much, he may become claustrophobic and pull back.

If a horse pulls back when tied to a hitching post or other object, try the following to get the horse to stop pulling:

✔ **Pull on the loose end of the safety knot to release the horse from being tied:** Be sure to take hold of the rope as you do that so the horse can't run away. Don't allow the horse to break the halter.

✔ **Step behind the horse (well out of kicking range) and shout at him:** The horse will move forward to get away from you.

Be aware that when one horse pulls back, the other horses tied with him at the same post often pull back, too.

If you have a horse who is a chronic puller, enlist the help of a professional horse trainer to break this difficult-to-change habit.

Biting

Most horses are very pleasant creatures, but occasionally, you may run across one who is the equine equivalent of a crabby 2-year-old. These grumpy-grouches may be wonderful when you're riding them, but they try to bite you when you handle them from the ground.

Horses usually bite humans for one of two reasons: to play or to send an aggressive message. Either way, the results are the same — an extremely painful bite that usually leaves black and blue marks on tender human skin.

Most horses are taught not to bite humans at a young age. Those who have not learned this lesson, however, must be trained in adulthood. If you have a horse who tries to bite you when you are grooming or leading him, follow these steps to break the habit:

✔ If your horse bites you or attempts to bite you, respond immediately by yelling "Quit!" and jerking once on the lead rope.

✔ Get to know your horse and anticipate when he may try to bite. If he bites when you are grooming him, let him bang his head into your raised

elbow as he turns around to bite. If he tries to bite you when you're leading him, hold your fist up near his mouth so he bangs into your knuckles
when he swings his head around to bite.

We like the idea of feeding treats to horses, because we think it helps develop
the bond between horse and human. However, if your horse is the nippy
type, we recommend that you don't give him treats by hand, and stick to
leaving goodies for him in his feeder.

Kicking

Kicking is a maneuver that nature gave horses to help protect them against
predators. Unfortunately, it's also a maneuver that gets used on humans now
and then. Although most horses don't go around kicking people, enough do
to make this behavior worth mentioning.

Most horses kick only when startled from behind, while others kick deliberately to keep humans from doing something the horse finds unpleasant.
Whatever the cause, a well-placed kick from a shod horse can do serious
damage to the human body.

Here are some pointers to keep yourself from getting kicked by a horse:

- **Never approach a horse directly from behind, because this area is one
  of a horse's blind spots:** Instead approach from a side angle, all the
  while speaking to the horse so he clearly knows you're coming.

- **If you must walk past a horse from behind, give the horse plenty of
  room:** Walk far enough away so that the horse's back leg can't reach
  you. If you don't have this much room, the next best alternative is to
  walk so close to the horse's hindquarters that you are nearly touching
  them. This way, if the horse moves to kick, you'll only be bumped by his
  hock and not kicked by his hoof.

- **If a horse turns his rump toward you suddenly, pinning his ears at the
  same time, the horse is threatening to kick you:** Yell "Quit!" as loud as
  you can and get out of range.

- **If you are grooming or saddling a horse and the horse pins his ears
  and kicks out at you, yell "Quit!" and slap the horse with an open
  hand on the shoulder or side:** Don't run away and leave the horse
  alone, which only reinforces the behavior. (If your horse always reacts
  this way when you groom a particular spot or tighten the cinch, consider that whatever you are doing may be causing the horse pain. Have a
  veterinarian check out the horse.)

- **If you find yourself dealing with a chronic kicker, get help from a professional trainer to fix this dangerous habit.**

Crowding

Well-trained horses learn at a young age to respect humans. They know that when a human is standing nearby, they shouldn't crowd or invade that person's space in any way.

Horses who haven't been taught this lesson, however, can be downright bratty when it comes to crowding. Although most horses don't have any intention of hurting you when they crowd, their sheer bulk can cause injury regardless of their intent.

If you find yourself dealing with a horse who repeatedly pushes into you when you are leading him, grooming him, or going into his stall or pasture, you have a crowder on your hands who needs professional help.

If your horse is generally well-behaved in this area, make sure that the horse stays that way by following these rules:

- **Make sure that your horse always gives way to you when you ask him to move:** When you push on your horse's shoulder or hindquarters from the side, he should willingly move away from you. Practice this movement with your horse every so often to remind the horse that he needs to respect your space.

- **Never allow your horse to push you up against a wall or other object:** If he does, yell "Quit!" at the horse and slap him with a flat palm on the shoulder or side.

- **Don't let your horse get away with crowding you when you're leading him:** If the horse starts coming into your space, use your right elbow to jab him in the shoulder.

Dragging

Few things are as aggravating as having a horse drag you when you lead him. Plenty of horses demonstrate this bad habit, and it requires considerable work to correct.

Try the following techniques to cope with a horse who likes to drag you:

- **Lead the horse in a bridle instead of a halter and lead rope:** The bridle gives you more control and makes the horse less likely to rush forward.

- **Keep the horse's head bent slightly to the left to keep the horse from pushing into you.**

- **Ask an experienced horseperson to help you affix a *stud chain* (an 8-inch chain made for use on horses) to the horse's halter, to go over the bridge of the nose:** This chain makes it uncomfortable for the horse to pull you along while you lead him.

If you are a newcomer to horses and find yourself handling a horse who repeatedly drags you whenever you try to walk alongside him, you have a serious problem. Have someone more experienced handle this horse and work on solving the problem before you try to lead the horse. The experienced handler can teach the horse not to drag and teach you what to do to avoid being dragged. Horses who are prone to dragging tend to pull this stunt even more with inexperienced horsepeople.

Lungeing Around

Riding is only one way of exercising your horse. You can also do something called lungeing, where you stand in the center of an imaginary 60-foot circle while your horse moves around you at a walk, trot, and canter.

Why lunge your horse? Can't you just ride the horse for exercise? You can, but then you'd be passing up on all the benefits that lungeing provides you and your horse. For example:

- ✔ **Lungeing is a way of providing controlled exercise to your horse on days that you can't ride:** It's safer than turning a horse out to run around on his own because with lungeing, you can control the horse's behavior and keep him from doing something to hurt himself.

- ✔ **Lungeing before riding helps a horse get rid of excess energy that can create problems when you are in the saddle.**

- ✔ **Lungeing teaches your horse to respect your authority and respond to voice commands.**

Tools for lungeing

Before you can lunge your horse, you must have the proper tools. These include:

- ✔ A 25- to 30-foot long cotton or nylon lunge line to attach to the horse and hold in your hand

- ✔ A halter, lungeing cavesson, or English snaffle bridle to go over the horse's head and attach to the lunge line

- ✔ A lunge whip to encourage the horse to move forward

- ✔ A secure area with good footing (not wet and slippery, and not hard) big enough to lunge your horse

- ✔ Riding gloves to help you keep a good grip on the lunge line and to protect your hands

Preparing the horse

Before you start lungeing the horse, you need to properly prepare and fit the equipment described in the previous section. Have an experienced horse-person who knows how to lunge help you the first few times, and follow these steps:

1. **If you plan ride your horse after lungeing him, tack the horse up in his saddle, tightening the girth or cinch securely.**

   If you ride in an English saddle, be sure that the stirrup irons are run up to the top of the leathers so the irons don't bounce against the horse when he's moving. To secure them there, wrap the leathers tightly around the irons.

2. **Consider outfitting your horse with protective leg wear (which we describe in Chapter 6).**

3a. **If you use a snaffle bridle, outfit the horse in the bridle, prepare the reins, and attach the lunge line to the bridle.**

   Secure the reins by putting them over the horse's head as if you were going to ride, twisting them a few times, unbuckling the throatlatch, and then rebuckling the throatlatch with the reins underneath so they don't swing when the horse moves.

   To attach the lunge line to the bridle, run the clip end of the lunge line through the left bit ring and up over the horse's head behind the ears. Clip the lunge line to the bit ring on the other side of the bridle.

3b. **If you're lungeing your horse with a halter, attach the lunge line to the halter.**

   Run the clip end of the lunge line through the ring on the left side of the halter. Pull the lunge line up over the horse's ears, and then clip it to the ring on the right side of the halter. Make sure that the halter is snug so that it doesn't slide sideways on the horse's head when you begin lungeing.

3c. **If you're using a lungeing cavesson, outfit the horse with the cavesson and attach the lunge line to the cavesson.**

   Simply clip the lunge line to the ring on the cavesson in the center of the top of the noseband, which should be about 4 inches behind the horse's nostrils. Make sure that the cavesson is snug on the horse's head so that it doesn't slide around.

Figure 13-6 shows how to rig up a horse for lungeing.

Before you attempt to lunge your horse, make sure that the horse has been trained to lunge. If you're not sure whether he's been lunged, ask an experienced horseperson to try lungeing the horse to see whether the animal knows what's expected of him.

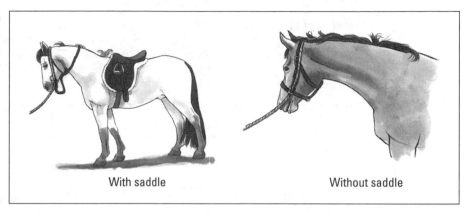

Figure 13-6:
The correct way to rig up a horse for lungeing with a saddle and snaffle bridle, and using a halter.

With saddle   Without saddle

Lungeing your horse

If your horse has been trained to lunge and is an obedient sort, lungeing can be an easy task, once you know what you're doing. Realize, though, that lungeing takes practice.

We strongly recommend that you have an experienced horseperson help you the first few times you lunge your horse to make sure that you and the horse are doing it right.

Take these steps when lungeing your horse:

1. **Prepare your horse we as describe in the previous section, and take your horse to a secure area with plenty of room to work.**

2. **Imagine a large circle, and position your horse so that he's prepared to move in a clockwise direction on that circle.**

   Hold the part of the lunge line attached to the horse's head in your right hand. Fold up the excess lunge line in your left hand. Hold the lunge whip in your left hand, too.

3. **Tell your horse "Ho!" and step away from the animal.**

   As you back up, feed out some of the excess lunge line so you don't pull on the horse's head.

4. **Back up until you're about 4 feet from the horse. Point the lunge whip toward the horse's hindquarters.**

   If your horse knows voice commands, tell him to "walk out." If not, cluck to the horse to get him to walk forward. As the horse starts to move, slowly back up until you're about 10 feet away from him.

5. **Adjust your position relative to the horse.**

   You should be standing at the top of an imaginary triangle. The horse's body makes up the base, and the lunge line and lunge whip the other two sides. Your body should be behind the horse's eye, at an angle. Staying in this position keeps the horse moving forward. See Figure 13-7 for the correct position while lungeing.

   Keep the horse walking in a clockwise direction for five minutes.

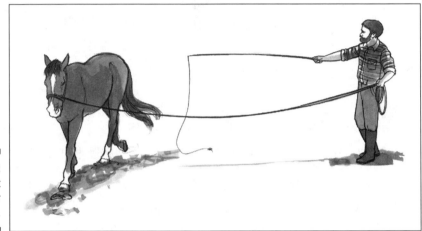

Figure 13-7:
The correct
position for
lungeing.

6. **Change directions.**

   Point the whip upright and tell the horse "Ho!" When the horse stops, slowly approach his head, taking up the slack in the lunge line as you go. Be sure to keep the whip pointing up so you don't confuse the horse.

7. **Place your hand on the lunge line about 4 inches from where it attaches to the horse's head.**

   Turn the horse around so he faces the opposite direction. Reverse the position of the lunge line and whip. You should now be holding the part of the lunge line attached to the horse in your left hand, and the excess lunge line and whip in your right.

8. **Ask the horse to "walk out" again, adjusting your position as in Step 5.**

   Work your horse at different speeds, changing direction every five minutes. To get the horse to go faster, tell the horse "Trot on" and then "Canter." If the horse doesn't know voice commands, cluck until the horse speeds up to the gait you're looking for. Cluck to the horse again if he breaks into a slower gait.

9. **To stop, step slightly out of your position so that you are even with the horse's head, and say "Ho!"**

   The horse should halt on command.

10. **If your horse has worked up a sweat on the lunge line, cool him down by walking him for at least 10-15 minutes.**

Things to remember when lungeing

Safety issues abound on the subject of lungeing. Keep all of these points in mind when exercising your horse this way:

- ✔ **Lunge your horse only in an enclosed area in case he somehow gets away from you.**

- ✔ **Get help while you're new to lungeing:** Make sure that your horse is quiet and well-behaved while lungeing before you start doing it on your own.

- ✔ **Don't lunge for long periods (20 minutes is more than enough), or too often (twice a week maximum):** Exercising in a tight circle is hard on the horse's legs. Give your horse plenty of walking breaks, especially if he's out of shape. If your horse isn't used to being lunged, build up slowly to longer work periods, starting out with a 10-minute session and moving up gradually in 5-minute increments per week.

- ✔ **Never loop, coil, or wrap the excess lunge line around your hand:** You can be seriously injured if the horse pulls away from you.

- ✔ **Some horses get pretty spunky when they're lungeing, so stay far enough away that you won't be kicked should the horse start frolicking on the lunge line.**

- ✔ **Be cautious with the lunge whip:** Don't use it to strike your horse, and be careful not to wave it around, especially in the horse's direction.

- ✔ **So as not to confuse your horse, try not to talk while you're lungeing except to give voice commands to your horse.**

- ✔ **When giving voice commands, carefully enunciate and differentiate each command so the horse can distinguish between them.**

Chapter 14

Choosing a Riding Style

· ·

In This Chapter

▶ Getting to know the disciplines

▶ Finding the best discipline for you

· ·

*O*ne of the coolest things about horseback riding is that you can ride in so many different ways. Humans have been riding horses for thousands of years, so they've had plenty of time to create a whole bunch of different styles (*disciplines* in horse lingo), many of which are still in use today.

Before you buy a horse or even take riding lessons, you have to figure out which discipline is for you. Don't confuse discipline with sport, however. One discipline can cover several different sports. For example, cutting is just one of many sports within the western riding discipline. For a rundown of the different equine sports, see Chapter 18.

In this chapter, we describe the most common forms of riding to help you get a handle on the style you want to pursue.

The Most Popular Ways to Ride

Nearly everyone who rides has a favorite riding discipline. As a budding equestrian, you need to find one, too, so you will know exactly how you'll be riding your horse. You don't have to be married to a discipline forever, but you should at least start with a commitment to riding in it. You can always switch to another discipline later on.

Your choice of a riding style is a very personal one. You should choose a discipline that you find attractive and feel comfortable in. The style you choose may be one that you've always admired from afar, or one that your friends participate in. Realize, however, that each discipline calls for different skills. You may have more talent for one than another.

Before you choose your riding discipline, do some research. Read up on the history of the discipline and the equine sports that ride in the discipline. Be sure to take some lessons in the discipline *before* you make the serious commitment of buying a horse trained in that style — and the tack to go with it. What looks good to you from the ground may not feel comfortable when you're in the saddle.

The most popular riding styles in the United States and Canada today are hunt seat, dressage, saddle seat, and western. The following sections tell you a bit about the history of each, the sports that utilize them, and some basics about riding the different styles.

Hunt seat

Few feelings are more exhilarating than the sensation of cantering along on a horse in a hunt-seat saddle. If you study this discipline, you'll discover that wonderful sensation. The English discipline of hunt seat gets its name from the British sport of fox hunting. Unlike fox hunting, most hunt-seat riding takes place in an arena, although plenty of hunt-seat riders also *hack* (ride on the trail). Hunt seat is probably the most popular discipline in the world.

If you want to jump with your horse, hunt-seat is the discipline for you. Some riders who master hunt seat eventually move on to a sport called *show jumping.* Show jumping is similar to hunt-seat competition, but it's not for the faint of heart because the jumps are higher, and time and speed are of the essence.

Its uses

Hunt-seat is the style of choice for many people who participate in horse shows. In hunt-seat competitions, judges rate riders *over fences* (evaluating the horse and/or rider for their skill over a course of jumps) and *on the flat* (judging horse and/or rider in the arena at the walk, trot, and canter). Competitive hunt-seat classes are held within different divisions determined by age and expertise of either the horse or rider.

People ride many different breeds in hunt seat, although Thoroughbreds are the horses you see most often in this discipline.

The tack

Logically enough, hunt-seat riding uses hunt-seat saddles. Varying only slightly in style from one to another (you see all-purpose saddles and show jumping saddles most commonly), these saddles allow close contact with the horse's body. The seat is rather shallow and the stirrups are kept relatively short.

Hunt-seat headgear usually consists of a single rein bridle with a bit that offers direct contact with the horse's mouth. One exception is the pelham bit, which uses two reins (see Chapter 6 for more information about the tack that riders use in hunt seat).

The ride

Hunt seat is an excellent discipline to study if you want to develop good balance on horseback. Because hunt-seat saddles are small, your margin for error is also small. You have to learn to ride well to ride hunt seat.

If you choose to ride hunt seat, judges will expect you to sit in the saddle — maintaining correct body position — as the horse walks. Figure 14-1 shows a hunt-seat rider in correct position. At the trot, you have to *sit the trot,* which means to sit firmly in the saddle. You must also *post the trot,* which is the action of lifting your rear end up out of the saddle and bringing it back down again, all to the rhythm of the horse's gait. At the canter, you lean slightly forward and move with the horse's body, with your seat firmly in the saddle.

Figure 14-1:
A rider in correct hunt-seat position.

If you plan to jump on horseback (and most hunt-seat riders do) you have to learn to maintain the *two-point position* while the horse actually negotiates the jump. The position requires that you bring your torso forward over the horse's neck while lifting your bottom off the saddle.

Dressage

Dressage, an English discipline, is one of the oldest riding styles in the world. Its roots lie in ancient European military maneuvers. Consequently, this type of riding has long been popular in Europe. Over the past decade, dressage has become rather popular in North America, too.

Its uses

Dressage is primarily a competitive discipline, although not in the same sense as other equine sports. Dressage competitors strive to achieve different skill levels, which are measured by tests. The dressage levels of mastery are called Introductory Level, First Level, Second Level, Third Level, Fourth Level, and Olympic Level. At dressage events, the riders with the highest scores receive ribbons, but most dressage riders care more about the quality of their own test scores rather than those of the other competitors.

The discipline of dressage is designed to focus on and emphasize the horse's natural movements. For both horse and rider, this discipline is one of the most difficult to master. Riders trained in dressage work very hard, which ultimately ranks them among the best riders in the world.

Warmbloods are the most popular breed for upper-level dressage, although plenty of riders compete in regional and local events on Quarter Horses, Thoroughbreds, Appaloosas, Morgans, Saddlebreds, and many other breeds.

You can apply many of the skills you learn in dressage to other riding disciplines, including hunt seat, western, and saddle seat.

The tack

The discipline of dressage calls for a dressage saddle, which looks much like a hunt-seat saddle to the untrained eye. Closer scrutiny reveals that the seat of a dressage saddle is deeper than that of a hunt-seat saddle. The flaps of a dressage saddle are also wider and at a greater angle to the seat. Finally, you wear the stirrups lower in dressage than in hunt seat.

As far as bridles go, dressage bridles don't vary too much from the bridles you see in hunt seat.

The ride

To master dressage, both you and your horse must be pretty athletic. Many people compare dressage to ballet because it calls for the same kind of grace and discipline from the horse. You have to become a very good rider to exact that sort of bearing from your horse.

If you pursue dressage, you practice riding at the walk, trot, and canter. At the trot, you're taught to *post* (move up and down in the saddle to the rhythm of the horse's movement), and also to sit firmly in the saddle at the trot. Figure 14-2 shows a dressage rider in correct position in the saddle.

Figure 14-2:
A dressage rider in correct position.

Western

Thanks to Hollywood, almost everyone is familiar with the discipline of western riding. Every cowboy movie showcases western riding (although not the best execution of it, we've noticed).

Both western riding and the western saddle are creations that arose in the American West. This relatively large saddle was the perfect invention for the men who worked cattle on the range from dawn to dusk and traveled long distances on horseback.

Its uses

Those who work cattle in the West still use western riding, but its biggest function is as a form of pleasure and show riding.

Western shows and rodeos take place around the country by the thousands each year, sporting classes such as western pleasure, trail, gymkhana, reining, roping, and cutting. In each of these sports, the western saddle and the style of riding associated with it is the only discipline permitted.

The discipline of western riding is also a favorite of those equestrians who ride for the sheer joy of it. Trail riders throughout North America ride in western saddles, primarily because of the saddle's comfort and the discipline's relaxed style.

The Quarter Horse has nearly cornered the western riding market, although breeds like the Appaloosa and Paint are also popular western horses. Because of the western saddle's design, you don't often see rangy Thoroughbreds and other high-withered breeds not suited to wearing the saddle in this discipline.

The tack

The tack you use in western riding is one of the neatest things about the discipline. The western saddle, with its high pommel and cantle, and its very distinct horn, differs considerably from the English saddle. This difference isn't surprising because the primary influences for the Western saddle came from Spain and Mexico, not Britain. The western saddle's stirrups are also very different in that they consist of large fenders, and are sewn directly onto the saddle's body. Unlike English saddles, the stirrups themselves are not made of iron, but are wooden with a leather covering.

Even the girth of a western saddle — more correctly called a *cinch* — is different. Unlike the English version, a part of the saddle called a *latigo strap* holds the western saddle on the horse. You must loop the strap through the girth and knot it high on the cinch ring.

Western bridles also differ considerably from their English counterparts. Typically, western bridles consist of a leather headstall and not much else. Some bridles bear brow bands and throatlatches, but many don't. The bit is almost always a curb bit — although snaffles are becoming more popular, and are usually used without curb shanks for training. A curb chain is present on every western bridle that bears curb shanks (see Chapter 6 for an explanation of the different parts of a western bridle).

The ride

If you like the idea of relaxing when you ride, western riding may be the discipline for you. You wear western stirrups long, and you learn to lean back slightly as you ride, keeping a loose rein on the horse. In this position, you and your horse can travel comfortably for hours. Figure 14-3 shows a western rider in correct position.

Figure 14-3:
A western
rider in
correct
position.

In the western discipline, the horse's gaits are known as the walk, jog, and lope, as opposed to walk, trot, and canter in the English disciplines. These gaits are considerably slower than what you experience when riding English. Generally speaking, if you ride a western horse, you experience an animal who has been trained to have quiet, leisurely gaits. The exception is a competitive rodeo horse trained to sprint around barrels and chase down cows.

Saddle seat

Saddle seat is considered an English discipline, although it's become uniquely American. You don't see as much saddle seat as the other English disciplines in most parts of the country, but this riding style nonetheless has its very dedicated followers.

Its uses

The roots of saddle seat riding lie in the American South, where the discipline is still popular today. You primarily see saddle seat on horses with high leg action, most often gaited horses like American Saddlebreds, Tennessee Walking Horses, and Racking Horses (see Chapter 4 for more information on gaited horses).

The main purpose of the saddle seat discipline is competition, although many saddle seat riders also enjoy trail riding. Shows for American gaited breeds always contain saddle seat classes, as do many shows for Morgans and Arabians. Saddle seat classes are judged on either the horse's action or the rider's position in the saddle (equitation). For a horse to be successful in saddle seat competition, he must be a very flashy animal.

The tack

Saddle seat riding uses a *show saddle,* which is a type of English saddle, although it's quite different from both the hunt-seat saddle and the dressage saddle. Show saddles are flatter than other English saddles, have a shallower seat, and feature a design that allows the horse's shoulders to move freely as the animal demonstrates high, front-end action. This design causes the rider to sit far behind the horse's withers, taking the rider's weight off the front part of the horse. The stirrups are worn rather long, similar to the length of the dressage rider's stirrups.

The bridle that saddle seat typically uses varies considerably from other English bridles. Called a *double bridle,* this piece of equipment features two bits and two sets of reins. One set of reins controls the curb bit, which you use to establish and maintain the horse's head set. The other set of reins controls a snaffle bit, which helps keep the horse's head up high. Riders need considerable dexterity and skill because they must use each set of reins separately instead of together, which is the usual tendency.

The ride

If you choose to ride saddle seat on a gaited horse, you'll notice the four-beat gaits of breeds such as the American Saddlebred, the Tennessee Walking Horse, and the Racking Horse provide a completely different experience than riding a so-called "trotting horse." The fact that you're sitting in a saddle that puts your legs out in front of you instead of beneath you like most other disciplines (see Figure 14-4) makes the ride even more unrivaled in feeling.

Figure 14-4:
A saddle seat rider in correct position.

The most exciting aspect of the saddle seat discipline is the way that it allows you to show off the horse you're riding. Sitting astride an animal who commands the attention of spectators with his flashy style and assertive presence is an exhilarating benefit of the saddle seat discipline.

Less-Popular (But Still Cool) Styles

Hunt seat, dressage, western, and saddle seat are the four most popular riding styles in the United States and Canada. However, they're certainly not the *only* styles of riding. Equestrians around the country use other riding forms, each with its own unique history and particular usage. Some of these styles are actual disciplines, while others don't require formal training.

If you want to pursue one of the actual disciplines we discuss here, you'll need to do some work finding a riding instructor who can teach them. Finding an instructor for a less-popular discipline isn't as easy as finding someone who gives western riding lessons, but the trouble of ferreting out an instructor may just be worth it to you when you come to appreciate the uniqueness of each type of riding.

Peruvian

Despite the fact that several American gaited breeds exist, Americans haven't cornered the market on gaited horses. The Peruvian Paso is a gaited breed that is becoming more popular in the United States of late (see Chapter 4 for more information on gaited horses).

Although you can also ride them in the more common disciplines, Peruvian Pasos have a discipline that's unique to the breed. Tradition dictates that you show these horses in their native discipline. Some purists insist on riding Peruvian Pasos in the breed's native tack at all times, even when merely going for a jaunt on the trail.

In Peru, people ride the Peruvian Paso in an incredibly comfortable saddle that has wide, flat skirts, a high pommel and cantle, and a leather-hooded stirrup. The traditional Peruvian Paso bridle is quite elaborate, featuring a bosal type halter, a piece called a *gamarilla,* which holds the bit, and a wide brow band known as a *tapa ojo.*

Riding a Peruvian Paso in his traditional tack is very fun, although you must specifically learn the Peruvian discipline. Many of the skills you learn in English and western riding aren't applicable in this discipline. Saddle seat riding probably bears the closest resemblance to the Peruvian discipline.

Australian

Not too long ago, North Americans discovered the wonders of the Australian stock saddle, a piece of tack that looks like a cross between a dressage saddle and a western saddle. Created by Australian riders who needed a light saddle with an easy seat for long rides through the outback, the Australian stock saddle has become the saddle of choice for many trail and endurance riders.

Australian stock saddles come in a few different styles, but each has two things in common: a comfortable seat for the rider, and a comfortable fit for the horse. Those who ride many hours on the trail in endurance and competitive trail rides describe the Australian stock saddle as ideal for their sport.

In North America, riders — depending on their preference — use English or western bridles with Australian stock saddles. The use of bridle isn't terribly important in this instance because riding in an Australian stock saddle doesn't call for the mastery of a new discipline. Riders who are experienced in hunt seat and dressage disciplines are most comfortable in an Australian stock saddle, although western riders also have little trouble adapting to it.

Sidesaddle

It's hard to imagine in this day and age that people used to consider it improper for a woman to sit astride a horse. Until the 20th century, however, this belief was essentially the social more when it came to riding.

For women, the answer to this expectation was something called the sidesaddle, a piece of equipment that allowed female riders a secure seat while keeping both legs on one side of the horse. In the sidesaddle, the left leg fits in the stirrup as it would in a conventional saddle, while the right leg rests over a fixed pommel situated on the left side of the saddle.

At first, society women simply rode sidesaddle when they needed to get from one place to another on horseback. Eventually, women were able to ride along on fox hunts, thanks to the invention of something called the *leapers horn,* which made them secure enough to sit a jumping horse.

Today, a relatively small group of female equestrians are keeping the tradition of sidesaddle alive, praising its elegance and historical significance. Using modern sidesaddles in either English or western design with corresponding bridles, they ride in arenas and on the trail in this discipline. They also show in antique saddles, most from the 1800s, while wearing period costumes appropriate to the saddle's age.

Sidesaddle calls for a skilled rider and a very obedient horse. Unlike astride disciplines, the aside discipline of sidesaddle doesn't permit the rider to give leg cues from the right. Sidesaddle riders must use a sidesaddle crop to direct the horse on the right side, while using standard leg pressure on the left. To learn this discipline, you need an instructor who is well versed in this form of riding.

Bareback

Before the invention of saddles, human beings rode bareback. This riding method worked well for transportation purposes. Humans didn't decide they needed saddles until they figured out they could wage war on horseback.

Today, many equestrians ride bareback. Bareback riding is not a discipline per se, but actually just another way of enjoying your horse. Riders who indulge in bareback riding don't usually ride *only* bareback, but do so for an occasional change of pace. Some even show in bareback riding classes, usually seen only at western shows.

Bareback riding makes you feel closer to your horse. When cantering along without a saddle, you almost feel as though you are one with the animal. Our ancient ancestors must have savored this exciting feeling.

Bareback riding is good for beginners because it helps create a secure and confident riding seat. You can't rely on the confines of a saddle to keep you on the horse when you are riding bareback. Instead, you must learn to balance in order to stay on. Another bonus of bareback riding is that it saves you time: You don't need to spend an extra 5 to 10 minutes saddling up your horse on the days you plan to ride bareback.

Although bareback riding can help you develop a good seat, the downside is that falling off a horse is much easier when you're riding bareback. Gripping the mane can help, but if your horse is bucking, spinning, or pulling some other athletic stunt, chances are that you're going to eat some dirt.

Driving

Humans have been putting the cart after the horse for millennia, and still do so today. For many elderly and physically challenged equestrians who are physically unable to ride — and for those who simply don't like to ride — driving is the equine sport of choice.

Many people hitch up their horses to carts and drive for the sheer joy of it, although others are serious competitors in the driving show ring. Several breed shows have driving classes that feature one or two horses pulling different types of vehicles, as well as events with six- to eight-horse draft teams hauling wagons the way they did before the advent of the automotive engine.

Horses must be specially trained to drive; some learn the style in their early preriding training. Horses who are trained to drive are taught to pull weight (instead of carry it), and they can be steered in a completely different way than when they're ridden. Drivers must train for this discipline as well. This training includes learning to handle the reins used in driving, which are very different from riding reins.

Chapter 15

Preparing to Ride

. . . .

In This Chapter

▶ Saddling up!

▶ Reining in!

. . . .

*U*nless you're wealthy — or starring in a movie — you won't have the luxury of having someone bring your saddled and bridled horse out to you every time you want to ride. No, the task of *tacking up,* as horse people call it, falls squarely upon your shoulders. Of course, in order to truly become an accomplished horseperson, you need to be able to tack up a horse anyway.

So how hard can this task be? You just toss the saddle on, stick the bit in the horse's mouth, and ride off, right? Wrong! In order to properly tack up a horse, you need to know what you're doing so the saddle sits in the right place on the horse's back, so the bit and bridle fit comfortably, and so the horse will let you near him with all this stuff in the first place!

Although the basics of tacking up for English and western riding are essentially the same, the differences are enough to make the process a bit confusing. We'll try to unravel all those straps and buckles for you in this chapter so you have a fundamental understanding of how to prepare a horse for riding.

Tacking on the Saddle and Accessories

The saddle and accessories always go on before the bridle when tacking up a horse; you need the horse's halter to secure him while you saddle up. After you bridle the horse, the halter comes off.

Before you attempt to tack up a horse on your own, have an experienced horseperson demonstrate the steps for you. After you watch the process a few times, you're ready to try it on your own — with supervision. Don't attempt to tack up a horse all by yourself until whomever is supervising you assures you that you have the process down pat.

Before you start saddling up, do the following:

- Tie your horse securely by his halter to a hitching post (using a quick release knot) or cross-ties.

- Groom your horse thoroughly, being careful to brush down the hairs on the back and the girth area (see Chapter 1 for a diagram showing the parts of the horse). Make sure that no pieces of dirt, bedding, or other foreign objects are stuck to your horse's back or girth area.

- Check your saddle blanket and girth or cinch to make sure that no burrs, sticks, or other items are clinging to the underside.

Know what you are doing when you put on a horse's saddle. Correctly positioning and fastening the saddle on your horse's back is extremely important. A poor saddling job can result in discomfort or injury to both you and your horse. The diagrams in Figure 15-1 show correct placement of English and western saddles.

Figure 15-1:
Correct placement of English and western saddles on the horse's back.

Western

English

English

First, familiarize yourself with the parts of the English saddle (refer to Chapter 6). Then, follow these steps to saddle a horse with an English saddle, beginning on the horse's left side (this protocol is important — all tasks concerning the horse's body begin with a left-side approach):

1. **Lay the pad over the horse's back.**

   Stand on the horse's left side and position the front of the pad a few inches above the horse's withers, at the base of the neck.

2. **Slide the pad backward a couple of inches so the front edge of the pad is still covering the withers.**

Don't slide the pad forward if you need to reposition it because doing so ruffles the hairs underneath, resulting in irritation to the horse while you ride. Check both sides of the horse to make sure that the amount of pad is even on the left and the right.

3. **Pick up the saddle.**

Grasp the front of the saddle in your left hand and the back of the saddle in your right. Make sure that the stirrup irons have been pushed up to the top of the stirrup leathers so they don't flop around while you handle the saddle.

4. **Place the saddle gently on the horse's back in the hollow just below the withers.**

About 3 inches of the pad should be showing in front of the saddle. To determine whether the saddle is correctly positioned on the horse's back, look to see whether the girth, when attached to the saddle, will fit just behind the horse's elbows (refer to Figure 15-1 for the correct position of a English saddle).

5. **Slide the girth straps on the left side of the saddle through the tab on your saddle pad (see Chapter 6 for a diagram that shows the parts of the English saddle).**

Go to the horse's right side and do the same.

6. **Fasten the girth to the right side of the saddle.**

You usually don't store English girths attached to the saddle, so your girth will probably be detached. Three girth straps hang there, but you only need two. The third one is just in case one of the other straps breaks.

Bring the girth over to the right side of the horse and fasten the girth's buckles to the two outside girth straps that are hanging from the saddle. Fasten the buckles about half way up each girth strap.

7. **Fasten the girth to the left side of the saddle.**

Move to the left side of the horse and reach underneath to grasp the girth. Follow the same buckling procedure that you did in Step 6. Be sure that the girth is resting just behind the horse's elbows, and that it isn't twisted. Buckle tight enough to make the girth snug.

8. **Gradually tighten the girth on the left side over a period of several minutes (so as not to shock the horse with one sharp pull) until it's snug enough that the saddle doesn't move.**

If you run out of holes on your left-side girth straps , begin tightening the buckles on the right. Figure 15-2 shows how you tighten an English girth.

Figure 15-2:
Tightening
the girth on
an English
saddle.

9. **Check your stirrup length.**

   Before you mount, it's best to determine whether your stirrups are the correct length for your legs. You can check pretty reliably by holding the reins in your left hand while sliding your right hand, palm down, under the flap of the saddle where the stirrup leather attaches to the saddle. Using your left hand, grasp the stirrup iron and pull it toward the crook of your arm, allowing the stirrup leather to lay flush against the bottom of your outstretched arm. If the stirrup iron fits snugly in the crook of your arm, the stirrups are most likely the correct length for your leg. If the stirrups are too long or too short, the problem will be obvious relative to your arm length.

   If your stirrups need lengthening or shortening, adjust them by using the buckle on the stirrup leather.

10. **Stretch the horse's legs to prevent pinching.**

    Standing at the front of the horse, pull the left leg toward you to stretch out the skin under the girth so it doesn't pinch the horse. Do the same with the horse's right foreleg.

You may need to repeat Step 8 after leading your horse around, before you mount. Many horses have a tendency to puff up their bellies by holding their breath while you tighten the girth. Before you get on, make sure that the girth is snug enough that it feels tight if you put your fingers between it and the horse's body. If you can't get your fingers in there, the girth is too tight and needs to be let out a notch.

Western

Before you start, familiarize yourself with the parts of the western saddle (refer to Chapter 6). Then follow these steps to saddle a horse with a western saddle:

1. **Lay the pad over the horse's back.**

   Stand on the horse's left side (this protocol is important — all tasks concerning the horse's body begin with a left-side approach) and position the front of the pad a few inches above the horse's withers, at the base of the neck.

2. **Slide the pad backward a couple of inches so the front edge of the pad is still covering the withers.**

   Don't slide the pad forward if you need to reposition it because doing so ruffles the hairs underneath, resulting in irritation to the horse while you ride. Check both sides of the horse to make sure that the amount of pad is even on the left and the right.

3. **Prepare the saddle.**

   On a western saddle, the cinch is permanently attached to the right side. Before you approach the horse, flip the cinch up and over so it drapes across the seat. Take the right stirrup and loop it over the saddle horn.

4. **Bring the saddle to the horse.**

   Grasp the front of the saddle in your left hand and the back of the saddle in your right. Approach the horse's left side.

5. **Place the saddle on the horse's back.**

   From the left side of the horse, swing the saddle up and over, and place it gently on the horse's back. The saddle should sit in the hollow just below the withers with about 3 inches of the pad showing in front. To determine whether the saddle is correctly positioned on the horse's back, look to see whether the cinch, when attached to the saddle, will fit just behind the horse's elbows (refer to Figure 15-1 for the correct position of a western saddle).

6. **Walk around to the right side of the horse and undrape the cinch so it hangs down.**

   Unloop the stirrup from the saddle horn and let it hang as well.

7. **Secure the saddle with the cinch.**

   From the left side of the horse, reach underneath and take up the cinch. Run the latigo strap through the ring of the cinch, and then feed the strap through the same dee ring on the saddle where it's attached (see Chapter 6 for a diagram showing the parts of the western saddle).

Continue to loop the latigo strap through the two rings until you have about 12 inches of free strap coming from the ring attached to the saddle. See Figure 15-3 to find out how to tie the knot.

8. **Check your stirrup length.**

Before you mount, determine whether your stirrups are the correct length for your legs. You can check this pretty reliably by holding the reins in your left hand while sliding your right hand, palm down, under the flap of the saddle where the stirrup leather attaches to the saddle. Using your left hand, grasp the stirrup and pull it toward the crook of your arm, allowing the stirrup leather to lay flush against the bottom of your outstetched arm. If the stirrup fits snugly in the crook of your arm, the stirrups are most likely the correct length for your leg. If the stirrups are too long or too short, the problem will be obvious relative to your arm length.

If your stirrups need lengthening or shortening, adjust them by using the buckle flap underneath the stirrup leather.

9. **Make sure that the cinch is snug enough that the saddle won't move, but not so snug that you can't fit the fingers of a flat hand between the cinch and the horse's body.**

To tighten the cinch, loosen the knot, and pull up on the outside layer of strap between the dee and cinch rings.

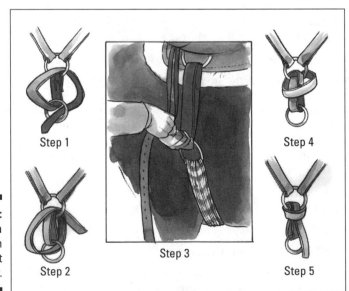

Figure 15-3:
You tie a western cinch knot this way.

Step 1

Step 2

Step 3

Step 4

Step 5

Check the cinch again after walking your horse a little and before mounting. You may need to retighten the cinch if your horse has a tendency to hold his breath when you cinched him up.

Putting on the Bridle

The bridle goes on last, because after you bridle your horse, you can't tie him up again until you finish with your ride.

Before you start to bridle your horse, do the following:

✔ Tie the horse securely by his halter to a hitching post (using a quick release knot) or cross-ties.

✔ Groom and saddle the horse.

✔ Check the bridle to make sure that the *noseband* (the part that goes around the nose) and *throatlatch* (the strap that fastens around the horse's jowls) on an English bridle are unbuckled. If you have a throat-latch on a western bridle, make sure that it's unbuckled, too.

✔ Have an experienced horseperson help you determine whether the bit size is correct, and how short the straps should be on the headstall, if your horse has never worn this particular bridle.

The steps for putting on an English and western bridle are nearly the same. Familiarize yourself with the parts of both bridles before you begin (refer to Chapter 6). Then, follow these steps to put on the bridle:

1. **Secure the horse with the halter.**

   Standing at the horse's left side, unbuckle the halter, slide the noseband off, and then rebuckle the halter around the horse's neck (Figure 15-4 shows how the halter fits around the horse's neck).

2. **Put the reins over the horse's head so they lay on the horse's neck.**

3. **Hold the bit and headstall and stand at the left side of your horse's head, facing the same direction that your horse is facing.**

   Grasp the top of the headstall in your right hand and the bit in your left hand. Let the bit lay against your outstretched fingers. Stand next to the horse's head, facing forward in the same direction as the horse.

4. **Place your right hand (still holding the headstall) just on top of the horse's head, behind the ears.**

   If you can't reach above the horse's head, you can instead reach your arm under the horse's jaw and around to the right side of the horse's head so your right hand and headstall are just above the horse's forehead, or above the bridge of his nose.

5. **Open the horse's mouth and insert the bit.**

   With your left thumb, gently press down on the inside corner of the horse's lip to open his mouth and gently guide the bit into the horse's mouth, being careful not to bang it against his front teeth. Raise the headstall in your right hand until the bit slides all the way in to the horse's mouth.

6. **Gently slide the headstall over the horse's ears.**

   The bridle is now in place.

7. **Buckle the throatlatch and noseband, if any.**

   English bridle: The throatlatch and noseband should be snug, but not so tight that you can't get three fingers between it and the horse.

   Western bridle: You probably won't have a noseband to tighten. If the bridle has a throatlatch, make sure that two fingers fit between the horse and the strap.

   Curb chain or strap: If one of these is attached to the bit, make sure that it's loose when you let the reins relax but makes contact with the horse's chin when you pull the bit shanks back at a 45-degree angle.

8. **Unbuckle the halter from your horse's neck.**

   If you plan to mount where you are, leave the reins over your horse's neck. If you want to lead your horse to another area for mounting, remove the reins from around your horse's neck and lead the horse by the reins.

Figure 15-4 shows how to put on English and western bridles.

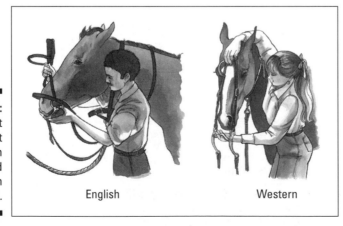

Figure 15-4:
The correct way to put on both an English and western bridle.

English

Western

Chapter 16

Handling Your Horse in the Saddle

● ●

In This Chapter

▶ Mounting your horse

▶ Holding the reins

▶ Taking riding lessons

▶ Coping with equine misbehavior

● ●

Something amazing happens when a human climbs aboard the back of a horse. If the rider knows how to communicate with the horse and if the horse is receptive, the resulting experience can be magical.

Achieving this oneness of horse and rider requires hard work. Images in popular culture make riding a horse look like a piece of cake. In actuality, it takes months of practice before you even have a sense of what you're doing.

It's never too late to develop riding skills. With plenty of hard (albeit fun) work, you can become as efficient a rider as any of those cowboy movie stars. But you have to start somewhere.

Getting into the Mind-Set

Before you get up on a horse for the first time (or if you've already been on a horse, make it the first time after reading this chapter), you need to have a basic understand of what riding is all about.

Chances are, you've probably never given much thought to why horses allow people to ride them, because most people just take for granted that horses carry people. But if you think about it, why *do* they?

The key to understanding why horses let humans ride them is *leadership*. Horses are herd animals who seek a leader in any social situation. Generally speaking, human beings have managed to convince the equine species that humans are worthy of that leadership position. So when a human gets up on a horse's back and tells that horse what to do, the horse obeys because he views the rider as his leader.

Of course, this scenario only works if the rider has the leadership qualities that the horse expects. If a rider gets up on a horse without a clue as to what to do and how to do it, the horse will quickly clue in and take over as leader himself.

Of course leadership has its responsibilities too. Leave your bad mood at the front gate when you ride. Your duties are to be patient, kind, and empathetic with your horse, all the while letting the animal know that you are the one in charge.

Take Riding Lessons First

Have you ever ridden a horse who ran away with you, tried to roll on you, rubbed you against a tree, or refused to move as soon as you got on? If not, you probably know someone who has.

Unfortunately, many first-time riders have this kind of experience and it sours them on horses forever. However, if they had taken riding lessons *before* they tried to go out on their own, their experiences may have been much better.

We can't overemphasize the need to take formal riding lessons before you go out and get yourself a horse or start riding regularly on your own. You probably wouldn't dream of going scuba diving without taking lessons first or even doing something as benign as golfing without finding out the rules of the game. With horses, rider training is doubly important — you have to understand the rules and develop the skills before you go it alone.

Where can you get lessons? You have a number of options:

✔ **Commercial stables:** Many commercial riding establishments offer riding lessons, usually in several disciplines. These facilities aren't hard to find — all you need to do is look in the phone book under "riding academies." Before you sign up, visit the stable and observe the lessons. Talk to the instructors and ask them about their experience. Look for instructors who have experience showing horses, have clients who are successful in the show ring, and have a certification by a riding instructor certification program (see Appendix B). If you like the stable and the instructors, sign up for one lesson. If the experience is good, plan to take at least several months worth of lessons.

✔ **Horseback vacations:** The term *dude ranch* conjures up images of city slickers slumped in western saddles, timidly hanging onto the saddle horn as their horses pick their way over steep mountain trails. But these days, dude ranches and other horseback-oriented vacation spots do more than give trail rides to those with only a casual interest in riding. You can take formal riding lessons at many of these places, provided you pick a facility that caters to beginners. A horseback vacation is actually a great place to get started because it not only combines a fun atmosphere with training, but also provides you with one or two weeks of intensive riding. You can follow up this instruction with more lessons when you get home (see Chapter 21 for details on ten great riding vacations).

✔ **Riding clubs:** Horse lovers tend to congregate, which is good news for neophytes who take an interest in horses. Although clubs that exist specifically to teach newcomers are usually aimed at children, they actually offer opportunities for adults, too. One example is the Pony Club, an excellent U.S. and British organization that teaches children (most of whom do *not* own their own horses) horsemanship and riding skills. If both you and your kid want to ride horses, sign your child up with your local Pony Club chapter and volunteer as an adult helper (see Appendix B for information on contacting the Pony Club). If you have a child of college age, consider getting involved with an intercollegiate college riding program.

✔ **An equine expert:** If you live in a very small town or a remote area, you may have trouble finding a commercial riding stable or riding club nearby. In this case, try to find someone locally who can help you with your riding. Ask other horse owners in your town to help you locate an experienced horseperson, such as a breeder, an equine veterinarian, or someone who shows extensively. Ask this expert whether you can hire him or her to teach you to ride. Most horsepeople are more than happy to help newcomers to the hobby provided those newcomers have a sincere and genuine interest.

What *not* to do:

✔ Don't go to a stable that rents out horses by the hour with no instruction. Remember those friends of yours who've been on the back of a runaway horse and rubbed off on trees? Most likely, it happened in this type of place. Owners at most rent-by-hour stables allow the horses to develop bad attitudes and dangerous habits. Such horses are bad news for beginning riders.

✔ Don't let an inexperienced friend give you lessons on his or her horse. If your friend is an experienced rider who owns a suitable horse for beginning riders, then by all means, ask your friend for help. But if your friend has only been riding a short time and has a horse he or she can barely control, politely decline the offer and opt for one of the alternatives we mention earlier.

The amount of time necessary for you to get the hang of riding depends on you. Some people pick it up faster than others. When you are to the point where you feel like you can competently control your horse, both inside and outside the arena, you know enough to begin doing some riding on your own. But remember: You can never know too much when it comes to riding. Heck, even the riders on the Olympic equestrian team still take lessons!

Shaping Up to Ride

You only need to be up on a horse once to discover that riding utilizes muscles that you never even knew you had. Although you don't need to be a super athlete to be a competent rider, the stronger and more flexible you are, the easier riding is on your body.

If you don't already have a regular exercise routine, now may be a good time to start one. (Be sure to talk to your doctor first.) Here are a few things to work on that will enhance your riding abilities:

- **Lose weight:** If you're overweight, it can be more difficult to mount, dismount, cue the horse, and stay comfortable when riding the horse's various gaits. Plus, your excess weight is a hardship for the horse.

- **Build muscle strength:** If you plan to ride English, you need a good amount of arm strength to maintain contact with the horse's mouth via the reins (because most men get sufficient arm strength genetically, women riders should take note!). You also need strong legs to cue the horse, *post* the trot (move up and down in the saddle with the rhythm of the horse's gait), and do a number of other tasks when you are riding.

- **Get flexible:** Most people notice soreness in their legs when they are first training to ride. That's because sitting stretched out across a horse's back creates a big pull on the upper, inner muscles of the thighs. Do stretching exercises for your legs and the rest of your body several times to a week to stay flexible for riding.

Swinging into the Saddle

Before you can ride, you have to get on. For most beginners, mounting is one of the greatest challenges of riding. Adults find it especially difficult because they have a lot more bulk to get up into than saddle than does a child.

As with most things related to horses, a prescribed method exists for mounting. Don't forget, human beings have had a long time to figure out the most efficient way to get up on a horse. Today's methods for mounting are the result of two millennia of trying.

Mounting your horse with great ease and decorum takes practice. In the beginning, we recommend that you have an experienced horse person spot you and make sure that you're doing it right. While this person is observing, have him or her hold onto your horse's bridle for the sake of safety.

Following are the steps for getting up on a horse, both for English and western riding.

Mounting English-style

Many English riders use a mounting block to get on their horses. The mounting block enables you to climb up nearly to the level of the horse's back, where you simply swing your leg over the saddle. A mounting block keeps the saddle from slipping during mounting.

Using a mounting block every time you get up on your horse is perfectly acceptable. However, even if you choose to do so, you should also know how to get on from the ground. If you get off or fall off of your horse out on the trail, or in a place where you don't have a mounting block, you could strand yourself if you don't know how to back get on.

To mount your horse from the ground follow these steps:

1. **Lead your horse to the area where you want to mount.**

   Choose the inside of the arena where you plan to ride, or another safe area.

2. **Position yourself and stay in control of the horse.**

   Place the reins over your horse's head and rest them on his neck. Stand at the horse's left shoulder, facing the back of the horse. The reins should be in your left hand. Grab a handful of mane at the base of the horse's neck with the same hand.

   Never release the reins while you're mounting. You need to keep control of your horse at all times.

3. **Using your right hand, grasp the stirrup iron and turn it toward you. Place your left foot in the stirrup.**

4. **Swing into the saddle.**

   Turn your body toward the horse as you grasp the cantle with your right hand. Bounce on your right leg two or three times and then launch yourself up into the air. Swing your right leg over the horse's hindquarters, being careful not to touch them, and land gently in the saddle.

5. **Place your right foot in the stirrup and gather up your reins.**

Western

Mounting in a western saddle is easier than mounting in an English saddle because western stirrups are relatively longer than English stirrups. Also, western saddles are less likely to slip than English saddles during mounting, and you have more to hold on to on a western saddle:

1. **Lead your horse to the area where you want to mount.**

   Choose the inside of the arena where you plan to ride, or another safe area.

2. **Position yourself and stay in control of the horse.**

   Place the reins over your horse's head. Stand at the horse's left shoulder, facing the back of the horse. The reins should be in your left hand. With the same hand, grab hold of the saddle horn.

   Never let go of the reins while you're mounting. You need to keep control of your horse at all times.

3. **Using your right hand, grasp the stirrup, turn it toward you, and place your left foot in the stirrup.**

4. **Swing into the saddle.**

   Turn your body toward the horse as you grasp the cantle with your right hand. Bounce on your right foot three times and then launch yourself up. Swing your right leg over the horse's hindquarters, being careful not to touch them, and land gently in the saddle.

5. **Place your right foot in the stirrup and gather up your reins.**

Riding Basics

Among the many things you practice when you take riding lessons are what we call *riding basics*. These are the fundamental elements you must know in order to successfully ride a horse.

Holding the reins

Just as you figured out how to hold a knife and fork as a child, you must now figure out the right way to hold the reins when you ride. Holding the reins properly is very important because the reins are one of the primary means of communication between you and your horse.

We describe how to hold the reins both English and western style. In addition to reading our description, we also recommend that you have a trainer or experienced horseperson show you how to do it.

English

Even though the term *reins* is plural, English snaffle bridles have one continuous rein that connects from one side of the bit to the other. The part of the rein that connects to the left side of the bit is the *left rein.* The part on the right side is the *right rein.*

English bridles call for two hands on the reins. When you ride English, you hold the left rein in your left hand and the right rein in your right hand.

To correctly pick up the reins, start with the reins resting on the horse's neck. Reach down and grasp the reins with your palms facing down and your thumbs next to each other. After you have the reins in your hands, rotate your wrists so that your thumbs are at the top (knuckles up) and the knuckles of your fingers are facing each other. Move your pinkies under each rein, so the rein rests between your pinkie and your ring finger. Hold your hands in a relaxed fist.

A common mistake many beginning English riders make is the tendency to balance themselves in the saddle by leaning against the reins. If you do this, you are in essence using the horse's mouth to help keep you in the saddle. This is not only considered poor riding, but it is unfair to the horse. Imagine having 100 pounds or more pulling on your mouth in an effort to keep from falling. Ouch! We know you don't want to do this to any horse you ride, so we suggest that you work hard at developing balance and security in the saddle so you won't feel the need to weigh heavy on the horse's mouth.

Western

Western reins are usually *split reins,* meaning that you have two separate reins, one attached to the right side of the bit, the other attached to the left . While you're still learning to ride, we recommend that you tie a knot in your western reins, right above the area where your hand would normally be when holding them. Knotted reins are safer for beginning riders because they won't fall out of reach should you drop them while riding.

Good footing

Before you get up on your horse and go, check the footing of the area where you plan to ride. If you plan to ride in an arena, be sure the dirt is loose — that is, not hard packed. Conversely, make sure the dirt isn't *so* loose that your horse will have to struggle through it.

Also, be certain that the footing is dry. Wet arenas are among the most dangerous places to ride, lunge, or turn out a horse. A horse can easily slip and fall on wet footing, seriously injuring himself or you in the process.

Western riding calls for the reins to be held in the left hand only. Theoretically, doing so frees up the right hand for roping, an important task for the cowboys who originated this style of riding.

You can hold western reins in one of two styles: traditional and California. These two styles exist purely as regional distinctions, with California style being most popular in California, of course. Either way is correct, although your riding instructor may prefer one instead of the other.

To ride traditional style, grasp the reins in your left fist, with the part of the reins that leads to the bit resting between your thumb and forefinger. As you hold the reins, the nail on your thumb should face skyward while the thumb itself points toward the horse's head.

To hold the reins California style, grasp the reins in your left fist, with your thumbnail upwards. The excess rein should be held in your right hand, which rests on your right thigh.

Position in the saddle

Many people don't realize how important seat position is when riding. Although experienced riders may seem to just casually sit up there, the fact of the matter is that it takes a certain amount of practice and concentration to attain the proper position.

The way you sit in the saddle affects both your comfort and your horse's comfort. It also determines how secure you are in the saddle. Riders with correct position in the saddle are less likely to fall off if the horse moves suddenly in an unexpected direction.

Your exact position in the saddle depends on the discipline you choose to ride in. However, the following basics apply to nearly everyone:

- **Your back:** Keep your back straight when you sit in the saddle. Don't hunch forward, slump your shoulders, or arch your back. Just sit up straight like you were told to do in grade school.

- **Your legs:** Generally speaking, your legs belong directly under you while you're in the saddle. They shouldn't thrust forward ahead of your body or lag behind. (An exception is saddle-seat riding, where the legs come out further ahead of the body than in other disciplines.) Furthermore, the balls of your feet (and nothing more) should rest in the stirrup, your toes should point up and straight ahead or slightly inward, and your heels should pointing down.

- **Your derriere:** Before you get on a horse and in the privacy of your own home, become familiar with your seat bones. These are the two bony points between your thighs and your buttocks (one on each side) that make contact with anything firm that you sit on, providing you are sitting up straight. When you're in the saddle, you should feel these two points against the seat of your saddle, which indicates that your posture is correct. If you don't feel your seat bones when you're riding, you are probably doing something wrong with your position. Ask a trainer, instructor, or experienced horseperson for help.

✔ **Your arms:** If you are riding English, your arms should be bent at the elbow creating a theoretical straight line from your elbow to the bit. Your hands should be held about 6 inches above the horse withers. If you are riding western, your left hand should be held a few inches above the saddle horn. Your left arm should be bent at approximately a 45-degree angle, while your right arm should be relaxed with your right hand resting on your right thigh.

Signaling the horse

After you're properly seated on the horse and are holding the reins, you're ready to start signaling the horse. Here is a list of basic riding commands that most horses understand:

✔ **Forward:** Squeeze the horse's sides with both your legs (using your thigh and calf muscles) at the same time. Make sure that your reins are relatively loose as you do. If the horse does not respond, you may need to gently tap the horse with your heels and make a kissing or clucking sound.

✔ **Stop:** Pull back on the reins with one steady motion as you say "Ho." Maintain the pull on the reins until the horse stops.

Bathroom breaks

Horses are always going to the bathroom at the most inopportune moments — usually when you are riding them. How should you handle this not-so-private moment while you're in the saddle?

Most horses prefer to stop in their tracks when the urge to defecate occurs. Many riders allow them to do so, waiting patiently until the horse finishes. Others, particularly those who show their horses, insist that the horse keep moving despite his bowel movement, because judges mark horses down if they stop to poop in the show ring. Depending on your personal feelings about this subject and whether you intend to show your horse, how you handle this situation is entirely up to you and your riding instructor.

When a horse needs to urinate, however, you have no choice: The horse must stand still in order to empty his bladder. If a horse you are riding starts to pee, stand up in the saddle to take your weight off the horse's back and make him more comfortable. Let the horse finish up his bathroom break before you ask him to move on.

- **Turn left:** You use both your legs and the reins to communicate this message.

  If you are riding English, pull back very slightly on only the left rein as you move your right leg back a little and apply some pressure. Your left leg applies pressure while staying stationary on the girth as a support for the horse to turn "around" it. After the horse completes the turn, relax your hands and legs.

  If you are riding western, move your left hand to the left so the right rein makes contact with the horse's neck (this is called *neck reining*). At the same time, move your right leg back a little behind the girth and apply some pressure to the horse's side. Your left legs applies pressure while staying in place on the girth as a support for the horse to turn "around" it. After the horse completes the turn, relax your hands and legs.

- **Turn right:** Turning right calls for the same commands as turning left, although in reverse. In English riding, pull back very slightly on only the right rein as you move your left leg back a little behind the girth and apply some pressure to the horse's side. In western riding, move your left hand to the right so the left rein makes contact with the horse's neck. At the same time, move your left leg back a little behind the girth and apply some pressure to the horse's body.

- **Back up:** Pull back on the reins in one steady motion at the same time you apply leg pressure to both sides of the horse. Make a kissing or clucking sound to the horse. Continue this command for the entire time that you want the horse to back up.

Coordinating the movements required to signal a horse takes practice. We recommend that you have an instructor, trainer, or experienced horseperson help you with these basic human-to-horse commands.

Riding the gaits

In Chapter 1, we discuss the different gaits of walk, trot, and canter that most riding horses are capable of.

As you begin to ride, you start out slow and work your way up to the faster gaits. Your first lesson is completely at the walk. As your seat and hands improve, your instructor moves you into a trot, and ultimately to a canter, or slow gallop.

If you're like most beginning riders, you're anxious to try riding a horse while it gallops. We don't blame you: After all, riding a galloping horse is an exhilarating feeling. But you need to be patient and work your way up to that moment when you're secure enough in your basic riding skills where you can handle that kind of speed. If you work hard at riding, you'll soon experience the glorious sensation of pounding hooves and the wind in your hair.

Riding the trail

Basic riding skills are just as necessary on the trail as they are in a riding arena. Out in the wilderness, you may find yourself in situations where you must turn your horse, back him up, and of course ask him to stop and go forward.

In addition to using your basic skills, you also need to use your head out on the trail. Stick to these trail basics to ensure the safety of your horse, other riders, and yourself:

✔ **Walk up and down hills.** Though your horse may want to, don't gallop downhill. Avoid the urge to trot uphill, too, if you can. The faster you go up or down a hill, the more dangerous it is. The practice is also bad for your horse's legs and it's a difficult habit to break after the horse is used to doing it.

Lean forward in the saddle when going uphill and lean back when going downhill. This helps your horse by shifting your weight off the end of the horse that is bearing most of the animal's weight.

✔ **Walk home.** Don't trot or canter during the last third of your journey home. Otherwise, your horse will think that rushing home is okay, and you soon have trouble controlling the horse when you turn toward the stable.

✔ **Negotiate obstacles.** Sooner or later, you and your horse are going to come across an obstacle on the trail that your horse won't want to deal with. It may be a fallen tree trunk, a mud puddle, or a big rock. Chances are, the obstacle will be running water because many horses are afraid to cross creeks and streams. You can't allow your horse to successfully avoid the obstacle, or your horse will soon figure out that he can dodge things he doesn't like instead of listening to you.

If your horse refuses to cross an obstacle, first, make sure it's safe to do so. Then get off and lead the horse through or over the obstacle. If this doesn't work, ask your trail buddy to take her horse over the obstacle. Chances are, your horse will follow. If not, don't risk your safety by engaging in a huge battle with your horse. Continue your ride in another direction, and when you get home to the stable, find an experienced horse person or trainer who can take your horse back on the trail to get the animal over his fear of that particular object.

✔ **Don't allow jigging.** *Jigging,* a cross between a walk and a trot, is something horses do when they're anxious to get home and don't want to walk. If your horse starts jigging and gets away with it, you soon have a chronic jigger on your hands. If your horse starts jigging, insist that the horse walk. If he won't walk, turn him around in a circle every time he starts to jig. Consistency is important to get the message of "no jigging" across to your horse.

✔ **No eating!** Imagine you're a horse on a trail ride. Everywhere you look, you see all kinds of grasses, flowers, and shrubbery, just waiting to be eaten. Walking on the trail must be the equine equivalent of strolling through a bakery.

Horses being horses, they're inclined to temptation and will reach out and try to snag a nibble at the first opportunity. However, as mean as it sounds, don't let your horse have anything to eat on the trail, for two reasons: First, many poisonous plants exist out there. Even one mouthful of the wrong thing can make your horse very sick. Second, if you let your horse eat on the trail whenever the mood strikes, pretty soon your entire ride will be spent with you sitting on top of a grazing horse.

✔ **Be safe at night.** When riding at dusk or at night, wear reflective clothing (a vest is best) so drivers can see you.

How long should you ride?

The answer to this question depends on a couple of things:

✔ **Your horse:** Horses are capable of going all day, provided they are properly conditioned. If you prefer to ride for an hour a day, once a day, slowly build your horse up to this level of conditioning. If you want to trail ride for hours on end several days a week, work your way up to this level over a period of months. If you only ride once a week (we recommend that you ride more often), don't expect your horse to go for hours on that day because he will be pretty out of shape and could even develop leg problems and something called *azoturia* (see Chapter 11). Also, we recommend that you limit arena riding to no more than one hour per day. Arena riding is hard on your horse's legs and can be a real bore for your horse.

Keep in mind that while a horse can walk for an extended time without tiring, faster gaits such as trotting and cantering take a lot more energy. Be careful about spending too much time at these faster gaits if your horse isn't properly conditioned. Also, don't ride your horse in tight circles or on hard ground for extended periods, which can do serious damage to his legs.

✔ **Your time:** Most horse lovers would be happy to spend most of their waking time in the saddle. However, unless you are a working cowboy, reality dictates that you'll be riding much less than that. We recommend that you ride as often as you can, for as long as you can, and take really long rides only on the trail and if your horse has been conditioned for such activity. The time you spend riding is not only good for your horse, it's good for your physical and mental well-being, too.

After You Ride

After you have your fill of riding for the day, you aren't completely finished with your horse. A couple of tasks remain.

Dismounting

Before you can do anything else in your life, you have to get off the horse or *dismount*. Dismounting is much easier than mounting because you don't have to battle gravity. However, you still need to dismount correctly for your own safety and the comfort of your horse.

Dismounting is virtually the same for both English and western riders:

1. **Bring your horse to a complete halt.**

2. **Take your right foot out of the stirrup and position your left hand.**

If you are riding in an English saddle, put the reins in your left hand, and grasp the horse's mane at the base of the neck with the same hand. Put your right hand on the pommel.

With a western saddle, grasp the saddle horn in your left hand as you continue to hold the reins.

3. **Swing your right leg over the horse's hindquarters — be careful not to touch the horse as you do —** *and* **at the same time, move your right hand to the cantle.**

4. **Turn so your stomach is flat against the horse and your legs are next to one another; remove your left foot from the stirrup.**

5. **Slowly slide down until your feet are touching the ground.**

Never let go of the reins while you are dismounting. You need to keep control of your horse at all times.

Untacking

After dismounting, lead your horse back to the hitching post or cross-ties where you left the halter. You are now going to remove the horse's tack. Untacking is basically the reverse procedure you followed when tacking up in Chapter 15.

If you ride English, be sure to *run up* the stirrup irons before you walk your horse back to his halter. The purpose of this is to keep the irons from banging against the horse's side as he walks. You can run up the irons by sliding them up the back strap of the stirrup leather so the irons lay flat against the saddle. Tuck the loop of stirrup leather through the stirrup iron to secure it.

Follow these steps to untack your horse:

1. **Restrain the horse with the halter.**

   Stand at the horse's left side. As you hold the reins in your left hand, buckle the halter strap around the horse's neck to restrain him (see Figure 15-4 in Chapter 15 for a diagram illustrating this). The halter should still be attached to the hitching post or cross-tie. Unbuckle the noseband and throatlatch, if any.

2. **Remove the bridle.**

   With your right hand, gently slide the headstall over the horse's ears so that the bridle comes off the horse's head.

   Be careful not to pull the bit out of the horse's mouth when you're removing the bridle. Let the horse open his mouth to drop the bit before you pull the bridle completely off the horse's head.

3. **Return the halter to its normal position.**

   Loop the headstall and reins over your shoulder or a nearby post. Unbuckle the part of the halter that is around the horse's neck and lower the noseband just enough to slip the halter over the horse's head. Then buckle it again. Be careful not to remove the halter strap completely from the horse's neck as you do, or you have no restraint on the horse!

4. **Remove (English) or untie (western) the saddle's girth.**

   With an English saddle, remove the girth by unbuckling first the left side of the girth, then the right. Remove the girth completely.

   If you are using a western saddle, untie the cinch knot first. Then, loop the latigo strap several times and tuck it into the dee ring. From the right side of the horse, lay the cinch over the seat of the saddle, and loop the right stirrup over the saddle horn.

5. **Remove the saddle.**

   Stand on the horse's left side, facing the saddle. Grasp the front of the saddle pad with your left hand and the back of the pad with your right. Lift the pad and saddle up together, up and off the horse's back.

6. **Put the saddle on a saddle rack.**

   The saddle pad should be on top of the saddle, with the wet underside of the pad facing up to dry. With an English saddle, you may want to lay the girth over the saddle pad, wet side up, to dry.

Cooling down

In the event that you haven't already walked your horse for at least 10 minutes at the end of your ride, you have to do so now.

Remove your horse's saddle and bridle as described in the preceding section, and take the horse for a walk around the stable by his halter. Keep walking until the horse is cool. You can tell whether the horse is cool by putting your hand on his chest. If the horse's chest is hot and sweaty, keep walking. The sweat should be dried from the most of the horse's body by the time you finish with your walk, and his breathing should be slow and back to normal.

For the benefit of your horse's health, never allow your horse to eat or drink until he's completely cooled down!

Grooming

Your horse needs to be groomed after you ride as well as before. Clean out your horse's feet and brush the horse down. If your horse sweats a lot during the ride, wash the horse off with a hose or sponge (see Chapter 9 for details).

Stuff Your Horse May Pull on You

Horses are a lot like children: They have a tendency to constantly test authority, just to make sure that it's still there. In your horse's mind, the best time to test your authority is when you are riding.

Many horses pull stunts just to see what they can get away with. In other cases, these behaviors stem from genuine fear, poor training, and insecurity on the horse's part. Either way, you need to call on your superior human intellect and leadership skills to convince the horse to change his behavior.

To constantly reinforce your horse's obedience, make sure that every move you make when riding is *your* idea, not the horse's.

Bucking

You've seen bucking broncos on TV. Although they may look ferocious, those horses are actually made to buck with the use of a device called a bucking strap, tied around their flanks. Rodeo riders make these horses perform by taking advantage of the horse's natural tendency to buck when something unpleasant or frightening is on the horse's back.

When an average saddle horse bucks, it isn't usually with the same force as a rodeo bronc. Nonetheless, even a moderate buck can still remove you from the saddle.

Average horses usually buck for one of two reasons: They have excess energy that they need to release, or they are in pain. If your horse bucks frequently when you ride, try giving the horse more exercise on a regular basis to release any pent up energy. If this doesn't help, have a veterinarian examine the horse to determine whether the animal is suffering from leg or back pain.

If you find yourself on a bucking horse, sit squarely in the saddle and try to pull the horse's head up with the reins. A horse needs to put his head down in order to buck.

If your horse bucks you off, be sure to get right back on (or have someone else get on) and continue riding, at least for a few minutes. You may not want to get back on board, you need to do this to keep the horse from thinking he can get out of work simply by unloading you.

Rearing

When a horse *rears,* he stands up on his hind legs, lifting his forefeet off the ground. Most horses rear when they are very afraid of something that is approaching them from the front, when a severe bit or hackamore is hurting their mouths, or when they are resisting the rider.

Rearing while being ridden is an extremely dangerous habit that you should not tolerate. If your horse rears with you when you ask him to do something he doesn't want to do, you should have a trainer work with the animal before you continue riding him.

Shying

Horses are prey animals by nature, and so they're always on the alert. If something spooks a horse, his first reaction is to shy away from the offending creature or object. Because shying usually comes along with quick and sudden movements in unexpected directions, riders sometimes become unseated.

Horses typically shy at the following objects: white plastic bags blowing in the wind, flags, balloons, umbrellas, and anything they haven't seen before and that they can't identify. They also get nervous when they see an object in a place where they haven't seen it before.

If your horse shies at something, the animal is most likely frightened of the object. Allow the frightened horse to turn and face the object to get a good look at it. After the horse has a moment to carefully focus on the object, he will most likely calm down. If the horse still refuses to pass the object, you may need to get off the horse and lead him past. For some reason, horses are much braver when they are being led than when they are being ridden. You can even try going over to the object and touching it yourself so your horse sees that it's harmless.

Many things on a riding trail can cause your horse to shy. Hikers with big orange backpacks, mountain bikers, and people walking their dogs are all potentially scary things to a horse. If you come across someone on the trail who your horse is nervous about, ask the person to please stand aside and refrain from moving so that the horse can pass. If the horse is still too frightened to approach the person, you may have to get off and lead the horse.

If the horse seems deathly afraid of something and refuses to calm down, take the horse away from the object so he doesn't become panicky and dangerous. Then, ask a trainer or experienced horseperson to help you work with the horse to get him over this particular fear.

Running away

Most well-trained horses wouldn't dream of running away with a rider, but on occasion, something can frighten a horse so badly that he takes off in a blind panic.

If you ever lose control of a horse who is running away with you, do your best to stay on without squeezing your legs against the horse (which only make the horse go faster). Pull back on the reins in a continuous motion, and say "Ho" over and over again in as calm a voice as you can muster. You can also try to turn the horse in a circle while he's running, because doing so is often a very good way to slow the animal down. Turn the animal by pulling the horse's head around using one rein as you apply pressure with the leg on the same side as the rein you are pulling.

If you have a horse who chronically runs away with you, you have a serious problem that should be handled by a professional trainer.

Refusing to move

Mules aren't the only animals who can be stubborn. Horses sometimes also refuse to budge. Because horses who are inclined to plant their feet are usually the kind who are good at sensing a lack of confidence in a rider, beginning riders often encounter this problem.

If you find your horse won't move when you first get up on his back, even though you apply leg pressure, you have a horse who isn't very responsive and is testing your authority. (Just to be on the safe side, have an experienced horseperson observe you to make sure that you aren't doing something wrong.) You can deal with this problem by kicking the horse with your heels and clucking or kissing to the horse to encourage the animal to move. If this doesn't work, get a trainer or experienced horseperson to help you deal with the problem. Spurs and a crop may do the job, but you need help to properly use these.

Another situation where a horse may refuse to move is if the animal is afraid of something up ahead. You can tell the difference between the two kinds of refusals by looking at the horse's body language. A frightened horse holds his head up high, rotates his ears forward, tenses his body, and shows the whites of his eyes. If this is the situation, follow our advice under the section "Shying." If the horse seems relaxed but simply refuses to move, you have a resister on your hands.

Refusing to leave the stable

A horse who refuses to leave the stable for a trail ride or fights you out on the trail in his attempts to get back home is considered *barn-sour*. Barn-sour horses are potentially dangerous and a real problem to retrain.

If you have a horse who is barn-sour, your first step is to make sure that the horse doesn't have a physical reason for his attitude. Have a vet examine the horse's mouth, poll, girth, and back to make sure that the animal isn't in pain.

If the horse is okay, then the attitude results from a lack of respect for rider authority. You need to gain the horse's obedience before you can expect the animal to allow you take him away from the barn, a place that he associates with food and security. Start by schooling the horse at home, in an arena. Practice moving forward, backing up, turning, and stopping. The horse should be following your commands completely before you attempt to take the animal out on the trail. When you go out for the first time after a couple of months of schooling, go with another rider for your own safety, just in case the horse misbehaves. Also, remind the horse throughout the ride that you're in charge by asking the horse to stop and back up.

When it's time to turn around and head for home, keep the horse's gait at a walk for the entire ride back to the stable. Avoid feeding the horse immediately after you return to the barn.

Barn-sour horses are notoriously hard to retrain. If none of the above work, you have to bring in a professional trainer.

Backing up when not asked

When a horse starts backing up even though you didn't ask him to, the horse is trying to resist you, probably because you asked him to do something that he doesn't want to do.

First, make sure that you're not inadvertently telling the horse to back up. Make sure that your reins are loose whenever you squeeze the horse to move forward.

If your reins are loose but the horse continues to back up, then the horse is trying to pull a fast one. To combat this maneuver, loosen your reins and prompt the horse forward by nudging him in the ribs with your heels. Keep nudging until the horse gives up and moves forward.

If backing up is a repeated problem with your horse, call in the services of a professional trainer for some help.

Falling off

Here's a fact: The longer and harder you ride, the more likely you are to fall off. Why? Because every time you get up on a horse's back, you're defying gravity. And occasionally, gravity retaliates.

Almost every serious rider has fallen off a horse at least once, most many more times than that. Riders who jump, barrel race, and participate in other strenuous equine sports are the ones who fall the most.

If you've never fallen off a horse, you probably imagine it being the most horrible thing that could possibly happen. You've heard horror stories, like the case of actor Christopher Reeve and tales of jockeys who lost their lives on the racetrack after plunging from the back of a horse. But serious accidents like these are in the minority when it comes to falling. Most people who fall off a horse don't sustain anything more than a bruise to their bodies — and egos!

When adults fall, they are more likely to break a bone than a child would be in the same situa tion, because older bones are more brittle. But if you are wearing a helmet and following the outlined safety precautions in this book, chances are good that you'll walk away from your fall with little more than dirt on your rear end and a few sore muscles.

Fighting with other horses

Horses have a social hierarchy complete with a distinct pecking order. So even though you think your riding buddy is the cat's meow, your horse may not feel the same way about your buddy's horse. The result: squabbling between the horses as you ride.

Most equine disagreements consist of flattened ears and benign threats between horses. However, these arguments sometimes get out of hand, resulting in one horse kicking or biting another, which can cause injury to a horse or rider.

If your horse shows an obvious dislike for another horse (or vice versa) while you're riding, do your best to keep the horses far away from one another. If your horse is the one making trouble by putting his ears back or threatening to kick, say "Quit!" and try to get your horse under control. Always keep a close eye on your horse (or the one who is doing the threatening), because equine grudges tend to be ongoing affairs.

If you have a horse that is particularly nasty to other horses — especially those who approach from behind — tie a red ribbon at the base of his tail as a warning to other riders.

Continuing Ed for You and Your Horse

The partnership between a horse and his rider is similar to a marriage: If you don't continuously work at the relationship, it probably won't succeed.

The way you keep your relationship with your horse healthy is to provide continuing education for both you and your horse. You can do so by entering into training with a professional (where you and your horse will be schooled), taking lessons as often as you can, or simply practicing your riding skills and schooling your horse. Spend some of your riding time reinforcing the commands your horse already knows while you practice giving them. Work in an arena once a week or so and execute turning, backing up, stopping, and other skills that you pick up in formal lessons.

Coping with Fear (Your Own)

We talk a lot about the horse's fear in this and other chapters of this book. But what about *your* fear?

If you are asking "What fear?" right about now, then good for you. You're probably one of those brave souls who has no qualms about getting up on a half-ton animal and trusting him with your life. But more than likely, you're one of the great majority of beginning adult riders who finds the notion of riding a horse a bit scary.

Being afraid to ride is okay, as long as fear doesn't keep you from trying. We feel confident that if you follow the advice in this book, you'll soon discover that your fears are unfounded and that riding a good horse is one of the most relaxing and enjoyable things anyone can do.

If you have a nagging reluctance, know that the more your riding skill increases, the more confident you'll feel on a horse's back. Remember, human beings have been riding horses for the past 4,000 years, and our species still survives!

Chapter 17

Keeping Things Safe

· ·

· ·

*H*orses are a real joy to be around, but the fact is, they are much bigger than you are. The average horse weighs almost ten times as much as the average human female. Consequently, humans have to be careful around horses to make sure that equine bulk doesn't end up somehow becoming a liability for the human body.

In this chapter, we give you all the details you need to be safe around horses, whether it be on the ground, in the saddle, alone, or with other riders. This chapter also gives you tips on how to keep your horse safe from himself, too!

When you've been around horses for a while, your comfort level grows, and you may start to cut corners with safety rules. Cutting corners — and many people certainly do — is never a good idea. When you start to slough off the rules and take shortcuts, you increase the probability of having an accident that may injure you, your horse, or both. *Don't allow yourself to get too comfortable.* Follow the safety rules we present here strictly, however at ease you become around horses.

Dressing for Safety

Believe it or not, the clothing you wear around horses and your safety go hand in hand. Wearing — or not wearing — something when handling these cumbersome beasts can mean the difference between an ambulance ride to the emergency room and going to bed that night unscathed.

Footwear

You should always wear protective footwear whenever you're around horses. Always wear heavy leather boots whether you plan to ride your horse or just plan a grooming session. Follow these rules to keep your tootsies safe:

- **Wear heavy boots when working with a horse on the ground:** Heavy boots are the footwear of choice for horse handlers, for good reason. Sooner or later, if you spend enough time around horses, one of these hulks is going to step on your foot. When he does, you'll have a few hundred pounds of pressure on your foot, conveniently punctuated with a weighty metal shoe. If you're wearing tennis shoes or sandals when this happens, you'll be walking around with a cane for some time. We recommend wearing equestrian boots for maximum protection (see Chapter 6 for details on equestrian footwear and where to purchase it).

- **Wear riding shoes or boots when you're in the saddle:** You may have seen people riding with tennis shoes on — a major no-no in our opinion. Riding shoes or boots made especially for equestrians are the safest footwear to don when riding. One reason is that these items have a heel that keeps your foot from sliding through the stirrup and trapping your leg, an important factor should you fall from your horse.

Helmet

Probably the most important part of your equestrian wardrobe is the safety helmet, because it protects your skull and brain. The safety helmet is a good idea when dealing with horses posessed of a difficult disposition on the ground, but when you're riding a horse, a safety helmet is an absolute must.

A safety helmet can protect you in the following ways:

- **On the ground:** If you're planning to be around a horse who is known for being difficult to handle in certain situations (freaks out while loading in a trailer, has a deadly fear of clippers, needs to be given some bad tasting medicine), wearing a helmet is a wise precaution. A helmet can protect your head if

  - A horse knocks you down and causes you to strike your noggin against the ground.

  - A horse accidentally whacks your head with his head (his skull is a lot harder than yours, believe us).

  - A horse rears up and mistakenly — or not — strikes your head with a hoof (ouch!).

> ✔ **In the saddle:** The fall from a horse's back is not a short one, and it can take place at a high rate of speed. In way too many instances, helmetless riders have fallen off their horses and hit their heads on a hard surface, sustaining permanent brain damage. Wearing a safety helmet designed specifically for equestrians can protect the single most important part of your body: your brain.

Wearing a safety helmet is especially important for children, whose heads tend to be more breakable than those of adults.

For more information about safety helmets, check out Chapter 6.

Long pants

The same people who ride around in tennis shoes usually ride in shorts, too, something we don't recommend. In fact, we're not really sure how people can stand riding in shorts. Bare skin only has to rub against a leather saddle for a few minutes to make you realize that shorts and riding don't go together. An occasional bareback rider can get away with riding in shorts, although this rider's skin doesn't stand a chance should he or she take a spill.

Jewelry

Even if you see yourself as a rhinestone cowboy (or cowgirl), don't wear jewelry around horses. Big rings, hanging earrings, necklaces, and bangle bracelets can be hazardous to a horseperson's health. Jewelry can catch on a horse's tack (equipment) when you're riding, and jewelry can catch on so many things at a stable that it's dangerous.

Riders often tell stories around stable water coolers of others who suffered serious injury because a piece of jewelry snagged on a horse shoe nail, a cross-tie ring, or a bridle shank. Don't wear this stuff when you're around horses. Besides, the other horse people at the stable will think you're odd if you show up decked out like Liberace.

Staying Safe on the Ground

The fact is that the majority of your time around horses is spent on the ground, not on the horse's back. You'll be grooming, feeding, and cleaning up on a regular basis. All this time spent in close proximity to your horse means greater odds of an accident occurring when on the ground.

That is one reason why ground safety with horses is so important. Another reason is that when you're on the ground, you are vulnerable to being stepped on, kicked, or knocked down. Sure, if something goes wrong while you're riding, the ground is a five-foot plunge away. But when you're handling a horse from terra firma, more stuff can happen besides falling.

Leading the horse

Leading — it sounds simple enough: Just walk with the lead rope and the horse follows. Right? Well, yeah, but what happens if something scares the horse from behind? If you're directly in front of the horse, you're going to get trampled.

Horse people have discovered that leading a horse from his left side, just at his shoulder, considerably reduces your chances of being stepped on or run over. If you lead a horse in this way, the worst thing your horse can do is step on your foot. Much better than being trampled, don't you think? (See Chapter 13 for an illustration showing the correct way to lead your horse.)

Here are some other points to remember when leading a horse:

- **Never wrap the lead line around your hand or hold the loops of the lead rope:** If the horse pulls back or takes off, he'll drag you. Instead, hold the part of the rope near the horse's head in your right hand and the loose end in your left hand.

- **Hold the lead rope close to the halter:** Doing so gives you better control over the horse's head and prevents you and the horse from tripping over slack in the line.

- **Never lead a horse with your hand in his halter:** If the horse pulls back or runs away, your hand can get caught and you can be dragged.

- **Walk, don't run:** When leading your horse through common stable areas, down streets, or in other places where you find people and horses, always walk your horse. Trotting your horse down the barn aisle on your way to the tie-up spot is rude and unsafe.

Dealing with feet

Horse people are always fussing with their horses' feet. Horses are constantly getting their feet cleaned, their fetlock (or ankle) hair clipped, or their hooves brushed with hoof polish.

The human urge when performing these hoof-related tasks is to kneel down on the ground next to the hoof. After all, from this vantage point, you can get your work done much more efficiently. The problem, though, is that kneeling close to a horse's foot puts you in a dangerous position from which you can't easily retreat. If the horse suddenly moves to the side, he'll likely step on you. If something scares him, you can even be trampled.

When you're fiddling with a horse's hoof, bend or crouch rather than kneel. By bending or crouching, you keep your feet beneath you, allowing you to move quickly if the horse's body comes your way.

Keep your head out of the field of motion of the horse's leg. In other words, don't put your head in an area where the horse can inadvertently conk you if he quickly jerks up his leg to remove a fly or reacts to the tickle of the clippers. As a child, one of your authors (okay, it was Audrey) stuck her head behind a horse's foreleg while clipping a fetlock and received a lump on her forehead roughly the size of Nevada for her trouble.

Remember, too, not to hold the hoof by the toe (the tip of the hoof) because this area doesn't give you enough control if the horse tries to pull the leg away from you. Also, if you hold the hoof only by the toe, you can lose your grip on the hoof and drop it on your own foot! Instead, keep your hand under the hoof or under the pastern (the area between the hoof and the ankle). Check out Chapter 1 for information about horse and hoof anatomy.

Horse moves

Horses typically make maneuvers that put humans in jeopardy — although to be fair to the horse, the poor creatures rarely mean to. Whether the move is accidental or not, you still need to know what to watch out for. If you're forewarned, you stand a better chance of getting out of the way in time:

✔ **Swinging body:** Remember these key points about equine physics: When a horse's front ends moves to the left, the back end concurrently moves to the right, and vice versa.

✔ **Head jerks:** If a horse wants you to get away from his head, he will jerk it upwards and sometimes to the side at the same time.

✔ **Sideways moves:** If a horse is afraid of something on his right-hand side, he will leap to the left, and vice versa.

✔ **Forward we go:** If something spooks a horse from behind, the horse will move forward — rapidly.

✔ **Backward ho:** If you approach a horse from the front holding something he wants to avoid (medication, dewormer, or a frightening object, for example), he will throw up his head, place all of his weight on his haunches, and back up at significant speed. If this happens, don't pull back on the lead rope because doing so only excites the horse more and causes further backing up. Just relax, hold the scary object behind your back, talk softly to the horse, and give the big guy a chance to settle down.

Close quarters

When you find yourself in close quarters with a horse, the reality of the horse's mass becomes much more apparent. Your comparatively minute human form can easily be squashed if a horse pins you up against a wall.

Horses who are well trained know not to encroach on a human's space. With these horses, you can merely push on the too-close body and cluck your tongue to get the horse to move over and give you some breathing room. Unfortunately, though, not all horses have learned this lesson, which is why you shouldn't take chances with your well-being by allowing a horse to pen you in.

Follow these simple rules to keep yourself out of harm's way in close quarters:

✔ **Don't ever wedge yourself between a horse and an unmoveable object:** Find a way to move the horse if you don't have enough room to gain access to that side of the horse.

✔ **Don't enter a box stall with a strange horse without finding out whether the animal is okay with your presence:** Nothing is more terrifying than finding yourself inside a small space with a horse who hates you.

✔ **Don't stand directly behind a horse you don't know:** The occurrence is rare, but occasionally a horse will kick out at a person walking or standing behind him, seriously injuring the person. If you need to pass closely behind a strange horse, make sure that the horse knows you're there, and then pass *very* close to the horse's body, nearly touching it. That way, if the horse tries to kick, you'll only make contact with the point of the hock (the "elbow" of the back leg) and not the full-force hoof.

✔ **Make sure that the horse has seen you:** When you approach a horse who's loose in a stall, speak to the animal first so that the horse turns around and looks at you before you enter. Gauge the horse's body language to make sure that the horse is calm and receptive to your approach. (See Chapter 2 to find out how to read equine body language.)

Tied horses

Many horses feel vulnerable when they are tied to a hitching post or cross-ties. Something about having their heads restrained can really set them off. To avoid accidents, follow these basic rules of safety around tied horses:

✔ **Short tie:** Whoever came up with the phrase "enough rope to hang himself" must have known a horse. If you tie a horse up at a hitching post with too much slack in the lead rope, the horse inevitably gets a foot hung up in the rope or ends up with the rope over his neck. Always tie a horse with a short rope (12 inches of slack is a good length) so he can't get himself into trouble.

- **Ducking under:** Never duck underneath a horse's neck to get to the other side (even though you may be tempted to and even if you've seen other horsepeople doing it). Instead, take the long way and walk around the horse's front or back. Although many horses don't mind a human walking under their necks, enough do that you could end up with a panicked horse and a seriously injured human.

- **The frontal approach:** All horses have the propensity to freak out and pull back when tied. If you've ever seen a horse throw all his weight on his hindquarters and rip a hitching post out of the ground, then you know that pulling back is a terrifying and dangerous habit (see Chapter 13 for information on dealing with horses who pull back). Some horses do it routinely, while others need serious provocation before pulling this stunt.

   To avoid instigating a horse to pull back, always be slow and quiet when approaching from the front. If you need to move toward the horse with an object in your hand, watch the horse's body language carefully to determine whether the horse is scared and a pull-back is imminent (see Chapter 2 for details on equine body language).

- **Use safety restraints:** When tying a horse to a hitching post or horse trailer, always use a safety knot (see Chapter 13 for details on how to tie a safety knot). A safety knot allows you to quickly release a panicking horse's lead rope. If you are cross-tying your horse, use quick release snaps on cross-ties and light ropes that break easily if the horse pulls back (see Chapter 13 for information on cross-ties).

- **If Mr. Horse gets loose:** Sometimes horses get loose when they are tied up. They either pull back and break a lead rope or halter, or pull away from the handler by ripping the lead rope out of the handler's hands. Sometimes, believe it or not, horses simply untie the knot with their dexterous lips!

However a horse manages to get loose, *do not* run after him. A chasing human only encourages a horse to run. And horses can run much faster than humans can, so if you decide to chase a horse, you will lose. In fact, you can make matters worse by scaring the horse into a street or other dangerous area. See Chapter 13 for more details on dealing with a loose horse.

Staying Safe in the Saddle

You can have plenty of fun riding a horse, but you need to keep safety in mind at all times if you are going to *continue* having fun. Getting hurt is a sure way to ruin the party.

When riding, several different safety angles come into play. Remembering all this stuff may take some concentration at first, but in time, it will become second nature.

Inspecting your tack before riding

Having quality tack (riding equipment) in good condition is pretty important if you want to have a safe ride. Just like the timing belt in your car's engine, tack can break at the most inopportune times if you don't regularly inspect it.

Before every ride, do a cursory inspection of your tack to make sure that no accidents are waiting to happen:

- ✔ **The bridle:** Check to make sure that all the buckles are tightly fastened and all the pieces are securely attached.

- ✔ **The girth:** On English saddles, inspect the buckles on both sides to make sure that they're securely fastened. On western saddles, be sure that the left latigo strap is snugly tied to the saddle ring, and the right latigo is securely buckled to the cinch (see Chapter 6 for diagrams showing the different parts of the saddle).

- ✔ **The stirrups:** On English saddles, check to make sure that the stirrup leathers are securely buckled and positioned on the stirrup bar. For western saddles, inspect the stirrup buckle to make sure that it's not loose (see Chapter 6 for diagrams showing the different parts of the saddle).

If you ride English, run your stirrup irons up the leathers so the irons are flush with the saddle skirt after you dismount from your horse. This move keeps your irons from catching on anything and banging around on your horse.

Riding with others

Riding is most fun when done in groups. Cruising the trail with your friends or riding around an arena with a buddy or two can be a blast. In situations where horses are kept at boarding stables and boarders share riding facilities, riding in groups is not usually a choice, it's mandatory simply because everyone is forced to use the same arenas at the same time.

Riders must take certain safety precautions when they're around other riders and horses. Following these rules helps keep you and your fellow equestrians safe and makes you a popular person around the barn!

Safety and etiquette

Riding is a dignified hobby, and riders are expected to behave a certain way when they are astride a horse. Nearly all of these expected behaviors are related to safety, and will keep you in good stead with those around you.

Follow these guidelines when riding on the trail or in an arena with other riders:

- ✔ **Stay back:** When you're riding in a head-to-tail situation, such as around the perimeter of an arena or on a trail ride, keep your horse several feet away from the horse in front of you. Most horses will tolerate another horse being behind, but some won't. As a result, crowding can end up with your horse being kicked and even seriously hurt.

  If you have a horse who kicks when other horses get too close, tie a red ribbon at the base of your horse's tail to warn other riders at horse shows, organized trail rides, or other events. Likewise, when you see a horse with a red ribbon in his tail, stay back! The ribbon is a warning that your horse may be kicked if you get too close.

- ✔ **Rear approach:** If you are on a trail and see a rider up ahead moving in the same direction that you are, do *not* run your horse up behind that rider. If you do, the rider's horse will almost certainly spook or take off, and you could be the cause of a serious accident. Instead, when you see a rider on the trail ahead, slow down to a walk or slow trot and make sure that the rider knows you're there before you pass.

  The same thing applies to the arena. If you are trotting or cantering and are going to pass a rider from the rear while that rider is at the walk (her horse is walking), give the rider and horse a wide berth so you don't upset the horse.

- ✔ **Passing:** When riding in an arena, you are bound to find yourself going in one direction while one or more riders are traveling the opposite way. When passing one another in a riding arena, riders use the *left shoulder to left shoulder* rule. When riders ride by one another, their left shoulders pass each other. To accomplish this feat, you may need to stay close to the rail so the approaching rider passes you on your left. Or, you may need to stay to the inside, away from the rail, in order to have the approaching rider pass you to the left. (To understand left shoulder to left shoulder passing, see Figure 17-1.)

- ✔ **Slow going:** When a cowboy wants to go for a ride in the movies, he leaps onto his horse and gallops off in a flurry. In the real world, equestrians don't behave this way unless they want to do harm to their horses and incur the wrath of everyone around them.

  When you first mount your horse, walk slowly to your point of destination, whether it be a riding arena or a local trail head. Don't trot or canter through the aisles of the stable, and don't stress your horse by tearing off into a gallop from a standstill. This behavior labels you as a yahoo and put you and your horse in all kinds of physical danger.

✔ **Be quiet:** Again, the movies come to mind. Yelling, hollering, and yee-hawing while on horseback is fine for actors in westerns, but in real life, doing so frightens your horse, annoys others, and makes you look like a dope. The only exception to this rule is when you're riding in gymkhana or some other competitive speed event where such vocalizations are considered acceptable because they encourage the horse to go faster (see Chapter 18 for more details on such events).

Figure 17-1:
Two riders passing left shoulder to left shoulder.

Chapter 18

Getting Competitive

● ●

● ●

*C*ompeting with your horse as your partner is one of the most fun and rewarding things you can do. When you show your horse, you put your best feet forward (both your own and your horse's), telling the world "Hey, look what we can do!"

Equine sports run the gamut from simple stuff you can do with just about any horse to complex events that require teams of horses. Some are easy to participate in; others call for a considerable investment of both money and time. To find the sport that is best for you — and your horse if you already have one — you need to do some research as well as some soul-searching. You can begin your search for the right competition for you and your horse by reading the descriptions we provide in this chapter. The descriptions should give you a good idea of what's out there.

Hunt Seat

Hunt seat is extremely popular in the United States and is the discipline you most often see when people are described as "riding English." These riders always use a hunt-seat saddle, with a seat that is inclined slightly forward (see Chapter 6 for details on the hunt-seat saddle).

The roots of hunt seat lie in the sport of British fox hunting. Fox hunters in Great Britain have ridden for a long time in the same type of saddles that hunt-seat riders use today. These saddles were designed for jumping and to provide close contact with the horse. The apparel worn in hunt-seat classes is based on British tradition, too. A hunt cap, hunt jacket, breeches, and high boots are the apparel judges expect to see in the show ring. This very traditional sport discourages individuality in appearance, so nearly all riders at a given show are dressed in almost exactly the same way.

Unlike fox hunting, hunt seat is primarily an arena sport, offering both jumping classes and *flat* classes, which are classes that don't involve jumping. If you choose to compete in hunt seat, you'll compete in a variety of classes. *Equitation* is one of these classes, where your riding form is judged either "on the flat" or over fences. In *hunters,* your horse's form and style over a course of fences is judged. The fences range anywhere from 2 to 4 feet, depending on the class. These classes are held within different divisions, based on the age and expertise of either the horse or the rider.

You can ride and compete on just about any breed in hunt-seat classes, although judges typically favor Thoroughbred and Thoroughbred-type horses because these are the types of horses traditionally used in the sport of fox hunting. Because jumping is an integral part of hunt-seat showing, you must become a proficient rider over fences.

Show Jumping

Show jumping is an Olympic discipline for daredevils. Both horse and rider have to be courageous to excel in this sport because show jumping demands that horse and rider teams negotiate some pretty high fences.

In show jumping, horse-and-rider teams are expected to jump a series of fences — ranging anywhere from 3 feet 6 inches in the novice classes to 6 feet or more in more advanced classes — as fast as they possibly can. In show jumping competition, the horse-and-rider team that can jump the highest fences with the least amount of *errors* (knocking down a rail or refusing a jump) in the fastest time is the winner.

Horses shown in show jumping are outfitted with close contact jumping saddles (a version of the hunt-seat saddle). Riders wear hunt caps, hunt jackets, breeches, and high boots. The color and styles of apparel in this class are not important and tend to vary from rider to rider.

Show jumping is an Olympic sport, and at the top levels, warmblood breeds (see Chapter 4 for more information about warmbloods) often compete in this event and have much success with it. At smaller local or regional shows, you may see other breeds in show jumping, too. Basically, any horse who is athletic enough to take the jumps can compete in this sport, regardless of breed. As a rider, you must also be athletic and pretty darn fearless.

Dressage

One of the oldest equine disciplines in the world, *dressage* dates back to training methods developed in ancient Greece. One of the Olympic disciplines, dressage has been a traditional favorite in Europe for centuries and is gaining considerable popularity in the United States.

Dressage consists of a series of subtle maneuvers that are meant to emphasize the horse's natural movement. Horse-and-rider teams perform in a rectangular-shaped arena that is marked with a series of letters. The purpose of these letters is to act as targets for particular movements during the dressage test. Think of dressage movements as the compulsory exercises in figure skating, with the letters functioning as spatial indicators of correct positioning of horse and rider.

A difficult discipline that calls for significant athleticism from both horse and rider, people often compare dressage to ballet because of its difficulty and corresponding beauty. Most dressage riders use a special dressage saddle with a deeper seat than the hunt-seat saddle (see Chapter 6 for more information on dressage saddles).

In dressage, horse-and-rider teams compete at different levels depending on their expertise. Judges score dressage participants on how perfectly the horse-and-rider team performs precise movements. The scores of competing riders are compared at the end of each competition, and the riders with the highest scores in each level receive awards. Though riders are technically competing with each other in these events, most are more concerned with improving their own individual score from show to show than beating out the other riders.

Dressage riders at the lower levels of competition can wear the same type of clothing seen in the hunt-seat arena: a hunt cap, hunt jacket, breeches and boots. In the upper levels, however, protocol dictates that dressage riders wear a black derby, white breeches, a black jacket, black high boots, and a white stock tie.

You can show horses of any breed in dressage, as long as they are physically and mentally capable of performing the required exercises. Thoroughbreds are popular in the sport, although you most commonly see warmbloods in the higher levels of dressage competition because of their extraordinary athleticism.

Saddle Seat

Saddle seat is one of the English disciplines, although the saddle for this type of riding is very different from a hunt-seat or dressage saddle. Show saddles, as saddle-seat saddles are called, have a flatter seat than other English saddles. The saddle's construction forces the rider to sit far behind the horse's withers (see Chapter 1 for a diagram showing the parts of the horse), thus taking the rider's weight off the front part of the horse and encouraging the animal to show off the high action of his front legs.

For a horse to be successful in this discipline, he must be a flashy creature with animated gaits. In fact, horses in this event often have the charm of Cary Grant, the grace of Fred Astaire, and the energy of Robin Williams. Horses are usually ridden with a double bridle (see Chapter 6 for a description of the double bridle). Saddle-seat riders are expected to wear derbies, jackets, and jodhpurs in the show ring.

You most commonly see the saddle-seat discipline at breed shows when people are riding gaited horses, such as the American Saddlebred, the Tennessee Walking Horse, and the Racking Horse. Some all-breed shows and single-breed shows also have saddle-seat classes for Arabians, Morgans, and some other high-stepping breeds. You see classes for saddle-seat riders at shows for gaited breeds, as well as at many single-breed and all-breed shows. A variety of different saddle-seat classes are usually offered, depending on the breed and type of show.

Judging in saddle-seat classes is typically on the horse's action or the rider's position in the saddle, depending on whether the class is a pleasure class (the horse is judged) or an equitation class (the rider is judged). The class you prefer to enter depends on a number of factors, including both your and your horse's abilities. Many riders enter both types of classes.

Western

The western discipline developed more than a hundred years ago in America from the cowboy's need for a safe and comfortable way to ride horses among vast herds of cattle. This legacy is not lost in the modern world today: Many western events — specifically rodeos — feature classes designed to test the cattle skills of today's horses and riders. Even those classes that don't involve actual cows have a basis in working with cattle.

In most western classes, you see a very specific type of horse. You won't find many lanky Thoroughbreds or cobby Welsh Ponies here. The Quarter Horse dominates this discipline, although other western-type breeds like the Paint and Appaloosa are also common.

Western pleasure

Western pleasure, along with its cousins western horsemanship and western equitation, are the most popular classes in western showing. In these events, riders demonstrate their own riding skills as well as the abilities of their horses. Horses in these events are expected to carry their riders quietly, comfortably, and obediently, all on a loose rein.

In western pleasure classes, horses are judged for their slow, steady movement and ability to carry their necks at the same level as their backs. The horse's conformation (the way he's physically constructed) weighs heavily in the judging because only horses built a certain way are capable of the movement required of a western pleasure horse. In western equitation classes, however, the emphasis is on the rider's riding skills and position in the saddle, rather than on the horse's conformation and movement. In horsemanship classes, riders must demonstrate that they can efficiently put their horses through a series of gaits and maneuvers. Horses in horsemanship classes must be obedient, responding quickly to their riders' cues.

Western riders must be good riders to be successful, and they must enjoy wearing a western hat! Both horse and rider apparel are important in these classes, especially in western pleasure. Expensive, silver-laden saddles and bridles are common, and riders are expected to wear a hat, fringed chaps, western boots, and a western vest or riding jacket.

Western showmanship

Many of the riders who compete in pleasure and horsemanship classes also participate in western showmanship classes. In western showmanship, competitors don't actually ride the horse. Instead, they handle the horse from the ground and present him to the judge. The judge evaluates the handler's ability to show off the horse (make him look his best). The horse's conformation is not judged, although having an attractive and obedient horse is certainly helpful.

Any western-type horse can compete in western showmanship. Horses wear a special show halter, and handlers are expected to wear a western hat, a western vest or show jacket, long pants (jeans or special slacks made just for this class), and western boots.

Gymkhana

The faint of heart need not apply for the exciting, fast-paced sport of gymkhana. If you decide to compete in gymkhana, you'll find yourself galloping at top speed across arenas, making sharp turns while trying to beat the clock.

You typically see two gymkhana games at horse shows and rodeos, where gymkhana is especially popular: barrel racing and pole bending. In barrel racing classes, metal or plastic barrels are usually set up in a clover pattern. The horse-and-rider team run through the pattern at top speed, making a complete turn around each barrel as they pass it. In pole bending classes, a series of poles are set up in a straight line, and the horse-and-rider team weave in and out of the poles at a gallop. The patterns for both barrel racing and pole bending are performed by one horse-and-rider team at a time. In order to pull this feat off, gymkhana horses are trained to make balanced turns and respond quickly to their riders, all the while going as fast as they possibly can.

Gymkhana is a popular sport for good reason: Not only is it exciting to perform and to watch, but it's accessible to many equestrians. Kids, especially, love gymkhana because it's so much fun (although it can be more dangerous than some of the other tamer western events). Gymkhana horses don't have to be expensive or highly trained to be successful at local events. Plus, costly tack and attire are not necessary, because no dress code is enforced in the ring. Both rider and horse simply need to be athletic and dedicated to the sport to succeed.

Reining

The sport of reining is a western event that arose from the discipline's working legacy. Originally used as a way to maneuver horses around cattle, reining has become a challenging sport that requires substantial training for both horse and rider. Reining horses are asked to perform spins, circles, and sliding stops at the slightest cue from the rider.

Reining horses are judged on their ability to execute the various reining maneuvers with ease and grace. In traditional reining classes, the horse-and-rider team performs maneuvers and patterns alone in an arena before a

---

Getting started in showing

So you want to show your horse. How exactly do you go about doing that?

First, before you do anything else, you have to start working with a trainer who teaches riders to compete in the sport of your choice, if you are not doing so already. If you have any hope of winning in the show ring, working with a trainer is mandatory. Sure, you can compete on your own if you want to, but you just won't do very well.

The other thing you need to do is to make sure that you have the right horse. The event descriptions in this chapter point out the different equine qualities necessary to successfully compete in each event. If you already have a horse and want to start showing him, find an event that suits your horse. If you don't have a horse yet but plan to get one to show, make sure that horse is already successfully competing in the type of event you are interested in — or at least has been trained to do so.

After you have the right skills and the right horse, your trainer will help you enter your first show and may even provide transportation for your horse to the event.

judge. A newer event called *freestyle reining* requires the horse-and-rider team to perform to music. A popular favorite among spectators, the horse-and-rider teams sometimes wear costumes that coincide with the rider's musical theme. For example, at a recent Quarter Horse show, a freestyle reining horse-and-rider team were *both* dressed like Madonna and performed their reining pattern to the song *Vogue*. In freestyle reining, the spectators usually decide which team wins the class with the help of an applause meter.

For a horse to be successful in reining, he must have good, balanced conformation and be very well trained in the discipline of western riding. Successful riders in this sport possess excellent horsemanship skills that allow them to communicate effectively with their mounts.

Other than the costumes for freestyle reining, reining horses and their riders require no special attire. Neat, well-cared for tack and western clothing is all that judges expect in the show ring.

Trail class

Good trail horses are willing to negotiate just about any obstacle you put in their way. This concept is the basis for the trail class you find at many western shows. In this arena event, horses have to cope with a variety of objects that could possibly show up on the trail.

Trail class exhibitors compete one at a time in an arena that is set up with an obstacle course. Typical obstacles include the following:

- A gate to open and close by the rider, on horseback
- A mailbox to open and shut by the rider
- A tarp or puddle of water for the horse to step through
- A small bridge for the horse to walk over
- Wooden poles on the ground for the horse to step over or between

For a horse to be successful in trail classes, the animal must be very obedient, responsive, and willing to trust the rider's judgment. The horse must also be proficient at a maneuver called the *side pass,* which allows the horse to move in and around pole obstacles by walking sideways. Good trail horses are also skilled at backing up on command.

Trail classes require no special apparel, although successful horse-and-rider teams usually wear show tack and western show attire.

Cow classes

Because cow classes are based on the working cowboy tradition, fancy tack and clothing are not expected in the ring. All that cow classes require is good working gear and typical western clothing.

A number of different cow classes exist. Some require no direct contact with the cow, while others are rough-and-tumble events that cause the cow quite a bit of angst (and which get many animal rights activists up in arms), and sometimes result in broken bones for the rider. If you are interested in showing in cow classes, gauge each sport individually and pick the one best-suited to you. Following is a review of the most popular cow classes that you commonly see at horse shows and rodeos.

Cutting

Cutting is one of the gentlest of the cattle classes, requiring no direct contact with the cow. The sport has its roots in the 19th century, when the task of cutting individual cattle from the herd was part of a cowhand's job. In those days, cutting was a basic skill for every cowboy and his horse.

Today, cutting has been refined to a delicate art. The horse-and-rider team are placed in a pen with a small herd of cattle and asked to separate two animals from the group. Because cattle will stick together at nearly any cost, separating two of them is a real challenge for the team. The horse and rider are judged on how fast and effectively they move the designated cows away from the group. Judges look for horses who are athletic and have innate "cow sense," which is almost a psychic ability to know what the cow is going to do next.

What's interesting about this sport is that the rider's primary job in cutting is to not interfere with the horse. The rider simply tells the horse which cow to cut, and the rest is up to the horse. After the horse knows which cow needs working, the rider lets the horse do his job.

Many cutting horse trainers believe that good cutting horses are born, not made. Several Quarter Horse bloodlines are said to have a strong inborn cow sense. Horses from these bloodlines make the best cutting competitors. Some special training is necessary, though, which goes for the rider, too. Access to cattle is also important and one of the greatest challenges for those who want to learn and show in this sport.

Team penning

Team penning is an exciting event that is rapidly growing in popularity. Unlike other western events, team penning calls for cooperation between several horse-and-rider teams. In team penning classes, three teams must sort three designated cows from a small herd and pen them in a paddock located at the opposite end of the arena. The penning is timed, and the fastest, most accurate team wins.

Two different judges officiate team penning classes, watching the action from different positions around the arena. Two timekeepers keep track of each team's time.

Much of the growing popularity of team penning is attributable to the fact that just about any horse can participate, as long as the horse is fast, obedient, and has good cow sense.

You need access to cattle and other horse-and-rider teams if you want to train and participate in team penning. You also need a horse who has some cow sense.

Calf roping

Roping is another cow class that sprung from the cowboy's job. In the Wild West, cowboys used ropes to capture and restrain calves at branding time out on the range. These days, most calf roping goes on in the performance arena at rodeos, where it is a timed event.

Riders can choose from two types of roping: single roping and team roping. In single roping, a horse-and-rider team chases down a calf in the arena until the rider gets a rope around the cow's neck. After the rope lands on the calf, the rider ties her to the saddle horn, the horse stops short, and the rider leaps off, runs to the calf and ties three of her legs together. The object is to accomplish the task in the shortest amount of time possible. Another version of single roping is called *breakaway roping,* and doesn't require the rider to tie the calf. As soon as the rope becomes snug on the calf's neck, it breaks away from the saddle horn and the timer stops the watch.

Competitive team roping is performed by two horse-and-rider teams. One team is considered the *heeler,* the other the *header.* The heeler's job is to rope the calf's back legs, while the header gets the rope around the calf's neck.

Roping calls for considerable training on the part of both horse and rider, in addition to physical strength. You also need access to calves to learn this sport.

Breed Events

One of the benefits of owning a registered purebred horse is the chance to compete in breed shows. Regional breed clubs represent just about every popular breed and they hold local shows at least once a year. These shows are a great way to meet people in your area and educate yourself about your chosen breed.

The classes that breed shows offer depend quite a bit on the particular breed being exhibited. Clubs emphasize different aspects of their breed's history and style. Breed shows proffer a wide variety of classes, each of which is specific to the type of horse being shown.

Although we don't have room here to name every possible class you will see at a breed show, a few popular classes are seen at a variety of different breed shows.

Halter classes

In halter classes — some of the most popular events at breed shows — horses are led into the ring wearing nothing but a fancy show halter. They are asked to stand and trot in front of the judge without a rider as the judge evaluates their conformation and movement.

The judge uses a *breed standard* when evaluating the horses in a halter class. The breed standard specifies the physical characteristics of a theoretical "perfect" example of the breed. (We say theoretical because in real life, you won't find a perfect horse — every horse has faults.) The judge has this standard committed to memory, and mentally compares each horse in the ring to this ideal.

Halter classes are typically broken down by age and gender. Horses as young as four months of age are shown in weanling classes that are divided by sex. Mares are judged together, as are stallions, and also geldings (see Chapter 1 for an explanation of these terms). Some shows even hold *Get of Sire* and *Get of Dam* classes, where several offspring of a particular stallion or mare are brought into the ring for evaluation, with the award going to the parent horse.

If you want to show your horse in breed halter classes, you must have an animal with exceptional conformation. You must also spend time training the horse to stand quietly in the ring during its evaluation. The horse has to also learn to trot alongside you without running you over. Judges don't look highly upon flattened handlers in the halter class.

Heritage classes

One of the most exciting breed classes for spectators and exhibitors alike is the *heritage class.* In heritage classes, both the horse and rider are decked out in dress that represents the breed's history.

Not all breeds have these classes, but the ones that do make the most of the event. In Appaloosa heritage classes, for example, riders wear Native American regalia, while the horses are tacked up in authentic Native American saddles, bridles, and other trappings. At Arabian breed shows, the heritage class features horses and riders wearing the spectacular native dress of the Bedouins. The cast of *Lawrence of Arabia* had nothing on the participants in these classes.

Some of the other breeds that feature heritage classes at their shows include the following:

- Morgan (early American tack and clothing)
- Andalusian (Spanish tack and apparel)
- Paso Fino (South American or other Hispanic tack and costume)
- Pony of the Americas (Native American tack and regalia)

In heritage classes, the emphasis is on the authenticity and attractiveness of the tack and dress. People usually make their own apparel and horse clothing for these classes, because no stores sell ready-made heritage class garb (although some specialty catalogs can provide many of the bangles and fabrics you need).

Other cool stuff

Breed shows can be plenty of fun to watch and participate in. All sorts of interesting classes can be found at these events. Here are a few examples:

- **Liberty class:** At Miniature Horse shows and some Arabian shows, spectators enjoy a liberty class where horses run loose in the show ring, one at a time, to show their stuff. The handler encourages the horse on display to trot and gallop around the arena so the judge can see him in his free state. The real fun begins when the judge instructs the handler to catch the horse and take him out of the ring. Handlers face disqualification if they don't capture the excited horse within two minutes.

- **Cobra of Mares:** At some of the larger Andalusian horse shows, the Cobra of Mares class is the highlight of the event. In this class, breeders present as many as 20 mares at a time in a single formation. Each formation of mares is shown in the arena with other formations of mares. The mares wear no halters, but are linked together with collars around their necks. Moving abreast, shoulder to shoulder, each Cobra of Mares is of one color, and is handled by one person, for whom the mares walk, trot, and maneuver in large turns. The largest Cobras, featuring many mares and their unweaned foals, are a sight to behold. The young horses have a tendency to gallop wildly around the arena, their mothers performing at its center.

  The Cobra of Mares has a rich legacy, based in Spanish tradition. In the Andalusian's native country, breeders use lines of mares to thrash grain in the field. This task is one of the few that the female horse is asked to perform, because her real job — in the eyes of her caretakers — is to bear young.

- **Nez Percé stake race:** Appaloosa shows offer the Nez Percé stake race, a game class. Although the game can be played like a standard pole bending class (see "Gymkhana" in this chapter), at shows where the entries are large, it is played in the traditional Nez Percé way.

   In the traditional Nez Percé stake race, two horse-and-rider teams compete against one another. The teams start together, bolting forward and running down the right side of a row of poles. When the team reaches the last pole, each horse turns on a dime and weaves back through them, and then weaves back again on the left side, toward the finish line. Perfection and speed are mandatory. A fallen pole means elimination, as does a failure to be first at the finish.

- **Classic Fino class:** Many Paso Fino breed shows feature a class where riders take horses over a wooden board so the judges (and spectators) can hear the cadence of the horse's four-beat gait. The Paso Fino's movement over a sounding board is reminiscent of the human dancing at a Spanish *flamenco* show!

Competing on the Trail

Not all equine competitions happen in a show ring. In olden days, most horseback riding took place out in the wilderness, on trails that had been forged by mounted travelers or by migrating game. Riding on these trails was both exciting and challenging, and only the toughest horses and riders survived the harshest journeys.

Decades later, horse people who appreciate this legacy developed two events that celebrate trail riding while also adding a competitive factor: endurance riding and competitive trail riding. This section looks at both of these sports.

Endurance riding

The sport of endurance riding has grown in popularity over the past 20 years. The sport's most noteworthy event, the Tevis Cup, is run in Northern California each year and receives international coverage. Hundreds of smaller, local events are conducted around North America every year.

The object of endurance riding is to cover a given number of miles on horseback in the shortest amount of time. Endurance competitions often consist of 50- to 100-mile-per-day rides, or multiday rides that usually cover 50 miles per day over a period of from four to six days. The horse-and-rider team that gets to the finish line first is the winner. (Mandatory veterinary checks are given throughout the competition, and only horses who are considered physically fit are allowed to finish the event.)

Endurance riding calls for a horse-and-rider team that is extremely fit and athletic. A team must undergo serious training in the form of conditioning over a period of months before it can compete in an endurance ride. This rigorous type of riding calls for a horse who is extremely well-conditioned and comfortable on the trail. Riders must be very fit, too. Imagine sitting in the saddle for 100 miles with only a few short breaks in between. Achieving that kind of muscle strength and stamina takes considerable work.

All lighter-weight horse breeds can participate in endurance competition, although Arabians dominate the sport because of their great capacity to travel long distances. Horses in endurance rides are dressed in any type of tack that the rider prefers, although most use specially made endurance saddles and halter/bridle combinations (see Chapter 6 for details on riding equipment).

Competitive trail

Another sport that takes place on the trail is an event called competitive trail riding. Competitive trail riding is for those riders who enjoy conditioning their horses for trail riding and want to hone it to a fine art. Competitive trail events consist of approximately 25- to 50-mile-per day rides through various terrains. Unlike endurance riding, competitive trail events are not races. Instead of using time as a determining factor, judges evaluate horses primarily on their physical condition, with their obedience to the rider along the trail also a factor in many events. Speed is not important, as long as the horse and rider complete the ride within the minimum and maximum time limits. A veterinarian and a lay judge periodically examine the horses throughout the ride to determine their fitness as the day progresses.

In order to compete successfully in competitive trail rides, horses must be comfortable being ridden on the trail, must be in excellent physical condition, and must be well trained and obedient. Riders need to be in good shape, too, because even a 25-mile ride can mean a minimum of five straight hours in the saddle.

Just about any breed can participate in competitive trail riding. The rider determines the type of tack he or she uses. Most riders use endurance saddles and halter/bridle combinations.

Cross-Country Jumping

The practice of jumping on horseback started centuries ago when horses were the only form of transportation, and tree-strewn trails were the only avenues of travel. Cross-country jumping most resembles the type of jumping riders practiced before automobiles and paved roadways became a part of everyday human existence.

In cross-country jumping, horse-and-rider teams are expected to travel over a given distance and negotiate a series of jump obstacles in the least amount of time. The obstacles on cross-country courses can be daunting: trenches filled with water, huge wooden fences, and combinations of the two are only some of the stuff put in the horse's way. The animal is expected to jump over whatever he encounters without the least bit of hesitation. (Incidentally, this is the event that actor Christopher Reeve was training for when he fell and seriously injured himself after his horse refused to jump an obstacle.) Just about any breed of horse can compete in cross-country jumping, as long as the animal is athletic and possesses considerable jumping ability.

Cross-country competitions can be held on their own or in conjunction with combined training events, because cross-country is actually the second phase of combined training (see "Combined Training" in the next section).

Combined Training

Combined training, one of the Olympic disciplines, is also known as *eventing* and *three-day eventing*. By any name, this activity is a challenging marathon that requires horses and riders to display a variety of skills. Many in the horse world consider this exercise to be the most difficult of all equine sports.

Combined training events consist of three days of competition. On the first day, the horse and rider perform a dressage test. On the second day, the horse-and-rider team negotiate a cross-country jumping course, which consists of a series of obstacles laid out over a distance through the countryside. On the third day, the team confronts a show jumping course. (For more information on the individual events, see "Dressage," "Cross-Country Jumping," and "Show Jumping" earlier in this chapter.) Because each of these days of competition exacts a toll on the horse-and-rider team's skills and energy level, combined training requires considerable stamina and versatility from both horse and rider.

To compete successfully in combined training, both rider and horse must be well trained, well conditioned, and eager to compete. A variety of good jumping breeds, like the Thoroughbred and warmblood breeds, are most often seen in combined training events. The type of clothing that riders wear depends on the phase. The dressage and open jumping phases call for dress typical for these sports, although the cross-country phase allows riders to utilize tack and apparel that suits the individual team. (Safety helmets are always worn in cross-country.)

Driving

For equestrians who prefer to be behind the horse instead of on top of him, driving is an attractive sport. Older riders and physically-challenged equestrians are especially drawn to competitive driving because it requires less athleticism than the riding disciplines.

Driving competitions call for one or more horses to pull a two- or four-wheel rig. Most driving competitions in the United States call for one or two horses to a rig, but draft breeds often show in six- to eight-horse hitches (see Chapter 4 for information on draft breeds).

Many breed clubs encourage driving, and usually offer driving classes in their shows. The Morgan, American Saddlebred, Miniature Horse , and Arabian are some of the light breeds that can be shown in breed-specific driving classes, while all the draft breeds are routinely shown in heavy hitches.

The judging of driving, or harness, classes occurs in a variety of ways, depending on the type of rig and breed of horse. Arena classes usually are made up of flashy, animated horses. This type of driving generally features gaited horses because of their high-stepping movement.

Driving marathons, which are the harness equivalents to cross-country jumping (see "Cross-Country Jumping" earlier in this chapter) — but without the jumping —, demand that horse teams pull rigs through a countryside course dotted with obstacles they must negotiate. Driving marathon teams must be extremely well conditioned.

Combined driving — another driving event — is an Olympic discipline that consists of three phases much like the combined training sport (see "Combined Training" earlier in this chapter). In combined driving, a team of two driven horses performs presentation and arena dressage on the first day, which consists of walking and trotting patterns. On the second day, the team performs a _marathon driving_ phase over a six-mile course. On the final day, the team must expertly negotiate an arena obstacle course consisting of cones set up in various patterns.

To compete in driving classes, horses must be specially trained to pull a rig. If you are serious about showing in this discipline, you must invest a good amount of money in a quality harness and rig in which to present your horse.

Getting your horse to the show

Before you can compete, you have to physically get your horse where he needs to go, which means hauling your horse in a horse trailer.

Some horse owners wouldn't dream of not owning a trailer. Others get by just fine by paying other horse owners or professional towers for the service whenever they need it. Either way, here are some important things to know about trailering:

✔ **Learning to trailer.** Trailering a horse requires skills. Find a trainer or experienced person to help you learn to load and unload your horse, and hitch the trailer. Practice before show day.

✔ **Loading the horse.** Not every horse is amenable to getting inside a trailer. Fear and/or poor training are at the root of most loading difficulties.

No matter how badly you want your horse to get into a trailer, you cannot physically force him to load. The only way that half-ton beast is going to get in that tin can is if he is properly trained to do so.

Practice loading your horse in and out of the trailer well before show day. If your horse refuses to load, get the help of a horse trainer. Don't try handling the situation on your own or letting someone get involved who is not very knowledgeable. Poor handling of a horse who refuses to load will only make the situation worse. If you are unable

to retrain the horse or need to load him in an emergency, call a veterinarian to sedate the horse.

✔ **Towing realities.** You need a powerful vehicle to haul a horse trailer. A loaded two-horse trailer weighs around 5,000 pounds or more. Don't try to pull this kind of weight with a standard SUV or pick-up truck. If you do, you are at serious risk for an accident.

✔ **Careful driving.** When you are pulling a trailer with a horse in back, keep in mind that the horse is struggling to keep his balance. Drive as carefully as you can, making your turns wide, slow, and gradual. Avoid short stops and quick accelerations.

✔ **Horse safety.** Horses can easily injure themselves when riding in a trailer. Dress your horse with shipping boots, a head bumper, and a light blanket if you'll be traveling in cold weather.

✔ **Trailer safety.** Whether you are using your own trailer or renting someone else's, make sure that the trailer is in good condition. Check to make sure that the floorboards are not rotted, that divider and door latches are working properly, and that the ramp springs are in good condition. Also, be sure that the trailer is big enough for your horse to travel in comfort and that it provides plenty of ventilation.

Chapter 19

Just for Fun

. . . .

In This Chapter

▶ Discovering trail riding

▶ Riding in parades

▶ Helping others through horses

▶ Going camping with your horse

. . . .

*T*he greatest thing about horses is how much you can do with them! The horse world is filled with all kinds of activities for those who ride — and even for those who don't like to climb on board but just enjoy being around horses.

In this chapter, we introduce you to several of the most popular and enjoyable noncompetitive equine activities. These activities are meant to let you spend time in your horse's company and have plenty of fun doing it. (For details on competitive activities, see Chapter 18.)

The Joy of Not Competing

Horse shows are a lot of fun, no question. But some not-so-great stuff comes along with showing your horse. Pressure is one of these unfortunate side effects. No matter how casual you are about your show career, you are still under considerable stress at times. Stress comes with assorted show-related pressures: getting your horse ready to show, getting to the show on time, and performing well after you get there. This kind of stress may not be what you are hoping to experience in your spare time! After all, most people have enough pressure in their jobs without inviting it into their weekends, too.

Showing costs money — sometimes a lot of money. If you want to achieve any modicum of success in the show ring, you need an above-average horse, show tack, special apparel, and a way to get your horse to the show grounds.

You can opt not to deal with the down side of showing and still have a good time with your horse. In fact, many people who *don't* show claim that they share a greater bond with their horses than show riders and *their* horses do. Without the pressures of showing, horse-and-rider teams often form more uncomplicated attachments.

Trail Riding

The number-one activity among horse owners throughout North America is trail riding, a hobby that takes both horse and rider into the wide open spaces simply for the sheer joy of it. Whether you live in the urban wilds of New York City or the untamed wilderness of the Pacific Northwestern forests, trail riding is something you and your horse can enjoy together.

What it is

Trail riding is a very old activity. Before the days of automobiles, riding a horse on the trail was usually the only way to get from point A to point B. Today, people trail ride just for the fun of it. Few activities are as relaxing and therapeutic as riding a horse out in the open. Horses have a way of helping humans feel connected to nature, and never is this more true than when you are riding on a shady, wooded trail or through a sweet-smelling meadow.

Trail riding is accessible to just about everyone because equestrian trails are abundant. Even big cities have large parks where riders can trail ride. New York City's Central Park and London's Hyde Park are just two examples. If only for a short time, city dwellers can get on their horses, get under the trees, and leave the concrete jungle behind.

Most suburban areas have equestrian trails, too, which a county parks department usually maintains. Suburban trails sometimes wind in and out of housing developments, with an occasional venture into a park or other undeveloped area. Some suburban trails even connect to wilderness trails, on which you can ride all day without seeing anything that reminds you of civilization.

But the best trails in the world to ride on are wilderness trails, hands down. Wilderness trails take you through the most pristine environments, from deserts to beaches to forests. Wilderness trails also offer the greatest opportunity for spotting wildlife, one of the greatest perks of trail riding.

How you do it

Trail riding is a pretty simple activity. You just locate a trail, saddle up your horse, mount up, and start riding. Trail rides can be as short as an hour or as long as an entire day. Some trail rides even stretch out over a week or more. You just have to decide how much trail riding you want to do.

Short rides don't call for much preparation. Your tacked-up horse and an idea of where you are going is all you really require. Assuming that trails are available in close proximity to where you keep your horse, you can probably ride to the trail head (the place where the trail starts). Otherwise, you need to trailer your horse to get there.

Don't forget your horse's comfort on the trail. Unless you're riding in extreme cold or desert heat, horse-eating insects are a problem in the wide-open spaces. Spray your horse with equine insect repellent before you go on your ride. If gnats are a problem in your area, you may even want to invest in a simple knitted or mesh bonnet that protects your horse's ears from these biting insects (available from tack stores and catalogs).

If you plan to take longer rides, be sure that both you and your horse have access to water (particularly important if the weather is hot) and that you know where you're going in advance. Of course, you can always just go exploring, but make sure that you have an idea of how to get back to where you started. Contrary to myth, horses don't always know the way back home, especially if you are on a trail the horse has never seen before.

What you need

One of the nicest things about trail riding is you don't need a bunch of fancy stuff to do it. Here are the basic trail riding requirements:

- ✔ **A horse:** The most obvious thing you need to trail ride is a horse. You don't have to have a fancy animal that costs as much as a Mercedes. All you need is a quiet, obedient mount who is comfortable being ridden out on the trail. If you plan to go on long rides, your mount must also be exceptionally physically fit.

- ✔ **Tack:** You can't ride your horse on the trail without a saddle and bridle, so these are basic necessities. You can use any kind of saddle for trail riding, although western saddles and endurance saddles are the most comfortable for longer rides and the tack of choice for those who do nothing but trail ride. The kind of bridle you use depends on what discipline you typically ride. Many trail riders use combination bridle/halters with attached lead ropes so they can safely tie their horses up during breaks on the trail. (See Chapter 6 for details on tack.)

Make sure that whatever kind of tack you use is in good repair before you head out on a trail ride.

- **Clothes:** A park ranger will arrest you if you try to trail ride in your skivvies, so clothes are a must. You'll need comfortable riding clothes if you plan to enjoy yourself. If you are riding in hot weather, wear a cool shirt that protects you from the sun but lets your skin breathe at the same time. In cold weather, wear layers of clothing to stay warm. Wear appropriate riding pants and high boots, paddock boots, or riding shoes for safety. And don't forget your helmet. Taking a spill while riding on the trail is a constant concern, so protection for your head is a must. Helmets also come in handy when you ride underneath low-lying branches.

- **Accessories:** All kinds of fun accessories are available to trail riders. The basic ones you need for longer rides are a saddle bag, a water bottle and holder, a hoof pick, and a small first-aid kit (see Chapter 10 for information on what a first-aid kit should contain). Your saddle bag can hold the hoof pick, the first-aid kit, your lunch, insect repellent, lip balm, and whatever other items you want to bring with you. The hoof pick is to remove any rocks that lodge in your horse's hooves. The water bottle and holder are for your hydrating needs, and the first-aid kit is to deal with any minor injuries (yours or your horse's) that occur on the trail.

If you own a cell phone, consider bringing it with you on trail rides. In an emergency situation on the trail, a cell phone can be a lifesaver.

- **A buddy or two:** Riding alone on the trail can be relaxing and enjoyable, but going with a friend is always best, especially when you are first starting out as a trail rider. If an emergency arises — such as your horse becoming seriously injured or you falling and becoming immobile — having another person with you can make a big difference in the eventual outcome.

Companionship is another reason to ride with a buddy. Trailing riding is a great way for horsy friends to enjoy each other's company.

Parades

If you've always wanted to participate in a parade but you couldn't walk and play the sousaphone at the same time, then a horse may be just the answer. Maybe you can ride and play the sousaphone, instead! Then again, maybe not; but have you ever seen a parade without horses in it? Probably not. Horses and parades go hand in hand. And as an equestrian, you automatically qualify to move from parade watcher to parade participant.

Riding in a parade can be tremendous fun. You and your horse are in the spotlight (along with your mounted comrades), and all you have to do is look good and wave!

What it is

The equestrian units you see in big parades are part of organized riding groups. The riders may be members of a youth riding club, representatives of a breed organization, or part of a horseback drill team group. The group's theme in the parade usually represents whatever the riding club is all about. For example, if the club is a military-style riding group for youngsters, the kids wear their uniforms and most likely carry flags. If the riders represent a local palomino horse club, all the horses are palominos tacked up in their finest garb.

How you do it

To become a participant in a big parade, you must be a member of an organized riding group, unless you are a celebrity and can justify participating on your individual merits! (If you have to think about whether you're a celebrity, chances are good that you're not.) In many smaller towns and cities, however, the parades are small and informal enough that individuals riders can also sign up.

If riding in big parades is for you, your first step is to join a local riding group. Of all the different kinds of riding groups, pick the one that best suits your age group and riding interests. Your parks and recreation department should be able to provide you with some names and numbers of riding groups in your area.

If you are joining an organized group primarily to do parade riding, make sure that parades are a regular part of their activities before you sign up!

Parade rides usually start early in the morning and last for several hours. The equestrian entries tend to be spaced apart in between other parade participants, and all participants start the parade route at a specific time. The equestrian entries are expected to ride through the entire parade route to the end with no breaks. You are on stage, after all, and parades don't have intermissions!

What you need

The basics of what you need to ride in a parade vary depending on your riding group. However, some basics are the same for all parade riders:

 ✔ **A good parade horse:** Parade riding is a blast for humans, but for some horses it can be nothing more than a series of nerve-wracking horrors. Marching bands, weird-looking floats, cheering crowds — all these things can drive certain horses to distraction. To have a good time riding in a parade, you need a horse who has a quiet personality and some experience with crowds and loud noises. Your riding group can help you mentally condition your horse for parades, but you need to start with an animal who is relatively calm to begin with.

If you want to ride in parades, you also need a horse who loads into a horse trailer easily. The I'm-not-going-in-that-trailer attitude just won't cut it on the morning you are rushing to get to the parade grounds on time.

✔ **Nice tack:** If you want to ride in parades on a regular basis, you should probably invest in a nice show saddle, complete with silver trimmings. Most — but not all — equestrians in parades ride in western show saddles. Check with your riding group to find out what type of tack your fellow members use for parades.

✔ **Fancy clothes:** Again, what you wear depends on whom you are riding with. If your group has a western theme, then some attractive western show clothes are in order. If you belong to a breed club, the group may prefer to dress in clothing that emphasizes the breed's heritage. And guess what you wear if your riding club is a military unit? If you said anything other than your uniform, drop and give us 50!

You don't have to own a horse trailer to participate in parades. Other people in your riding club will own trailers and your horse can double up with one of theirs when you need to take them to the parade grounds.

Drill Teams

If your favorite part of Hollywood westerns is when the cavalry charges the enemy, then drill team riding may be the hobby for you. Drilling on horseback is tons of fun and gives riders an opportunity to meet and socialize with others who enjoy the same activity.

What it is

Drilling on horseback is a very old activity, one that goes back all the way to the Roman legions and possibly before. In the old days, when horses were the primary vehicles of war, drilling was used to train mounted soldiers to follow commands with precision and obedience.

Today, drill team work is done mostly for fun. Riders who enjoy drilling get together and form clubs that practice at least once a week and sometimes more. They perform their precision drill work in parades, at county fairs, and during horse shows.

How you do it

Most drill teams consist of ten to twelve horse-and-rider duos, sometimes more. A drill caller gives drill commands that horse-and-rider teams follow. Each command requires a specific movement; when several horse-and-rider teams perform these moves in conjunction, the group ends up moving as a unit.

Because of its military foundation, drill-team work calls for discipline on the part of the rider and obedience on the part of the horse. You need to memorize each maneuver and have your horse execute it at the moment you hear the command. You rehearse exhibition drills, and after a few practices with your group, you know exactly what is coming from the drill caller. The drills you perform at exhibitions and horse shows are the same drills that you and your team have performed at home many times over.

What you need

One of the perks of drill-team work is that you don't need to invest a whole lot of money to participate in the activity. The following is all you need:

✔ **A cooperative horse:** Just about any horse can do drill-team work, as long as the animal is obedient and well mannered. Some horses really enjoy drill-team work and look forward to it (you can tell by their happy, relaxed attitude when they are working — see Chapter 2 for tips on reading equine body language). They like the excitement of working right next to other horses, as well as the quick movements and sharp turns that drill-team work requires.

Horses who don't like being in close proximity to other horses don't do well at drill-team work, and can even pose a danger to others if they have a tendency to kick or bite other equine participants.

✔ **Good tack:** You don't need fancy tack to ride in a drill team unless the riding group you belong to demands it. At least for practice, anyway, you can simply ride in a comfortable, well-fitted western saddle. (Some groups use English saddles or the old-style military McClellan saddles to more closely replicate the tack used by the cavalry.)

✔ **An outfit:** Drill teams are usually color-coordinated, so your group will probably tell you what you need to wear when the drill team is performing for the public. Some kind of hat will be in order (most likely a western one), plus a shirt and pants in specific colors or even designs. This outfit is unlikely to cost you much money. You may even be able to pull it together from stuff you already have in your wardrobe.

Hippotherapy

"It all goes back to your relationship with your mother; okay, next hippo please." Actually, strangely enough, *hippotherapy,* from the Greek word *hippos* meaning "horse," refers to horses and their incredible therapeutic effect on humans. People quickly forget a hard day at the office when they find themselves in the company of a horse. Teenagers who struggle with the difficulties of growing up find great solace in their equine companions. And those people who just need a four-legged friend to lean on once in a while have found that horses make wonderful best friends.

For some people, life offers even more challenges than just the everyday stuff that most of us deal with. For these physically and mentally challenged individuals, horses can provide an almost magical therapy.

What it is

Hippotherapy is a treatment that uses the movement and very essence of the horse's being to help those with physical and mental challenges develop better control over their bodies and minds. Specially trained therapists use hippotherapy in a controlled environment with the goal of improving the motor control and mental abilities of people with challenges. One aspect of hippotherapy called *therapeutic riding* actually teaches specific riding skills to physically-challenged persons.

Hippotherapy is usually conducted at special centers dedicated to providing this type of service to patients whose physicians refer them. The hippotherapy center owns or leases very quiet and easygoing horses used in these programs. Incredible stories abound of people overcoming their challenges with the help of these very special horses.

How you do it

Therapists specializing in physical, occupational, and emotional therapy perform the professional work of hippotherapy. But without specially-trained volunteers, most hippotherapy centers wouldn't exist. Volunteers are not only welcome in these programs — most facilities that offer hippotherapy desperately need them.

You don't need to own a horse to volunteer at a hippotherapy center, because most centers own or lease horses. In many cases, you don't even need horse-handling experience at all. The staff at hippotherapy centers train volunteers to do various jobs such as leading horses, *sidewalking* (walking alongside the mounted rider to provide support), grooming, tacking up, and cleaning tack.

Most hippotherapy facilities accept volunteers over the age of 14. Because young volunteers are welcome, hippotherapy centers are a great place for teens to learn about horsemanship while helping others in need.

To become a volunteer at a hippotherapy center, locate a facility in your area, call them, and offer your services. To find a center near you, you can contact the North American Riding for the Handicapped Association (see Appendix B), or look in your telephone directory under "riding academies."

What you need

Most centers don't require you to have horse experience. Of course, some experience is helpful, but volunteering is actually a good way to hone your own horse sense.

Vacationing with Your Horse

Can't get enough of your equine companion? Want to take that horse with you next time you go on vacation? Don't laugh — many people do just that, and have a great time, too! The practice of taking a horse along on vacation is becoming more and more popular every year. People are discovering that having their horse along on a trip — when they can do more than weekend riding — is just plain fun.

If your usual vacation spot is a beach in the Bahamas, you'll need to alter your plans a bit to accommodate your horse, but not by much. The number of neat places you can go with your horse in tow is amazing.

You can take your horse on vacation with you in one of two ways:

- You can go camping with your horse in specially designated horse-camping campgrounds or in the backcountry (where the paved roads don't go).
- You can trailer your critter to a horseback vacation resort that allows you to bring your own horse.

Horse camping

If you love regular camping, then you will *really* love horse camping. Few things are as wonderful as waking up on a dewy morning in your tent and hearing your horse munching his hay just outside.

Horse camping is not a new activity. Before the days of cars, plenty of people on long journeys were *forced* to horse camp! Today, horse camping is a recreational activity and quite enjoyable at that.

What it is

Horse camping is, simply, camping with horses. It has all the same elements as regular camping, except that your horse comes with you and you get to ride him on your camping trip. Horse camping can be done the same way as "car camping," where you drive up to your campsite, or the same way as backpacking, where you hike — or in this case ride, to your campsite.

Many people go horse camping in tents, with their horses tied or corralled nearby. Others bring RVs along so they can have a bit of luxury in the great outdoors. Many people think that the best horse camping comes when you sleep in a tent, though. When you tent camp, you stand a better chance of hearing your horse moving around through the night. Not only are you able to keep watch on your horse, but you also get neat, regular reminders that he's out there. Sure, if you're a light sleeper, you won't get a really good night's rest this way, but we think that knowing your horse is okay is better than sleeping like a rock. Save that for when you get home!

The biggest reason people take their horses camping is so they can go trail riding with them. Although most campers hike on camping trips, horse campers *ride*. Coming out of your tent in the morning, feeding the horses, cooking up your breakfast, and then heading out on the trail is a great feeling.

How you do it

Camping with horses is a little more complicated than camping without them. You need to trailer the horse to the campsite and then secure the horse so he doesn't wander off in the middle of the night.

Horse campers use a few different ways to keep their horses close to camp:

- **Campground corrals:** Campgrounds that are specially designated for horses often have permanent corrals made of pipe or other strong material. These corrals are usually secure, and your best bet when horse camping. When your horse is in a permanent corral, you tend to rest a little easier. You rarely see campground corrals in the backcountry, so keep that in mind if the security of a corral is important to you. (See Chapter 7 for details on what makes a corral safe.)

- **Portable corrals:** A number of different portable corrals are on the market, designed to keep camped-out horses from leaving the campsight of their own accord. These portable corrals fold up; you can store them in a truck or horse trailer — or even in a horse pack — and then put them together when you set up camp. Some of them come with electricity so the horse gets a mild shock if he tries to bust out. The benefits of portable corrals are that they allow the horse freedom to move about and lie down. The problem, however, is that they serve mostly as a mental barrier rather than a physical one. If a horse really wants to get out of a portable corral, he will — and that includes the electric ones.

✔ **Tie-outs:** Many horse campers opt to tie their horses to a tie-out, or picket, strung between two trees or staked to the ground. For a horse to be safely tied out or staked out, the animal must be used to this kind of restraint. Otherwise, the horse may get himself tangled up, panic, and incur serious injuries. The benefit of tying out a horse when camping is that tying gives you the freedom to camp wherever you like, knowing your horse is secure. The downside is that the horse is at risk for getting tangled in the line.

✔ **Trailer tying:** Some horse campers tie their horses to the rings on the side of a horse trailer with a lead rope (see Chapter 17 for details on how to tie horses). This method is good for keeping the horses nearby and under close watch, but the problem is that the horse can't lie down, something he needs to do to get valuable REM sleep (see Chapter 20 for information on how horses sleep).

✔ **Hobbles:** Hobbles, available at tack stores or through equine catalogs, work by attaching two of the horse's legs together so the horse can't move with any real speed. For horse camping, grazing hobbles are used to restrain the horse's forelegs. Hobbles won't stop a horse from wandering away completely — they only slow the horse down. You must get your horse used to wearing hobbles in advance so he won't panic when he feels his legs restrained. Horses wearing hobbles can lie down and sleep at night.

What you need

To really enjoy your horse camping expedition, you need the following:

✔ **A plan:** Embark on your camping trip with a solid idea of where you are going and how to get there. Make reservations at your campsite, if possible, and be sure to choose a campground that has drinkable water, which is available to your horse at all times. Horses need plenty of fresh water to stay healthy, especially in hot weather.

✔ **An experienced horse:** Horses who have never left the stable are not good candidates for horse camping. A horse should be used to traveling and riding on unfamiliar trails before you take him on an overnight trip. Your horse should also be relatively calm. Horses who frighten at the drop of a hat can be a hazard on a camping trip. The horse must load easily into a trailer, too, unless you want to begin and end your camping trip with a battle!

✔ **A horse trailer:** Unless you plan to ride from the stable to the campground, you need a horse trailer to pull your steed behind you. Make sure that your trailer is in good shape before you head out on a camping trip (see the trailering sidebar in Chapter 18).

✔ **Camping experience:** Don't make your horse camping experience your very first camping experience. Successful camping — especially tent camping — takes some practice. Learn how to do it on your own first before you add your horse to the mix.

✔ **Camping buddies:** Plan your horse camping trip to include a friend or two. Camping with friends is not only safer, but it's much more fun, too!

✔ **Camping gear for humans and horses:** Don't throw all your gear together in the last minute. Make a list a week before your trip so you won't forget to bring something important.

Besides your usual camping equipment, your horse needs you to bring some stuff for him too: a halter and lead rope, saddle, bridle, saddle pad, grooming tools, a first-aid kit for the road (see Chapters 9 and 10), a water bucket, a supply of your horse's usual food, and insect repellent.

Horse resorts

Horse resorts are resorts with facilities and activities that are horse friendly. They are ususaly located in wilderness areas, and feature homey, country-style themes. Many offer organized trail rides, riding lessons, and other horse activities. Many also offer a number of wonderful luxuries for non-horsy human guests.

Before you pick a horse resort for your vacation, do some research. First, figure out how far you want to drive to get there (remember, your horse will be in tow!). Then, start scoping out the horse resorts that are within that driving distance. You can also consider shipping your horse ahead of you by using a horse transportation company, and then flying to the resort yourself. This will cost you a bit of dough, though, so be prepared.

Before you make reservations at any horse resort, ask these questions.

✔ Can I bring my horse?

✔ What health certificates are required?

✔ Can you send me written information on the facility, including rates?

✔ Can you provide me with some guest references?

✔ Do you have what I want in a vacation?

Part VI
The Part of Tens

The 5th Wave   By Rich Tennant

"I thought you said he's been trained.
He just passed after I bid 1 No Trump."

In this part . . .

The Part of Tens is a hodgepodge of fun information regarding horses. In these chapters, we tackle some of the most common myths about the equine species. We also present you with a list of some of the best riding vacations around, where you can not only learn to ride but also have a great time doing it.

Chapter 20

Ten Horse Tales — Debunked!

· ·

In This Chapter

▶ How horses think

▶ Matters of equine health

▶ How horses meet their end

· ·

*G*iven how long horses have been a part of human culture, the fact that oodles of equine misinformation abound isn't surprising. Although the horse may not be as maligned as Sasquatch, the poor equine has suffered his share of urban myths.

As horse lovers, we're here to set the record straight regarding horses, their behavior, and various other stuff about them.

Horses Are Stupid

Horses are not the only non-human animal to suffer under this assumption. In fact, dogs seem to be the only species that isn't regularly thought of by humans as lacking in brain power.

The myth that horses are stupid is a result of human misunderstanding of equine behavior. Humans tend to judge other animals by themselves, or at the very least, by man's best friend, the dog. After watching and interacting with horses for a short time, you realize that these animals are smart — often smarter than we would like them to be.

Horses are not predators like dogs nor cognitive thinkers like humans. They are a prey species that has been designed by nature to function in a completely different way. The main purpose of nearly all of equine behavior is to survive in a potentially hostile environment. So, although horses may not be capable of sniffing out bombs like Beagles or understanding the exact meaning of human language, their behaviors all add up to brilliance at the job of survival.

Horses Will Run into a Burning Barn

We're not sure where this myth came from because we've never heard of a horse who ran toward a fire instead of away from it. Maybe somewhere, at some time, a horse or two *did* run back into a burning barn in a panic. Going back to the barn could make sense from the horse's perspective in certain circumstances, because horses who have lived their whole lives in box stalls (an unnatural way to keep a horse, by the way) associate those stalls with safety. The instinct to return to the place of safety during a frightening moment dominates a horse's thinking. A horse doesn't have the reasoning power to understand that the barn is no longer safe because fire will soon consume it.

Horses Always Sleep Standing Up

Because they are prey animals and need to make a quick getaway in times of emergency, horses have an amazing ability to doze on their feet. However, contrary to myth, they *do* lie down for heavy-duty shut-eye. In order for a horse to get the few hours of valuable REM sleep each day that is necessary for good health, he must either lie flat on his side, or in a recumbent position with his nose resting on the ground.

Horses Never Get Sick

Horses, as a species, are plagued with all kinds of health problems, many of which have been exacerbated by domestication. The average horse needs to be seen by a vet a couple of times a year for minor problems, but plenty of horses come down with at least one major illness in their lifetimes.

Horses Are Mean

If you've ever ridden a horse who has treated you unkindly, you're probably surprised to see meanness listed in this book as a myth. Unfortunately, a great many people have had unpleasant first-time experiences with horses. Then again, most people have their first riding experiences at poorly run, rent-by-the-hour stables (something we vehemently recommend against in this book). Not realizing that the horses at many of these establishments are poorly trained and badly treated, these first-time riders get up on the animal expecting to have a pleasant experience and end up traumatized because the horse tries to rub them off on a tree, run away with them, or get down on his knees and roll while they're in the saddle.

Horses who behave this way are reflecting the unkind and callous way they have been treated by the people responsible for their care and are by no means the norm in the horse world. The great majority of horses are gentle, friendly, and willing to do anything asked of them, provided they are given kindness and respect in return.

Horses Are Aloof

Human beings have a tendency to judge all other animals by the dog. Most dogs are happy, friendly, and demonstrative. When a dog likes you, you know it. That wagging tail and kissy tongue are hard to miss.

Horses, on the other hand are different. Dogs are easy when it comes to love. With a horse, you really have to earn it. And after you do earn that love and trust (and gaining such feeling from a horse is an honor and an accomplishment on your part), it will be expressed to you in subtle ways: a head gently pressed against your chest, a soft whinny, or a nuzzle with a velvet nose. Horses are not aloof; they are simply more discerning and more subtle in demonstrating affection than your average canine.

Horses Whinny a Lot, Just Like in the Movies

Next time you see a western, play close attention. You'll discover that the horses in the movie whinny every time they appear on screen. You won't see their mouths move, or witness any logical reason for their vocalizations. Instead, they'll just gallop into scenes, accompanied by the sound. Sometimes you'll hear the whinny as the horse comes to a sudden stop; other times, as the horse takes off at a mad gallop. Sometimes you'll hear the whinny when the horse is just standing there in the background, doing absolutely nothing.

In case you haven't figured it out by now, the horses in the movie are not actually whinnying. Their neighs are equine sound effects that have been added by the filmmakers for effect.

As you become more and more familiar with equine behavior, this constant cinematic whinnying will start to drive you crazy. You'll come to realize that horses only whinny for certain reasons: when they are anticipating being fed; when they are greeting a friend; or when they are engaged in courtship or parenthood. They don't whinny when their actor-rider needs to make a grand entrance; they don't whinny when the director wants to make sure that the audience knows they're watching a western; and they sure as heck don't whinny with their mouths closed!

They Shoot Horses, Don't They?

Well, they used to. A gunshot wound to the head was once the traditional way of putting a horse "out of its misery." In some very rural places, shooting is still the method of choice for destroying a horse. But for the most part, an injection administered by a veterinarian is the most widely used — and most humane — form of euthanasia for suffering equines these days.

Old Horses Go to the Glue Factory

This myth is a hundred years old or more, yet it still persists. In the old days, horses too old to work were sent to the glue factory for slaughter so their parts could be used to make glue. Today, natural glue is made mostly from the skin, bones, and hooves of cattle, which are by-products of the food animal industry.

Instead of going to the glue factory, unwanted horses these days are sent off to slaughter, where their meat is used mostly for human consumption in parts of Europe and Japan. Unlike the days of the glue factory, when only old horses were used for their parts, today's slaughterhouses receive horses of any age and condition. (See Chapter 12 for more information on equine slaughter.)

A Horse Who Breaks His Leg Must Be Destroyed

As recently as 20 years ago, this statement would have been true. Today, however, advancements in veterinary medicine have created a world where a fractured leg no longer means a death sentence.

Horses used to be destroyed when they broke a leg because mending a fractured leg was notoriously difficult. The fact that equine legs are too big for casting and the unavailability of general anesthesia, sterile conditions, equipment large enough to handle a horse, and surgeons capable of performing the delicate surgery made the procedure fail most of the time. Attempts to fix broken bones often resulted in infection in the affected leg or severe founder in the opposite hoof, a result of bearing all the weight of the horse while the broken leg was healing.

Nowadays, through much work and determination in the veterinary profession, a good number of veterinarians are skilled enough to perform the necessary surgery. Also, equipment and metal leg implants large enough for a horse needing care for a fracture are readily available.

Chapter 21

Ten Great Horse Vacations

*P*erhaps you're wondering how to best get started in riding. Maybe you've ridden a little already but want to spend some intensive time gaining even more knowledge. Or maybe you just want to spend an extended period of time in the saddle. Regardless of which of these scenarios describes you best, a horseback riding vacation may be exactly what you need.

Horseback vacations come in different styles. Some take place at resorts, where riding is only one of several activities you and your family can participate in. Others are intensive adventures where you ride for days on end while you see the countryside.

Spending time on a horseback vacation is a great way to learn to ride, provided you choose the right kind of vacation. A week-long, training-intensive vacation can provide an incredible opportunity to learn while you get away from it all. In this chapter, we outline ten different riding vacations around the world that are suitable for beginning to advanced riders. We're confident that you'll find any of these vacations a wonderful and enriching experience.

Luxury in the Golden State

If you want to learn to ride, but your spouse would rather golf and your kids just want to swim, then the Alisal Guest Ranch and Resort, located in the beautiful Santa Ynez Valley (just a two-hour drive north of Los Angeles) may be the spot for you.

The Alisal features daily picturesque trail rides that include a view of scenic Alisal Lake. Because the Alisal is also a working cattle ranch, you can see plenty of steers and even mule deer grazing on the hillsides. You can ride just for fun or request instruction with your ride. The Alisal's horses are gentle and well behaved, making them perfect mounts for first-time riders.

The accommodations at the resort consist of comfortable, western-style cottages and excellent dining. Non-riders can take advantage of the expansive golf course, petting zoo, heated swimming pool, tennis courts, and other amenities. For more information, contact the Alisal Guest Ranch and Resort, 1054 Alisal Road, Solvang, CA 93463; (800) 4-ALISAL; e-mail: alisal@alisal.com.

Riding among the Maples

Does having the beauty of New England as a backdrop to riding instruction sound good? If so, think about signing up for Equitour's Adult Trail Riding Clinic in South Woodstock, Vermont. At this six-day clinic, you'll spend your time perfecting your English riding. Morning arena work helps improve your seat and balance, while afternoon trail rides help you hone your skills.

Kedron Valley Inn in South Woodstock provides your dinner and overnight accommodations. For more information, contact Equitour, P.O. Box 807, Dubois, WY 82513; (800) 545-0019; e-mail: equitour@wyoming.com.

Irish Riding

Ireland is a perfect place to learn to ride hunt seat, especially when you do so at the Clonshire Equestrian Centre in County Limerick. Here you receive expert instruction from British-Horse-Society–approved instructors both in the arena and out in the Irish countryside. You also get a day off during the week to tour the sights of this historic area.

Your accommodations are at the comfortable Dunraven Arms Hotel, where non-riders in your family can hike, fish, and golf. For more information, contact Cross Country International, P.O. Box 1170, Millbrook, NY 12545; (800) 677-6077; e-mail: xcintl@aol.com.

Discovering Yellowstone

Nothing is better for the spirit than a trail ride though the stunning environs of Yellowstone National Park. Although many trail rides are too strenuous for beginning riders, the Yellowstone Backcountry Ride is perfect for those who are just beginning to master the art of riding.

The Yellowstone ride consists of six days of horseback touring through one of the most remarkable national parks in the United States. Riders camp out in tents at night and are fed breakfast, lunch, and dinner. The horses are quiet and well trained, and gaits are limited to walking and trotting, with an occasional canter. For more information, contact Boojum Expeditions, 14543 Kelly Canyon Road Bozeman, MT 59715; (800) 287-0125; e-mail: boojum@mcn.net.

Riding and Resting

Those who want to experience English riding while having access to all the luxuries of a modern resort will appreciate the Equestrian Centre and Resort at Penmerryl Farms, located in the Shenandoah Valley of Virginia. At this bed and breakfast style resort, you can practice the fine points of cross-country jumping, eventing, trail riding, and hunt seat.

When you want a break from your lessons, you can take a dip in the pool, a hike in the woods, or a swing at a tennis ball. For more information, contact The Equestrian Centre at Penmerryl Farm, P.O. Box 402, Greenville, VA 24440; (800) 808-6617; e-mail: equesctr@penmerryl.com.

Flavor of the Old West

Not far from Phoenix, Arizona, a place called Merv Griffin's Wickenburg Inn and Dude Ranch gives people from all over the world a taste of the old west. Here you can brush up on your western riding as you ride through the Sonoran desert, drive cattle, and even rope steer.

In addition to riding, you can visit the resort's arts and crafts studio, nature museum, or pools and spas. Other activities include mountain biking, jeep tours, and hiking. Because the inn offers so much to do besides ride, this vacation is excellent for the non-riders in your family. For more information, contact Merv Griffin's Wickenburg Inn and Dude Ranch, 34801 North Highway 89, Wickenburg, AZ 85390; (800) 942-5362; e-mail: wickinn@primenet.com.

Trail and Training in Spain

Does the idea of learning to ride in the romantic countryside of Spain appeal to you? Then the Epona Training and Trail Ride in southern Spain could be your dream vacation. You stay at the Epona estate, an 18th-century hacienda located between Carmona and Seville. In the mornings, you take lessons from British-Horse-Society–approved instructors, and in the afternoons, you trail ride though the Spanish countryside.

As though all these features aren't enough, your vacation includes a performance of classical dressage by the horses of *Real Escuela Andaluza del Arte Ecuestre*. For more information, contact Cross Country International, P.O. Box 1170, Millbrook, NY 12545; (800) 677-6077; e-mail: xcintl@aol.com.

Hunt Seat Riding in New York State

If you are serious about learning to ride hunt seat, consider spending several days at the Millbrook Equestrian Centre, located in Millbrook, New York, just north of New York City. Your spend your nights at a local inn, and your mornings are filled with riding instruction. In the afternoon, you have the chance to practice your skills as you ride on scenic trails.

Millbrook Equestrian Centre is one of only a few riding centers in the United States that is approved by the British Horse Society, which means their instructors have completed a three-year training program. For more information, contact Cross Country International, P.O. Box 1170, Millbrook, NY 12545; (800) 677-6077; e-mail: xcintl@aol.com.

Cowboy Riding

Many men — and a good many women — dream of mastering the skills of western riding. If you'd like to combine a week of cowboy living with intensive instruction in this discipline, check out Equitour's Old West Training Program near Kerrville, Texas. During the program, a National Cutting Horse Association champion schools you in western riding. After your basic skills are up to snuff, you're shown how to negotiate an obstacle course, and taught team penning and cutting. For more information, contact Equitour, P.O. Box 807, Dubois, WY 82513; (800) 545-0019; e-mail: equitour@wyoming.com.

G'Days in the Saddle

If you've been riding long enough to be comfortable at the trot and canter and know how to groom and tack up a horse, why not venture outback to experience Australia's high country in the Pub Crawl, a week-long ride through New South Wales? On the Pub Crawl, riders trek over 150 kilometers of rugged countryside, traveling from one quaint village to another.

You need to have a decent amount riding experience under your belt to tackle this vacation, although the many hours on the trail will greatly improve the skills you already have. For more information, contact Equitour, P.O. Box 807, Dubois, WY 82513; (800) 545-0019; e-mail: equitour@wyoming.com.

Part VII
Appendixes

The 5th Wave   By Rich Tennant

"He prefers it to trotting."

In This Part . . .

Horses For Dummies contains a pair of useful appendixes. Appendix A is a glossary that you can use to look up terms that you momentarily forget the meaning of. Appendix B is a collection of useful equine resources that you may want to look into as you continue to gain knowledge of things equine.

Appendix A

Glossary of Equine Terms

above the bit: an avoidance move where the horse places his mouth above the rider's hands on the reins to circumvent the pressure of the bit

abscess: a swollen pocket containing pus

acre: a unit of land measuring 4,840 square yards

action: the way a horse moves at the various gaits

aged: a horse over the age of 9 years

Banamine: brand-name for the painkiller flunixin, used by veterinarians

bale: a measurement of hay; made up of ten flakes

barn-sour: a horse who refuses to leave his stable or barn, or wants to return to the barn, when being ridden

behind the bit: an avoidance move where the horse places his head down to evade contact with the bit

Betadine: a patented antiseptic scrub

bomb proof: a horse who rarely spooks

bot fly: an insect that lays its eggs on the legs of horses, where they are ingested to begin a parasitic life cycle in the horse's stomach

brand: an identifying mark made on a horse either by burning the skin and removing the hair, or by using a freezing method that removes pigment from the coat

British Horse Society (BHS): a British organization that trains and certifies riding instructors in Europe and most recently, the United States.

breeder: a person who breeds purebred horses as a hobby or for a living

broodmare: a female horse used strictly for breeding

buck: when a horse jumps upward with an arched back, his head down, forelegs stiffened; hindlegs, and sometimes forelegs, lift off the ground

burro: A small member of the equine family; same as a donkey

bute: see phenylbutazone

by: fathered by

capped elbow: scarring or swelling of the point of the elbow

capped hock: scarring or swelling of the point of the hock

canter: English discipline term for a three-beat gait; same as a lope or slow gallop

cast: when a horse rolls against a wall or fence and becomes lodged there, requiring assistance to get up

Coggins test: blood test for equine infectious anemia (EIA)

cold-blooded: a heavy draft horse

colt: an intact male horse under the age of four years

dam: the mother of a horse

dapples: round, self-colored markings on a horse's coat

DMSO: dimethylsulfoxide; used in veterinary medicine as an anti-inflammatory agent

D.V.M.: Doctor of Veterinary Medicine

donkey: A small member of the equine family; same as a burro

easy keeper: a horse whose proper weight is easy to maintain

enteroliths: a stone formation in the intestine

equine infectious anemia (EIA): infectious disease of the blood characterized by depression, fever, weakness and anemia; also known as swamp fever

filly: a female horse under the age of 4 years

fistulous withers: infection of the withers often caused by a poor fitting saddle

flake: a measurement of hay; a bale of hay contains ten flakes

flexion test: a test of soundness, performed by a vet who flexes the leg for one minute before trotting the horse

Flehmen response: when a horse curls back his upper lip in response to a stimulating odor or taste

foal: a baby horse still at his mother's side

founder: condition of the foot caused by rotation of coffin bone; also known as laminitis

founder rings: rings in the hoof wall caused by laminitis

gallop: a three-beat gait; the fastest speed a horse can go

gelding: a castrated male horse

green: a horse who has little training and experience with a rider

gut sounds: the noises that can be heard in a horse's abdomen

gymkhana: rodeo events consisting of games like barrel racing and pole bending

hard keeper: a horse whose proper weight is difficult to maintain

head bumper: a pad placed on top of the horse's head to protect it during travel

headcollar: British term for *halter*

hoof tester: a device that vets use to measure the sensitivity of a horse's hoof

horse box: British term for *trailer*

horseperson: term for a man, woman, or child who has devoted considerable time and energy to learning about and being around horses

hotwalker: a mechanical, merry-go-round type device where horses can be attached for exercise; most hotwalkers can accommodate four horses at a time

in season: term for a mare who is in estrus, or heat

jog: Western term for a slow trot

lead, left or right: term for the foreleg that strikes the ground first at the canter

lipomas: fat tumor, always benign

lope: Western discipline term for a three-beat gait; same as canter or slow gallop

mare: a female horse over the age of 4 years

martingale: a leather device designed to control the position of the horse's head

moonblindness: equine recurrent uveitis (ERU), a disease affecting the eyes

mule: the offspring of a female horse and a male donkey

nerve block: an injection given in the leg to numb an area

paddock: a large enclosure

pony: a breed of small horse, usually under 14.2 hands in height

proud flesh: excess, raw, granulation tissue emanating from a healing wound

purebred: a breed of horse that produces consistent physical characteristics through generations of unmixed origin

phenylbutazone: an aspirin-like veterinary medication used for pain relief and reduction of inflammation and swelling; also known as bute

put down: euthanize

rogue: a poor-tempered horse

rolling: when a horse lies down on his side and rocks to and fro on his back

saddle rack: a stand designed to support a saddle when not in use

sire: the father of a horse

stallion: an intact male horse over the age of 4 years

stud book: a listing of breeding animals maintained by a registering organization

tie-down: Western term for a standing martingale, a leather device used to control the position of the horse's head while riding

trot: a two-beat gait

udder: the mare's mammary gland

V.M.D.: Veterinary Medical Doctor

weanling: a male or female horse who has been weaned from his or her mother but has not yet reached 1 year of age

yearling: a male or female horse in his or her first year

Appendix B

Equine Resources

●●●

*H*ere is a short list of resources to check out as your appetite for equine knowledge increases.

Breed Registries

Appaloosa Horse Club
P.O. Box 8403
Moscow, ID 83843-0903
(208) 882-5578
www.appaloosa.com

International Colored Appaloosa Association
P.O. Box 99
Shipshewana, IN 46565
(219) 825-3331
home.earthlink.net/~thelintons/ICAA/index.htm/

Arabian Horse Registry of America, Inc.
P.O. Box 173886
Denver, CO 80217-3886
(303) 450-4748
www.theregistry.org

American Miniature Horse Association
5601 South IH 35W
Alvarado, TX 76009
(817) 783-5600
www.amha.com

American Morgan Horse Association
P.O. Box 960
Shelburne, VT 05482-0960
(802) 985-4944
www.morganhorse.com

American Paint Horse Association
P.O. Box 961023
Fort Worth, TX 76161-0023
(817) 834-APHA
www.apha.com

American Quarter Horse Association
P.O. Box 200
Amarillo, TX 79168-0001
(806) 376-4811
www.aqha.com

Racking Horse Breeders Association of America
67 Horse Center Rd.
Decatur, AL 35603-9735
(256) 353-7225

American Saddlebred Horse Association
4093 Iron Works Parkway
Lexington, KY 40511-8434
(606) 259-2742

United States Trotting Association (Standardbreds)
750 Michigan Ave.
Columbus, OH 43215-1191
(614) 224-2291
www.ustrotting.com

Tennessee Walking Horse Breeders & Exhibitors Association
P. O. Box 286
Lewisburg, TN 37091-0286
(615) 359-1574

The Jockey Club (Thoroughbreds)
821 Corporate Dr.
Lexington, KY 40503-2794
(800) 444-8521
www.jockeyclub.com

Educational Organizations

Horse Industry Alliance
P.O. Box 200
Weatherford, TX 76086
(817) 598-0061
www.horseindustryalliance.com

United States Pony Clubs, Inc.
4071 Iron Works Pike
Lexington, KY 40511-8462
(606) 254-PONY
ponyclub.org

CHA - (Certified Horsemanship Association)
5318 Old Bullard Road
Tyler, TX 75703-3612
(800) 399-0138
www.cha-ahse.org/

Miscellaneous Equine Organizations

The Equine Connection National AAEP Locator Service
(800) GET-A-DVM
www.getadvm.com/equcon.html

American Riding Instructor Certification Program
P.O. Box 282
Alton Bay, NH 03810-0282
(603) 875-4000
www.win.net/aria/dircty.html

American Association of Equine Practitioners
4075 Iron Works Pike
Lexington, KY 40511
606-233-0147
www.aaep.org

American Farriers Association
4059 Iron Works Pike
Lexington, KY 40511-8434
(606) 233-7411

American Horse Council
1700 K Street, NW
Suite 300
Washington, DC 20006-3805
(202) 296-4031
www.horsecouncil.org

North American Riding for the Handicapped
P.O. Box 33150
Denver, CO 80233
(800) 369-RIDE
www.nasha.org

Pet Loss Hotlines

University of California, Davis
(916) 752-4200

Tufts University School of Veterinary Medicine (Massachusetts)
(508) 839-7966

Virginia-Maryland Regional College of Veterinary Medicine
(540) 231-8038

Michigan State University College of Veterinary Medicine
(517) 432-2696

Washington State University College of Veterinary Medicine
(509) 335-5704

Some Equine Rescue Groups

The Horse Protection League
5305 Eldridge St.
Arvada, CO 80002
(303) 526-2317
www.sni.net/hpl

Adopt-A-Horse Ltd., Inc.
7609 W. Josephine Road
Lake Placid, FL 33852
(941) 382-4483

American Standardbred Adoption Program
Route 1, Box 82
De Soto, WI 54624
(608) 689-2399

Equestrian Training Center Horse Rescue
Highway 225A
P.O. Box 770332
Ocala, FL 34474-0332
(904) 591-1066

Horse Lovers United Inc.
P.O. Box 2744
Salisbury, MD 21802-2744
(410) 749-3599

Some Horse Publications

Horse Illustrated
P.O. Box 6050
Mission Viejo, CA 92690
(949) 855-8822
www.animalnetwork.com/horses

Equus
656 Quince Orchard Rd., Suite 600
Gaithersburg, MD 20878
(301) 977-3900
www.cowles.com/magazines/mag/equus.html

Horses U.S.A.
P.O. Box 6050
Mission Viejo, CA 92690
(949) 855-8822

Horse & Rider
1597 Cole Boulevard, Suite 350
Golden, CO 80401
(800) 829-3340
www.cowles.com/magazines/mag/hor.html

Practical Horseman
6405 Flank Drive
Harrisburg, PA 17112
(800) 829-3340
www.cowles.com/magazines/mag/pra.html

Equine Equipment Catalogs

Stateline Tack
(800) 228-9208

Libertyville Saddle Shop
(800) 872-3353

Whitman Saddle Company
(800) 253-0852

Weise Equine Supply
(800) 869-4373

Index

• **F** •

• N •

• O •

• P •

• W •

• X •

• Y •

• Z •

Discover Dummies Online!

The Dummies Web Site is your fun and friendly online resource for the latest information about *For Dummies* books and your favorite topics. The Web site is the place to communicate with us, exchange ideas with other *For Dummies* readers, chat with authors, and have fun!

Ten Fun and Useful Things You Can Do at www.dummies.com

1. Win free *For Dummies* books and more!

2. Register your book and be entered in a prize drawing.

3. Meet your favorite authors through the IDG Books Worldwide Author Chat Series.

4. Exchange helpful information with other *For Dummies* readers.

5. Discover other great *For Dummies* books you must have!

6. Purchase Dummieswear® exclusively from our Web site.

7. Buy *For Dummies* books online.

8. Talk to us. Make comments, ask questions, get answers!

9. Download free software.

10. Find additional useful resources from authors.

Link directly to these ten fun and useful things at
http://www.dummies.com/10useful

For other technology titles from IDG Books Worldwide, go to
www.idgbooks.com

Not on the Web yet? It's easy to get started with *Dummies 101®: The Internet For Windows® 98* or *The Internet For Dummies®* at local retailers everywhere.

Find other *For Dummies* books on these topics:

Business • Career • Databases • Food & Beverage • Games • Gardening • Graphics • Hardware
Health & Fitness • Internet and the World Wide Web • Networking • Office Suites
Operating Systems • Personal Finance • Pets • Programming • Recreation • Sports
Spreadsheets • Teacher Resources • Test Prep • Word Processing

IDG BOOKS WORLDWIDE BOOK REGISTRATION

We want to hear from you!

Visit **http://my2cents.dummies.com** to register this book and tell us how you liked it!

- Get entered in our monthly prize giveaway.
- Give us feedback about this book — tell us what you like best, what you like least, or maybe what you'd like to ask the author and us to change!
- Let us know any other *For Dummies®* topics that interest you.

Your feedback helps us determine what books to publish, tells us what coverage to add as we revise our books, and lets us know whether we're meeting your needs as a *For Dummies* reader. You're our most valuable resource, and what you have to say is important to us!

Not on the Web yet? It's easy to get started with *Dummies 101®: The Internet For Windows® 98* or *The Internet For Dummies®* at local retailers everywhere.

Or let us know what you think by sending us a letter at the following address:

For Dummies Book Registration
Dummies Press
10475 Crosspoint Blvd.
Indianapolis, IN 46256

™

**BESTSELLING
BOOK SERIES**